W9-DFB-675

BORDERLINES IN BORDERLANDS

J. C. A. Stagg

BORDERLINES
IN
BORDERLANDS

JAMES MADISON AND THE SPANISH-
AMERICAN FRONTIER, 1776–1821

CABRINI COLLEGE LIBRARY
610 KING OF PRUSSIA ROAD
RADNOR, PA 19087

Yale University Press   New Haven & London

2293 + 2087

Published with assistance from the Annie Burr Lewis Fund and a
grant provided by the College and Graduate School of Arts and
Sciences of the University of Virginia.

Copyright © 2009 by Yale University.
All rights reserved.
This book may not be reproduced, in whole or in part, including
illustrations, in any form (beyond that copying permitted by Sections
107 and 108 of the U.S. Copyright Law and except by reviewers for
the public press), without written permission from the publishers.

Set in Galliard Old Style and Copperplate 33 types by
The Composing Room of Michigan, Inc.
Printed in the United States of America.

Library of Congress Cataloging-in-Publication Data

Stagg, J. C. A. (John Charles Anderson), 1945–
    Borderlines in borderlands : James Madison and the Spanish-
American frontier, 1776–1821 / J. C. A. Stagg.
        p. cm.
    Includes bibliographical references and index.
    ISBN 978-0-300-13905-1 (hardcover : alk. paper)   1. Madison,
James, 1751–1836—Political and social views.   2. Southern boundary
of the United States—History—18th century.   3. Southern
boundary of the United States—History—19th century.   4. East
Florida—History.   5. West Florida—History.   6. Texas—History—
To 1846.   7. United States—Territorial expansion.   8. United
States—Foreign relations—Spain.   9. Spain—Foreign relations—
United States.   10. Spain. Treaties, etc. United States, 1819 Feb. 22.
I. Title.
    E342.S69 2009
    973.5'1092—dc22   2008021326

A catalogue record for this book is available from the British Library.

This paper meets the requirements of ANSI/NISO Z39.48–1992
(Permanence of Paper).
It contains 30 percent postconsumer waste (PCW) and is certified by
the Forest Stewardship Council (FSC).

10 9 8 7 6 5 4 3 2 1

TO HOLLY AND THE GRANDCHILDREN:
CHARLOTTE, ALEX, ELIYAHU, AND CHANA

CONTENTS

ACKNOWLEDGMENTS

It is customary, in addressing one's obligations, to note that while the writing of a book is very much a solitary vice, it cannot be done at all without the consent and the cooperation of others. Certainly that is the case here. My greatest debt of gratitude over the years has been to my colleagues on *The Papers of James Madison* at the University of Virginia— David Mattern, Mary Hackett, Angela Kreider, Jeanne Cross, Ellen Barber, Anne Colony, Mary-Parke Johnson, Sue Perdue, and Sarah Marshall. They have assisted me in countless ways, but mainly by tolerating with patient good humor my single-minded pursuit of one particular aspect of the career of James Madison, even when it seemed to be to the exclusion of other matters they doubtless thought were far more important. But as they concentrated on these other matters, they laid the essential foundation for the vastly improved understanding of James Madison and his times that scholars of the early American republic have been able to provide in recent years.

A similar debt is due to friends and colleagues who have worked to produce the modern editions of the papers of the Founding Fathers, particularly Barbara Oberg, Ellen Cohn, Jeff Looney, John Catanzariti, Dick Ryerson, Jim Taylor, Bill Abbot, Dorothy Twohig, Phil Chase, Ted Crackel, and Stan Katz. Collectively, their labors have contributed not merely to this slender tome but, more important, to providing historians of early America with documentary resources of unparalleled richness, which have yet to be as fully appreciated as they might be. On a more personal note, friends and acquaintances have assisted me by critiquing drafts, gathering remote materials at a distance, assisting with Spanish translations, and simply providing the companionship that helps preserve one's sanity in trying times. It is, therefore, with particular gratitude that I recall in this context the contributions of Jim Banner, Ken Lockridge, Roger Kennedy, Jim Cusick, Mary-Ann Lugo, Brian and Karen Parshall, Hans-Peter and Gerti Stoffel, Lew Gould, Lew Ware, Philip and Therese Rousseau, and Joe Kett. At the University of Virginia, the College of Arts and Sciences generously awarded me a sabbatical leave in the spring of 2005, and the dean, Edward Ayers, now president of the University of Richmond, greatly enhanced its value by relieving me of teaching duties for an additional semester. Peter Onuf also helped by making Charlottesville an outstanding center for the study of the early American republic, even if there is not, as he sometimes likes to imagine, any such thing as the "Virginia school" of American history. And two of our students, Peter Kastor and James Lewis, have shared my interests in matters relating to the Spanish-American empire. Their scholarship and their example have greatly improved my own questions and arguments. Otherwise, as they say, any and all errors and misconceptions in the book are entirely my own responsibility.

In preparing the manuscript for publication, I have been greatly aided by the staff of Yale University Press, particularly Chris Rogers, Laura Davulis, and Jessie Hunnicutt. Chris obtained valuable readers' reports, and Jessie polished my prose style. The maps were expertly drawn by Rick Britton, and Susan Holbrooke Perdue compiled the index. Funds for these purposes were generously provided by the College and Graduate School of Arts and Sciences at the University of Virginia as well as by the Corcoran Department of History.

On a more personal note, I owe the deepest debt of gratitude to Holly Shulman for her dedication over the years to all the important things that have made it possible for me not only to produce this book but also to share a life with a truly wonderful companion.

BORDERLINES IN BORDERLANDS

INTRODUCTION

By the dawn of the twenty-first century, national boundaries had become an increasingly confusing, fluid, and even intangible phenomenon. In an age of mass migration, globalization, and instantaneous communication, the once familiar and seemingly reassuring lines drawn around the maps of nation-states had taken on an air of unreality as it became progressively easier for individuals and businesses to cross (or to violate) them, while at the same time it became harder and harder for governments to justify and to police them. Indeed, scholars inhabiting many disciplines now routinely talk of an oxymoronic world of "post-territorial" states in which physical borders and frontiers have become "an archaic spatial feature."[1] And if it is not much better than a mere truism to observe that the ability of a government to define and to control its borders is a fair reflection of its capacities to project power and to vindicate its interests more generally, then even the most powerful nation-states have become steadily less powerful.[2] Nowhere, of course, is this more true than in the case of the southern border of the United States itself, where the lines demarcating the jurisdictions of Florida, Louisiana, Texas, New Mexico, Arizona, and California have almost dissolved into thin air, leaving the reality of the sovereignty of the government in Washington, DC, a concept more hollow than hallowed, even as political leaders of all stripes continue to insist that the borders of the nation must be better controlled, if not closed altogether.[3]

An account of how this state of affairs originated in the earliest days of the republic might be a significant contribution to both American historiography and contemporary political debate, but this study was not initially undertaken to fulfill either of those purposes. It arose, instead, from a more prosaic need to solve certain problems I encountered in preparing *The Papers of James Madison* for publication, particularly the presidential series of the edition. Madison's two terms in the White House between 1809 and 1817 have always been the most unsatisfying, and perhaps the most difficult, aspect of his long public career for historians to interpret. Successive generations of scholars have never ceased to wonder how the creative statesman who "fathered" both the Federal Constitution and the Bill of Rights, to say nothing of the Republican Party of the 1790s, could be as incompetent and as unsuccessful as he seemed to be as a chief executive. The conventional solution for that conundrum has been to argue that there were, in effect, two different James Madisons, a notion that has permitted his biographers to describe how the effective and influential legislator and politician of the years before 1800 was, essentially, in control of circumstances and events before they proceed to deplore how the less effective administrator and executive of the years after 1801 was overwhelmed by the turmoil of the Age of Napoleon.[4] Such a formulation, however, begs more questions than it can answer, and more recent investigators have come to doubt whether there were really two different Madisons at all. More intensive analyses of Madison's political thinking and behavior have left some historians, at least, more impressed with the overall continuities in his public career between 1780 and 1817 than they are persuaded by the view that this most thoughtful and intellectually rigorous member of the founding generation was simply tossed about by forces he could neither understand nor control during his years in Washington after the start of the nineteenth century.[5]

Yet the notion that there were two Madisons has permeated even the study of Madison's presidency itself. The predominant image of the fourth president is that of the weak and indecisive statesman who handled the disputes with Great Britain over maritime rights so badly that he lost control of his policies to a congressional faction of "War Hawks," whose members, after November 1811, stampeded him into a conflict which he did not want and which he then mismanaged to the extent that he remains to this day the only president ever to have been driven from the nation's capital by an invading army.[6] And for much of the twentieth century, historians described a somewhat similar situation with respect to Madison's conduct in the nation's disputes with Spain over the boundaries of the Louisiana Purchase: namely, that he pursued some dubious claims to the borderland territories of West Florida, East Florida, and Texas in ways that implicated him in illegal revolutions in the first two of these Spanish provinces—the former being successful and the latter unsuccessful—as well as led him into an attempt to seize Texas by means of an equally illegal and unsuccessful filibuster. The questionable nature of these actions, however, was not their worst aspect. Rather, the problem was they were simply unnecessary. Historians schooled in Frederick Jackson Turner's theories about the inexorable nature of the westward movement across the North American continent maintained that it might have been better for Madison to have done nothing at all about trying to make good on the claims to the Spanish borderlands and to have waited, instead, for the inevitable demographic growth and geographic expansion of the nation's frontier settlements to pull the northernmost provinces of the Spanish-American empire into the Union without the costs of revolution and the risks of conflict and war.[7]

More recently, though, what earlier historians had regarded as Madison's pointless ineptitude in the matter of the Spanish borderlands has been reinterpreted as evidence of a more malign and sinister intent on his part. Some scholars have come to believe that, far from stumbling into poorly considered and unwise efforts to enlarge the boundaries of the nation, Madison instead deliberately and purposefully adopted policies to subvert the Spanish authorities in the borderland territories as the means to accomplish his expansionist goals. The main evidence for such an argument is the indisputable fact that in the summer of 1810 Madison sent executive agents into all three of the Spanish provinces—East Florida, West Florida, and Texas—with instructions that envisioned their incorporation, to varying degrees, into the Union after the displacement of their colonial regimes.[8] For a generation that, after the 1970s, had become all too familiar with exposés of the "covert operations" of the U.S. government abroad, especially in Central and South America, Madison's actions in the Spanish borderlands between 1810 and 1813 suddenly came to be seen in a new and disconcerting light. Far from being dismissible as evidence of mere folly, they indicated instead a hitherto undetected determination and ruthlessness on the part of this seemingly most mild and unassuming of presidents. In this process of reinterpretation, the "Father of the Constitution" and hapless commander in chief was transformed, with barely an apology to Nathan Hale, into the founding father of the Central Intelligence Agency.[9]

It is not necessary to belabor the point that these two contradictory portraits of Madison as president cannot be easily reconciled, if they can be reconciled at all. Rather, it is much more reasonable to assume that they are both incorrect in significant ways and that it should be the task of further research to determine how they might be modified. The purpose of this book, however, is to focus almost exclusively on re-examining Madison's conduct toward Spain and its borderland possessions.[10] This topic has been far less intensively studied than the more familiar one of Madison's Anglo-American diplomacy, and the larger significance of the fourth president's actions here has yet to be comprehensively assessed. There can, of course, be no denying that Madison's dealings with Spain were, at times, both clumsy and ineffective, but it can be demonstrated, in ways that it has not yet been, that at no time after 1809 did Madison ever assume that the nation's territorial disputes with Spain could be solved by means that were other than legal, and that as a consequence only a settlement consistent with the law of nations could give the United States good title to the territories in question. Moreover, in the longer run, with the negotiation of the Transcontinental Treaty in 1819, the United States accomplished its most important territorial goals with respect to Spain—and much more, particularly with the acquisition of a boundary line on the Pacific Ocean. By 1821 significant portions of the northern borderlands of Spanish America had thus become the bordered lands of the new American republic.[11] But in what ways, exactly, had Madison contributed to that outcome?

The story of American territorial aggrandizement at the expense of Spain also forms part of the larger narrative of American expansionism—the series of stages whereby the United States grew from a nation initially bounded by the Mississippi River in the west and the 31st parallel in the south into the far greater "imperial" republic that by 1848 had come to extend from the Atlantic coast to the Pacific Ocean and from the Gulf of

Mexico to Canada. Historians have long realized that this expansionism was a multifaceted phenomenon, arising from concrete state interests involving security and control over land as well as the need for Americans to gain access to resources, rivers, ports, and markets—to say nothing of the ambition, greed, idealism, patriotism, religious chauvinism, and racial contempt for local and indigenous populations that also fueled and justified the acquisition of this territory.[12] In taking these factors into consideration for the purpose of framing more broad-gauge explanations for American expansionism, many scholars have also concluded that the annexation of several parts of the Spanish borderlands to the United States by 1821 might well be seen as an early instance of the "destiny" of the republic becoming "manifest" long before the term *Manifest Destiny* was coined by John L. O'Sullivan (or Jane McManus Storm Cazneau) in 1845.[13] But was there really a "Madisonian" sense of Manifest Destiny, and how might that sense have informed the decisions Madison made in the course of his efforts to enlarge the United States? To raise these questions is not to deny that many citizens of the early republic sensed that a great destiny might await their country, but it will hardly do for historians to invoke the vague notion of an incipient Manifest Destiny in an overtly anachronistic fashion as the best way to explain the politics of American expansionism in the first quarter of the nineteenth century. In these matters the processes of decision and policy making need to be described more precisely than they have been.[14]

For this purpose, we need a new way of thinking about the ideological origins of early American expansionism.[15] Rather than explain this phenomenon as Manifest Destiny before the fact, it might be better to regard it as an outgrowth of the ideology of American continentalism—a worldview that arose in the middle decades of the eighteenth century and one that rested on the belief that a secure and independent United States would not so much be "the great nation of futurity" as it should be the successor state to the rival European empires of North America.[16] This view, long in the making, received its first significant political expression in the territorial provisions of the Model Treaty of 1776. It was only partially vindicated in the boundary arrangements of the 1783 Peace of Paris before being subsequently rejuvenated and reinforced with the Louisiana Purchase of 1803, whereby the United States acquired a title to what remained at that time of France's claims to a North American empire. And it finally assumed truly continental dimensions in 1819 when the republic chose in the Transcontinental Treaty of that year to consolidate its hitherto tenuous claims to a coastline on the Pacific Ocean instead of merely annexing additional adjacent southwestern territory in the form of Texas. Each of these episodes confirms the extent to which the leaders of the early republic understood the problems of national security in terms of geographical expansion, and by the time a Pacific coastline had been secured, the geopolitical situation of the nation had been radically transformed. No longer could the republic be threatened, as the American colonies had been, by the European empires that had earlier held sway in North America, and it was in this international environment of greatly increased security that ideas about expansion, both retrospective and prospective, could be romanticized as inevitable and largely uncontested—or, to put it another way, that the expansionist destiny of the nation could become not only "manifest" but also "exceptionalist."[17]

That historians have slighted this dimension of the problem of early American expansionism can probably be attributed to the lingering influence of Henry Adams. Long after scholars rejected, or moved beyond, most of Adams's major interpretive themes, they continued to draw on the account of American relations with Spain between 1801 and 1817 that he provided in his classic *History of the United States during the Administrations of Thomas Jefferson and James Madison*.[18] Few would deny even today, more than a century after its appearance, that Adams's analysis of the seemingly puzzling and often paradoxical elements in the policies of both Jefferson and Madison has yet to be surpassed in terms of its polished style and ironical wit, but regarding his analysis of the American quest for the Spanish borderlands, it has been less seldom noted just how far, or why, Adams perversely pushed his own fondness for paradox.[19] Not only did he insinuate that Jefferson, after 1803, chose to sacrifice a relatively strong claim to Texas as part of Louisiana in order to pursue a far weaker one to Florida—an argument that was the reverse of the president's own conclusions on the subject—but he also summed up the essence of Jefferson's Spanish diplomacy in a wonderfully epigrammatic formulation that has served ever since to impede further study of the subject—namely, that between 1800 and 1803 "Spain had retroceded West Florida to France without knowing it, that France had sold it to the United States without suspecting it, that the United States had bought it without paying for it, and that neither France nor Spain, though the original contracting parties, were competent to decide the meaning of their own contract."[20] That elegant sound-bite could also summarize nearly two decades of complex, if not tortured, diplomacy in three capitals between 1803 and 1821, and so skillfully did Adams impart the impression that the means of American policy were almost never clearly related to its ostensible ends that he seemed to be suggesting that Jefferson and Madison might have had motives other than their stated ones for demanding that Madrid relinquish the Spanish borderlands to the United States.

To conclude that Adams believed that Jefferson and Madison acted on the basis of hidden agendas may be to risk misreading his philosophy of history.[21] Subsequent generations of historians, nevertheless, have devoted a good deal of effort to identifying what those hidden agendas and motives might have been, thus giving rise to a heavy emphasis on the role of cultural, demographic, material, and political factors in their explanations for this aspect of Jefferson's quest for an "empire of liberty" in the American Southwest.[22] Yet Adams, for all the complexity and subtlety of his narrative, oversimplified the nature of the controversy over the borderlands. The problem was not that the United States wrongly insisted that Spain had assigned West Florida and Texas to France in 1800 and that these provinces were already included in Louisiana as it was purchased by the United States in 1803. The United States, strictly speaking, made no such claim, but it did insist that Spain had been obliged by treaty to cede these territories to France and that France was obliged, also by treaty, to ensure their delivery to the United States. Nor was the problem that the American claim to the borderlands was indisputable. It could be disputed, and Spain did so consistently, though not always coherently, up until 1819.[23] Adams, however, simply accepted the arguments of Spain as correct and ignored the fact that the United States, by signing a treaty in 1803 that contained the same definition of Louisiana that France had sought to establish in 1800, had also acquired a claim under the law of nations to the territories it was to seek from Spain.[24] The United States, moreover, had an equally good right as Spain under that same law of nations to construe the meaning of its contract with France.[25] The problem of American diplomacy after 1803, therefore, was one of persuading Spain to accept the claims of the United States to the borderlands as legitimate under international law.

It is, moreover, difficult to avoid the suspicion that Adams, in some sense, knew this, or at least that he should have known it. Shortly before his grandfather, John Quincy Adams, signed the treaty with Spain settling the boundaries of Louisiana in February 1819, there appeared in the *City of Washington Gazette* a lengthy account of the 1803 negotiations that contended that the American diplomats in Paris—Robert R. Livingston and James Monroe—knew full well that neither West Florida nor Texas was included in Louisiana and that by manipulating their dispatches to create the opposite impression, they had led the United States into pursuing under "false pretenses" a "wicked and contemptible policy" toward Madrid.[26] Realizing that the publication of this article represented a last-minute effort to derail his negotiations, John Quincy Adams indignantly recorded in his diary that its contents did not "really affect the question at all." Instead, he maintained, they proved that the negotiators in Paris did indeed take the boundaries described in 1803 from the 1800 treaty of retrocession and that these had been drawn "with the express intention on the part of France to take possession of the whole of the original Colony of Louisiana, as granted in Crozat's charter."[27] "Whether Spain meant the same thing, or understood the article as importing so much may be questioned," he added, but he also stressed that "both parties knew that if a question of construction upon the article should arise between them, the effective construction would be that of France."[28] Events had proved that the matter was not so simple, but Adams also included in his diary evidence that France had long regarded West Florida as part of Louisiana and had intended to act on that assumption whenever it suited France's purposes. That Henry Adams had no affection for his celebrated grandfather has long been known to students of the Adams family, but historians of the early republic have never paused to consider how far Henry's antipathies might also have colored his interpretation of the policies of Jefferson and Madison that John Quincy Adams brought to a successful conclusion in 1819, two years after the fourth president had departed the political stage.[29] Consequently, scholars will always risk misinterpreting American policy toward Spain after 1803 if they discount the extent to which the

United States believed it had valid claims under international law to the borderlands and conducted its diplomacy in accordance with that belief.

Be that as it may, getting the story in Washington right is only half the problem of understanding the American quest for the Spanish borderlands. An equally significant matter is the question of how policy made in Washington played out in the affected regions of the borderlands themselves. Students of the subject encounter here a formidable historiography originated more than eighty years ago by Herbert Eugene Bolton as a result of his belief that the Spanish borderlands should be regarded as being as important in the history of the American frontier as the narrative of the westward movement from the Atlantic to the Pacific.[30] Bolton, not coincidentally, was also a student of Frederick Jackson Turner, and like Turner he, too, mentored many students in the course of expanding this particular field of knowledge.[31] The middle decades of the twentieth century saw something of a pause in the activities of the Boltonians, but their cumulative influence can now be seen in the recent upsurge in the publication of case studies, or micro-histories, of many borderland communities and regions.[32] The findings of these studies are also beginning to be synthesized with scholarship inspired by other conceptualizations of regional and international history, including the newer fields of "transnational" and global history.[33] These latter fields, in turn, have been shaped by two important interdisciplinary perspectives on early modern history. One is the dependency theory and "world systems" approach of Immanuel Wallerstein.[34] The other comes from the schools of "Atlantic history" under the direction of Bernard Bailyn in the Atlantic History Seminar at Harvard University and Jack P. Greene in the Program in Atlantic History, Culture, and Society at Johns Hopkins University.[35] The perspectives of historical and cultural geographers, most notably Donald W. Meinig, on the stages of American national development have also been influential.[36]

To reference these new conceptualizations, however, is not to claim that the phenomenon of American expansionism in the early nineteenth century can be neatly encapsulated within any one of their formulations. The matter, perhaps unfortunately, is too complicated for so expedient a solution.[37] Nevertheless, this more recent scholarship can suggest potentially fruitful lines of inquiry to inform the study of how the Spanish borderlands became part of the United States. How far, for example, were the policies made in Washington advanced, or hindered, by developments within and along the borderlands themselves or by changes in the relationships between states in the Atlantic network of nations? In these contexts, it is necessary to regard borderlands and frontiers not merely as reflecting lines on maps that were in dispute between the metropolitan centers of Madrid, Paris, and Washington but also as embodying more indeterminate geographical zones characterized by conflict and other interactions between their various populations, including American, British, French, and Spanish settlers, African slaves, and indigenous Indian peoples. This latter definition must be observed in order to accord these local populations an appropriate degree of agency in influencing, if not always determining, their own fates in the struggles between empires and nation-states. It also needs to be insisted on to make the point that at times the policies devised in metropolitan centers had little or no effect on outcomes in the peripheral borderland regions.[38] Yet in the case of the United States, these recent efforts to rewrite the history of the nation as merely one part of a larger Atlantic and transnational "history without borders" should not be pushed too far.[39] Nation-states, even those with the "rough edges" of contested borders, can exercise significant power both as independent agents in their own right and as interdependent actors in the larger international arena, and it was in the course of acting thus as "a nation among nations" that the United States drew boundaries of its own choosing in the Spanish borderlands as these regions were incorporated into an expanding American republic.[40]

It is with these perspectives in mind that I have attempted to describe the developments that occurred in West Florida, East Florida, and Texas between 1810 and 1813. My goal has been to understand why the United States succeeded, somewhat inadvertently, in annexing most of West Florida during that period, why it failed to secure East Florida at all before 1819, and why in the process of settling its disputes with Spain it consented to abandon the claim to Texas in order to obtain a boundary line farther to the north that extended to the Pacific Ocean. In each of these three cases, the Madison administration dispatched executive agents to the Spanish province in question—William Wykoff, Jr., to West Florida, George Mathews and John McKee to East Florida, and William Shaler to Texas—

on a series of errands to determine the future relationship of the region to the United States. The outcomes of these errands into the borderlands have yet to be properly understood by historians, in no small part because three of these agents—Mathews, McKee, and Shaler—went into the borderlands on errands of their own, which ultimately came into conflict with those of the administration in Washington.[41] In the course of describing how these conflicting errands affected administration policy, it has been my purpose to provide a clearer sense of the linkages between policy making at the center of American government and the developments that unfolded at the peripheries of the American polity in the early nineteenth century. If the United States ultimately succeeded in expanding its boundaries through the processes thus described, it did so as much because of contingent developments over which it had little control as it did because of its intention, first openly proclaimed in the Model Treaty of 1776, that its southern border be made to extend from the east coast of the Florida peninsula to the Mississippi River.

In the final analysis, these issues bring us to the much more difficult question of how historians might write accounts of the infinite varieties of the American national experience. Manifestly, it is not enough merely to provide ever more detailed accounts of national politics in Washington alone. But the alternative of trying to draw larger patterns from a rapidly proliferating number of local or regional case studies is probably not the answer either.[42] There seems to be too much variety or complexity in such studies to make that course an entirely satisfactory means for furnishing a synthesis of the nation's experiences, but that does not mean we should simply abandon any effort to address the problem. In the matter of understanding American expansion at the expense of Spain in the early nineteenth century, it seems preferable to try and readjust our comprehension of the balance between the narratives we might construct of events at the center of the nation and those at its peripheries in order to clarify the dynamics of the processes at work here. Yet it is in the course of clarifying our understanding of the balance between these conflicting narratives that the role of individuals, particularly those who wield executive power, becomes more rather than less important. The conduct of a nation's foreign policy, by its very nature, depends heavily on the ability of its policy makers and executives to assimilate considerable quantities of ambiguous and incomplete data concerning international relations in their broadest dimensions, to weigh contingent and imponderable factors, to plot courses of action, and to implement and to adjust them when policy collides with unforeseen realities—as it invariably does. It is, in short, the task of individuals placed in these situations "to hold the world in their minds" and to act accordingly.[43]

That being the case, the role of Madison in the early nineteenth century, irrespective of whether he be regarded as a "successful" president, becomes far more important than most historians have been inclined to suspect. In the person of its fourth president the United States possessed a chief executive who was more than capable of absorbing very considerable amounts of information and processing it in complex ways. Yet at the same time, Madison, by virtue of both his intellectual training and his personal temperament, was usually driven to organize that information into reasonably predictable and stable cognition patterns in order to make knowledge serve the purposes of policy making. And few scholars would now deny that Madison did indeed possess an unusually distinctive ability to extract larger issues and questions of broad significance from the confusion and swirl of the daily occurrences that confronted him. That ability had served him quite well in his career as a legislative politician in the years before 1800. It was, perhaps, to serve him less well after 1801 in the realms of diplomacy and international affairs, where developments and outcomes were more likely to be influenced by unpredictable turns of events far beyond his control, but at all times Madison's decisions and actions were the product of a coherent and consistent way of viewing the world that changed relatively little over the course of his lifetime. In that sense, there was only one James Madison, not two. It might be objected, of course, that to reduce our understanding of American expansionism in the early nineteenth century to the perspectives of a single individual risks privileging an excessive reductionism at the expense of a more desirable and satisfying complexity. More certainly, the result might seem to be too short a book on what is necessarily a very large and complicated subject. Yet, despite its limitations, a close study of the thought and actions of James Madison can still tell us more than we have ever previously understood about our local, national, international, and transnational histories.

1

A TROUBLESOME NEIGHBOR

In various ways, therefore, may Spain promote or oppose our political interests with several other Countries; and we shall, I think, either find her in
America a very convenient Neighbour, or a very troublesome one.

—John Jay to the Continental Congress, 3 August 1786

The pursuit of the Spanish borderlands of East Florida, West
Florida, and Texas was a dominating, if not obsessive, concern for three
presidents of the Virginia Dynasty: Thomas Jefferson, James Madison, and
James Monroe. Their quest extended from the early days of Jefferson's first
administration to the eve of Monroe's second, and on that account historians have usually regarded it as an inevitable consequence of the ascendancy of Virginia and southern interests in national politics after 1801.[1] So
sectional a perspective on how the United States came to acquire the Spanish territories it had by 1821 is not entirely misplaced, but it has imposed
some distortions on our understanding of why this territory was sought at
all. Among them is the belief that American interest in the borderlands developed largely after 1795, after the boundaries between American and
Spanish claims east of the Mississippi River were adjusted in the Pinckney
Treaty of that year and after reports began to circulate that France would
recover its former colony of Louisiana from Spain. In 1800, France regained
Louisiana "with the same extent that it now has in the hands of Spain and
that it had when France possessed it" before 1763. Three years later, France
sold Louisiana to the United States, in a treaty containing the same defini-

tion of its extent that had been established in 1800.[2] The Virginian presidents then devoted nearly two decades of effort to determine how much of the Spanish borderlands might have been included in the territory purchased in 1803. Of necessity, their diplomacy was conducted as a series of disputes over the limits of Louisiana, but behind the diplomacy were American concerns about, and interests in, the Spanish borderlands that had long predated the treaties of 1795, 1800, and 1803.

The deep background to the borderland disputes between Spain and the United States can be traced in the history of European rivalries in the New World that began after the first voyage of Christopher Columbus in 1492 and culminated in the expulsion by Great Britain of the French and Spanish empires from the eastern half of the North American mainland in 1763.[3] The more immediate origins of the story are to be found in the deliberations of the Second Continental Congress after May 1775, when the delegates of the thirteen mainland colonies began to consider what sort of political arrangements would replace British rule in the event of the colonies turning independent. In these matters, Benjamin Franklin and John Adams often took the lead. As early as July 1775, Franklin's first proposal for articles of confederation assumed that *all* British colonies in North America would seek "the Advantages of our Union," and Adams seconded him by demonstrating that questions about declaring independence, forming a confederation, and future diplomatic strategies were so integrally related that they "ought to go hand in hand." As Adams pointed out, Great Britain would neither redress colonial grievances nor recognize America as "a distinct state" until Americans themselves had "set up a Republican government, something like that of Holland," and foreign states would hardly acknowledge such a confederation before "we had acknowledged ourselves and taken our station among them as a sovereign power, and independent Nation."[4]

That Adams sought to supplement the Declaration of Independence and the Articles of Confederation with a "Plan of Treaties" that assumed Congress could avoid political and military alliances in favor of commercial agreements is well known. Far less remarked upon, however, has been his concern, also shared by Franklin, that the basis of the emerging union should be enlarged by providing for the inclusion of not only the thirteen mainland colonies but also the remaining British possessions of Canada,

East and West Florida, and Bermuda. For that reason, both the first draft and the final text of his Model Treaty stated that "its true intent and Meaning" was that the United States "shall have the sole, exclusive, undivided, and perpetual Possession of all the Countries, Cities, and Towns, on the said Continent [of North America], and of all the Islands near to it, which are now, or lately were, under the Jurisdiction of or subject to the King or Crown of Great Britain, whenever the same can be invaded and conquered by the said united States, or shall in any manner submit to or shall be united or confederated with the said united States."[5] Or, to put it more succinctly, the original concept of the Union as it was discussed in 1775–76 was that it should be the successor state to Great Britain in North America and include all the American territories of its empire as defined in the 1763 Peace of Paris.

To achieve that goal Congress attempted to create a federal union, or more precisely a confederated republic, that right from the outset envisaged and required future expansion, both to consolidate the nation and to reinforce an emergent sense of American identity.[6] Realizing the vision, however, was problematic. It was not clear in 1776 whether Canada, which had long been regarded as a dangerous threat to the American colonies, could become the fourteenth state or whether it would remain a base for British military operations. The matter was eventually finessed by the stipulation that "Canada acceding to this confederation, and adjoining in the measures of the United States, shall be admitted into, and be entitled to all the advantages of this Union."[7] The future of East and West Florida, whose possession before 1763 had been disputed by France and Spain, raised other issues. These provinces posed a less immediate military threat than Canada, but they remained under the control of their British governors and never sent delegates to Philadelphia.[8] And in light of reports received after July 1776 that France and Spain might soon be at war with Great Britain, it became questionable whether Congress should attempt to claim or to occupy these Gulf Coast colonies, should it need financial or military assistance from Paris and Madrid. Their fate, therefore, was left to depend on circumstances, yet they too could be admitted to the Union if nine states so decided.[9] Regardless of its actual size, though, the new confederation believed that the power of its commerce would compel international diplomatic recognition and thereby permit Congress to commence dealings with the European state system, or the "sort of republic" of European nations that Emmerich de Vattel had described in his widely read and influential 1758 treatise, *The Law of Nations; or, The Principles of the Law of Nature, Applied to the Conduct and Affairs of Nations and of Sovereigns.*[10]

These hopes barely survived the summer of 1776 and the need for greater and greater amounts of foreign aid to win the War for Independence, but Congress would always return to them whenever possible. Insofar as their goals involved Florida, the delegates tacitly reasserted their claims when they drafted instructions in September 1776 for their commissioners in Europe, directing them to seek recognition from France and Spain. In anticipation that Charles III of Spain might be "disinclined" to the American cause by an "apprehension of danger" to his South American dominions, Congress offered "the strongest Assurances" that these dominions would not suffer "molestation" from the United States. It made no comparable statement with respect to the king's interests and territories in North America. Realizing three months later this bid needed improving, Congress promised, in return for an alliance and a treaty of commerce, "to assist in reducing to the possession of Spain the town and harbour of Pensacola, *provided the citizens and inhabitants of the United States shall have the free and uninterrupted navigation of the Mississippi and use of the harbour of Pensacola.*"[11] This was a concession, but a limited one. It assumed that both West Florida and the navigation of the Mississippi belonged to the United States as a matter of right, derived from the peace of 1763, and that if Spain received Pensacola with American aid, it should offer an equivalent in return. And it did not necessarily preclude the possibility that Spain might return Pensacola to the United States after the establishment of American independence.

The signing of the Franco-American alliance in February 1778 began developments that would further undermine the notion that the Union should include Florida. In the articles of the treaty, the Bourbon monarchy of France did not openly challenge the territorial pretensions of the United States, but with due regard to the terms of its Family Compact with the Spanish Bourbons as well as the need to persuade them either to mediate the conflict with Great Britain or, failing that, to join to the alliance, Louis XVI reserved the right of Spain to prescribe the conditions on which it might act.[12] Consequently, when France pressed Congress after February 1779 to define its goals in a peace settlement with Great Britain, its minister, Conrad-Alexandre Gérard, made it clear to the delegates that the goals should be acceptable to Spain. That meant Congress would have to abandon its claims not only to East and West Florida and to the right to navigate the Mississippi but also to the territory between the Appalachian Mountains and the east bank of the Mississippi. The states, individually and collectively, claimed this last region by virtue of both their colonial charters and the settlement of 1763, but Spain intended to reclaim it as Luisiana Oriental, part of a vast territory between the Appalachian and Rocky mountains where Madrid refused to acknowledge the pretensions of other nations.

Congress balked at such concessions. To the extent it was prepared to contemplate a settlement excluding Florida, it insisted on the retention of both the territory extending to the Mississippi and the right to navigate the river. It also demanded "adequate compensation" for Florida in the form of a subsidy and a guarantee of its other territorial claims. Even that was too much of a compromise for some to accept, and delegates from the Southern states wished to compel Spain to accept American claims to both Florida and the Mississippi. The matter was precariously resolved by August 1779 when Congress agreed to negotiate with Spain on the basis that the United States might obtain Canada, Nova Scotia, Bermuda, Florida, and the Mississippi at the end of the war, but that if Spain should demand Florida and the exclusive navigation of the Mississippi south of the 1763 boundary line on the 31st parallel, the United States, in return, would receive a free port, or ports, in West Florida, a subsidy for the duration of the war, and a guarantee of its territory.[13] John Jay was then selected as minister to Madrid to see if Spain would accept these terms.

As Jay arrived in Madrid, James Madison, in March 1780, took up a seat in Congress as a delegate from Virginia. He was not yet thirty years of age, but he quickly mastered congressional business by becoming well informed on all issues before him.[14] How much he knew about Spain and its American empire, though, is difficult to tell. As a young boy compiling his commonplace book, he had transcribed from Francis Bacon the observation that "Spaniards had been noted to be of very small dispatch" and that if the French were wiser than they seemed, "Spaniards seem wiser than they are."[15] Later in his life Madison doubtless experienced many occasions on which he must have savored the pungency of such witticisms, but in 1780 it is unlikely he gave them very much thought. There is no evidence at this time, or at any other stage of his public career, that he ever really mastered Spanish, but it is quite probable he had read accounts in both English and French of the Spanish voyages of exploration and settlement in the New World.[16] More certainly, he would have been familiar with the treatment of these subjects by the celebrated Edinburgh historian William Robertson, whose approach to them, informed by a combination of providential Calvinism and the progressive social theories of the Scottish Enlightenment, Madison had absorbed at the College of New Jersey at Princeton after 1769.

From Robertson, Madison would have acquired a historically grounded perspective on the role of Spain and its empire in the rise of the early modern European state system, and he may well have absorbed Robertson's view that the decline of Spain under its later Habsburg rulers reflected a lack of resources to manage its vast American territories, which in turn had led to its overreliance on American gold and silver as opposed to a more diversified commercial economy.[17] And while Robertson subscribed, to some extent, to widely held notions about Spain and Spanish America suffering from problems of "priestcraft," and had also expressed doubts about how far the New World could be regarded as an environment that nurtured human progress, he was by no means a severely unrelenting critic of all things Spanish. He carefully cultivated relationships with prominent Spanish officials for research purposes, and he often tempered his reservations about Spanish America with praise for the reforms and "wise regulations" of the Spanish Bourbons, particularly those of Charles III, which had done much to restore the international standing of Spain after the defeats it had sustained during the Seven Years' War.[18] Madison, too, regarded Charles III as an enlightened ruler with a significant ability to influence both American and European affairs, and neither he nor anyone else could have predicted the extent of the collapse and the misfortunes Spain would experience under his successors, Charles IV and Ferdinand VII.[19]

By 1780 Madison had also gained some experience with the practical issues likely to arise from Spain's participation in the War for Independence.

In January 1778 he had joined the Virginia Council of State as an advisor to Governor Patrick Henry, and on his first day in office he found himself reading correspondence between Henry and the governor of Spanish Louisiana about how the latter might assist America. Henry wanted supplies—wool, linen, and money—which were lacking in Virginia and which he hoped might come from New Orleans through trade on the Mississippi. Henry took this plea one step further by suggesting that Spain consider "whether by uniting West Florida to the Confederation of the States of America, the English settlements [in the West Indies] will not be reduced to an extremity, and whether the progress of their rivalry with Spain would not cease."[20] Governor Bernardo de Gálvez was not opposed to the possibility that West Florida might at least be detached from Great Britain if not handed over to the United States, but neither Virginia nor Congress authorized any military activities on the Mississippi in 1778 that would have allowed him to act on it.[21] Later that year, though, Congress did ask Virginia to provide galleys for an attack on East Florida. Two vessels were located, but Henry reported that one of them could not "without great danger of Sinking be sent to Sea."[22]

After Spain declared war on Great Britain in June 1779, Madison's reactions to suggestions that the United States assist Spain in seizing Florida were mixed. He was aware Congress had its own claims in the region, but of more importance by 1780 was the view that the Spanish occupation of Pensacola and St. Augustine would do little immediately to advance the independence of the American states. "It would be much more for the credit" of Spain, Madison noted, "as well as for the common good, if instead of wasting their time & resources in these separate and unimportant enterprises, they would join heartily with the French in attacking the enemy where success could produce the desired effect," namely by defeating the Royal Navy squadron in the Caribbean under the command of Admiral George B. Rodney before it could furnish reinforcements to British garrisons in New York and elsewhere.[23] But when it came to American and Virginian interests in West Florida and on the Mississippi, Madison was soon to learn he could not afford to be so dismissive of such seemingly "separate and unimportant" matters.

In October 1780 Congress reaffirmed the instructions it had issued to Jay in 1779, and it fell to Madison to write a report justifying the decision.[24] Shortly before he did so, Madison met with the secretary of the French legation, François de Barbé-Marbois, whose task it was to get Congress to induce Spain to recognize the United States and join the 1778 alliance, particularly by renouncing once and for all its pretensions to Luisiana Oriental, navigation of the Mississippi, and access to the Gulf Coast through West Florida. That Madison desired all these objectives Barbé-Marbois saw as proof that he embodied "too many of the ambitious principles adopted by Virginia," but the secretary also conceded that Madison worked hard in his report "to remove all expressions that might displease His Catholic Majesty."[25] Madison tried to persuade Spain to accept Congress as an ally, but at the same time he rebutted the objections to U.S. claims that Jay would likely encounter in Madrid. His report, accordingly, was cast as a sustained defense of the territorial ambitions of the United States, in which Madison at once recapitulated past American thinking on the issues at stake while pointing to the ways in which he and others would approach them in the future.

At the heart of the report were conclusions Madison drew from the case for independence and the Model Treaty, namely that the confederated states were the rightful successors to Great Britain's North American empire and that Britain had acquired its territories not for itself but for all Americans. Even if Spain were to occupy "small spots" of this formerly British domain, as it had done by taking Baton Rouge, Mobile, and Natchez late in 1779 and early 1780, that would not, Madison believed, be sufficient for it to repossess all the "circumjacent territory"—indeed, Virginians under George Rogers Clark had also captured similar "spots" in the Illinois and Wabash regions. As for Luisiana Oriental, Madison claimed it under the colonial charters of the states, dismissing as he did so the view that the British Proclamation Line of 1763 restricting settlement west of the Appalachians was anything more than a temporary regulation that had no bearing on the matter of right, as both France and Spain were to contend. To relinquish the region to Spain, moreover, would divide the members of the confederation against themselves, deprive them of an essential source of future revenue, and violate the rights of their citizens who had already founded settlements there. Madison further maintained that France, in several articles of the 1778 alliance, had already guaranteed the territorial claims of Congress. If Spain were to say otherwise, it, and not the

United States, would be responsible for the failure to form a triple alliance against Great Britain.[26]

As far as the claims to navigation of the Mississippi and to free ports in West Florida were concerned, Madison asserted that even if Spain were to control both banks of the Mississippi to its mouth, this would not trump the American case. On that score, he invoked the law of nations, as Vattel had summarized it, to the effect that when two nations at peace held different portions of a river, each was entitled to a right of "innocent passage" on the whole, subject to only "a moderate toll" collected for trade regulation by the power at the river mouth. The claim to free ports in West Florida, furthermore, derived from the right and the necessity to make the navigation of the Mississippi meaningful in a commercial sense. Otherwise, he pointed out, commerce on the river, by its very nature, could only be a mere trade to New Orleans and not beyond. By insisting trade must mean "foreign trade" and ocean-borne commerce, Madison was able to advance an argument that territorial rights of some sort in West Florida were inseparable from the navigation of the Mississippi, and he even went so far as to state that the inhabitants of inland Georgia would need equivalent privileges, if not formal rights, for access to rivers in West Florida if they were to trade with the outside world as well.[27] All of these were arguments that Madison, and Jefferson and Monroe too, would draw on and recycle on many occasions over the next forty years as they engaged in their borderlands diplomacy with Spain.

Of no less significance was Madison's penultimate argument for requiring Spain to grant Americans access to the Gulf Coast. Should Spain deny this right, Americans in the trans-Appalachian West would have no choice but to seek their commercial outlets in Canada, through the northern Mississippi (which was believed to originate in Canada), the Great Lakes, and the St. Lawrence River, where the trade would come under British control (Madison was assuming here for the purposes of diplomatic bargaining that the United States would not obtain Canada without recognition and assistance from Spain). The northern route, Madison admitted, was not as "advantageous" as that to the Gulf Coast, but it was "far from an impracticable [one]." And should it to come into operation, he predicted the consequences. "So fair a prospect," he wrote, "would not escape the commercial sagacity of [Great Britain]. She would embrace it with avidity; she would cherish it with the most studious care; and should she succeed in fixing it in that channel, the loss of her exclusive possession of the trade of the United States might prove a much less decisive blow to her maritime preeminence and tyranny than has been calculated."[28] That argument rested on a widely held American belief that the growth of colonial trade throughout the eighteenth century had allowed Great Britain to rise as a world power, but it was far more than a mere debating point to use against Spain. It also reflected Madison's awareness that the power that commanded access to America's inland waterways could control its external trade. He was never to lose sight of that point, and more than three decades later, in 1812, it would eventually lead him into a war with Great Britain over the future of Canada itself.[29]

Considered as a whole, therefore, Madison's report for Jay constructed a case for territorial expansion that required American control of all the critical strategic points between the Gulf Coast and the St. Lawrence River. Its contents, which might be described as a hardheaded adaptation of the tenets of eighteenth-century mercantilism to the geographical realities of North America, thus positioned its author as a Virginian spokesman for a continentalist vision of America's future.[30] The report also made him in this respect an important successor to Benjamin Franklin. A quarter of a century earlier, the Pennsylvania statesman, along with many other colonial Americans and British imperial officials and writers (including Daniel Coxe, William Douglass, Thomas Jefferys, Archibald Kennedy, James Logan, John Mitchell, Daniel Neal, John Oldmixon, William Shirley, and Arthur Young), had made the argument for territorial growth, the expansion of settlement, and—in the case of Franklin alone—intercolonial union as the best responses to the situation that prevailed between 1702 and 1763, when all of the major strategic points necessary for control of the North American hinterland were in the hands of the French and Spanish Bourbons.[31] By 1780, after Great Britain replaced the Bourbons in the eastern half of North America following 1763 and then exercised its preponderance of power there in ways that propelled the American colonies into independence, Madison had seen just how clearly that legacy from the past could continue to affect the future of the new nation.

Jay acknowledged receipt of Madison's report in April 1781, but it did little to help the diplomat. The Spanish minister of state, the conde de

Floridablanca, made it clear that Spain was in no hurry to recognize America and that questions of financial assistance would require Congress to drop its other claims as well. Floridablanca thus laid down the position that the territorial settlement to the war should leave Spain with not only the Mississippi and Luisiana Oriental but also Florida, to ensure its control of the Gulf Coast and the routes to its colonies in Mexico and South America.[32] Moreover, within a few weeks of reaffirming the instructions Madison had defended in October 1780, Congress abandoned them, in part because of pressure from the delegates of South Carolina and Georgia, who feared that diplomatic maneuvers by the European powers following the formation of the League of Armed Neutrality in 1780 might lead to a mediated peace on the basis of the *uti possidetis*. That, in effect, risked leaving much of Florida in the hands of Great Britain, an outcome the Georgia delegation declared to be "utterly inadmissible by these States." Rather than accept that possibility, Georgia was willing to concede to Spain both the "entire navigation" of the Mississippi and a considerable portion of the territory to the east, provided Spain made an alliance with the United States, offered financial aid, and would not accept a peace in Europe until Congress could agree to its terms.[33]

Madison opposed this retreat. Concessions to Spain were premature, he believed, partly because insufficient time had passed for Congress to learn of the response to his arguments in Madrid, and partly because he feared that the exposure of divisions among the states would "do a mischief" by depriving them of "the weight of unanimity to reinforce [their] position."[34] Yet Madison hardly suspected at this stage that it might be Spain's policy to divide Congress. Its "mysterious & reserved" reluctance to treat with Jay did not greatly worry him, and he regarded its "backwardness in the article of money as intended to alarm us into concessions rather than as the effect of a real indifference to our fate or to an alliance with us." He therefore refused to indulge in "any distrust" of this prospective ally, relying on the reputation of Charles III "for steadiness and probity" as well as on his own assessment that Spain's interest in defeating Great Britain would ultimately compel it to join France in the alliance with America.[35] Even the Virginia Assembly came to share the concerns of South Carolina and Georgia, however, and it directed its delegates to modify Jay's instructions to the extent of withdrawing the demands for navigation of the Mississippi and for a free port, if Spain absolutely insisted, provided such concessions did not affect Virginia's claim to the river as its own western boundary. Madison had no choice but to follow the assembly, though in preparing new instructions for Jay, he tried to strengthen his hand by linking the concessions to Spain's accepting the right of the states to navigate the Mississippi north of the 31st parallel. Congress adopted this policy in May 1781, and Madison could only hope it would remove Spain's objections to recognizing and aiding the United States.[36]

Again, Madison was to be disappointed. At the same time that Congress dispatched its concessions to Madrid, Spanish forces under Governor Gálvez captured Pensacola from Great Britain. Virginians generally expected the Bourbon allies to follow this success with further operations in the New World that would contribute to the liberation of Charleston and Savannah from the British occupation they had endured since 1780.[37] They learned instead not only that Spain allowed the British troops surrendered at Pensacola to be sent to New York where they might be used against American forces but also that France intended to withdraw naval vessels from the Caribbean to humor Spain, as Madison put it, "on the subject of her hobby horse," the reduction of Gibraltar.[38] That France could behave in this way alerted him to the reality that Louis XVI might not have "that absolute sway in the Cabinet" of Spain as Madison had supposed, and the lesson was reinforced in August 1781 when he heard that Spain had sent a force of some eight to ten thousand troops off on another "hobby horse," the capture of Minorca.[39] This expedition, unlike that against Gibraltar, resulted in a Spanish victory, but Madison doubted it would do much "to hasten a peace." Its real purpose was to adjust the balance of power in Europe, from which outcome, he concluded, the United States would only benefit if it disposed the rulers of Europe "to reject the Uti possidetis as the basis of a pacification" in America.[40]

If Madison worried about a settlement based on the uti possidetis of 1781 —which could have left New York, South Carolina, and Georgia, to say nothing of Canada and East Florida, in British hands—it was not for long. The battle of Yorktown in October 1781 ended the war in North America, without Spain making a treaty with Congress. That situation left France and the United States, as principals in the 1778 alliance, free to negotiate with Great Britain without the United States having to deal directly with the conditions that bound France in its 1779 treaty with Spain, namely that

France would support Spain's territorial position in America and in Central America as well as its demands for Gibraltar and Minorca. Starting from that position in January 1782, Madison took a prominent role in shaping diplomatic strategies for the American commissioners in Europe. And, as had been the case with his October 1780 report, he staked out his ground on the Model Treaty by arguing that the United States, "as independent sovereignties," had succeeded to "whatever territorial rights" had belonged to Great Britain before 1776. That meant not only that Congress could demand British recognition of the independence of the states it represented but also that it might yet acquire the territories it had failed to occupy during the war, including Canada and Florida. By making these claims, Madison and his fellow delegates were trying to deprive Great Britain of any territory in North America on the grounds that its retention of Canada and Florida would be "imminently dangerous to our peace" and would expose the republic to foreign encroachments on its trade and territory.[41]

The realities were very different. The story told by Jay's dispatches, as Madison himself put it, was one of "*insulting delays disappointments* and *tergiversations*," multiplied by "dilatory pretexts no less inconsistent with [Spain's] own professions than disrespectful to the U.S."[42] By April 1782 no delegate in Congress was under any illusion that Spain would not demand the restoration of both East and West Florida and insist on its claims to the Mississippi and Luisiana Oriental. Madison was quick to point out that the concessions offered to Spain in 1781 were "the price of the advantages promised by an early & intimate alliance," but that "if this Alliance is to be protracted till the conclusion of the War, during a continuance of which only, it can be necessary, the reason of the Sacrifice will no longer exist." He hinted Congress might withdraw the concessions it had offered to Spain in 1781, but it did not do so, out of concern that the result would be a quarrel with France. Madison was also aware that to revise yet again the instructions for Jay risked reopening divisions among the states over the future national domain at a time when the financial position of Congress could hardly afford any reduction in its size. Nevertheless, he wished to extract something from Spain and suggested that Congress seek a "more liberal" treaty by stipulating for greater financial aid, commercial concessions and free ports in Spain's colonies, and a relaxation of its stand on the Mississippi.[43]

The peace negotiations hardly conformed to these expectations. Spain continued to delay recognizing the United States, and Madison approved of Jay's decision to leave Madrid and continue his diplomacy in Paris, in the larger forum of all the nations participating in the war against Great Britain. Their diplomats hammered out preliminary articles of peace by November 1782. Canada and Florida were not transferred to the United States; the former remained with Great Britain, while the latter was restored to Spain with a boundary line on the 31st parallel. The other terms, however, especially a western boundary on the Mississippi and a right to navigate the river recognized by Great Britain, as well as fishing rights and concessions for New England in Labrador and Newfoundland, were more satisfactory.[44] Their reception in Philadelphia, accordingly, was somewhat mixed, with Madison reporting that although the delegates welcomed the prospect of peace, there were "various circumstances" relating to the treaty articles "which check our confidence in them, as there are some which will *detract from our joy* if they should be *finally established*."[45]

What worried the delegates were the means whereby the boundaries of the United States had been determined. Jay, unable to make better progress in Paris than in Madrid and learning that France would support Spain rather than the United States on boundary questions and disputes over the Mississippi, persuaded his fellow commissioners to violate the spirit of the 1778 alliance, as well as the explicit direction of Congress that they should coordinate their diplomacy with France, by entering into secret and separate negotiations with Great Britain. Great Britain offered these negotiations in an effort to split the 1778 alliance, and it very nearly succeeded in doing so by tempting the Americans with the terms they had long sought on the western boundary and the Mississippi. In fact, so great was Jay's anxiety to secure these advantages that he even went so far, in a secret treaty article, to offer Great Britain an enlarged West Florida if it would retake the province from Spain before the signing of the peace treaty. Great Britain declined the opportunity and made separate arrangements with Spain regarding Florida and Minorca, but when the details were revealed in Philadelphia, Madison was appalled.[46]

Some delegates felt that Spain deserved no special consideration from the United States, but Madison's position was more complicated. Although he had been irritated by Spain's refusal to recognize the United

States, he did appreciate that Madrid had provided some financial assistance to Congress and that the expenditures of Spanish forces in the Caribbean and on the Gulf Coast had also been of benefit to Virginia.[47] And Madison could not approve of the risk of breaching the 1778 alliance that Jay had taken by negotiating separately with Great Britain, especially when one of the consequences could have been an expanded British West Florida on the southern border of the new nation. That outcome involved "considerations of both national honor & national security," and Madison regarded it as unnecessarily hostile to Spain as well as amounting to "a dishonorable alliance" with Great Britain "against the interests of our friends." Yet he also found the subject "infinitely perplexing," as he did not wish to appear to repudiate the peace treaty or even its negotiators, particularly when any criticisms of the latter might have inflamed sectional tensions in Congress. The best solution Madison could suggest was that Congress disclose to France the details of the secret article on West Florida—to repair any damage to the alliance and, more important, to prevent Great Britain from being able to divide France and the United States in the future.[48]

Toward the end of his term in Congress, while waiting for the peace treaty to arrive, Madison paused to reflect on some of the difficulties he and other delegates had encountered in conducting their business. Among them he noted their general lack of information on "the law of nations, treaties Negociations &c," which, he suggested, might be remedied if Congress established a reference library to help make its proceedings "conformable to propriety." Accordingly, Madison proposed that Congress purchase some 550 titles, including several on the history of Spain and its American colonies. The information they contained was necessary, he believed, not only to compile a history of the United States but also to controvert "future pretensions [against] its rights from Spain or other powers which had shared in the discoveries & possessions of the New World."[49] Future events verified Madison's prediction about Spain. While that nation finally recognized the United States at the end of 1783, it rejected the treaty article that sanctioned American navigation rights on the Mississippi, and in 1784 it closed the river to Americans altogether. Spain also refused to accept the boundaries established in 1783, both on the Mississippi and on the line between Florida and Georgia; the former, it insisted, should be moved eastward toward the Appalachians, while the latter should be located further northward.[50] Those decisions gave rise to new sources of friction between the two nations, some of which were to persist into the nineteenth century.

Madison was to be involved in all these disputes, although between 1783 and 1786 he acted as a member of the Virginia Assembly and not as a delegate in Congress. The experience he had accumulated in Philadelphia led some delegates to suggest that he might be sent to Madrid, but Madison, who was never willing to make a crossing of the Atlantic, preferred to work in Richmond.[51] From the vantage point of the Virginia Assembly, the main problems to settle were the Mississippi boundary and the navigation of the river. These were critical because of their importance to Kentucky, where a movement to separate from Virginia had been under way since 1779. The difficulty was that some Kentucky leaders began to suggest, if not to threaten, that unless Virginia and Congress could secure both the Mississippi boundary and the navigation of the river, the district might be compelled to leave the Union.[52] The alternatives, they hinted, were either to join with Spain in order to secure the navigation to New Orleans or to turn to Great Britain to obtain access to the northern reaches of the Mississippi, the Great Lakes, and the St. Lawrence—just as Madison had predicted in 1780 and as Vermont was already doing during the course of its quarrels with New York and New Hampshire over whether it could join the Union as a separate state.[53]

The very seriousness of these issues led Madison after 1783 to harden his attitude toward Spain, the more so as that nation ceased to be a potential friend and became instead the source of intractable problems. In response, Madison came to refer to Spain in harsher and more contemptuous terms, describing it on one occasion as a nation notorious for its "impotency, who has *given no proof* of a regard *for us* and the *genius of whose government religion & manners* unfit them, of all the *nations in Christendom*," for any treaty with the United States.[54] Yet a treaty with Spain was still necessary, and as far as the vital American claims to the Mississippi boundary and navigation were concerned, Madison ceased to argue for them as legacies from the British imperial past. These were now treaty rights of an independent nation, and to the extent that treaty rights under the law of nations could be seen as compatible with the laws of nature, Madison defended them in terms of natural law. As he told Lafayette in 1785, "Nature has given the use of the Mississippi to those who may settle on its waters, as she gave the United States their independence." Since Great Britain "could not defeat the latter, neither will Spain the former. Nature seems on all sides to be reasserting those rights which have so long been trampled on by tyranny & bigotry," and should the United States ever consent to "the occlusion of the Mississippi, they would be guilty of treason against the very law under which they obtained & hold their national existence." To reinforce such arguments, Madison relied extensively on the law of nations and the writings of Vattel in particular for relevant historical precedents.[55]

At times, Madison could also speak and write as if hostilities with Spain were inevitable, if Madrid continued denying American claims. The United States, he told Jefferson in Paris in 1784, was "already a power not to be despised by Spain," and he predicted the future security of its North American possessions would "depend more on our peaceableness, than on her own power."[56] Usually, though, he was more cautious. Madison was well aware Congress lacked the political will and the resources to settle foreign disputes by force, and he privately acknowledged that Florida and Louisiana were better secured to Spain by American weakness than they were threatened by American strength. War under those circumstances, as he pointed out to Monroe in 1785, was "more than all things to be deprecated," especially if it risked dividing France and the United States in ways that would allow Great Britain to meddle in the American interior from Canada.[57] To avoid that danger, Madison preferred to put forward arguments—which he intended Jefferson and the marquis de Lafayette to circulate to French and Spanish officials in Europe—that appealed to Spain to transcend its "folly" toward the United States by adopting a liberal trade policy on the Mississippi that would transform New Orleans into "the Grand Cairo of the New World."[58]

Yet as Madison continued to argue for access to New Orleans, he did not abandon his earlier thinking about the importance of Florida, even though it was now the task of American diplomacy to persuade Spain to accept the boundary on the 31st parallel rather than to push it to the Gulf Coast. That problem notwithstanding, Madison reminded Jefferson in 1784 that Americans needed not only the Mississippi but also the right to use the "Spanish shores" of the river below the 31st parallel and to have an "entrepot of our own" there. If Spain was not prepared to designate New Orleans as a free port, "some territorial privileges" would become as "indispensable to the use of the river as this is to the prosperity of the western country." Here Madison identified "the Englishman's turn" on the island of New Orleans, about "six leagues below the town," as "the fittest for our purpose," and he described "point Coupe," to the north, "as the highest to which vessels can ascend with tolerable ease." But he also mentioned Baton Rouge in West Florida "as a convenient station" where vessels might be moored and an American merchant community established. He even indulged the hope that Spain would allow Americans to survey the areas concerned to facilitate "a deliberate choice," and he hinted at the possibility of making a purchase, assuming that whatever price Spain might ask, it "[could] not well exceed the benefit to be obtained." To avoid the disputes that might arise in the event of these proposals being put into effect, he further suggested that Spain and the United States establish a "joint tribunal" to adjudicate them. That Spain had previously agreed to a similar tribunal in its 1648 treaty with Holland led him to assume that Madrid could find no good reason under the law of nations to deny the same to the United States.[59]

Given Spain's record of reluctance in its dealings with the United States, these were optimistic goals, but Madison remained willing to believe that the nation's diplomats might accomplish them. Americans and Spaniards on the disputed boundaries were less confident, however. Even as they rejected the 1783 treaty lines, Spanish officials on the Gulf Coast were aware their northern and eastern borders were too thinly settled to withstand pressures from American immigrants, and the governors of Florida and Louisiana responded by allowing selected groups of Americans to settle in Spanish territory on terms that included generous land grants and religious toleration for Protestants as well as the promise of their being able to use the Mississippi.[60] That the success of these policies was mixed at best was less important in the minds of many Americans than the fact that their intent was clearly to weaken the position of the United States on its own frontiers. Madison was less alarmed than most on this score, though he agreed that "a watchful eye" should be kept on all such Spanish ventures. Otherwise, he was inclined to compare them with "the experiment tried by the Roman Empire on its decline," adding with a touch of contempt that the consequences of that experiment were "sufficiently known and would have escaped the attention of no other politicians than those of Spain."[61]

Rather more serious, though, were encroachments by American officials, speculators, and settlers on territory claimed or held by Spain. Their activities dragged the United States into several conflicts simultaneously: with Spain; with southern states with claims to lands occupied by the Chickasaw, Choctaw, and Creek Indian nations; and with the Indian nations themselves as they turned to Spain for assistance and protection.[62] In 1785 the Georgia Assembly even went so far as to extend its authority into the area between the 31st parallel and the Yazoo River by creating a new jurisdiction, Bourbon County. This region had been conquered by Governor Gálvez in 1779, then ceded to the United States by Great Britain in 1783, and it was now in dispute with Spain. These circumstances led to violence, or near violence, by both sides. The commissioners of the Georgia Assembly threatened the commander of the Spanish garrison at Natchez, and Gálvez, who was now viceroy in New Spain, ordered their expulsion and the breaking up of the county.[63] The incident foreshadowed confrontations Madison would face after 1801 as secretary of state and as president. His responses to them were always governed by his understanding of how far the claims of the American parties involved could be reconciled with both fundamental law and the law of nations. Thus when he heard of the actions of the Georgia Assembly, Madison was appalled that any state "could be so guilty of so flagrant an outrage on the foederal Constitution, or of so imprudent a mode of pursuing their claims against a foreign Nation."[64]

Yet the more Madison contemplated these quarrels with Spain, the more it became apparent to him that the United States lacked the capacity to resolve them. The problem was not merely that Congress lacked the financial and military resources to vindicate its claims or even that Spain would not negotiate. In 1785, Madrid dispatched Diego de Gardoqui y Arriquibar to New York to make a treaty with Jay, who now held the position of secretary of foreign affairs in Congress. Gardoqui's instructions precluded any compromise on the navigation and boundary of the Mississippi, and he was also to contend for a West Florida border extending up the Flint River to the Highwassee and Tennessee rivers and from there to the point where the Ohio River met the Mississippi. In return, he could accept a boundary between East Florida and Georgia on the 31st parallel as well as offer trade concessions in Europe and a defensive alliance that included a mutual guarantee of territory.[65] When Congress would not agree, Jay, in an effort to prevent a rupture that might lead to war, sought to make a treaty that would have closed the Mississippi to Americans for twenty-five to thirty years in exchange for the commercial concessions in Europe and the mutual guarantee of territory. For this, the consent of nine states was necessary, but no more than seven northern states ever backed the idea. The result was a bitter sectional debate that paralyzed Congress to the point of seriously destabilizing the Union.[66]

Madison was adamantly opposed to Jay's concessions. He did not share the secretary's concern that failure to make a treaty necessarily risked war, and he scorned the value of a mutual guarantee of territory. That proposal would only draw the United States into "the labyrinth of *European politics* from which we ought religiously to keep ourselves as free as possible," and Madison could hardly believe that "the arm of *Spain*" could save the nation anyway.[67] But Madison's real objections to an agreement with Gardoqui arose from its impact on domestic politics. The idea that the Mississippi border and navigation might be exchanged for trade concessions in Europe by the fiat of a less-than-constitutional majority jeopardized sectional comity in several ways. It was bad enough that the interests of southern planters might be sacrificed for the benefit of northern merchants, but Madison also feared that western regions, particularly Kentucky, would conclude that they too had been betrayed and would follow the example of Vermont by turning to Great Britain. That Madrid was willing to make a treaty to that effect he could attribute to no other motive than its desire "*to work a total* separation of *interest and affection between* the *western and eastern settlements* and to *foment* the jealousy *between the eastern & southern states*." The future growth of the American West would be stunted and the Mississippi closed, all to promote "the general *security of Spanish America*."[68] And even more worrying from Madison's point of view was his fear that Gardoqui and Jay had so aroused sectional antagonisms that it would become impossible to persuade the states, especially Virginia, to adopt the constitutional changes that by 1786 he believed were necessary to save the Union.[69]

It was to pursue this last goal that Madison returned to Congress in February 1787.[70] He lost little time in seeking out Gardoqui for an assessment of the Spanish problem. After an exchange of pleasantries to the effect that Spain and the United States should live in harmony, Gardoqui explained his position on the Mississippi, telling Madison "with an air of ostensible jocoseness" that "the people of Kentucky would make good Spanish subjects, and that they would become such for the sake of the privilege annexed to that character." He also rejected the view that there was any case under the law of nations for Americans to share the Mississippi, remarking as he did so that Spain had "exclusive possession" of "a great proportion" of the territory on both sides of the river. When Madison asked, "*How much?*" Gardoqui replied, "At least as far as the Ohio." The Virginian had a higher estimate of the loyalty of Kentuckians to the Union than did Gardoqui, and upon hearing that the northern border of West Florida was on the Ohio, he recorded that he could only "smile."[71] Nevertheless, there could be no mistaking the seriousness of the problem. Madison's solution was to propose that Congress shift the negotiation to Europe, where he assumed that Jefferson might undertake a special mission to Madrid, supported by the good offices of France. When Jay opposed the idea, however, he was happy enough to let the matter rest until after the meeting of the Federal Convention in Philadelphia in May 1787.[72]

The Federal Constitution of September 1787 did not satisfy Madison in all respects, but the provisions of the treaty clause in the second section of its second article at least promised to prevent a repetition of the problems of the Jay-Gardoqui negotiations. Even though one of the most serious defects of the old confederation (according to Madison)—equality of state representation regardless of state population size—was preserved in the new Senate, Congress lost the initiative in making treaties to the president, and the Senate could approve them only by a two-thirds vote as opposed to a mere majority.[73] After the new government commenced its operations in the spring of 1789, George Washington considered resuming the negotiations with Gardoqui, and he sought Madison's counsel by sending him a series of questions about how to recover the ground that had been conceded by Jay. As Madison had done, the president worried that to surrender the Mississippi could "occasion—certainly—the separation of the Western territory."[74] That Washington took no further action on the matter suggests that Madison probably advised him against doing so until Jefferson had returned from Paris and taken up the duties of the newly created State Department.

Jefferson's views about Spanish problems were usually very similar to those of Madison, though this was not always to be the case throughout the course of their collaboration over the next twenty years. Nevertheless, by 1790 Jefferson agreed that the United States was entitled to the Mississippi boundary and navigation, both by treaty and by the laws of nature, and he understood the importance of vindicating those rights to ensure an orderly transition for Kentucky into statehood in the Union. He also realized that the navigation of the Mississippi required some sort of territorial concession from Spain below the 31st parallel to provide for an American entrepôt on the Gulf Coast.[75] But within weeks of his taking office and before he could commence any diplomacy at all, Jefferson was confronted with a crisis that portended a radical transformation of the context in which American policy toward Spain had previously been made. That crisis resulted from the simultaneous efforts of Great Britain and Spain to establish trading posts at Nootka Sound on Vancouver Island, where the latter nation claimed rights by virtue of prior discovery and the former denied them on the grounds that they had not been made effective. At issue here was Madrid's contention that it alone had the right to colonize the Pacific coast, and London wished to exploit the dispute to undermine Spain's recently strengthened position in North America. For the Washington administration, though, the immediate subject for discussion was how to respond to the problems of an impending war between Great Britain and Spain.[76]

The difficulties of such a war for the United States could hardly be understated, especially if its ally France should enter on the side of Spain, but the question that shaped the deliberations of the administration was whether to grant British troops the right of passage across American territory in the event of Great Britain attacking Spanish possessions on the Gulf Coast. Should such passage be granted, and assuming that British troop movements would be accompanied by naval operations in the Gulf of Mexico, the United States, in the event of a British victory, risked being completely encircled by Great Britain—from Canada, down the Mississippi to New Orleans, and across to East Florida. The replies of Washington's cabinet members to a hypothetical British request for troop passage from Canada to the Gulf Coast have been repeatedly discussed by historians, but far less attention has been paid to their implications for American policy toward Florida and Louisiana.[77] Before making his response, Jefferson consulted with Madison, and in offering his suggestions to the president he explicitly mentioned that they reflected Madison's thinking as well as his own.[78]

If the Nootka Sound crisis resulted in an Anglo-Spanish war, both Jefferson and Madison believed that Great Britain would emerge victorious and that it would at least attack, and probably take, Florida and Louisiana. Whether the United States itself should then risk war to escape the dangers of British encirclement, however, depended on whether France became a party to the war. Even if France did participate, Jefferson and Madison worried that the costs to the United States would be too high, and if Spain fought alone, they admitted that "our situation [would be] rendered worse." Rather than recommend a course of action for that dilemma, they opted for delay, hoping that Great Britain might not attack Florida and Louisiana or that she might fail to take them. If Great Britain did take these Spanish colonies, though, Jefferson and Madison realized the United States "should have to re-take them" and bear all the costs and risks of war. To reach this conclusion was to anticipate the worst possible outcome, but before that point was reached they chose to suppose that Spain might understand it could not prevent Great Britain from capturing Florida and Louisiana. They suggested that Spain might consider granting independence to those colonies, in which case France, Spain, and the United States could then join together in guaranteeing their independence. A triple alliance to remove the Spanish borderlands as an object of British policy might, therefore, spare the United States from a war—if, as Jefferson and Madison conceded, "G[reat] B[ritain] respects our weight in a war."[79]

When Jefferson came to consider the question of how he might negotiate directly with Spain, however, he instructed William Carmichael, Jay's former secretary who had remained in Madrid as American chargé d'affaires, to present them in ways that might advance the American goal of securing the Mississippi and, perhaps, even of obtaining Florida itself. To accomplish this, Jefferson directed Carmichael to insinuate that the United States might act in conjunction with Great Britain, in which case the former would receive at least Florida and the island of New Orleans in return.

To avert that outcome, Spain would have to accept the necessity of granting the Mississippi to the United States as well as a port near its mouth "to secure our vessels, and protect our navigation," including a separate jurisdiction "to avoid the danger of broils." And to be entirely certain of keeping Florida and Louisiana out of British hands, Spain could also choose (and Jefferson stressed the element of "*choice*" here) to cede Florida to the United States, in return for which Spain would receive an American guarantee of its possessions west of the Mississippi.[80] In short, while adopting a policy of procrastination to avoid an irrevocable commitment in the event of an Anglo-Spanish war, Jefferson also attempted, by indirect means, to turn the crisis into an advantage by securing some longer-term American policy goals against Spain. It was a tactic he would attempt again after 1801.

The peaceful resolution of the Nootka Sound crisis in October 1790 allowed Jefferson to return to the diplomacy of the Mississippi question. To the extent Madison played an active role here, it was largely by writing to correspondents in Kentucky to assure them that the Washington administration would make every effort to secure them the river and that they, in turn, should discourage any thoughts among their fellow westerners of secession or of using force to gain access to New Orleans.[81] For his part, Jefferson worked to restart negotiations, though he had made little progress by the time he retired from the State Department in December 1793. Before he left office, however, the secretary of state found himself paying as much attention to problems on the still-unsettled Florida border as he did to business in Madrid. The governors of Louisiana and West Florida continued to invite Americans into their territories, and after 1792 Baron François Hector de Carondelet in New Orleans, in particular, became unusually aggressive in stepping up Spain's policy of cultivating southern Indian nations in order to counter the efforts of newly appointed federal Indian agents to place these nations under the protection of the United States. At the same time, conflicts between the governments of East Florida and Georgia, also centering on the Creek Indians, intensified and were compounded by the inability of any of the affected authorities, American or Spanish, to reach understandings about how to handle other issues, such as the return of escaped slaves, criminals, and military deserters.[82]

These matters came to a head in 1794 when Washington, to avert the possibility of a rupture, sent an extraordinary mission to Madrid, entrusting it to Thomas Pinckney of South Carolina. The chances for its success did not at first seem promising, but developments resulting from the French Revolution, in both Europe and America, created pressures that led Spain to reconsider its stance toward the United States. The execution of Louis XVI in January 1793 dissolved the Family Compact between the French and Spanish Bourbons and replaced it with an Anglo-Spanish alliance that proved to be a disaster for Madrid. Among the consequences of this reversal of Spain's traditional policy were the efforts of the first French republican minister to the United States, Citizen Edmond-Charles Genet, to promote filibusters against Florida and Louisiana from American soil, and by early 1795 French armies had invaded northern Spain.[83] Another undesirable result of the Franco-Spanish war was the transfer of much of the trade of Spain's borderland colonies to Great Britain and the United States. Confronted thus with the prospect of diplomatic failure on a grand scale and suspecting that the treaty Jay had negotiated with Great Britain in November 1794 might mark the beginning of an Anglo-American rapprochement, Charles IV and his minister, Manuel de Godoy, attempted to salvage their situation by ending the alliance with Great Britain in order to restore the former connection with France. As they did so, they also granted the United States many of the demands it had been making since 1780.[84]

Accordingly, Pinckney was able to conclude a treaty with Spain at San Lorenzo in October 1795. Under its provisions Spain finally accepted the 1783 boundary lines on both the 31st parallel and the Mississippi. It also conceded the navigation of the river, though it did so as a "privilege" rather than as the right that Americans claimed they already had by virtue of the settlements of 1763 and 1783. Spain did not, as Madison would have wished, grant a territorial concession in West Florida for an entrepôt accompanied by arrangements for adjudicating disputes between Americans and Spaniards, but it did consent to a deposit, or its equivalent, for the purpose of allowing exports through New Orleans. In addition, Spain undertook to restrain the Indian nations within its territories from hostilities against the United States, and it regularized trade on a most-favored-nation basis.[85] In Philadelphia, Madison did not learn of Pinckney's success until late February 1796. The news, he wrote Monroe, gave "general joy," and he described the boundary and commercial articles of the treaty as "very satisfactory." Indeed, so eager was Madison to see Pinckney's treaty in force that he would allow nothing to jeopardize its success, even when the price of its ratification included the simultaneous implementation of Jay's treaty with Great Britain, an agreement that Madison deplored as a dishonorable contrast to the victory that had been won in Madrid.[86]

Pinckney's Treaty might have reduced the tensions between Spain and the United States, but it did not entirely end them. As Spain and France resumed their traditional alliance, the latter began negotiations to recover its former colony of Louisiana with the boundaries it had claimed before 1763.[87] It did so, moreover, at a time when France and the United States were in a state of undeclared war as a result of the Jay Treaty. These circumstances ensured that Spain's Gulf Coast possessions would remain an object of concern for Americans, the more so after Spain declared war on Great Britain in October 1796. Considerations arising from that state of affairs, as well as the desire for speculative gain, led William Blount, the Federalist senator from Tennessee, to plan a filibuster in 1797 to seize Spanish military posts in West Florida and Louisiana.[88] His plans were derailed by his expulsion from the Senate and a subsequent trial for impeachment, but as the administration of John Adams stepped up its preparations for a possible war with France, Alexander Hamilton, in his capacity as inspector general of the U.S. Army, also contemplated the seizure of Florida and Louisiana. By 1799 Hamilton could write that he had "long been in the habit of considering the acquisition of those countries as essential to the permanency of the Union," and his ambitions may have extended even further, to Mexico and Peru—or as he put it, "to squint at South America."[89]

Madison probably never suspected how far Hamilton might have "squinted." He certainly feared Adams would pick a war with Spain, but not so much for territory as to provide opportunities for privateering to American merchantmen deprived of commercial outlets after 1798.[90] Nevertheless, after Madison took up his duties as secretary of state in Jefferson's first administration in May 1801, he inherited the same borderlands problem Hamilton had proposed to solve by war. By that date there was an abundance of evidence that France had obtained the "retrocession" of Louisiana from Spain, and Hamilton contributed to it by sending Madison a letter he had received from Paris to that effect. Madison returned it, remarking only that its contents had been "previously signified to [the State] Department from several sources, as an event believed to have taken place."[91] The event in question had occurred in October 1800, on the day after France and the United States had agreed to end their undeclared war by dissolving their 1778 alliance and leaving for future discussion their unsettled disputes over France's liability for spoliations committed during its course.[92] The contents of the Franco-Spanish Treaty of San Ildefonso remained unknown, however, as did the exact extent of the territories its signatories might have understood to be included under the description of "Louisiana."

Herein lay the problem that was to dominate American relations with Spain for the next twenty years. In October 1800 Spain returned to France "the Colony or Province of Louisiana with the same extent that it now has in the hands of Spain, and that it had when France possessed it; and Such as it should be after the Treaties subsequently entered into between Spain and other states." The last clause of this article was intended to accommodate the modifications made to Louisiana by the treaties of 1783 and 1795, but the preceding clauses reflected the inability of France and Spain to resolve disputes over the extent of their respective claims in Louisiana before the territorial cessions made to Spain and Great Britain in 1762–63. By virtue of voyages of exploration made from Canada and in the Gulf of Mexico in the last quarter of the seventeenth century, France maintained that it had possessed territories to both the east and the west of the Mississippi. On the east, French claims covered that portion of the province Great Britain had designated as West Florida as far eastward as the Perdido River and included such originally French settlements as Mobile, Biloxi, and Dauphin Island; on the west, France's claims embraced their settlements at Bayou Pierre and Natchitoches as well as the region that Spain had administered as Texas as far westward as the Rio Grande.[93]

In November 1762 a border was drawn at the Iberville River to separate Florida from New Orleans in order to transfer the former to Great Britain. The unresolved Franco-Spanish boundary disputes west of the Mississippi ceased to matter as Spain simply assumed control over all the territories in question.[94] After Spain regained West Florida in 1783, it administered the former British province and Louisiana as parts of an extended jurisdiction with two governors who reported to Madrid through the captain-general and governor of Cuba at Havana.[95] But when France embarked on its quest for Louisiana after 1795, its intent was plainly to recover, one way or another, all of the territories it had previously claimed on both sides of the Mississippi and to acquire East Florida as well. At first, Spain would consent to return only New Orleans and Louisiana west of the Mississippi, but it eventually agreed to honor a further request for the territory between the Mississippi and Mobile Bay, which France demanded as "part of Louisiana before the treaty of peace of 1763."[96] Hence the final wording of the retrocession clause in October 1800 when Spain returned Louisiana not only "with the same extent that it now has in the hands of Spain" but also with the same extent "that it had when France possessed it." That West Florida was not formally delivered to France along with New Orleans and Louisiana west of the Mississippi River before 1803 was Madrid's way of protesting against Napoleon's further demand for East Florida—to which France had no good historical claim whatsoever—but as late as November 1802 the French foreign minister, Charles Maurice de Talleyrand-Périgord, even as he tried to restrain the First Consul's problematic ambition for East Florida, continued to assert that "West Florida suffices for the desired enlargement of Louisiana" and would complete "the retrocession of the French colony, such as it was given to Spain."[97]

That was the situation inherited by Jefferson and Madison in 1801. Their response was to instruct their diplomats in Europe—Robert R. Livingston in France and Charles Pinckney in Spain—to purchase the island of New Orleans and East and West Florida from whichever nation actually possessed them.[98] As Jefferson was to note, "Whatever power, other than ourselves, holds the country east of the Mississippi becomes our natural enemy."[99] Florida was also necessary to protect the navigation of the Mississippi as well as to ensure access to other rivers flowing to the Gulf Coast for settlers moving southward from Tennessee and westward from Georgia. The clarity of well-defined or "natural" borders with ports, however, was far more important than the intrinsic value of any land that might be obtained. Florida itself had too much sandy soil and too many pine forests to be of much value as an agricultural or revenue resource.[100] The priority of controlling access to ports and rivers was further confirmed in October 1802 when the Spanish authorities, in apparent violation of the 1795 treaty, revoked the right of deposit at New Orleans without providing any equivalent facility.[101] The episode could only have reminded Jefferson and Madison of why they had tried to insist before 1795 that the right to navigate the Mississippi could hardly be kept distinct from the question of territorial and jurisdictional rights for Americans in West Florida.

In April 1803 France offered to sell New Orleans and Louisiana to the United States. Livingston and Monroe—who had recently arrived in Paris bearing instructions from Madison—hesitated, knowing that their briefs did not cover territory west of the Mississippi.[102] But after conversations with French officials that provided a basis for believing that France had regained a valid title to Florida between the Mississippi and the Perdido, they agreed to the purchase, subject to the condition that the 1800 retrocession clause be included in the treaty as proof that the United States had acquired the French claim to West Florida and that France would sanction that understanding.[103] The two diplomats then embarked on a course of research using archives and maps to furnish additional historical underpinnings for that contention. When Jefferson and Madison received the news, they too had questions about what had been purchased, and they commenced their own inquiries. By August 1803 the president was convinced the United States had acquired in Louisiana a "substantial" claim to West Florida as well as rights in Texas that "may be strongly maintained," conclusions he reinforced over the next several weeks as he compiled a history of French exploration and settlement on the Gulf Coast and in the Mississippi valley after 1673.[104] That document was based largely on French sources, and it has often been dismissed—when it is even noticed at all—as little more than a meaningless example of its author's not-inconsiderable talent for finding convenient rationalizations for his purposes.[105] To so conclude, however, is to misunderstand the significance of the president's decision. By accepting Louisiana as it had been defined by France in 1800 and 1803, Jefferson deliberately staked out the position that the United States was the rightful heir to France's remaining claims to a North American empire, just as Congress, in the Model Treaty of 1776, had asserted that it was the sole legatee of Great Britain's American empire of 1763.[106] Indeed, one of the main advantages of the 1803 purchase was not so much that it enlarged American territory westward to the Rocky Mountains but that it also furnished the administration, albeit at a greater financial cost than Jefferson would have liked, with the opportunity to continue the quest for a border on the Gulf Coast.

The Spanish minister to the United States, Carlos Martínez de Yrujo, promptly attacked the validity of the Louisiana Purchase on a variety of grounds, including one that Napoleon had promised Spain never to alienate the colony, and Madison soon came to learn that Madrid did "not include any territory E[ast] of the Mississippi except the Island of N[ew] O[rleans] in the idea of Louisiana." That reaction scarcely bothered him. Believing that France would support the United States, he concluded that it would be "an easy matter to take possession [of West Florida] according to our idea. The mode alone can beget a question."[107] But when Congress assumed that Spain would shortly vacate the province and sought to supply "the mode" by authorizing the administration to establish a customs house at Mobile Bay in February 1804, Yrujo sent Madison an angry critique of the notion that France had acquired West Florida, and he denounced Congress for legislating an "atrocious libel" on the good faith and integrity of the United States.[108] Madison cautioned the minister to use more "decorous" language, but Yrujo was unrepentant, which amounted to a virtual rupture between the State Department and the Spanish legation.[109] Madison had personal reasons to regret the development inasmuch as Yrujo's wife, Sally McKean, was both the daughter of the governor of Pennsylvania and a close friend of Dolley Payne Madison.

The unpleasantness of this exchange was one reason that convinced Madison to shift the diplomacy for securing West Florida from Washington to Europe, and by April 1804 he and Jefferson had devised a strategy for doing so. They did not expect that Spain would readily accept their claims, and they counted instead on France exercising considerable influence on their behalf in Madrid at a time when it seemed almost inevitable that Spain would sooner or later be drawn into the war that had recently broken out between France and Great Britain. Jefferson and Madison, moreover, did not particularly wish to entrust their diplomacy to Pinckney, in part because they had lost confidence in his abilities and in part because they were reluctant to allow the Spanish foreign ministry too many opportunities to attack the American case and create the impression throughout Europe that it was without merit. The task was therefore assigned to Monroe in an extraordinary mission that the administration hoped would lead to a comprehensive settlement of all its outstanding disputes with Spain.[110]

Monroe's principal goal was to obtain both East and West Florida in order to secure Louisiana by extending American control over the northern coast of the Gulf of Mexico. He was to accomplish this in two stages: first, by persuading Madrid that West Florida to the Perdido River was part of Louisiana, in return for which the United States would establish its new western boundary somewhere between the Sabine and Colorado rivers rather than on the Rio Grande and draw the lines in ways that, while excluding Spain from access to the Mississippi and Missouri rivers, would leave "a spacious interval between our settlements and those of Spain"; and second, by offering a financial inducement if Spain would cede to the United States the remainder of West Florida between the Perdido and Apalachicola rivers as well as the province of East Florida.[111] Initially, the idea was to pay Spain $1 million for East Florida, but by April 1804 the monetary sum was replaced by an offer to assume Spain's liability for its so-called French spoliations.[112] These claims had resulted from the use of Spanish ports by French naval vessels and privateers during the Quasi-War of the late 1790s, and in a convention Pinckney had negotiated in August 1802, he and the Spanish secretary of state, Pedro Cevallos Guerra, had been unable to agree on how this breach of Spain's neutral obligations toward the United States might be settled.[113] Rather than simply seizing East Florida in retaliation or as an act of reprisal, the United States, instead, offered to assume the claims on behalf of its own citizens and made an attachment on East Florida for the purpose of fulfilling them.[114]

Monroe did not reach Madrid until January 1805, but even before he had done so his mission was doomed. France retreated from its position that West Florida could be regarded as part of Louisiana, particularly after Spain joined it in the war against Great Britain in December 1804.[115] Thereafter, Napoleon was always to pay more regard to his own needs with respect to Spain than he did to those of the United States. For Madison, this was an unwelcome development that weakened Monroe's hand. The problem was not that he regarded the American claims as unsound so much as that he understood they rested on a historical reading of the retrocession clause that, in turn, depended on the intentions of France and Spain in 1800 and on how those intentions should be construed under the law of nations. As he reminded Jefferson, the claim to West Florida had to be supported by "those rigid notions of technical law" that often had "too little weight in national questions generally," and should Paris and Madrid mutually agree that West Florida had never been included in Louisiana, "the world would decide that France having sold us the territory of a third party, which she had no right to sell, that party having even remonstrated [against] the whole transaction, the right of the U.S." would be limited "to a demand on France to procure & convey the territory, or to remit pro tanto the price, or to dissolve the bargain altogether."[116]

Madison did not suppose France would return even some of the money that had been paid for Louisiana, but that matter only highlighted another problem with Monroe's mission: that he was not empowered to offer enough money to induce either France or Spain to begin considering his demands. He could promise no cash payment, and it would take a lengthy period to determine the value of the French spoliations, even if Spain agreed to such calculations being done. But Spain continued to reject all liability, pointing out as it did so that Americans should collect any compensation for French spoliations in Paris, where Livingston and Monroe had established a spoliations commission at the same time that they had signed the Louisiana Purchase.[117] Nor would Spain consider submitting the dispute to arbitration. The result was that Monroe passed five frustrating months in Aranjuez, near Madrid, until May 1805, during which time Cevallos spurned every proposal he and Pinckney put forward, "in terms," as Monroe reported, "the most explicit and at the same time not the most respectful." Worse was the fact that Cevallos omitted to offer any counterproposals. From Madrid's point of view, not only was there nothing to settle, but there was not even anything to discuss.[118]

When Madison learned of these developments in August 1805, he was hardly surprised. His pride was more than a little irritated that Cevallos would treat the honor of the republic so roughly, and he realized that Monroe's failure seemed to leave only a choice between going to war with Spain or doing nothing beyond preserving the status quo and reasserting American claims at a later date. His inclination was for the latter, especially if he could find ways of retaliating at the same time against the colonial commerce of all belligerent nations guilty of infringements on American rights and interests.[119] Jefferson had no desire for war either, but he wanted to do more than merely reserve American claims. He suggested that Spain be threatened with an Anglo-American alliance if it did not settle, the same tactic he had suggested in 1790 and had also contemplated in 1802 in the event of it being necessary to guarantee American access to New Orleans from Spain before Napoleon took over Louisiana.[120] Madison disagreed. Throughout 1805 relations with Great Britain had deteriorated as that nation stepped up its impressments of American seamen and its seizures of American vessels engaged in neutral trade with France and Spain. On these issues, the secretary of state was unwilling to make the concessions that he assumed London would demand in a treaty.[121] Jefferson, nevertheless, pursued the idea because he believed Spain would never satisfy the United States unless it was exposed to greater pressures that would have maximum effect only in the context of the European war. Indeed, should that war end in the near future, the president feared that the opportunity to talk Spain into a treaty would be lost for a very long time.[122]

The next move came from Paris, however. In August 1805, the American minister to France, John Armstrong, was given a hint that Talleyrand, and possibly Napoleon as well, might be interested in arranging a settlement between Spain and the United States. The proposed terms on border problems were essentially the same as those Monroe had put forward at Madrid; the differences were that the United States would pay Spain $10 million, that Spain would not be liable for the French spoliations, and that the United States would assume all debts owed by Spain to American citizens by issuing bills of credit for Spain's American colonies. Armstrong had no doubt the initiative was a "job" to extract American money for France at Spain's expense, and he was later to remark that to pay up to $10 million for East Florida was "a great deal of money for pine trees & sand hills."[123] Even so, Jefferson responded positively. After deciding that the war in Europe would continue for at least another year, the president agreed to resume negotiations—with "France as the Mediator" and "the price of the Floridas as the means." Of the money, he wrote: "We need not care who gets that: and an enlargement of the sum we had thought of may be the bait to France, while the Guadaloupe [River, between the Colorado and Medina Rivers] as the Western boundary may be the soother of Spain providing for our spoliated citizens in some effectual way."[124] What Madison thought is less clear. He was not sorry to see Jefferson abandon the idea of a British alliance, but the president also made his decision alone late in the fall of 1805, at a time when Madison was in Philadelphia accompanying his wife as she underwent medical treatment for an ulcerated knee.

That decision required extensive planning for the financial arrangements to accompany the negotiation of a treaty in Paris. The secretary of the Treasury, Albert Gallatin, was uncomfortable with the entire scheme, however, partly because of its potential to derange his carefully calibrated programs of balanced budgets and debt retirement, and partly because he disliked the idea of issuing treasury bills for Spanish America. He estimated he could afford no more than $2 million in cash to pay for additional territory, and he grudgingly agreed that he might find at least $4 million to cover Spain's spoliation liabilities.[125] In December 1805 Jefferson sought the $2 million appropriation from Congress but without being entirely candid about its ultimate purpose. He obtained it four months later, at the cost of provoking a rebellion in the ranks of his supporters, led by John Randolph of Roanoke, who denounced the proposal as corrupt and attempted to prove the charge by quoting Madison as saying, "France wanted money & must have it."[126] The secretary of state denied he had said any such thing, but Randolph was hardly wrong about where the money would go. Accordingly, in March 1806 Madison drafted fresh instructions, which included an outline for a convention with Spain. The territory to be acquired was East and West Florida; the western boundary of Louisiana could be located on either the Colorado or Guadaloupe rivers, again with a provision for a neutral zone between American and Spanish settlements; and the negotiators were allowed considerable discretion as to how they settled the spoliations but were encouraged to avoid promising treasury bills for Spanish America.[127] Of necessity, Armstrong would be the main negotiator, but to assist him Jefferson and Madison also sent to Paris their new minister-designate for Spain, James Bowdoin of Massachusetts, who could take up his duties in Madrid once the treaty had been concluded.

Armstrong and Bowdoin were no more successful than Monroe and Pinckney. As had been the case in 1805, Spain immediately indicated its unwillingness to part with Florida. Madrid did not assume that Napoleon would necessarily render decisions in its favor, and it only reluctantly sent a minister to Paris. It was, moreover, impossible for the Americans to determine whether that minister, Eugenio Izquierdo, had been empowered to enter into a treaty or whether his goal was merely to protract the proceedings in order to prevent an outcome to them.[128] Armstrong and Bowdoin also mishandled their assignment by engaging in bitter personal quarrels to the point that they could not cooperate on anything.[129] For his part, Napoleon proved to be more interested in trying to persuade Spain to invade Portugal than he was in pressing it to settle with the United States. He also came to doubt that the United States would pay as much money as Talleyrand might have liked, and in the summer of 1806 he turned his attention to Germany, where in short order between July and November he established the Confederation of the Rhine, abolished the Holy Roman Empire, and defeated Prussia—after which he accelerated his maritime war against Great Britain and laid the foundation for his Continental System by issuing the Berlin Decree.[130]

By May 1807, it was clear nothing would be achieved, but the discussions dragged on because no one would end them. That situation troubled Madison because he feared that the absence of a treaty with Spain risked elevating incidents on the unsettled borders to the causes of a more serious conflict, as had nearly been the case in the fall of 1806 when American and Spanish troops occupied parts of the region in dispute between Louisiana and Mexico. The avoidance of war on that occasion owed more to the efforts of Brig. Gen. James Wilkinson and Col. Simón de Herrara, the army commanders on the ground—who established an unofficial "Neutral Ground" between the Sabine River and the Calcasieu River in Louisiana—than it did to anything the diplomats attempted in Madrid, Paris, or Washington.[131] Only the shock of the attack on the USS *Chesapeake* by the British warship *Leopard* in June 1807 ended this state of affairs. The urgency of the crisis with Great Britain, as Madison might have guessed, overtook the quarrels with Spain, and in July 1807 he finally wrote to Armstrong and Bowdoin and directed them to cease their efforts to purchase a treaty on the borderlands.[132]

The failure in Paris demonstrated that the outcomes of Madison's Spanish diplomacy were increasingly dependent on events in Europe, where he and Jefferson had assumed that French military victories, in conjunction with the difficulties Spain would experience in contending against Great Britain, would promote their views in Madrid. But events in Europe could also jeopardize Madison's quest for the borderlands, as he realized when he read a February 1808 letter from Armstrong reporting "an extraordinary turn" in American relations with France. The development to which the minister referred was not merely Napoleon's decision to start confiscating American vessels under the Milan Decree of December 1807 but also a statement by Talleyrand's successor as foreign minister, Jean-Baptiste Nompère de Champagny, that any future French support for a territorial settlement with Spain would be dependent on the United States cooperating with France's war against Great Britain, particularly by a strict observance of the Berlin Decree. Since the purpose of that decree was to end all neutral trade with Great Britain, the United States could hardly have acquiesced without either going to war with Britain itself or accepting that London would probably initiate a war by way of retaliation for such conduct. If the United States failed to follow French policy, however, the result would be, Armstrong learned, the sequestration of all American property in France.[133]

When he decided to adopt this policy, Champagny may not have known that the Embargo of December 1807 had already effectively "sequestered" most American property in American ports, so the impact of his threat was less dramatic than he might have calculated. It was, nonetheless, highly offensive. Madison certainly found it so, and he instructed Armstrong to communicate this to Champagny. As for the matter of French support for the acquisition of Florida, Madison responded that the United States would not depart from its policy of neutrality toward the European belligerents and that it would not become a party to their wars "for the purpose of obtaining a separate and particular object, however interesting to them." That did not preclude, though, the possibility that the United States might undertake a "precautionary occupation" of Florida should "the hostile designs of Great Britain" toward Spain make it necessary. This was a measure Madison believed France could hardly oppose, and he reminded Armstrong that Napoleon had never indicated he would disapprove of it.[134] But what Madison did not know when he wrote this directive on 2 May 1808 was that Napoleon had recently invaded Spain and overthrown its monarchy—by imprisoning Ferdinand VII in Bayonne after he had replaced his father, Charles IV—in order to establish his own brother, Joseph Bonaparte, as King of Spain and the Indies. Nor did Madison know on 2 May that a crowd in Madrid had already risen up against *el rey intruso* and the French usurpation in the first stage of a popular revolt against the Napoleonic empire in Europe, which would ultimately lead to further revolutions against the prospect of its extension to Spanish America.[135]

Madison had not been unaware that Napoleon might intervene in Spain. The emperor, after all, had invaded Portugal in 1807, a development that led Great Britain to send an expeditionary force to that country and also to send the Portuguese royal family to Brazil at the end of the year.[136] Madison's reactions to the events of May 1808, therefore, required him to consider their implications for Spanish America as a whole as well as their impact in the borderlands. How far would France seek to extend its influence, if not direct control, over Spanish America, and would Spanish Americans accept or reject that situation? Even more troubling was the prospect that Great Britain would respond by trying to emancipate Spanish America from its mother country, a policy he had long known London to be interested in but which it had not yet attempted in any serious way. As Madison told Armstrong in September 1808, "It is well understood here, that in the event of a French family being established on the Spanish throne," the whole of Spanish America would "revolt under the patronage of Great Britain."[137] But if Great Britain managed to gain access to the markets and resources of a rebellious Spanish America, the consequences for the United States would be extremely serious. The impact of the Embargo on the British imperial economy would be immediately reduced, as would the administration's longer-term ability to employ any form of economic coercion to persuade London to respect its definitions of American neutral rights.[138]

Madison therefore waited on news from Spain, which he often found difficult to assess. When Spanish loyalists drove Joseph Bonaparte (albeit briefly) from Madrid after the Battle of Bailén in July 1808, Madison even wondered whether Napoleon might not find "the tide at length turning against him."[139] But until the answer to that question was clearer, there could be no question of the United States recognizing either Joseph or the Supreme Central Junta that was organizing the resistance against him. As he reminded Gallatin shortly thereafter, "To acknowledge the new and local power set up in Spain would be an infatuation to which the most stupid or the most wicked only could suggest."[140] What Madison desired most here was "authentic information" about developments in Spain, as he was reluctant to rely on accounts coming from British newspapers, which the American minister in London, William Pinkney, believed exaggerated the strength and the significance of the Spanish resistance.[141] An alternative perspective from Madrid was provided by the American chargé d'affaires, George W. Erving, who right from the outset was deeply impressed by the intensity of the popular hostility to the French invasion and the rule of Joseph. In the matter of military operations, Erving readily conceded the superiority of the French. He frequently reported how their better-organized and better-disciplined forces could defeat the resistance, but in the long run he could not see how either Joseph or Napoleon could effectively govern Spain under such circumstances.[142]

However "authentic" this information might have seemed, it embodied a perspective Madison was unable to share. After he replaced Jefferson in the presidency in March 1809, he ignored efforts made by the Supreme Central Junta to secure American acknowledgment of its cause, and he refused formal recognition of the diplomatic representatives it sent to the United States, Valentín de Foronda and Luis de Onís, even though they both claimed to have the authority to negotiate the disputes Madison still wished to settle. His decisions here were governed in part by his distrust of the surviving representatives of the Bourbon regime in Spain and in part by his wish to maintain American neutrality in the European war, but underlying these concerns was a deep skepticism that the Spanish resistance could ultimately prevail.[143] As late as November 1809, Erving continued to maintain that the Supreme Central Junta, with support from the forces of Great Britain, with whom it had allied in August 1808, could succeed, though he admitted that the conflict would be "long & obstinate."[144] Madison passively dissented from this point of view. While he never suggested to Erving that he should ignore the resistance, he did wonder whether the chargé, by continually following the movements of the Supreme Central Junta, had not become too persuaded of its view of the situation and thus made a serious misjudgment. Jefferson tried to reinforce this impression by pointing out that Erving had "erred in principle, by not taking his stand with the government of Spain de facto." The former president, very probably recollecting the positive role that Joseph Bonaparte had played in 1800 in ending the Quasi-War with France, regretted the error and reminded his successor that the emperor's brother "has been said to be well disposed towards us."[145]

To Madison, that last point seemed less important than the possibility that Napoleon might now revive his earlier dreams for a French-American empire, first by demanding Cuba from Spain and then by offering to settle the boundaries of Florida and Louisiana in return for an American agreement not to seek trading privileges in Spanish America. He recalled that Napoleon had attempted to terminate American trade to St. Domingue while trying to subdue the island in 1803, and he feared that if the emperor should make similarly restrictive terms the condition of a boundary settlement, it would present him with "a dilemma not very pleasant."[146] Yet by the beginning of 1810, it seemed Madison might face that dilemma, or something very like it. In a series of rapid moves starting late in 1809, French armies advanced into Andalusia, where they captured Seville and besieged Cádiz, both of them critical cities that connected metropolitan Spain to Spanish America. These reverses forced the Supreme Central Junta to retreat to the Isla de Léon in the harbor of Cádiz, where in January 1810 it relinquished its authority to a Regency Council. The Council summoned a *Cortes* (parliament) for the purpose of reorganizing the resistance, but not even Erving could believe this would now save Spain. He admitted as much in what would prove to be his final dispatches to the State Department, and in February 1810 he left for home.[147] When the news crossed the Atlantic, the consequences were manifold. In April 1810, the *cabildo* (town council) of Caracas in Venezuela, also assuming that Napoleon would now reduce Spain, repudiated the Cádiz Regency and embarked on a course that would lead it by July 1811 to become the first major Spanish-American colony to declare its independence.[148] After reading of these developments in Washington in June 1810, Madison reached the same conclusion: that the fall of Spain was inevitable and the days of its American empire were numbered. But if so, what would be the outcome of the still-unsettled boundary disputes with Spain in the borderlands?

2

WEST FLORIDA

To form for themselves an independent Government is out of the
question!

—W. C. C. Claiborne to William Wykoff, Jr., 14 June 1810

As news from Cádiz and Caracas appeared in the newspapers of
June 1810, the governor of the Orleans Territory, William C. C. Claiborne,
arrived in Washington, where he was to be a guest of the president. His
visit had been planned months earlier, after the death of his second wife
in November 1809, and it had nothing to do with the emerging crisis in
Spanish America. The governor was merely exhausted after having spent
nearly seven years at a geographically remote posting in an arduous climate that had taken a considerable toll on his personal life. He had sought
permission to leave New Orleans to settle his accounts and deal with family business in Virginia, and perhaps he had hopes of obtaining a new and
more comfortable government position.[1] But he would have immediately
grasped the significance of the accounts in the newspapers. The fate of
Spain and its empire had always been a subject of daily concern to him as
an administrator whose territory shared disputed borders with Spanish
West Florida and Texas. The difficulties these circumstances had created
for him as he labored to integrate Orleans into the Union had long led him
to look forward to the day when these outposts of Spanish power on the
Gulf Coast might disappear from the map altogether.[2] In June 1810, Claiborne, like Madison, sensed this day had now come.

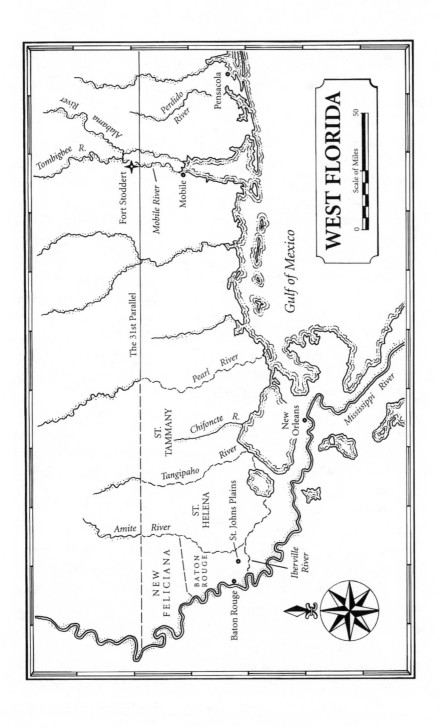

WEST FLORIDA

Scale of Miles

0   50

Gulf of Mexico

Pensacola

Perdido River

Alabama River

Tombigbee R.

Fort Stoddert

Mobile River

Mobile

The 31st Parallel

Pearl River

ST. TAMMANY

Chifoncte R.

Tangipaho River

New Orleans

Mississippi River

Amite River

ST. HELENA

St. Johns Plains

NEW FELICIANA

BATON ROUGE

Baton Rouge

Iberville River

In 1803, France had delivered New Orleans and Louisiana west of the Mississippi to the United States, but it made no attempt to turn over any of the territories comprised in its claim to Louisiana east of the river. Spain had declined to relinquish them, and its colonial administrators remained at their posts between the Mississippi and Perdido rivers, most conspicuously at Baton Rouge and Mobile, as well as at Pensacola. Some even remained in New Orleans itself, including Sebastián Calvo de la Puerta y O'Farrill, the marqués de Casa Calvo who had recently been appointed boundary commissioner for Spain, and Juan Ventura Morales, the intendant for Luisiana who had been responsible for withdrawing the right of deposit from Americans in New Orleans in October 1802.[3] Following the example of their superiors in Madrid, these officials denied the validity of the Louisiana Purchase and particularly the claim that it had included West Florida to the Perdido. Consequently, when Claiborne considered issuing a proclamation defining the extent of his jurisdiction in January 1804, he eventually decided against it after he learned Casa Calvo and Morales would almost certainly contest whatever territorial limits he claimed as being under his control.[4] Insofar as the problem involved West Florida, the Spanish officials were backed by the outgoing French colonial prefect Pierre Clément de Laussat, who declared he did not believe himself authorized to transfer to the United States any territory east of the Mississippi other than New Orleans.[5] West of the Mississippi, the situation was rather less contentious, but no Spanish official would support the notion that Claiborne might exercise any authority beyond the Sabine River, and certainly not in Texas as far west as the Rio Grande.

Initially, Claiborne tried to avoid entanglement in such "diplomatic" quarrels, but his position made that impossible.[6] Any contact with Casa Calvo and Morales, or even with any Spanish subject residing in the Orleans Territory, required the governor to engage in varieties of "local diplomacy"—routine, day-to-day decisions that might have international repercussions—in the course of carrying out his duties.[7] Madison instructed him to persuade the Spanish officials to depart, preferably to other parts of their empire such as Cuba or Mexico, but they refused.[8] Casa Calvo remained in New Orleans, conducting himself as a "high diplomatic character" by maintaining a military guard whose members often came into conflict with American citizens.[9] Morales had fewer pretensions, but he was widely despised for being immoral and corrupt. He reinforced that reputation by engaging in land speculation in the territories in dispute between Spain and the United States, even going so far as to open offices for that purpose in New Orleans and Pensacola. Claiborne was mortified to have to report that his buyers included many prominent Americans.[10] It had also been policy since 1785 for Spanish officials to grant small plots of land—averaging about five hundred acres—to encourage settlement, as opposed to speculation, in Spain's Gulf Coast territories, and local officials in West Florida continued that practice too, at least until 1806, when, in reaction to the Kemper revolt of 1804, they began to restrict it.[11] Consequently, the legitimacy of land titles in West Florida became a complex and contentious matter, which Morales only made worse. By issuing grants on a grand scale in his capacity of intendant, he exercised a sovereign right that challenged the American claim to West Florida, and he created at the same time groups of American settlers with vested interests in supporting Spain. Among them were Daniel Clark and his associates in New Orleans, who also became the most prominent opposition faction in the Orleans Territory to Claiborne's administration.[12]

Frustrated, the governor wondered whether Morales might be driven out of New Orleans as a common-law nuisance, but Madison's reaction was much more extreme.[13] In the fall of 1805 he inquired whether it would be possible to indict Americans who had purchased land from Morales under the Logan Act of 1799 on the assumption that their commercial dealings with a Spanish official amounted to a form of unauthorized diplomacy. The secretary of state abandoned the idea after being advised against it by his chief clerk.[14] Casa Calvo posed problems of a different sort, making life difficult for Claiborne by constantly insinuating that the Louisiana Purchase was only a temporary arrangement and that American rule on the Gulf Coast would not long endure. In particular, he spread rumors to the effect that while negotiations between Spain and the United States in Europe might result in the United States receiving both East and West Florida, the price would be the return of New Orleans and all of Louisiana west of the Mississippi to Spain.[15] The combined effect of the presence and activities of Casa Calvo and Morales in New Orleans was thus to call into question every aspect of American control over the Orleans Territory, thereby heightening the governor's anxieties about the loyalties of its polyglot population.[16] Claiborne endured these provocations for three years before Casa Calvo and Morales finally agreed to depart in 1806.

Even then, the governor's difficulties were scarcely eased. Casa Calvo and Morales relocated to Pensacola, where the Spanish governor, Juan Vicente Folch y Jaun, proved himself to be a worthy pupil of Casa Calvo inasmuch as when he came to New Orleans—as he frequently did after visiting Baton Rouge—he would insist on receiving as much diplomatic respect as the former boundary commissioner had demanded.[17] Folch also attempted to improve Spain's military position in West Florida by building roads in the province and by rearranging and reinforcing his troops in the forts at Mobile and Pensacola whenever he could.[18] Claiborne had to treat him carefully, in part because New Orleans depended on West Florida for supplies and in part because Spain's policy of conducting its Indian trade in the region to the east of the Pearl River through the British firm of John Forbes and Company was an important element in a frontier balance of power that could not be disturbed without jeopardizing the security of American settlers in the Mississippi Territory and in western Georgia.[19] Claiborne would have been happy to see Folch leave, but for as long as the status of West Florida remained in dispute he found that Madison, in Washington, would instruct him to negotiate with his Spanish counterpart over such matters as the construction of postal roads through West Florida to improve the American mail service to New Orleans.[20] To the extent Folch's consent required the United States to accept that Spain exercised effective control in West Florida, he was willing to grant it, but by occasionally obstructing or delaying the mails he could also underscore the difficulties the United States encountered in making good on its territorial claims.[21]

More difficult than the subject of postal roads was the question of to what extent American vessels might have access to the port and river at Mobile Bay in order to reach the Mississippi Territory north of the boundary line on the 31st parallel. On several occasions before mid-1810, the Spanish garrison at Mobile had refused to allow American vessels passage up the river to supply Fort Stoddert, a U.S. Army post just above the boundary with West Florida. These episodes produced confrontations that risked provoking wider military conflicts, but for that very reason neither

Spain nor the United States was prepared to push them to their ultimate conclusion.[22] Almost as serious, though, were disputes over the terms on which American civilians might use the Gulf Coast river mouths for migration and peaceful commerce. As had been the case with the Mississippi between 1784 and 1795, the United States claimed a "natural right" to reach the Gulf of Mexico on rivers originating in American territory, particularly the Tombigbee and Alabama rivers. Spanish officials never conceded this "right," but they were prepared to allow trade that was subject to the collection of export and import duties, usually as high as 12 percent each way. These rates were regarded by merchants and settlers alike as ruinous if not prohibitive, and Claiborne appealed to Folch on several occasions to abolish them, albeit without success.[23] The power to impose duties also involved the issue of sovereignty over West Florida, thus leading one group of Mississippi settlers to petition Congress for relief in November 1809 by asking, "Are We Americans or Spaniards? Shall we support the Republic of the United States, or the Spanish Monarchy?"[24] Further petitions on this subject were presented in the spring of 1810, and while Madison reaffirmed the "natural right" of Americans to use the rivers in question, he declined to take any action to avoid the danger of "controversies with the Creeks & Spaniards."[25]

The question of commercial rights became more serious as Americans settled in West Florida in increasing numbers in the first decade of the nineteenth century. The effects of this migration were felt not so much in the eastern section of the province between the Pearl and Apalachicola rivers as in the area between the Pearl and Mississippi rivers. In the region east of the Pearl the population grew slowly, probably amounting to not much more than four thousand by 1810—excluding the Spanish garrisons in Mobile and Pensacola—and it consisted for the most part of small handfuls of families in scattered communities separated by impenetrably dense cane breaks, cypress swamps, and crocodile-infested rivers and streams. The land was poor—sandy soil where it was not marshy—and the economy, devoted largely to the exchange of frontier products such as livestock, timber, food, and deerskins, was relatively undeveloped. This "poor sand-bank and quagmire," as the Scottish merchant James Innerarity described it, was nevertheless of considerable strategic significance. By virtue of its rivers and bays and their proximity to more populous and prosperous settlements in western Georgia and the Mississippi Territory, it was essential to the development of the American frontier itself, and for that reason alone it was not an area that Americans believed should remain dependent on "the pleasure of a foreign monarch."[26]

The settlements east of the Pearl River had little contact with those farther to the west. By 1810 the population of the region between the Pearl and Mississippi rivers had risen to about fifteen thousand, mostly Americans who were concentrated in the Feliciana and Baton Rouge districts, where they had sought out rich river-bottom lands with access to waterways for the export of slave-produced cotton and sugar. Here the impact of Jefferson's Embargo of 1807, followed by the Non-intercourse Law of 1809, proved to be substantial, and by depressing both cotton and land prices it created many difficulties for those Americans who were under Spanish rule in the region below the 31st parallel.[27] To ease the consequences of Washington's policies, Folch appealed to Claiborne to exempt West Floridians from them, but Claiborne had to refuse, knowing full well that to tolerate trade through Spanish outlets would permit American products to pass into the hands of Spain's ally, Great Britain.[28] Inevitably, though, the prolonged duration of the maritime crisis with Great Britain after December 1807 gave rise to smuggling through Spanish territory, and that development threatened to retard the growth of Orleans by diverting American migration into West Florida. That situation, as former U.S. senator John Adair of Kentucky pointed out to Madison shortly before he assumed the presidency, was potentially dangerous. What might happen, Adair asked, if Great Britain were to intervene on the Gulf Coast by offering "Independence, alliance, and Commerce" to the people of the adjoining territories? Should it do so, he feared it would "at once give the British interest [in West Florida] a decided ascendancy," to say nothing of producing "intreague, cabals and heart burnings" against American authority all along the southwestern frontier. "The proper management" of the people of West Florida "at this moment," Adair warned, therefore became a matter "all important to the Union."[29]

Adair's concerns weighed heavily on the minds of Madison and Claiborne when they met in June 1810. Both the governor and the president assumed that Spain had "yielded" to Napoleon—or would very shortly do so—and that the Cádiz Regency would be reduced to no more than "a little local committee." Once the authority of the Spanish Bourbons had been rendered defunct by the Napoleonic conquest, they anticipated that "the people of Florida" would be "assailed by a host of intriguers" in the form of "a French party and an English party" whose adherents would seek to attach the province either to France or to Great Britain. And while there might not have seemed to be much basis for fearing the activities of a "French party"—Claiborne observed that a "connection with France" would be opposed by all "the honest prejudices" of the country—recent influxes of French refugees (originally from Haiti and expelled from Cuba after Napoleon's invasion of Spain) had created concern throughout Orleans and West Florida about their potential influence should either Joseph Bonaparte or his brother attempt to rule Spanish America directly. Settlers of British and Loyalist descent were also numerous, but if they were to seek "the protection of Great Britain," the governor predicted, it would be a "curse" that would bring London into immediate conflict with Washington. West Florida would then become "a seat of war."[30]

To prevent these contingencies from coming to pass, Madison decided, first, to warn Great Britain against meddling in West Florida. On 13 June 1810 the American minister in London was told to inform the British government that the United States believed that the alliance between Spain and Britain was about to be "terminated by events in Europe," that the ties between Madrid and its American colonies were "on the point of dissolution," and that any future British challenge to the American claim to West Florida would be regarded as "unjust and unfriendly."[31] The next day, 14 June, the president took steps to vindicate the claim that the United States had a good title to West Florida extending to the Perdido. He authorized Claiborne to write to his friend William Wykoff, Jr., a well-connected territorial judge who resided near Baton Rouge, to direct him to contact prominent American settlers in the districts between the Mississippi and Pearl rivers for the purpose of organizing a convention to invite the United States to take possession of West Florida as the successor to the expiring Spanish regime. Madison presumed that the invitation would strengthen the American claim and that the utility of a convention would be to certify that its request reflected the wishes of the inhabitants of Florida "as far at least as the Perdido." He allowed the governor to grant the local leaders some discretion in the matter but insisted that they scout "everything like French or English influence." And under no circumstances should they "form for themselves an independent government." That step was "out of the question!" because it would undermine the American claim to West Florida, to say nothing of the fact that the province was hardly viable as an independent state anyway. As the governor pointed out, "The paucity of their numbers, their insular situation, and circumscribed limits forbid the idea!" In short, Wykoff's task was to steer the views of his neighbors across the Mississippi River in the "right direction" to ensure the peaceful and uncontested extension of American authority over West Florida.[32]

Claiborne's letter would have taken at least three weeks to reach its destination, but before it had done so West Floridians took steps of their own in response to the news from Spain and Venezuela. Sometime in late May or early June 1810, John Hunter Johnson, the son of an old British settler of 1775, and some other planters from St. Francisville in the Feliciana district visited Tomas Estevan, the Spanish commandant at Bayou Sarah, to demand that he summon a convention to discuss measures to "restore public tranquility." Estevan agreed, and on 23 June a crowd estimated at more than five hundred assembled at the plantation of Alexander Stirling and elected four "respectable and influential neighbors"—Johnson, William Barrow, John Mills, and John Rhea—as delegates to coordinate with like-minded men from the Baton Rouge, St. Helena, Chifoncté, and Christiana districts and meet in a general council to administer the government for the common good in a time of crisis. According to one account there was also talk of electing a governor, a secretary, and a council of three "to take possession of the country in behalf of Ferdinand VII, if he should again be restored to the throne of old Spain."[33] Two weeks later, similar events in Baton Rouge, including a meeting at the house of Samuel Fulton, who had written to Madison as long ago as 20 April alerting him to the impending crisis of legitimacy for the Spanish regime, resulted in the election of five more delegates—Philip Hicky, Thomas Lilley, Manuel Lopéz, John Morgan, and Edmund Hawes. And on 14 July, another five delegates were chosen from St. Helena, Tanchipaho (St. Tammany), and Chifoncté—John Leonard, Joseph Thomas, William Spiller, Benjamin Williams, and William Cooper.[34] These fourteen delegates would eventually meet in a convention at St. Johns Plains near Baton Rouge on 25 July 1810.

Such developments did not necessarily reflect any long-standing or clearly articulated desire to overthrow the Spanish regime. To all outward appearances, they paralleled the creation of loyalist juntas that was occurring in many other Spanish dominions after 1808 to carry on the government during the confinement of Ferdinand VII in France. At that time West Florida, too, had been the scene of meetings between local officials and settlers during which the latter called for the introduction of popular participation into public affairs.[35] And it would be inaccurate to say that relations between settlers and officials in West Florida after 1803 had been consistently characterized by conflict and hostility. Even the revolt led by Reuben Kemper and his brothers in 1804 was much more a manifestation of isolated personal grievances and frontier lawlessness than it was a popular or coherent political protest.[36] Occasionally Spanish officials worried about the possibility of an American invasion, especially at times of heightened tension between Washington and Madrid, but for the most part they concentrated on developing working relationships with those leading American settlers whose consent and cooperation they required for a peaceful administration.[37] After 1805, certainly, some of these Americans were unhappy about a more restrictive land-grant policy that had been introduced as a consequence of the Kemper revolt, and there were also complaints about the practice of bribery in the administration of local justice, but not even the 23 June meeting in Feliciana, where such discontent was most keenly felt, called for the end of Spain's rule, as long as its officials were willing to cooperate with local community leaders.[38] Moreover, four of the ten delegates elected in July—Cooper, Hicky, Lilley, and Leonard—were from British or American Loyalist backgrounds, and events were to prove that López was no rebel either. Their election also took place with the consent of the Spanish commandant at Baton Rouge, Carlos deHault DeLassus, who then retroactively sanctioned the earlier meeting at Feliciana.[39]

Nevertheless, as would be the case with loyalist juntas in Spain and elsewhere in Spanish America, these actions concealed as much as they revealed, and the prospect of the imminent collapse of the Bourbon regime compelled both West Floridians and Americans in the surrounding neighborhoods to begin exploring the implications of that development. That they were doing so became clear in the contents of a draft "constitution" that began circulating after mid-July 1810. Apparently drawn up by Edward Randolph, the postmaster of Pinckneyville, Mississippi Territory, in conjunction with John Hunter Johnson and the other delegates from Feliciana, this document predicted, as had Claiborne and Madison, that the "political ties" binding West Florida to Madrid would be dissolved by events in Europe. Even so, it did not call on West Floridians to abandon their own allegiances to Spain but merely stated that these could not be transferred to "the present ruler of the French nation, or to any King, Prince or Sovereign who may be placed by him on the throne of Spain." But because "distant provinces no longer cherished or protected by the mother country" also had "a right to institute for themselves such forms of government as they may think conducive to their safety and happiness," the Randolph-Feliciana plan began to lay the groundwork for an autonomous, if not exactly independent, province of West Florida by providing for the continuation of the local government under the supervision of an elected governor, a secretary, and a council of three who could, if necessary, call out the militia, lay taxes, declare war, regulate commerce, naturalize foreigners, and even "enter into confederacy with other states." Questions about the long-term future were left open, however, with the governor and council to decide sometime in the next three years whether to summon a convention with "full powers to form a constitution for the better government of this Commonwealth."[40]

Whether the Randolph-Feliciana plan had been influenced by knowledge of Claiborne's 14 June letter to Wykoff is impossible to tell. As Madison would have wished, it did not declare West Florida independent, and it allowed for the possibility of the province joining the Union, though it also provided for an autonomous government that could have laid claim to far more sovereign powers than the president would have felt necessary for it to have in order to issue the invitation he sought for the United States to fill the vacuum about to emerge from the collapse of Spain. It also seems clear that to the extent there was knowledge of Claiborne's directive from Washington, it was understood to mean that the administration desired any convention that might meet to issue a declaration of independence as a preliminary to discussions about how West Florida might be taken into the United States.[41] That step not only was the opposite of what Madison wanted but also seemed too radical, or too dangerous, for many West Floridians to avow openly at this point. Even American settlers who did desire to join the Union were not clear how that might be accomplished, or, more seriously, they were unsure whether the United States still had a valid claim to the province after having failed twice to vindicate it in negotiations in Madrid and Paris and having done nothing more since to make it effective. As delegate William Barrow, who, in fact, despaired whether the United States could ever find a way of getting possession of West Florida, complained when the convention met, "We have found people disposed to involve us in civil war by declaring Independence and calling the U. States to aid, without knowing whether they would or not."[42]

With opinions uncertain and divided as to how to proceed, the convention acted with great caution after 25 July. The delegates were, as Barrow pointed out, "in a measure strangers to one another," and one of the first orders of their business was a proposal that they take an oath of allegiance to Ferdinand VII. Barrow confessed surprise at "finding men to believe that it was essential to be done," but others apparently felt differently. After some discussion "only one appeared to be in favor of it"—almost certainly Manuel Lopéz—but that meant no delegate could be confident that any discussion would not be reported to the Spanish authorities. "Then we thought it proper," Barrow added, "not to say much on any subject."[43] The delegates took the oath and turned to the more "immediate object" of promoting "the safety, honor, & happiness of his Majesty's province of West Florida" by considering such matters as the "redress of existing grievances," including defense and settlement policy as well as regulations governing roads, slaves, livestock, weights and measures, fees charged by officials, and measures to keep out French exiles from Cuba. Committees were formed on these subjects, and the convention extended its reach on 27 July by proposing that it take over the costs of administering West Florida—a step justified as relieving "the burthens of the mother Country, engaged as she is at present in a dubious Contest for her own preservation"—and by considering the creation of a new court system. All this was done with the consent of DeLassus, to whom the delegates sent a loyal address in which they also offered to pay his salary. They did not, however, think it necessary at this stage to trouble His Excellency "with a detail of [their] proceedings" and deliberations, "in which the greatest unanimity has prevailed." The convention then adjourned until 13 August.[44]

As had been the case with the meetings before 25 July, there was more to these transactions than met the eye. According to the governor of the Mississippi Territory, David Holmes, who sent a former member of his executive council, Joshua G. Baker, to report to him from Baton Rouge, "a correct Opinion . . . of the real Views and Wishes" of DeLassus and the delegates could not be gained "from their public and official Acts." Majority sentiment in the convention, Holmes informed the State Department, favored incorporation into the United States, while DeLassus had only acquiesced in its meeting for want of a better alternative as he waited for Folch to return to Pensacola from Havana and bring a military force to "put an end to [its] deliberations."[45] When the convention reassembled on 13 August, however, DeLassus merely sent the delegates a reply to their address, declaring much of it to be "tranquilizing and satisfactory" and only mildly complaining about the appearance of "seditious Pasquinades" that "hoisted the standard of Independence" throughout the province on the same day he had ordered the militia to turn out for the defense of the country against "French Machinations." The commandant also declined the convention's salary offer, "being very satisfied," he said, with the pay he received from Ferdinand VII.[46] The delegates, nevertheless, pushed on, preparing in the week after 15 August statements of their grievances and their recommendations for reform. These they presented on 22 August in the form of an ordinance in which, even as they conceded that the convention derived its authority from DeLassus's having consented to its meeting, they declared themselves "for the time being, the guardians both of the publick interests, and of the rights of the individual members of their community."[47]

The ordinance asserted the convention's control over settlement policy by allowing "all free persons of good character" to settle in West Florida with their slaves and other "moveable property" and to receive "the same privileges and rights with the permanent inhabitants" (that is to say that they would be eligible to receive land grants on the same basis as settlers before 1804 had done). The convention also created a militia for the four districts of the province between the Mississippi and Pearl rivers. More significantly, it established a new court system, including a superior tribunal consisting of the governor and three judges to be elected by the delegates, as well as district courts to be run by local commandants as presiding judges in conjunction with local *alcaldes* (mayors) as associate judges. Since the local commandants and alcaldes were to be elected once the ordinance had gone into effect, this new system would transfer much of the control over local government and justice away from officials appointed by the Spanish authorities and give it to popularly elected officials. Admittedly, it could be argued that recent events in the Iberian Peninsula—which had disrupted the normal functioning of a legal system that depended on appeals and reviews in Spain—required the creation of new judicial institutions, but these provisions in the ordinance, nonetheless, also amounted to a real revolution in the government of the province.[48]

Other articles in the ordinance were intended to end abuses in landgrant policy by prescribing the duties of the registrar of land claims and requiring that official to keep open records, and to avoid the problems of bribery by paying the registrar a salary from the treasury. To finance these changes the convention assumed the right to impose direct taxes on land and slaves and to collect indirect taxes on the conveyance of merchandise and by granting licenses for the running of taverns and the ownership of billiard tables.[49] Only one delegate dissented from these proposals—Manuel Lopéz, who pointed out that the local commandant had been deprived of virtually all of his prerogatives in such matters as naming magistrates, levying taxes, and the selling and granting of royal lands.[50] DeLassus did not disagree, but as he told a meeting of his fellow Spanish officials on 21 August, he lacked the means to mount an effective opposition. Requests he had made in June for additional military resources and money had not been answered, and he had been asked by "the better known residents" to avoid the risk of bloodshed, which would only provoke further "insults" to Spanish authority.[51] Consequently, the governor accepted the ordinance, subject to its being approved by the captain-general in Cuba. He then united with the delegates in sending addresses to that effect to his superior in Havana and to the inhabitants of Baton Rouge.[52]

While this somewhat deceptive charade was being played out, Joshua

Baker, the observer sent by Governor Holmes, returned to the Mississippi Territory, accompanied by William Barrow. The delegate's assignment was to learn whether the Mississippi governor had received authority from the administration to act under "any circumstances that might occur," and particularly whether the United States might take West Florida "under its protection," as this was what the convention believed that the majority of the settlers wanted.[53] Barrow's requests were supported by correspondence he bore from other convention members, including a letter from John Hunter Johnson predicting that DeLassus would eventually repudiate the concessions he had made to the delegates and then crush their proceedings by force. That development, Barrow said, would produce "serious commotions," as the convention was not prepared to retrace its steps. More pointedly, Johnson asked Holmes whether the convention should declare independence and seek the aid of the United States. His question betrayed the convention's uncertainty about whether the United States would receive an independent West Florida, but if it did, Johnson added, the delegates wished to impose some conditions, namely that all Spanish land titles in the province be confirmed and that settlers continue to be entitled to receive as much land as the Spanish had been prepared to grant them.[54] Holmes was not unsympathetic, but he had to tell Barrow he had not received instructions to take "any active part in the affairs of West Florida." He could only offer to report news to Washington and express the view that he, too, was extremely concerned about possible developments below the boundary line.[55]

Holmes's position left the convention with little option but to continue discussions with DeLassus. The delegates, accordingly, remained in session for another week, passing additional resolutions to secure their control over the militia and all local offices as well as granting themselves the authority to borrow money on the credit and revenue of the province "whenever the public service may require." The convention then adjourned until 1 November, partly to implement the measures it had already adopted and partly to broaden the bases of its support by making arrangements to adjust the number of delegates allocated to the regions between Feliciana and the Pearl River in order to grant them "equal representation . . . according to the number of their Inhabitants." For the period of their recess, the delegates appointed a committee of three to act for them in dealings with the

Spanish authorities, and they further authorized the president of the convention, John Rhea, to summon any six delegates to exercise full powers "in case of emergency."[56] For the next three weeks, both the Spanish officials and the delegates continued to operate on a basis of mutual suspicion and distrust. DeLassus delayed carrying out some of the details of the agreement reached on 22 August—he failed to sign the ordinance of that date establishing the convention's measures as law pending the approval of the captain-general in Cuba—and he was frequently reported as having declared that he did not consider himself bound by its terms anyway.[57]

For their part, the delegates went about the task of reorganizing the militia and the local government, all the while continuing to proclaim their loyalty to Ferdinand VII. On 20 September the militia commander in the Baton Rouge district, Philemon Thomas, intercepted letters from DeLassus to Folch in which the former had requested military assistance from the latter to put down the insurrection of the self-appointed officials who had usurped his authority. Two days later, John Rhea convened a meeting with five other delegates—Johnson, Barrow, Mills, Hicky, and Lilley—at St. Francisville to decide on the convention's response. They promptly passed resolutions condemning DeLassus as "unworthy of their confidence" and stripping him of his executive powers. They then instructed Thomas to gather his available forces and seize the Spanish fort at Baton Rouge, a task he accomplished with relatively little difficulty and the loss of only two Spanish lives—including that of Louis de Grand Pré, a grandson of DeLassus's predecessor as commandant—in the early morning hours of 23 September. DeLassus attempted to lead a resistance, but according to one account he was knocked down "with the butt end of a musket" and placed in irons. Three days later, on 26 September, ten convention members reassembled at Baton Rouge and declared West Florida to be independent of Spain.[58]

In releasing its declaration, the convention justified its action as a reasonable response to DeLassus's decision to break the "compact" he had agreed to on 22 August. Thus did they claim to have preserved their "good faith" and "inviolable fidelity" to Ferdinand VII and Spain until such time as DeLassus chose to "pervert" the compact into an "engine of destruction by encouraging, in the most perfidious manner, the violation of ordinances sanctioned and established by himself as the law of the land." To avoid "the evils of a state of anarchy" that would result, the convention dissolved its allegiance to Spain in order to establish a "free and independent state" that could provide security for the inhabitants of West Florida. That task, however, could only be accomplished if West Florida assumed the status of "a sovereign and independent nation" with the power to provide for the common defense, to form treaties, to establish commerce, and to call on "all foreign nations" to respect the declaration by "acknowledging our independence, and giving us such aid as may be consistent with the laws and usages of nations." The declaration presumed that all laws and ordinances in force before 26 September would remain in effect, but that after that date any acts not authorized by the convention would be "null and void."[59]

The parallels between the actions of 26 September 1810 and those taken in the United States on 4 July 1776 were intentional and too obvious to be missed, but the realities behind the decisions of the convention were very different inasmuch as the delegates were *not* seeking to establish a "free and independent state" in West Florida. When John Rhea and five other delegates assembled on 22 September to authorize the seizure of the fort at Baton Rouge, they also sent a letter to Governor Holmes informing him of their somewhat contradictory intentions to make "an unqualified declaration of Independence" as proof of an "unalterable determination to assert [their] rights as an integral part of the United States," and stating that if Holmes could put "any body of Militia immediately in motion . . . under the pretext of preserving tranquility" in his own territory, it could not "fail to favor [their] views," as it would "give a check to the tories, and serve to animate the honest tho' timid Americans." Even better, if Holmes could prevail upon some gunboats in the Mississippi River "to drop down to the neighborhood of Baton Rouge, the Dons would be parilised."[60] When Rhea later forwarded Holmes the 26 September declaration, he requested that it be sent to Madison as testimony of the convention's belief that it was administration policy to take West Florida "under immediate & special protection, as an integral & inalienable portion of the United States."[61]

Two weeks later, on 10 October, Rhea raised the same matter with the State Department, pointing to all of Madison's diplomatic correspondence since 1803, and specifically the instructions he had issued in March 1806 for the Armstrong-Bowdoin negotiations in Paris, as evidence that West Florida belonged to the Union and requesting that the province either be admitted as a state or be attached to a neighboring territory (preferably Orleans rather than Mississippi). On this occasion, Rhea repeated the condition that the convention had attempted to stipulate earlier about the confirmation of Spanish land titles, but he also anticipated the possibility that the convention might have to undertake military operations to defend West Florida, for which purpose he sought an immediate loan of $100,000, subject to its being kept secret from the ministers of foreign nations. To expedite matters the convention wished to send an envoy to Washington but offered to delay doing so until it received some indication of whether its actions would be approved. And to secure that approval Rhea warned that "without the most direct and unequivocal assurances of the views and wishes of the American Government," the "weak and unprotected situation" of the convention would compel it to "look to some foreign Government for support." Implicit in these requests was the assumption that the West Florida declaration of independence would serve to acquit the United States of suspicions that it had conspired with the convention to subvert Spanish rule, and that if Madison were to accept the declaration in that light, he could then disregard any claims to the province that Spain or France might continue to assert. The newly independent Gulf Coast nation, however, would also be equally free to negotiate for its terms of entry into the Union.[62] Considered as a whole, therefore, the actions of the delegates between 22 September and 10 October were not the preliminaries to the establishment of a new nation but rather a series of hastily improvised expedients to force the United States to settle the West Florida problem—on West Floridian terms—before Folch could organize a counteroffensive to crush the convention.

To say that these developments came as an unwelcome surprise to Madison would be an understatement. After assuming that he had given events a "right direction" in West Florida in June, the president had left Washington on 9 July for his annual summer retreat at Montpelier, where he read a few days later a letter from Governor Holmes that could have only reinforced the concerns he had discussed earlier with Claiborne. Spanish authority in West Florida, Holmes reported, was on the brink of collapse, resulting not only in the formation of parties devoted to American, British, French, and Spanish interests but also in the establishment of local "neighborhood police" forces whose operations were both "inefficient" and "unjust." Holmes admitted he was worried, to some extent, about British intervention in West Florida, but he was, in fact, much more concerned that "Anarchy and confusion" throughout the province would encourage a slave revolt that might spread to Mississippi. Should it do so, he predicted, "we shall be placed in a very unpleasant if not precarious situation" in which the "respectable" and "well disposed" sections of the community would be overwhelmed. In response, the president authorized the governor to prepare his militia for service in the event "either of foreign interference with W[est]. F[lorida]. or of internal convulsion" and to keep "a wakeful eye to occurrences & appearances" in the province. He also directed the State Department to inform Holmes of Wykoff's mission to West Florida and to encourage him to cooperate "in diffusing the impressions we wish to be made there."[63]

Secretary of State Robert Smith implemented these directives on 21 July. For the next two months Madison remained in touch with developments in West Florida through accounts published in the newspapers, especially the administration journal the *National Intelligencer,* and through letters sent to him by executive-department secretaries and clerks from the nation's capital, albeit at the remove of about one month because of the time required for mail from the Gulf Coast to reach Washington and then be transmitted to Montpelier. To the extent these communications dealt with the deliberations of the convention at Baton Rouge, the president discerned no cause for alarm over events in the region between the Mississippi and Pearl rivers. By August 1810 even Holmes seemed to be less worried than he had been in June, and he dutifully reported the sentiments and wishes of the convention delegates, who were sympathetic to the United States, and told how they had successfully taken control of much of the provincial government away from DeLassus. The governor's letters left no doubt that the convention's professions of loyalty to Ferdinand VII were purely tactical and that the delegates at some point would seek the protection of the United States, but he gave no grounds to expect that this would be preceded by a declaration of independence.[64] The president, accordingly, waited for the invitation he had sought and sensed it would come later in the year, closer to the time when Congress would reassemble in December. He also continued to anticipate the fall of Cádiz and probably believed that this event would inspire the convention to act.[65] Madison did note the West Floridian concern about Spanish land titles, but he doubted whether he could act on that subject before a meeting of Congress. He also inquired of his colleagues in the Treasury and War departments about how he might extend American authority over West Florida following an invitation to do so.[66] It was his assumption that some aspects of the situation would be covered by the 1803 legislation that had authorized the earlier occupation of Louisiana, but the more "difficult question" was how to ensure "the preservation of peace." Receiving no clear answer to that question, the president made no decision about it before he left Montpelier on 3 October to return to Washington.[67]

The first indication Madison received that the plans he had made in June had gone awry came with the publication of a hastily inserted postscript in the 19 October issue of the *National Intelligencer*. The item was based on an account of the seizure of the Spanish fort at Baton Rouge that had been printed in the 26 September issue of the Natchez *Weekly Chronicle*, published in the Mississippi Territory. Additional details in the *National Intelligencer* postscript, most notably the descriptions of the death of Louis de Grand Pré and of DeLassus being knocked down "with the butt end of a musket," suggested, however, that the State Department had also received at that time a letter from Governor Holmes. That communication, dated 26 September, was largely a cover letter for some reports of events at Baton Rouge between 23 and 26 September, including a description of the fate of DeLassus using the exact wording that had appeared in the *National Intelligencer*.[68] Madison was bewildered by this turn of events. Writing to Jefferson on 19 October, the president informed his predecessor that "the Crisis in W. Florida, as you will see, has come home to our feelings and interests." But, he complained, "the successful party at Baton Rouge has not yet made any communication or invitation to this Govt."[69]

As Madison explored the implications of this news, he started to worry. The West Florida convention, he predicted, would now certainly "Call in, either our Aid or that of G[reat] B[ritain], whose conduct at the Caraccas gives notice of her propensity to fish in troubled waters." In Madison's

mind, events in West Florida remained linked to those in Venezuela because at the same time that he had authorized Claiborne to send Wykoff
to Baton Rouge, the State Department had also sent an agent, Robert
Lowry of Baltimore, to Caracas. It had done so partly because the Caracas junta had sent agents to both London and Washington in June 1810
to purchase arms and supplies, and partly because it would be useful to receive up-to-date information from Spain's rebellious colonies in South
America in the event of their declaring their independence and desiring to
establish trade relations with the United States.[70] Lowry had reached
Venezuela at the end of August, but he came too late, as Madison learned
on 14 October, to pre-empt the decision of the Caracas junta to seek closer
commercial relations with Great Britain, particularly an agreement it had
made with the secretary of the British governor in Curaçao that granted
British merchants preferential treatment in the customs house at the
Venezuelan port of La Guaira in exchange for Venezuelan vessels being
admitted to British West Indian ports on the same terms as British vessels.[71] This apparent willingness of Great Britain to subvert Bourbon authority in Spanish America even as it fought to uphold it in Spain itself
was proof that London was prepared to "fish in troubled waters." And on
17 October the editor of the *National Intelligencer,* Joseph Gales, Jr.,
asked the president, during a conversation, whether he was not worried
that Americans might soon become involved in West Florida in ways similar to those in which Great Britain had become involved in Venezuela.[72]

Madison told Gales that "he imagined measures had been adopted"
to prevent this kind of involvement in West Florida, but by 19 October
it seemed as if those measures had not been adequate. The president tacitly admitted as much by voicing to Gales his concern that there were indeed some elements in the West Florida population—whom he identified
as "the British party, together with the refugees from justice, deserters
from the United States Army, and land-jobbers"—who might be able to
prevent the province from coming under American jurisdiction.[73] If so,
how might he respond? "The Country to the Perdido," he pointed out to
Jefferson, "being our own, may be fairly, taken possession of, if it can be
done without violence, above all if there be danger of its passing into the
hands of a third & dangerous party." But even here there were difficulties.
Could the president, Madison wondered, extend the territorial laws of the

United States over West Florida without the consent of Congress, and were these laws adequate to cover whatever emergencies might arise? And would not such an attempt, at so close a time to when Congress was supposed to meet anyway, be open "to the charge of being premature & disrespectful, if not of being illegal?"[74]

Three days later, on October 22, the situation was clarified with the arrival of further information in the form of a letter from Holmes, written on 3 October. Among its enclosures was the West Florida declaration of independence, coupled with the convention's request for American protection, as well as four other documents bearing news more alarming than anything that had hitherto reached Washington from the Gulf Coast. Holmes began by telling the State Department that its 21 July instructions had not been franked at the Washington, DC, post office before 1 August and that they should have reached him by 24 August. They had not arrived, however, until 29 September. As a consequence, he had not been able to have the territorial militia in "a state for any service that might be called for" as the president had wished. (Nor had Holmes, for the same reason, been able to supply the West Florida convention with accurate information about the real intentions of the administration.) Even worse was the announcement that events in West Florida had now "assumed Very serious and determined Aspect." Not only had the convention declared independence and gathered a "considerable force" at Baton Rouge, but Holmes also believed that settlers in the lower portions of the province were "inimical to the New Order of things." They, too, were reported to be gathering forces, though the governor hoped they would not be able to undertake a counteroffensive in the absence of any assistance from Folch in Pensacola. Nevertheless, he mentioned that "Royalists" were intriguing for the support of Indian nations in the Mississippi Territory, and that fears of a slave revolt were widespread. As soon as he had received his orders of 21 July, Holmes had mobilized the territorial militia and requested aid from the nearest U.S. Army posts, but he admitted that he had taken these steps more to guard against dangers from slaves than he did with a view to intervening in West Florida. In fact, he had even given express orders that none of the military forces he had organized was to cross the boundary line into West Florida, on which subject he confessed himself to be at a loss and sought "special instructions" from the president.[75]

Holmes's letter led the president to summon his cabinet for a meeting that was held at some point between 22 and 25 October. That meeting, Gales recorded in his diary, went into "close session for at least three hours," and its outcome was the decision that the United States had no alternative but to occupy West Florida immediately.[76] A proclamation to that effect was drafted by the attorney general on 26 October, though Madison revised it the next day, removing some ill-considered phrasing that described how "a crisis [had] at length arrived subversive of the order of things under the Spanish authorities" in West Florida "and substituting in lieu thereof a self created independent Government." That last clause too had to be deleted, as even the slightest hint of acknowledgment of an independent regime on the Gulf Coast threatened to call into question the main justifications for an American occupation, namely that West Florida to the Perdido had been included in the Louisiana Purchase of 1803, that the province should have been delivered at that time, and that "the acquiescence of the United States in the temporary continuance of the said Territory under the Spanish Authority was not the result of any distrust of their title . . . but was occasioned by their conciliatory views, and by a confidence in the justice of their cause." That the transfer of West Florida had been "too long delayed" was not, therefore, the fault of the United States, which now had to take possession in order to preempt "events ultimately contravening the views" of both Madrid and Washington. In the meantime, the proclamation continued, "the tranquility and security of our adjoining territories are endangered, and new facilities given to violations of our Revenue and Commercial laws, and of those prohibiting the introduction of Slaves."[77]

A variety of considerations underlay the president's decision and the justifications he gave for it. If Madison had been worried about the propensity of Great Britain to "fish in troubled waters" in Venezuela so that it might give an "éclat" to "British commercial favors" and thus "strengthen their party" there, as he put it to Joseph Gales, it did not take much for him to imagine what London might make of the opportunities presented in West Florida, where there was now a government that claimed the authority to form treaties, establish commerce, and provide for the common defense, and where Holmes had given him reason to believe there was a "British party" that might offer it some encouragement.[78] And John Rhea had as good as warned him that if he did not respond to events in West Florida, the convention would, in effect, turn to Great Britain for assistance.[79] In addition, Madison could not be entirely sure, as he confessed to William Pinkney, that when news of the West Florida declaration of independence reached London, Great Britain would not simply seize the province "either with or without the privity of her allies in Cadiz."[80] There were, moreover, serious issues arising from the law of nations that Madison needed to consider if he were to act in ways consistent with the claim that the United States had held a valid title to West Florida since 1803. Among them was the possibility that if France continued to maintain, as it had since 1804, that West Florida had not been included in either the 1800 retrocession treaty or the 1803 Louisiana treaty, then at some future time a French government might argue that it still possessed some territorial claims on the Gulf Coast.[81] It was to deal with that prospect that Madison stopped short of an outright annexation of West Florida as opposed to an occupation, after which, he promised, it would "not cease to be a subject of fair and friendly negotiation and adjustment."

The requirements of international law also ruled out the possibility that Madison might have recognized the West Florida government for the purpose of taking the province into the Union by treaty. According to authorities on the law of nations, most notably Vattel, the United States could not have made a treaty with West Florida without destroying the basis of its own claim to the territory by virtue of the 1803 agreement with France. Nations already bound by one treaty on a subject were not free to make a second, conflicting treaty on the same subject. In such instances, the second treaty was "void."[82] Furthermore, any American treaty with West Florida would almost certainly be regarded by France and Great Britain as a usurpation of Spanish rights, if not an unprovoked act of war against the Regency in Cádiz. To avoid that impression and the dangers it might create, Madison decided to ignore the West Florida convention on the grounds that it was not a sovereign body "competent to enter into any compact."[83] After weighing these matters, the president concluded he could not afford to risk even the remotest possibility of jeopardizing the American claim to West Florida by delaying his response until after the meeting of Congress in six weeks time. If he did not act immediately and if the West Florida convention were allowed to consolidate its authority on the Gulf Coast, other nations would conclude that the United States had abandoned its title to the province and was "insensible" to the "importance of the stake" there.[84]

The task of implementing the 27 October proclamation was entrusted to Claiborne, who, after attending to his personal affairs, had returned to the capital at the same time as Madison. In instructions also dated 27 October but not made public before the first week of December, the governor was directed, first, to go to Natchez, in the Mississippi Territory, from where he was to distribute copies of the president's proclamation in English, French, and Spanish as well as communicate it to nearby Spanish governors, presumably in Cuba, East Florida, and Texas, accompanied by letters of "a conciliatory tendency." He was next to travel to Washington, Mississippi Territory, to meet with Governor Holmes and make arrangements for the possible employment of troops supplied from U.S. Army posts and the Mississippi militia. Only after that was he to enter West Florida itself. For the purposes of establishing American authority, Claiborne was to treat West Florida as part of Orleans Territory—or as "Eastern Louisiana," as the *National Intelligencer* later came to describe it—and he was to organize its militia, establish courts and parishes, maintain order, and secure the inhabitants' "liberty, property, and religion" accordingly. If further measures were necessary, Claiborne could assume that the Orleans Territorial legislature was competent to provide them. And if the occupation should be "opposed by force"—by which the administration meant resistance from the West Florida convention—the governor could respond to it with the assistance of U.S. Army and Mississippi militia forces. But if "any particular place, however small, [should] remain in possession of a Spanish force"—that is, Mobile—he was not "to employ force against it" but merely to report the fact to the State Department.[85] In short, Madison was not prepared to risk the consequences of inaction over West Florida, but he took possession of the province in ways that minimized the danger of provoking war with Spain at the same time.

Claiborne did not reach his specified destinations until the first week of December 1810. By that date, he found himself confronting not merely the West Florida convention that had declared independence but a body that by 22 November had written a new constitution, transformed itself into a legislature, and elected a governor—Fulwar Skipwith, the former

U.S. consul general in Paris between 1794 and 1809 who had recently settled in the province and taken possession of the land, slaves, saw mill, and
steam press of the Montesano plantation.[86] Skipwith had played no part
in the early stages of the settler movement to establish popular control
over the Spanish officials, but the leading Americans in the province—impressed by his experience, by his connections with the administration, and
by his relation by marriage to the family of Thomas Jefferson—had has-
tened to attach him to their cause by nominating him for a judgeship in
August. DeLassus, who almost certainly saw in Skipwith's attributes
grounds for suspicion, had declined to accept the nomination for the quite
proper reason that Skipwith had not yet fulfilled the two-year residence
requirement for officeholders.[87] The convention had insisted, nevertheless,
on using Skipwith's services, and he was almost certainly selected as governor in the belief that he would be the most eligible American resident
to negotiate the terms of West Florida's entry into the Union with the administration. Difficulties arose, therefore, when Skipwith and the West
Florida government learned that Claiborne's task was not to negotiate but
simply to incorporate the new nation into his own territorial jurisdiction
without any reference to the terms West Floridians had sought to exact
from Washington.

Consequently, West Floridians were at first inclined to dismiss the president's 27 October proclamation as a forgery, and some of the messen-
gers Claiborne had sent from Natchez to distribute it were arrested.
Skipwith shared that attitude, and he also declined to meet with Claiborne,
insisting instead that the governor should pay the first call on him. That
stand was, in part, the result of pique and pride, but there is no reason to
doubt that Skipwith sincerely believed that it had been Madison's wish for
West Florida to declare its independence before joining the Union and
that the president had created the convention for that purpose.[88] Through
some delicate meetings mediated by Governor Holmes in the second week
of December, Claiborne was able to explain that the United States would
neither recognize an independent West Floridian nation nor consider the
terms of its inclusion in the Union to be subject to negotiation.[89] Skipwith
was angered by the misunderstanding. He drafted two letters to Madison
to protest what he regarded as "the harsh & hostile conduct" of Claiborne, and more pointedly he regretted that Claiborne had not delayed his

actions until such time as the West Florida government had been given the opportunity to remove the Spanish garrison at Mobile, thereby permitting it to acquire all of West Florida to the Perdido River. Eventually, however, he came to accept that his position could not be allowed to imperil the greater goal of West Florida's inclusion in the United States. He withheld his letters of protest to Madison, and thereafter the House and Senate of the West Florida Assembly simply ceased to meet.[90] Nevertheless, Skipwith's sense that he had been manipulated and misused lingered, and he pointed out to personal friends in Washington that they—and others in the administration as well—might have treated him with greater consideration by informing him of the true nature of Madison's wishes.[91]

As a result of Claiborne's efforts, by the time Congress assembled in Washington in the first week of December 1810, the independent nation of West Florida was on the point of passing out of existence. On the assumption that Claiborne would be able to occupy West Florida without too much difficulty, the administration expected to face only one immediate problem: the reaction of legislators and foreign diplomats to what would become a fait accompli after Madison had revealed it in his annual message to Congress on 5 December. To the extent foreign diplomats had anticipated the possibility of American intervention in West Florida, Secretary of State Robert Smith had already told the French minister, in November 1810, that members of the administration were "strangers to everything that [had] happened" in the province and that "the Americans who [had] appeared there either as agents or leaders [were] enemies of the Executive," motivated by the hope of obtaining from "a new government considerable concessions of lands."[92] That remark was not misleading insofar as it had not been Madison's intention to encourage West Floridian independence, and the president also had good reason to suppose that concerns about Spanish land titles had played some role in the decisions of the convention. It was, nonetheless, an unfair statement inasmuch as there was genuine misunderstanding in West Florida about what the administration had expected of the convention, and Madison had provided no guidance about how its members might respond to the problem of the Spanish authorities, who, instead of becoming defunct as he had assumed, might attempt to crush them by force. In that sense, the secretary of state made the West Florida convention a scapegoat for what proved to be a misjudgment on the part of the president, namely that the regime of the Spanish Bourbons would collapse sometime in 1810.

As for Congress, the *National Intelligencer,* in a preview of the likely contents of the president's annual message on 1 December, hinted that while West Florida might raise "considerations of some importance," they would not require "any immediate act of the legislature."[93] Four days later, Madison informed Congress he had occupied West Florida to the Perdido and extended to the region "the laws provided for the Territory of Orleans." He added that he presumed the legislators would be convinced of the necessity for his actions and that they might supply "whatever provisions may be due, to the essential rights and equitable interests of the people, thus brought into the bosom of the American family." Madison said little more than that, however. He did not explain further what he might have understood bringing West Florida into the "American family" would mean in constitutional and legal terms, nor did the documents he attached to his annual message explain why he had occupied the province in the first place.[94] The legislators saw nothing of the alarming letter Governor Holmes had sent to the State Department on 3 October, and they received in addition to the president's proclamation and instructions of 27 October no more than copies of the West Florida declaration of independence, accompanied by John Rhea's requests to Holmes and to Robert Smith that the province be taken into the Union. The clerical copies of the latter documents, moreover, were described as having been enclosed in a 17 October letter from Holmes, even though it would have been perfectly obvious to any reader of the *National Intelligencer* that the administration must have received earlier versions of these communications in order for the president to have made the decisions he had by 27 October.[95]

Congress was not troubled by this discrepancy about the matter of dates. Instead, both houses immediately commenced lengthy debates about the constitutional and practical implications of the occupation of West Florida. In the Senate, discussion centered on the issues of how far the United States could be said to have had a good claim to West Florida under the 1803 Louisiana Purchase treaty and whether the president could still continue to negotiate with foreign powers over the status of a region that was now under the jurisdiction of the Orleans Territory. Federalist senators, in particular, found Madison's actions and arguments on these counts to be both illegal and defective, and they succeeded in forcing the administration to respond by publishing lengthy defenses of the American title to West Florida in the *National Intelligencer*.[96] In the House of Representatives, the debate took a different course as members there assumed that West Florida, as part of the Orleans Territory, would be included in a bill intended to advance that territory toward statehood in the Union. That consideration provoked a variety of reactions—ranging from questions about how Madison could regard part of a state to be subject to "negotiation and adjustment" with foreign nations to concerns expressed by members from Tennessee and the delegate from the Mississippi Territory that the new state would control the outlets of both the Mississippi River and Mobile Bay. Rather that accept that possibility, they proposed that West Florida either be included in an expanded Mississippi Territory that might be immediately admitted to the Union or become a separate territory altogether. The complexity of these matters was so great that no solution to them was reached. The bill to advance Orleans to statehood was passed, but only after West Florida had been excluded from its limits.[97] The session thus ended in March 1811 with West Florida in a legal limbo. It remained under the Orleans Territory without being part of it.

Confusing though that outcome might have been, Madison probably regarded it as not unsatisfactory, at least for the time being. It gave the United States effective control over the American population in the most settled region of West Florida bordering on the Mississippi River while allowing the president some flexibility about how he might respond to international reactions to the American occupation. It also gave him time to deal with those parts of West Florida that Claiborne had been directed not to occupy for fear of risking war with Spain, namely Mobile. In June 1810, the president had not been unmindful that the extension of American authority into the thinly populated region between the Pearl and Perdido rivers would pose problems, and Claiborne had directed Wykoff to take "some pains to prepare for the occasion the minds of the more influential characters in the vicinity of Mobile."[98] Just how that might be done was not immediately clear, but one week later, on 20 June, the administration requested Senator William Harris Crawford of Georgia to select an agent to go "without delay into East Florida, and also into West Florida, as far as Pensacola" to gather information on "the several parties in the Country" and to spread the message that should the local settlers declare their independence from Spain, "their incorporation into our Union would coincide with the sentiments and policy of the United States."[99] When Crawford received this request, on 17 July, he had no idea whom he might choose until he met by chance with George Mathews, a former governor of Georgia, who was intending to make a business trip to Pensacola anyway. After discussing the matter with him and warning the administration that the illegible and often illiterate "orthography" of the old governor was "proverbial among us" and that his "manuscripts sometimes require a Key" to decipher their meaning, Crawford entered Mathews's name on the blank commission he had received from the State Department. Madison subsequently declared himself to be "perfectly satisfied" with this choice.[100]

Mathews first went to Pensacola, only to find his entry to the town prevented "by the prevalence of a contagious fever." He then went to Mobile, where he met with Folch and explained the president's views. The Spanish governor accepted readily enough that Spain and the United States might agree to the extent that neither nation would wish to see any other European power—that is, France or Great Britain—take over Spain's American possessions, but otherwise he showed no interest in discussing the notion that West Florida might enter the Union.[101] In July, Crawford had predicted that Mathews would be able to complete his mission by mid-September; in fact, the administration did not receive the news about his meeting with Folch before November 1810, by which time Mathews had departed for St. Augustine to carry out his instructions with respect to East Florida. And although Mathews eventually came to Washington in January 1811 to make a personal report on his findings, the obstacles he encountered, coupled with the fact that he was an infrequent correspondent at best, meant that throughout the final months of 1810 the administration lacked the means to influence events in West Florida east of the Pearl River to the extent it would have wished. The result was that during this interval, the initiative there was seized by settlers in the Mississippi Territory.

For those settlers, the most immediate benefit of the crisis at Cádiz was the prospect of ending the situation that had permitted Spanish officials to control and to tax the movement of people and goods up and down Mobile Bay. Even before Claiborne had dispatched Wykoff to Baton Rouge, Joseph Pulaski Kennedy, a major in the Mississippi territorial militia and a lawyer well connected to politically prominent families in Georgia, had sent an emissary into Mobile in the first week of June to lay the groundwork for the replacement of Spanish rule there.[102] Kennedy, along with Reuben Kemper and his brothers, who had participated in an unsuccessful rebellion in West Florida in 1804, belonged to the Mobile Society, an organization that, as Kennedy put it, had "its origin in the oppression which we have suffered from the Spanish Government in detaining a country which the Supreme law of the State has declared to be ours."[103] Members of the society made few efforts to conceal their plans, and they invariably spoke as if these would have the blessing of the United States. Indeed, so casual and so confident were they about their success that the first the commander of the U.S. Army forces at Fort Stoddert, Lieut. Col. Richard Sparks, knew of their plans was when he was informed by his Spanish counterpart at Mobile that Kennedy and his associates intended to seize the arms and the ammunition in the fort to enable them to capture Mobile while at the same time denying Sparks the means of preventing them from doing so.[104] That this plan was illegal according to the provisions of the 1794 Neutrality Law was of little concern to Kennedy, who maintained that because the United States recognized neither the minister of the loyalist resistance in Spain nor the rule of Joseph Bonaparte, West Florida belonged to no nation to which the United States was obligated, and therefore the Mobile Society was entitled to seize the province. Kennedy also went so far as to predict to Harry Toulmin, the U.S. territorial judge in Washington County, Mississippi Territory, that no jury would convict him, or any other American, for participating in a filibuster against Mobile anyway.[105]

When Madison learned, in the second week of August, of the ways in which Kennedy intended to pervert his policy of not taking sides in the struggle for control of Spain, he was annoyed.[106] He lost no time in ordering the War Department to reinforce U.S. Army posts in the Mississippi Territory and directing the State Department to alert Governor Holmes to the need to enforce the 1794 neutrality legislation. In doing so, the president assumed these measures could be implemented in conjunction with those he had put into effect for West Florida in July, and he took pains to insist that Lieut. Col. Sparks obtain the evidence in the possession of the Spanish authorities in Mobile "to support any legal proceedings that may become proper, agst. guilty individuals."[107] As Madison had enjoyed a friendship of several years standing with Toulmin, he also went out of his way to thank the judge for bringing Kennedy's plans to his attention. There could be no doubt, the president added, of their "unlawfulness" or of "the duty of the Executive to employ force if necessary . . . and to make examples of the Authors." This was not the time, he continued, for "private individuals" to take national policy into their own hands, nor should they "distrust the dispositions of the Govt.," even if these were necessarily regulated by "the limits of its authority, and by the actual (that is, present) state of our foreign relations."[108]

For the remainder of the period between mid-August and the first week of October, Madison devoted more time to the potential problems of a filibuster against Mobile than he did to the difficulties that arose in the West Florida convention. He discussed the details of troop mobilization with the Secretary of War, but at that juncture neither he nor Eustis had reason to suspect there was any connection between the plans of the Mobile Society and the actions of the convention at Baton Rouge. It was also possible for them to doubt that the plans of the Mobile Society would materialize once its members became aware that the administration was contemplating acting against them.[109] Whatever comfort Madison might have derived from that conclusion was jeopardized, however, by the actions of the convention after it had declared independence. As part of their strategies to preempt a counterrevolution headed by Folch, the delegates, on 10 and 11 October, had sent an address to the people of Mobile and Pensacola, inviting them to authorize the convention to act on their behalf or to send deputations of their own to Baton Rouge. They had, moreover, entrusted the delivery of that message to Col. Reuben Kemper and Maj. Joseph White.[110] According to Toulmin, White was "held in esteem by the Spaniards" but Kemper, most certainly, was not. White was also prevented by sickness from discharging his mission, and when Kemper traveled to Fort Stoddert, the rumor that he was about to descend on Mobile with a force of 1,600 men provoked "the utmost panic" among the settlers there.[111]

Toulmin, who met Kemper at Fort Stoddert at the end of October, personally doubted that the colonel would do anything rash, but he was far less sure about Kennedy, who seemed, he informed Madison, "very solicitous to impress the idea, that as the Convention has now become the ruling power in Florida, it will be lawful to leave the [Mississippi] territory and serve under their banners against Mobile."[112] He was also aware of the possibility that two or three hundred men in Mississippi might assemble for that purpose and that several men from Fort Stoddert might join them as well. To prevent these developments, Toulmin embarked on an extended campaign against the organization of a filibuster. As soon as he learned of the West Florida declaration of independence, the judge impaneled a grand jury in Washington County, Mississippi Territory, whose members he swore to uphold the law and to whom he presented a lengthy case against an attack on any Spanish possessions. Well aware of the potential for conflict in the region, Toulmin demonstrated that however oppressive the Spanish duties at Mobile might be, they could not justify an act of war, nor was it the business of American settlers to take the law into their own hands, regardless of the merits of the argument that West Florida might have been illegally occupied by Spain since 1803. To go filibustering to redeem that situation, Toulmin argued, would be to reduce American citizens to the level of Aaron Burr, and they could not assume that the president would similarly sink to accomplishing his policy goals by "recourse to the instrumentality of an obscure conspiracy."[113] Toulmin then conveyed the same arguments to all the militia captains in Washington County by means of a circular, in which he also enclosed the letter he had received from Madison thanking him for alerting the administration to the illegal activities contemplated by Kennedy.[114]

After taking these steps by the first week in November, Toulmin reported to Madison that he felt confident there would be no filibuster into Spanish territory, but the president was unwilling to leave anything to chance. He sent further orders to Holmes in the Mississippi Territory to take all necessary steps "with the utmost rigor of the law" to suppress filibustering, adding that any seizure of Mobile would be "utterly repugnant to his wishes and contrary to the motive which induced the executive to occupy the Territory of West Florida."[115] By the end of the month, Toulmin, too, had become less positive about his earlier prediction. In the

intervening weeks Kemper and Kennedy had met, and the judge concluded that they might attack Mobile after all. Together with his son-in-
law, U.S. Army Captain Edmund Pendleton Gaines, he resolved to meet
with them to explain "the impolicy and rashness of proceeding in the enterprize."[116] Before he could do so, however, he received a letter, written
on 22 November, from James Innerarity, the Pensacola agent of the British
firm of John Forbes and Company, who had met with Folch and learned
that the governor's thinking about future relations between West Florida
and the United States had undergone a considerable change. In light of
the seriousness of the situation in the province and in order to "save the
effusion of blood," Folch declared that he was willing to abolish the duties at Mobile "on American goods passing up and down the river," provided Toulmin could notify him that "the expedition under Kemper and
Kennedy is entirely laid aside and abandoned by all the inhabitants" of the
Mississippi Territory. According to Innerarity, the governor went even
further by hinting that one reason for his decision was his expectation that
Americans and West Floridians would "*probably soon become citizens of the
same community*."[117] In other words, Folch was now thinking about surrendering West Florida east of the Pearl River to the United States.

Toulmin and Gaines were more than willing to respond positively. The
captain went to Mobile to meet with Folch, who provided him with a letter on 25 November abolishing the duties at Mobile from that date. The
judge gave extensive publicity to Folch's decision and hoped it would prevent a filibuster.[118] His wishes were granted to the extent that the Mobile
Society was unable to muster a large enough party to risk attacking either
the Spanish fort or the store of John Forbes and Company at Mobile Bay,
possibly because success in these enterprises could by no means be guaranteed without the backing of the United States.[119] A smaller party led by
Kemper and Kennedy did, however, raid a Spanish settlement on Saw Mill
Creek. Folch was able to arrest some of its members, whom he sent to
Havana for imprisonment. And on the Pascagoula River, a group of Americans led by Sterling Duprée decided to follow the example set at Baton
Rouge by declaring their independence and attacking a nearby settlement
of French refugees.[120] For such lawlessness, Toulmin issued arrest war-
rants for Kemper, Kennedy, and other members of the Mobile Society.
There ensued for several months thereafter a bitter vendetta between

Toulmin and the supporters of Kemper and Kennedy, which culminated in an attempt by the latter in the spring of 1812 to have the judge removed by impeachment.[121]

After successfully chastising some of the small raiding parties around the Mobile region, Folch, nevertheless, remained true to the promise he had implied in his meeting with James Innerarity on 22 November. On 2 December he wrote letters from Mobile to Governor Holmes and the secretary of state, offering to relinquish West Florida to the United States on the conditions that he would not receive any assistance or directions from his superiors in Havana and Veracruz within the month and that the administration would direct Sparks and the U.S. Army forces at Fort Stoddert to suppress any future raids by Kemper, who would have to be confined to the limits of Baton Rouge. The governor mailed this information to Washington and entrusted copies of his correspondence to John McKee, a former U.S. Indian agent to the Choctaw Nation, for delivery in person. It was to be McKee's role to give the administration "every information that it ought to possess" from "an eye-witness to all that has passed in this part of the province and the adjacent country."[122] Three days later, McKee set out from Fort Stoddert through the Creek country to Knoxville, Tennessee, to make the journey to Washington.

3

EAST FLORIDA

I learned from [General Mathews] that he had been for some time in treaty with the house of Panton & Forbes of Pensacola, for the purchase of a tract of Country, owned by them in the vicinity of St. Marks, and would shortly set out for the former place to close the contract.

—[William Harris Crawford] to Robert Smith, 27 July 1810

McKee arrived in Washington on 14 January 1811, where he and Mathews would meet with the president and the secretary of state.[1] But even before McKee could discuss Folch's offer, Madison had taken further action. He did so because of the reaction of the British chargé d'affaires, John Philip Morier, to the occupation of West Florida. Partly by inclination and partly because of his low diplomatic status, Morier had been slow to react to both the news of the West Florida revolt and the contents of Madison's annual message, but on 15 December 1810 he delivered a strongly worded and sarcastic protest against the president's proclamation of 27 October. Dismissing the members of the West Florida convention as "a band of desperadoes who are known here by the contemptuous appellation of land-jobbers," Morier pointed out that the "manifestly doubtful" title of the United States to West Florida could not justify the American occupation, and he wondered why the administration had not adjusted matters with the Spanish authorities who possessed "the actual sovereignty" over the province as the president had promised in his proclamation. He then announced that Great Britain could not view the occu-

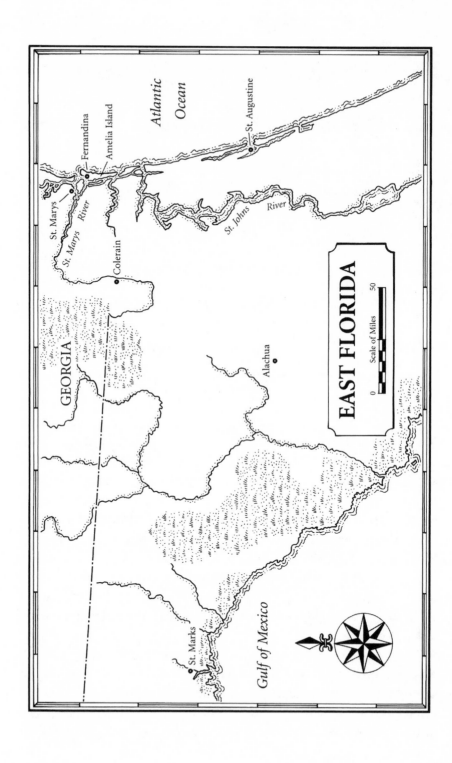

EAST FLORIDA

Scale of Miles

0   50

Atlantic
Ocean

St. Augustine

Fernandina
Amelia Island

St. Marys

St. Marys River

Colerain

St. Johns River

GEORGIA

Alachua

Gulf of Mexico

St. Marks

pation "with indifference" and demanded an explanation to satisfy his government of the "pacific disposition" of the United States toward its Spanish ally. More ominously, Morier stated that Great Britain would intervene and attempt to mediate Spain's disputes with the United States. After he had failed to receive a reply within the week, Morier repeated his demand for an explanation.[2]

Madison knew the chargé's remarks about British intervention could not have been authorized by his government, but as long ago as June 1810 the administration had warned London against questioning American claims to Florida, and there could be no question of allowing it to do so now. Accordingly, on 3 January 1811 Madison sent Morier's notes to Congress, accompanied by those copies of Folch's correspondence with McKee that had arrived by mail and that offered to surrender West Florida under the conditions the Spanish governor had specified. The president requested Congress to retort Morier's language by issuing a declaration to the effect that the United States "could not see, without serious inquietude, any part of a neighbouring territory in which they have in different respects so deep and so just a concern, pass from the hands of Spain, into those of any other Foreign power." He also sought legislation authorizing him to "to take temporary possession" of any part of the territory east of the Perdido River by providing for the government "of the same" in anticipation of a possible "subversion of the Spanish authorities within the territory in question, and an apprehended occupation thereof by any other foreign power." And by extending his gaze to all of the country "adjoining the United States Eastward of the River Perdido," Madison was suggesting he would consider the occupation of East Florida to secure the position he had staked out in West Florida.[3]

Since Madison designated his message as "confidential," Congress debated it behind closed doors. Within the week, and with Henry Clay of Kentucky taking the initiative, the Senate framed a resolution and a bill along the lines of the president's request. Progress was slower in the House of Representatives, where members delayed matters by discussing procedural and substantive amendments that sought either to justify the president's policy or to control it by compelling him to return Floridian territory to Spain after the period of "temporary" occupation had ended.[4] Concerned, perhaps, about the tenor of the debate, Madison, on 10 January 1811, sent Congress another message that emphasized his concern about British meddling in Florida. He also forwarded a copy of a letter written in February 1810 by Luis de Onís to Captain-General Vicente Emparán in Caracas, which had recently been obtained by executive agent Robert Lowry in Venezuela. The Spanish minister had then been worried the administration would recognize Joseph Bonaparte as king of Spain, and by a series of what Madison referred to as "misrepresentations and suggestions," he had even supposed the United States was willing to enter into an alliance with Denmark, France, Russia, and Sweden against Great Britain and the Supreme Central Junta of Spain. Nothing could have been further from Madison's mind, but that was not the point. The problem was Onís's suggestion that Great Britain and Spain, in order to thwart the United States, should send naval vessels to its coasts and an army "near to Louisiana" to separate and divide "these provinces" into "two or three republics," which would thereafter "remain in a state of perfect Nullity." Once the Union had been dismembered, Onís foretold that "the republic of the north"—by which he presumably meant a regional confederation centered on New England—"would be our friend," from which Great Britain and Spain could draw "all the supplies" they needed while other parts of the former United States would "perish from Poverty and quarrels among themselves."[5]

This threat, although more alarming in prospect than it was in reality, may have had some effect, and within five days the House of Representatives had joined with the Senate in granting the president his 3 January request. The "No Transfer" resolution of 15 January 1811 declared that the United States "under the peculiar circumstances" of the "existing crisis" in Spain and its American empire could not see "without serious inquietude" any part of Florida pass to "any other foreign power." Coupled with the resolution was a bill appropriating $100,000 to permit the president to employ the armed forces "to take possession of, and occupy" any Spanish territory east of the Perdido River "in case an arrangement has been, or shall be, made with the local authority for delivering up possession of the same . . . or in the event of an attempt to occupy the said territory . . . by any foreign government." That bill also authorized the president to establish a temporary government in the affected area until Congress made other provisions. The legislature then debated, and subsequently passed, a further law requiring that neither the resolution nor the law of 15 January 1811 should be published before the end of the next session of Congress—an event not likely to occur before 4 March 1812 at the earliest—unless the president decided otherwise.[6]

Immediately after the passage of the law of 15 January, the administration implemented its provisions with respect to Folch's offer of December 1810. By that time, Mathews had also arrived in Washington from his fall mission to Florida, and Robert Smith suggested that the former Georgia governor should be sent back there to negotiate with Folch and that McKee might accompany him as a secretary.[7] McKee had other ideas. His immediate concern, as he informed James Innerarity at Mobile, was "money," by which he meant, at least, that he should be reimbursed for the sum of $500 he had spent on the hire of horses and the protection of a soldier while making the journey from Fort Stoddert to Washington.[8] In the longer term, though, his goal was to regain some form of public employment, preferably as agent to the Choctaw Indians, a position from which he had been dismissed in 1802, possibly for suspected involvement in the Blount conspiracy of 1797.[9] Since then, McKee had been engaged in a variety of enterprises, including acting at times as a representative of John Forbes and Company to the Choctaw, and he had also contemplated forming partnerships with Forbes to purchase Indian lands on the Apalachicola River with the "special permission & authority of the Spanish Government."[10] And in light of the fact that McKee also mentioned to James Innerarity that he had written to Forbes while he was en route to the capital, it would seem McKee was still interested in such business ventures. He even hoped that Forbes, who was in Charleston at the time, might be able to meet him in Washington for discussions of matters of mutual interest.[11]

Forbes never came to Washington, but that McKee had John Forbes and Company's business interests on his mind is confirmed by his reporting to James Innerarity that while in the capital he had "a few skirmishes" with members of the administration about the firm's "Anglocism." This misconception, he declared, he placed in "a proper point of view," namely that Forbes and his associates were "honest peacable English merchants & men of Honor above being intriguers or spies for any Government—and without any strong prejudices against ours."[12] Mathews would not have quarreled with these claims. He, too, had plans for doing business with Forbes, and among his reasons for accepting the assignment to Florida from Crawford in July 1810, in addition to his belief that the region should become part of the United States, was that he was already heading for Pensacola to sign a contract with Forbes's agent there—John Innerarity, Jr., brother of James—for "a tract of Country, owned by them in the vicinity of St. Marks."[13] Forbes had received several such tracts from the Lower Creek and Seminole Indians after 1804 in return for services he had rendered to them in facilitating land sales to the United States that paid off their tribal debts (owed mostly to Forbes's company). He secured good title to these tracts from the Spanish authorities—subject to the proviso that he could not alienate land from them without "express consent"— and he was planning to sell parts of them off to speculators while developing others with slaves and settlers from the Loyalist community in the Bahamas and from his homeland of Scotland.[14]

McKee must have been concerned that the administration would be alarmed at his business connections with Forbes—and at those of Mathews as well—but in reality times had changed somewhat since the days when American governments had worried so very greatly about the activities of Loyalist merchants trading with Indians in the borderlands under license from Spain. The very magnitude of the indebtedness of the southern Indians, including the Choctaw, to John Forbes and Company had long since led both Forbes and McKee to the realization that the debts could only be redeemed if the Indians sold their lands to the United States, and the Jefferson administration had not hesitated to avail itself of Forbes's cooperation in negotiating several important land-cession treaties with the southern Indians between 1804 and 1806.[15] Viewed in that light, John Forbes and Company had become a useful instrument for American policy makers, and it was by no means impossible that its agents, in the event of any future conflict with Spain or even Great Britain, could continue to play a positive role by helping to ensure the neutrality of Indian tribes that were still numerous and powerful along the southwestern frontier.

Considerations of these sorts, coupled with the fact that McKee seemed to enjoy the confidence of Folch, probably played into Madison's decision—made by 26 January 1811—to send Mathews and McKee back to the Gulf Coast, accompanied by Ralph Isaacs, who was to provide secretarial services to compensate for the eccentric "orthography" of Mathews that Crawford had earlier warned about. Their primary task was to make an arrangement with Folch that would have allowed the United States not only to take complete possession of West Florida between the Pearl and Perdido rivers but also to occupy the remainder of the province to the Apalachicola River. In the event of Folch or some other "local authority" offering these terms, McKee and Mathews could accept them, and they could also agree to the "re-delivery" of territory at a future period "to the lawful sovereign" if Folch so insisted. And if Folch should "unexpectedly and pertinaciously insist," they could even agree to the "re-delivery" to Spain of Florida west of the Pearl River, provided the stipulation did not "impair or affect the right or title of the United States to the same." As executive agents, McKee and Mathews could also negotiate terms relating to land titles and debts to the extent these were "clearly sanctioned" by Spanish law, and they could continue the Spanish local functionaries in office as well as extend to all settlers the right of religious toleration. But if no agreement could be reached and there was reason to suspect "an existing design in any foreign Power" to occupy Florida, the agents could, "on the first undoubted manifestation" of the approach of a force for that purpose, "pre-occupy" the territory "to the entire exclusion of any armament that may be advancing to take possession of it."[16]

The wording of these instructions was also applied to East Florida, subject to Mathews and McKee exercising a proper discretion based on an "accurate knowledge of the precise state of things there." In other words, should the agents discover "an intention" in its governor or "in the existing local authority, amicably to surrender that province into the possession of the United States," they could accept it in the same manner in which they were to receive West Florida. "And in case of the actual appearance of any attempt to take possession" of East Florida "by a foreign power," the agents were to pursue "the same effective measures . . . for the exclusion of the foreign force."[17] The use of that language, however, raises the question of how far Madison had reason to believe that the situation in East Florida was comparable to that in West Florida and how far future developments in East Florida might replay those he had just dealt with in West Florida. Some insight into that problem can be gleaned from a brief report Mathews wrote for the State Department upon arriving in Washington after his mission to Florida. After leaving Mobile in the fall of 1810, Mathews had headed for St. Augustine, where he planned to contact Governor Enrique White, just as he had sought out Folch. Mathews and White never met, however, probably because of advice Mathews received from a local resident, Andrew Atkinson, that if he were to raise the subject of his mission with the governor, he would probably "die in chains in the Moro Castle [in Havana]."[18] Apparently taking the warning to heart, Mathews decided to bypass White in favor of seeking out "Gentlemen of influence" in East Florida from whom he could learn whether there was some other way in which the province might be taken into the Union.

How many gentlemen Mathews met, what he told them, and what they said to him is not entirely clear. According to George F. J. Clarke, who held the offices of magistrate and surveyor general in Fernandina on Amelia Island, among Mathews's contacts on his mission were James Hall, an American-born doctor whom White had recently expelled from East Florida (probably for espionage), and James Seagrove, formerly a U.S. agent to the Creek Indians, who had settled in St. Marys, Georgia, from where he had written a letter to Madison as long ago as September 1805 advising him on how the United States might seize the province in the event of a diplomatic rupture with Spain.[19] From Clarke and his informants White learned by January 1811 that Mathews had told Seagrove he would shortly return to East Florida "to aid and assist" in a revolution that was "sup[p]osed to be nearly ripe" and that Seagrove "had in his desk . . . an order from the Secretary of State of the same import, and that it was only necessary for a few of the inhabitants of this side of the [St. Marys] River to gather and declare independency, and call across the river for protection, to afford him [Mathews] a pretext for acting, and he would immediately support them with a sufficient strength for their purpose."[20] Mathews may well have talked in this manner, though if he did so he had gone further than the administration had intended in the summer of 1810 when it sought an agent to do no more than inform East Floridians of its good will and tell them that "in the event of a political separation from the parent country, their incorporation into our Union would coincide with the sentiments and the policy of the United States."[21] The administration's instructions had been entirely silent about how East Florida might enter the Union, but because the United States claimed the province as compensation for unmet spoliations and not by right of treaty—as it did West Florida—it was a fair inference that should East Florida separate from Spain, it would be free to open negotiations to join the United States.

This last assumption helps explain the report Mathews wrote for the State Department. Its contents made no reference to any meetings with Hall or Seagrove, but Mathews did provide Madison and Robert Smith with the names of five "Gentlemen of influence" who he said were sympathetic to American policy: John Houstoun McIntosh, a member of a prominent Georgia family who had settled in East Florida in 1803; Fernando de la Maza Arredondo, Sr., a native of Spain who had amassed a fortune through slave trading; Andrew Atkinson, a merchant and planter from Georgia and South Carolina who resided on the St. John's River; George Fleming, an Irish immigrant planter based near St. Augustine; and Justo Lopez, the commander of the small Spanish garrison on Amelia Island and a friend of Atkinson's. It is unlikely all of these men met together with Mathews as opposed to his talking with them individually or in smaller groups, but they, along with "a large majority" of the people of East Florida, Mathews believed, wished to join the United States. They had expectations, he added, "of soon declareing [sic] for themselves" and they appeared "only to be waiting to hear the fate of Cadiz." Once they learned the city had fallen to France and had declared their independence, it was the intention of "those who will be foremost in it" to seize the fort at St. Augustine, the Castillo de San Marcos, "by surprise." They did not seek the active assistance of the United States for that purpose, only asking instead, as Mathews put it, "to see some Military force, of ours on that frontier" which "would have a tendancy [sic] to awe what British influence there is in the province and give confidence to those friendly to us." The military aspects of the operation were not expected to be difficult anyway, as Mathews reported that there were only about 150 Spanish troops at St. Augustine and "not any Navil [sic] force in the Province." Beyond that, these would-be revolutionaries desired no more than that the United States pay the debts Spain owed to its troops and "make some provision in land for each family."[22]

In short, what Mathews conveyed to Madison in January 1811 was the impression that events in Spain in 1810 had created in East Florida, just as they had in West Florida, a climate of opinion that disposed some promi-

nent settlers and officials to consider assuming an autonomous, or even independent, status in order to avoid falling under the control of Joseph
Bonaparte (and, indirectly, under that of Napoleon).[23] Admittedly, there
were far fewer Americans in East Florida than there were in West Florida—
in 1811 the total population (white and black but excluding Indians) was
only 3,690[24]—but Mathews believed that the locals were capable of stag-
ing their own revolt or coup d'état with little direct outside assistance,
making the United States a largely passive beneficiary, provided Madison
followed the suggestions in his report. For that purpose Mathews had also
proposed to the president that it would be "advisable to have some person on whome [sic], he can depend near the Governments of the Floridys
to avail themselves of any occurrence that may occur."[25] That Madison
adopted this understanding of the situation in East Florida and concluded
that Mathews would be a suitable person to be "near the Governments of
the Floridys" is clear from the contents of both the "No Transfer" resolution and legislation of 15 January 1811 and the instructions issued to
McKee and Mathews eleven days later. On that basis, the two agents left
Washington on a joint mission that, if successful, promised to give the
United States effective control over all remaining Spanish territories between St. Augustine and the Pearl River.

Further evidence that Mathews's report provided the basis for Madison's
policy could be found in the instructions issued to the American armed
forces on the southern frontier. In early January 1811 the War Department
ordered Lieut. Col. Thomas Adam Smith of the Regiment of Riflemen to
move troops from Coleraine in the southwestern corner of Camden
County, Georgia, to St. Marys, and on 26 January Smith was directed to
assist McKee and Mathews in the event of their making an agreement for
the delivery of territory, specifically by taking possession of "such military
posts within the said territory as by an arrangement with the local authority may be agreed to be surrendered."[26] The order did not assume that
Smith's troops would bring about the surrender of those posts, nor did
Secretary of War Eustis inform Smith that McKee and Mathews might call
upon him to "pre-occupy" territory against a foreign power. Smith, however, was absent from his post on other business by March 1811 and was
not to return to St. Marys for another year, and in the interim the War De-

partment neither took steps to hasten his return nor informed his second in command, Maj. Jacinct Laval, about the assignment of McKee and Mathews. These omissions suggest that the administration believed that the mission of their agents would be peaceful and that American troops would only be involved after the transfer of territory had taken place, either by negotiation with White or after East Floridian rebels had established their independence.

Orders for the preparation of gunboats were also sent in January 1811 to Commodore Hugh George Campbell at Charleston, South Carolina, where he commanded a detachment charged with suppressing smuggling and slave trading from Amelia Island across the St. Marys River into Georgia. But these orders were largely concerned with the prevention of illegal trade, and they formed part of a series of directives that had commenced as long ago as October 1810 and were to continue intermittently throughout 1811 without their being explicitly connected to the movements of Mathews and McKee. Campbell, moreover, like Laval, was never informed about their mission, and in all the communications he received from the Navy Department he was instructed to coordinate his activities not with the agents but with the U.S. customs collector at Savannah, Georgia.[27] Nor can it be supposed that the emphasis on suppressing illegal trade in Campbell's orders might have been a pretext to conceal a naval buildup for the agents' benefit. The Amelia Island–St. Marys River region had always been notorious as a place where British merchants and others could evade American trade laws, and as early as 2 November 1810 Madison had proclaimed his intention to impose new trade restrictions on Great Britain if that nation did not remove its Orders in Council against American shipping within three months.[28] Congress had also been considering legislation to enforce that policy before McKee and Mathews had arrived in Washington and before any planning for their mission had taken place.[29]

Navy Department policy, therefore, was not conducted in ways that were central for the success of Mathews and McKee. That fact was confirmed by Mathews himself in late February 1811 when he and McKee stopped at St. Marys while en route to Mobile for negotiations with Folch. Once back in St. Marys, Mathews re-established contact with the gentlemen who had been "disposid to Sarve our goverment" and whose names he had mentioned to the administration. But after surveying the scene on the Florida-Georgia border, where he noted signs of increasing British commercial activity that made East Florida of "more importans to the U.S. evarey day," Mathews also reported that "thare has not one soldier arived, or one armed Visil or a gun Boat in this river," and for that reason both he and his gentlemen friends concluded that it would be premature or "not proper to attempt Eny thing at present."[30] By this remark Mathews was indicating that the conditions for the internal revolution in East Florida he had described in January were not yet in place. The agent was not unduly bothered by that situation, but he was troubled by another matter that promised to jeopardize any mission in East Florida that might be undertaken after he and McKee had completed their business with Folch. As he reread their instructions, Mathews noted that "our Comition only goes to West Florade while our Instruction imbrace East Florade."[31]

The expression was as cryptic as the grammar and spelling were crude, but Mathews had belatedly realized that the paragraph in the instructions relating to East Florida was not a proper credential to display to any authority in the province—either to the Spanish governor or to a successor regime—for the purpose of making a treaty with the United States. The fact that Mathews still had no reason to suppose White might negotiate with him in ways similar to those that Folch had proposed to McKee was less important than the possibility that this situation could change after the mission to Folch was over. Here Mathews would have been assuming that the transfer to the United States of all of West Florida extending to the Apalachicola River would persuade White that any efforts he might make to preserve East Florida for Spain were futile, meaning, therefore, that the governor would then have no alternative but to follow the example set by his counterpart in Mobile. In those circumstances, McKee and Mathews would need a commission that explicitly sanctioned their making a treaty with whatever authority could fairly claim to control the province. But until that point had been reached, Mathews was more concerned with West Florida than with East Florida. He and McKee departed for the former province on 26 February, assuming that troops and gunboats, as well as a new commission, would arrive at St. Marys by the time of their anticipated return on 20 April 1811.[32]

Mathews's letter reached Washington on 18 March 1811.[33] The administration made no response. More than likely, neither the president nor the secretary of state saw any need to act at this stage. Madison and Robert Smith were also preoccupied with other matters. For reasons that were personal, professional, and political, their relationship had never been comfortable, and it was now about to break down completely. The day after Mathews's letter arrived in the State Department, on 19 March, Madison tried to rid himself of Smith by dispatching him to St. Petersburg as minister to Russia. Initially, Smith indicated he would accept, but after some reflection and a brutally frank conversation with Madison during which the president called into question both his competence and his honesty, he rejected the offer and left Washington on 6 April 1811. The fact of Smith's departure, to say nothing of the obviously angry and possibly vindictive mood in which he quit his post, however, was both embarrassing and potentially dangerous for the administration, and for some time thereafter Madison was more concerned with the political fallout from Smith's departure and its bearing on relations with Great Britain than he was with Spanish issues.[34] The implementation of policy for the borderlands thus fell by the wayside until Smith's successor in the State Department, James Monroe, could deal with it.

Monroe did not turn his attention to Florida until June 1811. By then the mission to negotiate with Folch had failed. In preparation for their arrival in West Florida, Mathews and McKee had sent Isaacs on ahead for a meeting with Folch, at which the secretary learned in late February that the governor had changed his mind about relinquishing West Florida to the United States. Since December 1810 he had received financial aid from Veracruz along with orders to retain his province "until the last extremity." Folch noted as well, and not without a certain irony, that the American occupation of Baton Rouge had also relieved him from the immediate danger of filibusters organized by Kennedy and the Mobile Society and that his circumstances were now much improved.[35] Mathews and McKee were unwilling to accept this statement, preferring to believe that this "new ground" was no more than "a finesse" reflecting Folch's wish "to enhance his own value on the occasion." They pressed on in the belief that personal meetings, coupled with a "frank expression" of the administration's views, would convince the governor that his original offer was "reconcilable with the interest & honor of Spain" as well as being in the best interests of West Florida and its officials. It was to no avail. When they met with Folch after 21 March 1811, he remained firm in refusing to make any arrangement with them.[36]

After he had reviewed this correspondence, Monroe decided at the end of June to terminate the mission of the agents insofar as it related to West Florida and to transfer oversight of affairs in the Mobile and Pensacola regions to Claiborne in New Orleans. As for East Florida, he was inclined to tell Mathews to continue the mission there if circumstances warranted it, but as he reached that conclusion Monroe either overlooked or ignored Mathews's February request that he be given a new commission. The secretary of state then changed his mind and withheld the letters he had just drafted.[37] His reasons for doing so can be easily surmised. Emboldened by Folch's rejection of Mathews and McKee, Spanish officials in West Florida reasserted their authority by denying American vessels passage up the Mobile River to supply Fort Stoddert. A fresh crisis on the Gulf Coast loomed, threatening an armed clash with Spain. Worse, as McKee reported from Fort Stoddert, it seemed not impossible that Folch would consider retaking Baton Rouge, and he believed that the governor had written to the Spanish ambassador in London seeking British assistance for that purpose. He therefore warned the administration to expect "serious embarrassments in this quarter."[38] That development coincided with the decision of one of the Federalist senators from New England to reveal the secret Congressional proceedings of January 1811 relating to the missions of the agents. Madison's intentions with regard to Spain and Florida were thus published in the *Hartford Connecticut Mirror* in the last week of June, after which they were broadcast throughout the nation by other newspapers. Even the administration's own journal, the *National Intelligencer*, printed the story, though not without casting severe aspersions on the morals of the legislator who had "treacherously" divulged it.[39]

The timing of this revelation was no accident. It was common knowledge that a new minister from Great Britain, Augustus John Foster, would arrive in Washington at any moment. Since it could also be fairly predicted he would make some sort of protest against Madison's occupation of West Florida, the administration could only be further embarrassed by the disclosure of its plans to get control over what was left of Spain's possessions on the Gulf Coast and the Florida peninsula. Moreover, news coming out of London under 1 and 5 July 1811 datelines that arrived not too long after Foster did conveyed the more alarming story that Great Britain was sending a squadron of naval vessels under the command of Rear Admiral Sir Joseph Yorke to American waters. The squadron was said to be "large enough to blow the entire American navy out of the water," and who could say that Yorke, whatever his assignment might be, would not make a call in a Florida port?[40] Confronted with the prospect of simultaneous crises with both Great Britain and Spain, Monroe concluded that it would be premature and imprudent to end the missions of Mathews and McKee. And by withholding the letters he had recently drafted, the secretary of state left standing the instructions issued by his predecessor on 26 January.

Foster arrived in Washington on 2 July 1811 and lost no time in taking up the matter of Florida. His instructions were to protest "the ungenerous and unprovoked Seizure" of West Florida and to "instantly remonstrate" at any attempt on East Florida, but without using "hostile or menacing language" that would commit Great Britain to vindicate "the Rights of Spain" by force. That decision, Lord Wellesley told him, "must be determined by future Considerations."[41] Originally, it had been Foster's plan to commence his mission with an attack on Madison's occupation of West Florida, but the publication of the January congressional proceedings about East Florida led him to expand his notes and conversations with Monroe into a critique of all American actions along the Gulf Coast. On the matter of West Florida, nothing was achieved. The British minister continued the line of argument Morier had made in December 1810 and in return had to endure with "real pain" the "most profligate arguments" from Monroe that the United States had a valid claim to the province, that it had not assisted the rebels there, and that Madison had occupied the province to protect Spain's officials from being overrun by those rebels. Like Morier, Foster found that last claim to be "extraordinary." On the matter of East Florida, Foster presented no note, but in conversations he outlined a situation—which he hardly considered hypothetical—that if another Fulwar Skipwith should appear at the head of a band of insurgents in East Florida, what guarantee did Great Britain have that the United States would not succumb to "a fresh impulse of humanity" by occupying that province too? Monroe evaded the question by pointing out that he had played no role in the decisions of January, but he did assure Foster that the "most positive orders" had been given to American military officers "not to commit any hostility against the Spaniards."[42]

One month later—in September 1811, when both Madison and Monroe were in Virginia on vacation and after Foster had received a letter from Onís in Philadelphia complaining about the recent appearances of Mathews at St. Marys—Foster did write to the secretary of state to inquire under what authority the agent was acting when he was reported as having offered land, religious liberty, and debt relief to the people of East Florida in return for their abandoning their allegiance to Spain. Receiving no answer, Foster wrote to Rear Admiral Herbert Sawyer, the Royal Navy commander on the West Indian station, to suggest that he might assist the Spanish authorities by sending vessels to cruise off Amelia Island. In doing so, Foster was aware he was going beyond his instructions, but his conversations with Monroe in July had led him to conclude that the administration would seize East Florida by means similar to those he believed had been employed in West Florida. To prevent such a move, he had already recommended that Great Britain make a "direct threat" of war, and he had sought permission to deliver this message to Monroe. Foster also advocated placing an agent in New Orleans to gather information on American intrigues against Spanish territory and proposed that British military officials and colonial governors in the West Indies make offers of aid "in a very public manner" to the governors in Mobile and St. Augustine. Nothing less, the minister was convinced, would restrain the administration and its supporters from further encroachments on Spain's possessions.[43]

Shortly before the diplomats began their exchange of notes, Mathews returned to St. Marys. His stay in Mobile had been prolonged by the time he and McKee had spent trying to persuade Folch to cede West Florida, and neither agent was willing to accept the governor's refusal as final. To them, it still seemed Folch's circumstances were sufficiently desperate to require him, sooner or later, to make a deal with the United States. Accordingly, Mathews went to Pensacola to pursue a claim to some "negroes" in which he had an interest and where he sought at the same time to acquire "a better understanding" of Folch's thinking.[44] In May 1811, the governor was relieved of his command in order to answer questions in

Havana about his recent conduct, but that development only encouraged the agents to believe they might find another Spanish official to make the deal they had just been refused.[45] Mathews also made a reconnaissance of the Mobile Bay region in case the United States should have to undertake military operations there, while McKee withdrew to Fort Stoddert, from where he requested that the administration clarify a problem in its instructions that had brought him and Mathews into conflict with Brig. Gen. Wade Hampton. The general had contended that the agents could not requisition troops to occupy Spanish territory unless the request had his prior approval. McKee could see no reason for this, but he duly reported the facts of the case, along with a hint that Lieut. Col. Leonard Covington might be a more cooperative officer for him and Mathews to work with in the future.[46]

For these reasons Mathews did not set out for St. Marys until 19 May, and then only after he had learned that Governor White had died in St. Augustine on 13 April. He reached his destination on 9 June but was confined to bed for more than two weeks by a bout of malaria.[47] By the time he had recovered at the end of June, he found that the situation in East Florida had not developed in the ways he had anticipated in his January report. Admittedly, there were now four gunboats and two hundred American troops on the north side of the St. Marys River, but Mathews immediately dismissed these forces as too few to "pre-occupy" East Florida or "to repel a large force" from there. That last remark reflected the unwelcome news that White's interim successor, Juan José Estrada, was no more willing to consider delivering the province to the United States than White had been and that he might soon be reinforced by a British regiment of black troops from Jamaica. Should such a force arrive, Mathews felt sure that "the best class of inhabitants would flock to the American standard," but he admitted there were "renagadoes" in East Florida "who would joyfully hail their approach & join their banners."[48] Given that Spanish methods of colonial defense frequently relied on employing local blacks in the militia, that would mean, though Mathews did not say so, there could be no internal revolution for independence without the leading merchants and planters in the province running the risk of civil war and slave revolt.[49]

Anxiety on that account was not the only source of Mathews's concern.

The other problem was that support inside East Florida for a revolt against Spain had dissipated. It did so for a variety of reasons. Estrada was aware of the intrigues surrounding Mathews's earlier visit, and he had talked with both Arredondo and McIntosh, who agreed "to drop all further animosities and conspiracies and live as peaceable, good citizens."[50] Equally important was a boom in the local economy spurred by an expansion of British trade with Spanish America and also the current news of a succession of British and Spanish victories over the French in Spain. Newspapers from Georgia, as well as the *National Intelligencer* from Washington, provided detailed accounts of French setbacks in the Peninsula War, and although Mathews tried to put them in the most positive light he could, the settlers of East Florida were "much flush'd with the partial success obtain'd over the French" which "caus'd them to assume a tone different from the one held last fall."[51] If the fall of Cádiz was supposed to be the signal for a rejection of Spanish authority in East Florida, that day was now receding into the future. Mathews noted too that smuggling into the United States, much of it abetted by British merchants, was increasing, but that situation only underscored "the vast importance of Florida to the U. States in a commercial view."[52] The agent was at a loss as to his next move, but beyond suggesting the need for aid from "volunteers" from Georgia, the only idea he could come up with was to make a personal visit to East Florida. "By being a spectator of what is going on," he wrote, "I can better for[e]see & provide for events than by the best information I can obtain here."[53]

Mathews never provided any account of his movements and contacts over the next month, but there is no doubt he met again with McIntosh. However, if McIntosh's recollections of his meetings with Mathews can be trusted, the agent would have learned that McIntosh was no longer so well disposed to serve the interests of the United States as he had appeared to be in January. Indeed, according to McIntosh, his first responses to the news that the administration would be "friendly to any party in Florida who would depose the Spanish authorities, and declare themselves desirous of becoming citizens of the United States" had been cautious and noncommittal. As a condition for holding land in East Florida, McIntosh had sworn an oath of allegiance to Spain, and he pointed out to Mathews that there were "great difficulties in attempting to bring about a revolt in

Florida: that the population was much spread, and composed of men of various political opinions" and that "the impregnable castle of St. Augustine would render abortive any attempt which a handful of men, without artillery and proper resources, might make to revolutionize the Province."[54] If McIntosh still felt that way in July 1811, even after he had learned of Mathews's January instructions, he was probably not likely to be persuaded otherwise on the basis of there now being four gunboats and two hundred troops in southern Georgia. That he was not so persuaded is suggested by his decision, immediately after meeting again with Mathews, to disclose the details of the agent's instructions, first to William Craig, a magistrate at St. Johns, and then to Estrada.[55] Yet it is unlikely that McIntosh entirely discouraged Mathews either. He told Craig about Mathews's plans without telling the magistrate he would also pass them on to the governor— perhaps as a way of testing Craig's reaction to them—and he told Estrada in order to prove that he was adhering to his recent promise to be a "peaceable, good" citizen. Besides, he also wanted Estrada to grant him permission to move his family back to Georgia for the education of his children. At best, McIntosh was keeping his options open, and he probably told Mathews he wanted to see a greater commitment of resources from the United States for the removal of the Spanish regime.

That last problem was the subject of Mathews's next letter to Washington, written on 3 August 1811. He now discounted the rumors about the "African" regiment from Jamaica but confirmed that "the quiet possession of E. Florida" could not be gained by an "amicable negociation with the powers that exist," pointing out that while many inhabitants were "ripe for revolt, they [were] however incompetent to effect a thorough revolution without external aid." Mathews then sought that aid, asking for arms, swords, and artillery to be sent to Point Petre, "subject to [his] order," so he could assist the settlers in launching a revolution "with a fair prospect of success." He promised to be "most discreet" and "prevent the U. States from being committed." And although he was not actually prepared to "vouch for the event," he thought there would be "but little danger." In offering these suggestions, there can be no doubt that Mathews was going beyond anything contemplated under his instructions. Had the original intent of those instructions been to sanction the organization of a revolution, Mathews would never have bothered to write as he did on 3

August; indeed, the reason he wrote that letter was to redefine the purpose of his mission. He therefore explicitly requested "to be favord with a reply to this . . . confided to the proper Departments only" and not communicated to him by letters from "clerks." Here Mathews assumed he could rely on the "political sagacity" of the secretary of state to grasp his meaning.[56] In other words, Mathews wanted Monroe to write a confidential letter to Crawford endorsing his proposals.

Mathews waited more than two months for a reply. Being impatient and impulsive, he did not find the wait easy, and in September his thoughts turned back to the unsuccessful negotiations with Folch earlier in the year. By now, it seemed clear that neither Folch nor any other Spanish official would volunteer to relinquish Mobile and Pensacola in the immediate future, so Mathews wrote to McKee at Fort Stoddert, urging him to go to Mobile and seek out two Irish priests of the Capuchin order, James Coleman and Francis Lennon, to attach them "to our cause." The "holy Fathers" should be convinced, Mathews wrote, that the time had come for them to cease serving as "very able props to a tottering government." Mathews assumed the priests could be persuaded to switch their loyalties from the Spanish regime once they understood "the superior advantages they would enjoy under a government conducted upon principles of rational liberty & calculated to ensure social happiness." If that prospect should not be sufficiently attractive, he suggested that there were "other inviting allurements" that might be useful in getting the priests to see that they could make "God's word a sinecure" under American rule as well as they could under the Spanish regime. Exactly what Mathews might have meant by this is uncertain. He declined to go into further detail in case some "impertinent curiosity" might make off with his letter, but it would seem he was now trying to lay the groundwork for the future subversion of the Spanish authorities in both Mobile and Pensacola.[57]

As for East Florida, by October Mathews had become so eager to learn how his 3 August letter had been received that he made an urgent visit to Crawford, probably to see whether he had heard from Monroe and certainly to give him a copy of the letter before the senator departed for the first session of the Twelfth Congress, which Madison, in the last week of July, had summoned to assemble in November. Mathews accompanied this copy with a further letter, dated 14 October, in which he again lamented that "the early favorable presages to our mission so soon vanish'd in W. Florida," and he recapitulated the reasons for his bringing about a revolution in East Florida—mainly to stop smuggling and to keep the province out of the hands of Great Britain. He also added that if the administration should find it inconvenient to send him the arms he had requested, the officers of "the gunboats now riding at anchor in these waters, at and near St. Marys, could easily, and that without inconvenience to their service, furnish arms and accoutrements that would render great facility to the business." To make the prospect of changing the East Florida regime more palatable, Mathews stressed that the fortifications at St. Augustine were "weak and decayed," that the troops there were without ammunition, and that little more than half of them should be considered "effective."[58]

Enclosed with Mathews's 14 October letter was a pseudonymous account of developments in East Florida, which the agent must have found very troubling. Among them was the rumor that the Cortes in Cadiz had recently conveyed "all the vacant Land in that Province; whether ceded or unceded by the Indians" to Richard Raynal Keene, formerly the son-in-law of Luther Martin of Maryland, who had become a Spanish subject and who, for the past two years, had been seeking an extensive grant of land between the Bay of Tampa and San Marcos de Apalache, where he planned to grow cotton and establish a naval stores industry.[59] Mathews admitted he did not normally give credence to rumors, but he believed that the administration should be aware of the difficulties Keene's grants might pose for any future American occupation of the Gulf Coast. What Mathews did *not* say, however, was that if Keene received the land he had requested, his grant would overlap, or conflict, with the earlier grants Forbes had received from the Creek and Lower Seminole Indians, in which Mathews (and McKee) had already taken an interest.[60] It is possible Mathews felt it was unnecessary for him to say anything about his personal affairs at this juncture, but his pseudonymous source did not fail to point out that a revolution would be "the most effectual mode" of destroying any grant given to Keene. That source also concluded his communication with the warning that unless Mathews or the U.S. Army commander at Point Petre had "instructions to afford the friends of our Country at least an indirect aid, no change will take place in E. Florida."[61]

Yet another reason Mathews visited Crawford was to check on a report he had received from McKee that, according to Hampton, Madison had revoked their "joint power" to act in Florida.[62] Unwilling to believe it, Mathews declared he had not allowed the rumor to interrupt his duties, and Crawford could have certainly confirmed for him that the instructions of January 1811 were still in effect. But Crawford would have been unable to tell him any more than that, and at the end of their meeting the senator left for Washington, where he delivered Mathews's October letters to the State Department on 5 November. In the previous week, however, Monroe had resumed discussions with Foster over Florida. Knowing full well he had yet to respond to the minister's September inquiry about what Mathews was doing at St. Marys, the secretary of state sent his chief clerk, John Graham, to apologize for the omission and to explain that he had "unluckily left [Foster's] letter behind him at his house in the Country" when he had returned to the capital. That apology he repeated in person when he met with Foster on 30 October for a talk "of a very serious nature" that the minister had requested on Florida. During the course of their conversation, Monroe stated that Mathews had been sent to St. Marys not to seduce East Floridians into overthrowing Spanish rule but "to watch the conduct of the Captain-General at Cuba, who it was supposed might have been disposed to resent the measures pursued in West Florida."[63]

It would be a mistake to characterize this statement as a lie to conceal from Foster that the administration now wished Mathews to organize a revolution along the lines he had suggested on 3 August. Certainly, Monroe did not disclose the full range of considerations informing the instructions under which Mathews was acting—he was under no obligation to do this, and to have done so would have been unwise—but the explanation he gave Foster was not totally inconsistent with those instructions either. It is also necessary to stress that on 30 October the State Department had received no communication from Mathews dated later than 28 June—when the agent had done little more than write of his confusion at discovering that the situation in East Florida had changed significantly since his earlier visit there. Monroe had not read, or responded to, Mathews's 3 August letter for the simple reason that it never reached Washington. It had miscarried in the mails, and the copy delivered by Crawford on

5 November is the only surviving text.[64] There was, therefore, no need for Monroe to comment on, much less refute, allegations made by Foster and Onís that Mathews was orchestrating a revolution in East Florida when the administration neither intended for him to nor had any evidence that he was already doing so.

Nevertheless, the 30 October conversation between Foster and Monroe was considerably more heated than their earlier exchanges. The reason was that the administration had just learned that in June 1811 the Regency in Cádiz had agreed to discuss an offer from Great Britain to mediate disputes between Spain and its American colonies. In return for agreeing to the discussions, Spain wanted loans while Great Britain desired to expand and legalize its access to the trade of Spanish America. And should the mediation be unsuccessful, London promised to assist Cádiz in returning its wayward American colonies "to their duty." The *National Intelligencer* denounced these proposals as "perfectly visionary" and "a fruitless & dangerous undertaking," but it would be difficult to underestimate their impact on an administration that was still defending its occupation of West Florida, that was hopeful East Florida might yet declare its own independence, and whose president was about to send Congress a message recommending preparations for war as the only way to resist Great Britain's monopolization of all American trade through its Orders in Council.[65] Even as Foster and Monroe were meeting, Madison was inserting in his annual message a paragraph on Spanish America in "anticipation of unfriendly views originating in the misguided councils or ambition" of Spain and Great Britain. He deleted it, however, after Gallatin pointed out it would needlessly "hurt the pride" of Spain as "an improper interference" in its concerns.[66] Even so, there is no doubt Madison placed the worst possible interpretation on the British initiative, and he did not assume that what was publicly known of it described its full extent. Treaties invariably contained secret clauses, and Madison, as he later admitted to Foster, feared that eventually "Spain would be obliged to make common cause with England" in any war with the United States.[67]

It was against this background that Foster, instead of warning the administration off from further encroachments on Spanish territory, found himself listening to Monroe "very warmly" inveighing against "the interference of Great Britain with respect to East Florida." The secretary of

state again defended the basis of the American interest in the province—
as the only pledge available to the United States for the payment of unsettled spoliations—and he further hinted that Foster's concern with the
subject merely masked his own government's wish to annex the province
because of its proximity to the West Indies. That, Monroe asserted, could
not be tolerated by the United States, which would under the circumstances be entitled to seize the province regardless of the consequences.
Foster could only rejoin that Great Britain had better uses for its forces
than to send them to East Florida, and he eventually managed to extract
some remarks from the secretary to the effect that despite its right to do
so, the United States would not commence hostilities against Florida.[68]
Three days after this conversation, on 2 November, Monroe sent Foster a
note in response to his September letter. It merely restated the long-standing grounds for the American claim to East Florida. About Mathews, it
said nothing, and it concluded with a recapitulation of what was now publicly known about the policy adopted in January 1811—that the United
States might occupy East Florida in the event of it being offered by a "local
authority" or to prevent a foreign attack and that the province would be
held subject to "future and friendly negotiation."[69]

Only after these exchanges did the administration examine the October
communications Crawford had delivered from Mathews. That Madison
had been informed by at least some of their contents he revealed in a 17
November letter to his minister in Paris, Joel Barlow, warning him "there
[was] good reason to believe that an agent (Keene) for certain grasping
land Jobbers of N. Orleans & possibly elsewhere, has been treating with
the Cortes for the vacant lands in E. Florida." The president could only
trust that France would accept the inevitability of both East and West
Florida coming to the United States and that Napoleon would not resur-
rect his "unworthy" policy of trying "to extract money from the occasion"
because, he added, "without our occupancy, that of G[reat]. B[ritain].
would be interposed."[70] As for what London was doing, the news was
disturbing. The State Department had received letters from Cádiz and
Havana reporting signs of closer cooperation between Spain and Great
Britain, including the story that the two allies would send a total of eigh-
teen thousand troops to Cuba, from where they were "destined for Vera-
Cruz *as it is said*" to assist the Viceroy in Mexico to suppress the indepen-

dence movement there.[71] If such a force did materialize on the southern frontiers of the United States, Madison took it for granted that he would have to occupy East Florida, though he did not predict what Great Britain might then do. But, he continued, "the game she will play with Cuba may be more readily conjectured," even if "like most of her others it may in the end be a losing one."[72]

Despite the possibility that Great Britain might occupy Cuba, the administration made no response to Mathews's request for the authority and resources to organize a revolt in East Florida. Its failure to do so, though, was not proof that Madison and Monroe wanted him to act anyway in order to spare them the responsibility for initiating hostilities against Spain. Such a decision would have been too cynical a violation of the law of nations for Madison to have approved. It was enough that the nation was already mobilizing for one war, and it was by no means uncommon for cabinet members to ignore letters containing suggestions the administration did not wish to adopt. In fact, it was almost standard practice for executive departments to disregard such letters when they advocated policies that exceeded the instructions their writers had originally received. From the perspective of the administration, it was the responsibility of agents to remain bound by instructions until informed otherwise. Consequently, Monroe never wrote to Mathews at all, which meant that the agent's August request was *not* approved. Administration policy, therefore, remained unchanged: Mathews was to remain at his post to observe developments in East Florida; McKee was to do the same at Fort Stoddert; and they could only act under the conditions specified in their instructions.[73] That this was the administration's intention was confirmed by Monroe when he sent his 2 November letter to Foster to Congress on 9 December 1811. From there it was reprinted in the *National Intelligencer* and in other newspapers for all the world to read—Mathews included.[74]

At some point after December 1811, Mathews was informed about, or read, the newspaper version of Monroe's 2 November letter to Foster. There can be little doubt he failed to understand that its contents, considered in conjunction with the absence of any response to his requests, meant that his task was to continue following his original instructions. But it is not likely, either, that he ever believed Monroe's communications with Foster amounted to a tacit authorization for him to orchestrate a revolution in East Florida in which the armed forces of the United States and "volunteers" from Georgia might participate. Monroe had not written his 2 November letter for that reason, and Mathews's conduct and correspondence thereafter suggest, even as he embarked on the course he had outlined in August, that he was never totally confident the administration was committed to his actions. The problem of obtaining Madison's consent never ceased to trouble him, and he was to seek it repeatedly throughout the next four months.[75] When he failed to get it, he resorted to the more audacious gamble of trying first to seize East Florida and then, with the assistance of McKee, to subvert the Spanish authorities in Mobile and Pensacola in the hope that their efforts, if successful, would be accepted by the administration as the fulfillment of the instructions it had issued in January 1811.

That Mathews experienced considerable difficulty in raising forces to take control of St. Augustine has long been known to historians.[76] By November 1811, too, he had fallen ill again, and Isaacs at times feared "the old general" was on the point of death.[77] Mathews also found that he could not count on as much assistance from his "Gentlemen of influence" as he had once hoped, though he did resume discussions yet again with McIntosh, who eventually came to convince himself that Monroe's 2 November 1811 letter to Foster could be adduced as proof that the administration was committed to supporting any efforts Mathews might make to take possession of East Florida.[78] Mathews also recruited McIntosh's overseer, John Boog, to the cause, along with a small handful of other men residing on both sides of the St. Marys River, among them being Lodovick Ashley, Archibald Clark, George Cook, William Kelley, Benjamin Sands, and Francis Young. James Hall and James Seagrove continued to encourage him, though if Seagrove had ever told Mathews that in 1805 he had advised Madison that the "easy" conquest of East Florida would require a force of not less than two thousand regulars and militia as well as three hundred mounted militiamen, fifty artillery men, and half a dozen gun boats, the agent might well have given up in despair.[79] He did not give up, but at times he did despair and was heard to complain that "if *five* Floridians or even *three* would join him, he could then go on and command in his service the United States forces in the neighborhood."[80]

The problem was that Mathews could not even be sure about the U.S. forces. He had received no reply to his letter of 14 October 1811, so he wrote again to Crawford to suggest "the propriety of sending on here a company of artillery" as well as "the arms heretofore recommended" or "an order to the commanding officer of the gun-boats." Apparently not hearing from the senator either, Mathews wrote to Monroe on 23 January 1812, pointing out that it was "indispensably necessary" for the administration to comply with his requests if it had "any serious objects in view" in East Florida. This was not the language of a man who believed that the administration was supporting his revolution, and Mathews knew his position was deteriorating. If he did not take St. Augustine soon, the "Dons" might get "a small reinforcement" there, which would be "productive of great inconvenience." After he had finished the letter, he added a postscript announcing that his fears were already confirmed by the news that the Cádiz Regency had just appointed Col. Sebastian Kindelán y Oregon, a military engineer in Cuba, to be the next governor of East Florida. Mathews was "well acquainted" with this "gentleman of handsome talents and military experience." Kindelán had met with Mathews in 1795, as an envoy of Governor Juan Nepomuceno de Quesada, to discuss the status of dissident East Floridians who had fled across the St. Marys River and to request that Mathews arrest any Georgians who assisted them. Mathews might well have wondered whether Kindelán was not about to make the same request of him again, but more immediately he dreaded that the new governor would repair the drawbridge at St. Augustine, "which will render the fort difficult to be taken." Monroe ignored this letter too. It sat in his office until the first week of August 1812, when it was belatedly turned over to the War Department.[81] By then, though, Mathews had less than one month to live.

The continuing silence from Monroe drove Mathews, in mid-February 1812, to the town of Jefferson in Camden County, where he met with the governor of Georgia, David B. Mitchell, to whom he explained his mission. Mitchell was by no means hostile to the notion that Spain should be expelled from East Florida, but he was stunned by what Mathews told him. This was the first he had heard that the administration was even contemplating taking the province, and he could only wonder—and not be a little offended at the same time—about why he had not been informed of a project that was of major concern to his state and that could hardly be executed without its support. But regardless of his personal views, there was little Mitchell could do. He could order the ranking local militia officer, Brig. Gen. John Floyd, to ready his troops, but it would take time to prepare men and supplies for a campaign to reduce St. Augustine, a city that had been captured only once—briefly in 1686—since its foundation in 1565. Moreover, the governor could not order the militia to undertake operations outside of Georgia, much less in a foreign territory, without a directive from the president. And Mitchell had received no such communication from Madison, even though like every other governor he was already engaged in mobilizing his state for war with Great Britain.[82]

The outcome in Jefferson left Mathews with only two possibilities: to continue recruiting for volunteers from East Florida and Georgia, and to get control over the U.S. Army and Navy forces at St. Marys and Point Petre. He had some limited success with the first, and by March 1812 he had assembled a force of about 120 Georgians—mostly "waggoners and carters" with little military training, according to a contemptuous description later provided by Foster—and a smaller number of East Floridians.[83] Among them, though, was McIntosh, who finally committed himself to the project Mathews had been urging on him since 1810. Why McIntosh took the plunge can only be conjectured. He may well have been worn down by the more persistent and far stronger personality of Mathews, and he was undoubtedly much more of an American at heart than he was a good Spanish subject. In the long run, he did not wish to see his children grow up under the rule of Spain, and as he wrote somewhat extravagantly to Representative George M. Troup in Washington, he preferred to leave them with the legacy of the "rights and privileges" of American citizens rather than with the wealth of "the mines of Peru." McIntosh may also have realized that if it was only a matter of time before Spain lost East Florida anyway, he could no longer indefinitely postpone the choice about whether he was going to be on the winning or the losing side. Even so, he was unable to vindicate his decision by any strongly held convictions. Instead, he fell back on his quarrel with Estrada from the previous summer over the relocation of his family to Georgia and maintained that the governor's unwillingness to accommodate him was a sufficiently serious breach of contract to justify his turning rebel.[84]

The U.S. forces were a more difficult problem, which Mathews approached with circumspection. He met, first, with Commodore Campbell in late February seeking muskets, bayonets, pistols, and swords for fifty men but learned instead that Campbell had never received any information from the Navy Department about his mission or orders to assist him. Nevertheless, Campbell was willing to be persuaded, albeit reluctantly, that Mathews's instructions took precedence over his own, and he agreed to provide the equipment when Mathews formally requested it on 11 March.[85] As for Maj. Laval, with whom Mathews had been sharing accommodations in St. Marys, he left him to the last. He disliked Laval and knew that the major returned the antipathy. In terms of their backgrounds and personalities, the two men were totally incompatible, and Laval had long suspected that Mathews was plotting something improper. On 10 March 1812, Mathews and McIntosh received a tip from Henly Wylly, a half-pay British officer working on behalf of British and Spanish interests, that Great Britain was about to send black troops to East Florida. Wylly urged the Americans "not to delay, *not for one* day, the accomplishment of their object."[86] If this was a way of tricking Mathews into acting before he was properly prepared—and it almost certainly was—Mathews fell for it, and on that basis he finally asked Laval to supply him with arms and ammunition as well as 140 men from his command.[87] The major refused, pointing out that Mathews's instructions did not authorize him to overthrow the government of East Florida. The fury of Mathews's reaction led him briefly to reconsider by offering fifty troops instead, but when he learned Mathews wanted them to serve not as a regular army detachment but as disguised volunteers in a Patriot Army, he reverted to his original position. That subterfuge, for Laval, only confirmed the illegality of Mathews's request.[88]

At the same time that Mathews was making his plans in St. Marys, he was also keeping McKee at Fort Stoddert posted on developments in East Florida, and on 6 March 1812 he wrote again to his fellow agent, stating that by the time McKee received the letter, a revolution would have taken place and East Florida would have become "an Independent nation." Among the first acts of that new nation would be the appointment and recruitment of men "for revolutionizing Pensacola & Mobile or reducing them by force." Mathews announced that he intended to accompany this army on a march "through the Creek nation of which they will be apprised but not of the Motives, but will suppose they are to protect our citizens on Mobile." In conjunction with that operation, McKee was directed to go into Pensacola to use his "influence with Fathers Coleman & Lennon & the rest of [his] friends & prepare them for a revolt from the Spanish government." He was, Mathews stressed, to "exert" himself, "as the Government will expect much from us."[89]

It was to take McKee a while to act on this directive, but in the interim Mathews and McIntosh, as late as 12 March 1812, still hoped to seize the fort and the governor at St. Augustine "by surprise" within the next few days, before they were driven to conclude the next day that Laval had made this impossible.[90] Mathews refused to accept defeat. He told McIntosh he had received arms from the United States "ready for our use" and then came up with a hastily improvised scheme to attack Fernandina on Amelia Island, which the Patriots, with the assistance of Campbell's gunboats, carried out by 17 March, when Lopez surrendered the fort there.[91] On 14 March, the morning the attack began, Mathews sent the State Department a rambling and incoherent letter stating that he was about to exercise "as sound a discretion as [his] judgment was capable of" about "the intent & meaning" of his January 1811 instructions. What the letter did *not* make plain was Mathews's intention to remove the Spanish authorities in both East and West Florida by force. Instead, the letter implied that East Florida had already declared its independence and that Mathews had been engaged in a fruitless effort to obtain ammunition and troops from Laval to "preoccupy defend & hold" the province "by force" against a foreign invasion. Mathews provided little in the way of evidence to substantiate these claims—beyond the 10 March note Wylly had sent to McIntosh—and the greater part of his letter was an angry catalog of complaints against Laval, whose behavior had made it impossible for him to take St. Augustine. Mathews demanded Laval's removal and furnished evidence of his misconduct to justify doing so. He also reminded the administration—again—that it was more than time for it "to send on immediately" the artillery and infantry he had requested earlier if it ever wanted to secure possession of East Florida.[92]

It was to take nearly a month and several more letters before the administration was able to clarify what Mathews's 14 March letter had left unsaid. On 21 March the agent forwarded articles he had negotiated three days earlier with the "constituted authorities" of East Florida at Fernandina as the "local authority" ceding the province to the United States. Mathews decided to withhold the final text until all of East Florida had been conquered, but he did include a draft treaty. Its six articles, in some respects, followed his instructions quite closely. They ceded the province to the United States and obligated the administration to accept it as an "integral part" of the Union by extending to it protection and religious liberty. The treaty also guaranteed all existing Spanish land titles, offered land grants to all who had participated in the revolution, and provided for the United States to pay debts owed to Spanish officers and soldiers. It even allowed these soldiers to join the U.S. Army at their equivalent ranks and remunerations. More interestingly, though, the treaty made little attempt to justify the break with Cádiz. Nowhere did it protest loudly against misrule or tyranny from Spain, nor did it claim that the revolution had originated in any "disgust" for the Bourbon cause there, for which Mathews and the Patriots expressed only their good wishes for its future success. This omission was a tacit confession that there was no significant support for a revolution in East Florida and that Mathews was trying to avoid grounds for political disputes among its people as he went about changing their government for them.[93]

The treaty was also problematic in other ways. Although East Florida was to join the Union, Mathews agreed to establish it as a free port for the coming year. That would exempt the province from American trade law, including the administration's policy of nonintercourse against Great Britain.[94] Mathews justified this concession to permit the United States to receive revenue and supplies, especially for its Indian trade, from Great Britain, but more important was his wish to reconcile the wealthier members of the British and Spanish communities in East Florida, such as the Arredondo family and the agents of John Forbes and Company, to the revolution.[95] Indeed, John Forbes himself had written to McKee from Nassau in late February 1812 to inform him that he had *already* received assurances from Mathews that "our establishment in East Florida would meet with every protection in the event of that Province being occupied."[96] The treaty also committed the United States to occupying Mobile and Pensacola as a means of defending East Florida.[97] To square that provision with the contents of Monroe's 2 November 1811 letter to Foster, however, Mathews did allow for territory to be restored to Spain by negotiation, provided that Spain re-established its independence from France, that it fully compensated the United States for unsettled spoliations and for all damages that had resulted from the withdrawal of the deposit at New Orleans in 1802, that it reimbursed the United States for all costs incurred in its occupation of Spanish territory, and that a majority of the citizens of East Florida agreed to return to Spanish rule.[98]

One week later, on 28 March, Mathews reported that the Patriots had marched on St. Augustine and were on the point of taking it. His confidence rested on the hope that William Craig, whom he had not previously considered to be a Patriot, would facilitate the surrender of the fort. He mentioned, too, that Lieut. Col. Smith had returned to his post and supplied him with troops denied him by Laval and that Smith would occupy all territory ceded to the United States. Mathews also ordered Campbell to send gunboats to St. Augustine to regulate trade and control access to its harbor. He repeated—yet again—his requests for artillery and infantry to defend East Florida.[99] Some two weeks later, St. Augustine had not fallen, but Mathews, far from showing signs of concern, only became more optimistic. Indeed, if Commodore Campbell is to be believed, Mathews became "sanguine beyond Conception," possibly to the point of taking leave of his senses.[100] On 16 April 1812, he wrote to Madison and Monroe announcing he would complete his mission in both East and West Florida. He also talked of going on to "revolutionize" Mexico before coming to rest in Peru. He forwarded another copy of the articles ceding East Florida, rehearsed the obstacles he had overcome, and commended those who had made the revolution possible. He offered suggestions for the government of East Florida, including the recommendation that the territory have a sole judge rather than a bench of district judges. McIntosh, as "a man of large property" and a "leading character in the revolution," wanted to be governor, but Mathews hinted that Floyd might be better. Seagrove, as an "old Servant of '76," could be surveyor, and his ever-faithful secretary Isaacs, to whom Mathews affectionately referred as "the King of the Jews," deserved to be attorney general. Finally, he drew Madison's attention to the requirement that he accept the reduction of Mobile and Pensacola as a prerequisite for the admission of East Florida to the Union. He then awaited the applause of a grateful nation, but the reception of his news was not to be what he wanted.[101]

Communications from St. Marys usually took between sixteen and twenty-one days to reach the capital, and even if Mathews's 14 March letter to Monroe had arrived by 1 April, its contents would not have made much sense to either the president or the secretary of state.[102] Without additional information from East Florida at hand, they could not have surmised much more than that something had happened, or was about to, but what? It would not have been clear whether there had been a successful revolution in East Florida or whether foreign troops had landed in the province. Certainly, the administration was aware of the possibility of further developments on the Florida-Georgia frontier, as the secretary of the Navy, Paul Hamilton, had alerted Campbell on 28 March that St. Marys was about to become "a scene of active operations." But by that statement Hamilton referred to no more than the new embargo on American trade (which was a prelude to a rupture with Great Britain) that Madison was about to request from Congress on 1 April 1812. When that measure became law three days later, Hamilton wrote again to Campbell, directing him to enforce the embargo wherever possible, but *not* in places "within the jurisdiction of a foreign state, which we are on no pretext to violate."[103] In short, the administration was not looking toward any immediate outbreak of conflict with Spain in East Florida.

As for Mobile and Pensacola, the administration was expecting new developments even less there. Indeed, so quiet did the situation seem to be in West Florida that Monroe, on 2 January 1812, had written to McKee at Fort Stoddert terminating his mission on the Gulf Coast and directing him to notify Claiborne in New Orleans accordingly.[104] McKee did not receive this letter until 14 May 1812, and in the intervening period he made some efforts, albeit of a rather halfhearted nature, to implement the directions he had received earlier from Mathews. He doubted there was much sentiment for a change in Mobile, but he nevertheless contacted James Innerarity there, predicting that East Florida was about to fall to the United States and asking him to use his influence with the Spanish authorities to see if they would meet him "on the ground proposed by Governor Folch" in December 1810.[105] McKee was to report his activities to

Monroe in a highly selective way, however, writing to describe rumors of discontent among the Creek Indians, sending an account of a new Spanish governor to replace Folch, and only in passing alluding to the fact that he was making "another effort to renew negotiations with the Spanish authorities on the basis of Governor Folch's letter to your predecessor (Decr. 1810)."[106] Entirely missing from these letters was any reference to the steps he and Mathews had been discussing to "revolutionize" Mobile and Pensacola, to say nothing of the plans Mathews had been making for St. Augustine.

In fact, it was not from either Mathews or McKee that the administration was to learn the full extent of their plans. The missing pieces in the picture were to be provided first by Foster in Washington, then by Benjamin Hawkins, U.S. agent to the Creek Indians in Georgia. On 2 April 1812, Foster, who had received very full accounts of Mathews's seizure of Fernandina from a local English merchant, Joseph Hibberson, called at the State Department to register a protest. Monroe was caught unawares. He explained at great length that Mathews had no authority for such actions, but he would not promise a disavowal of them until he received letters from the agent himself confirming Foster's claims.[107] Two days later, on 4 April, the War Department received a letter from Hawkins, dated 23 March 1812, describing how he had forwarded Mathews's 6 March letter, with its directions for subverting the Spanish authorities at Mobile and Pensacola, to McKee at Fort Stoddert and providing a description of Mathews's plans to march an East Floridian army through the Creek country to "protect the white people on Mobile from any injury from the revolt of Florida." Hawkins assumed Mathews was acting in accordance with instructions he had received from Washington, and he promised his full cooperation, but he did point out to Secretary of War Eustis that he had received no orders in relation to Mathews's mission.[108]

It seems most likely, therefore, that Mathews's 14 March letter to Monroe did not reach the capital until the same time as Hawkins's 23 March letter to Eustis. But it was Hawkins's letter that clarified what Mathews had left unsaid, while also lending plausibility to the allegations made by Foster.[109] The administration was horrified. It took immediate action by repudiating Mathews and transferring his duties on the Florida border to Governor Mitchell of Georgia, both decisions being made on the same day, 4 April 1812. Mitchell was given directions to restore "the state of things in [East Florida] which existed before the late transactions," meaning the return to Spain of "Amelia Island and other such parts, if any, of East Florida as may have been taken."[110] In Madison's eyes, Hawkins's account would have been incontestable proof that Mathews and McKee had now departed very far from both the spirit and the letter of their January 1811 instructions. Even worse was the fact that the administration was reading about the plans of their agents to overthrow the Spanish authorities in Mobile and Pensacola for the first time. Once a full awareness of the situation had sunk in, repudiation of the East Florida revolution was the only option—if the administration wished to avoid a series of developments that formed no part of its policies, most notably a war with Spain accompanied by an Indian war on the southern frontier of the nation on the eve of an impending war with Great Britain.[111]

At the time that Madison repudiated Mathews and transferred his mission to Mitchell, he left only one recorded comment on the situation, namely that "in E. Florida, Mathews has been playing a tragic-comedy in the face of common sense, as well as his instructions. His extravagances place us in the most distressing dilemma."[112] The president hardly bothered to list the "extravagances," but it is not difficult to surmise what was distressing him. Almost the least of it was the fact that Mathews had placed the administration in precisely the position Madison had tried to place Great Britain when, on 9 March 1812 and five days before the attack on Fernandina, he had sent Congress the letters of a British agent, John Henry, who was believed to have conspired with New England Federalists to break up the Union during the Embargo crisis of 1807–9.[113] That embarrassment was bad enough, but far worse was the more ridiculous claim, implicitly made by Mathews, that a small band of rebels on Amelia Island might exercise effective sovereignty over East Florida without controlling St. Augustine. The question of accepting the province under such circumstances could not even rise to the level of serious consideration.[114] Consequently, the agent had not only undercut the president's case for war against Great Britain at a critical moment but also acted in ways that destroyed Madison's long-standing hope that East Florida might be acquired in ways that would pass muster under international law.

The problem now was how to respond to the situation Mathews had created. Difficulties arose almost immediately in the implementation of the decisions made on 4 April. In addition to returning territory seized by Mathews, Mitchell was directed to negotiate "a full understanding" with the Spanish authorities to ensure the Patriots were not subjected to reprisals for the belief that their revolt had been officially sanctioned. But the letter for Mitchell was delayed until the War Department sent the State Department copies of new orders to Lieut. Col. Smith informing him that in the future he was to take directions from Mitchell and not Mathews. No such order emerged from the office of the adjutant general before 9 April, and then it erred by telling Smith to withdraw from East Florida "immediately." That command was in conflict with the letter to Mitchell, in which the governor had been told he could use "discretion" in issuing orders to Smith. The mistake was corrected the next day and the letter mailed on 11 April, but as a consequence it did not reach the capital of Georgia, Milledgeville, until eleven days later.[115] Mitchell left immediately for St. Marys to commence negotiations with Estrada, but he had some questions, which he forwarded to Washington on 2 May. What measures might he take and what resources would he have if Great Britain should land troops in East Florida? What would he do if the Patriots refused to obey him or refused to return any territory? And would his authority extend over Campbell?[116] The matter of his authority over Campbell was a problem because the Navy Department, after learning of the role the gunboats had played at Fernandina, had written to the commodore on 8 April telling him not to take orders from Mathews. The news reached St. Marys at the same time that Mitchell did. It made Campbell "the happiest of mortals," and he promptly withdrew his gunboats from Spanish waters.[117]

The administration anticipated some of Mitchell's concerns. On 2 May, the same day he had written from St. Marys, Monroe sent him a letter informing him that as "affairs with Great Britain" were now at the point of "rupture," policy toward East Florida would have to be changed. The "danger" was that Great Britain would occupy the province, "which it is the duty of this Government to prevent." Monroe might have added here—though he did not—that because of Mathews's actions, Spain might allow British troops into East Florida, and that if it did, the agent would have brought about the very situation his mission had been intended to prevent. But the secretary of state was careful not to criticize one Georgia governor to another. Mathews's "patriotism" was not to be doubted, even as it subjected the administration to "much embarrassment." Nevertheless, the news that the Patriots had advanced to St. Augustine indicated that "the revolutionary party . . . [had] gone further, than was anticipated, making an accommodation between the Spanish authorities, and that party, very difficult, if not impracticable." The dilemmas seemed insurmountable. To restore East Florida to Spain, "in the expectation of immediately retaking it" in the event of war with Great Britain, was "absurd." To retain it after disavowing Mathews would be "inconsistent," and to abandon the Patriots who had followed Mathews in good faith was "impossible." Nevertheless, Monroe believed he had an "honorable" solution. Justice still dictated the restoration of East Florida to Spain, and it could be retaken after the outbreak of war. But in return for restoring the province, Mitchell was now to consider it his "sacred duty" to obligate the Spanish authorities not to punish the Patriots. If he had doubts Estrada would not agree, he could consider it "a sufficient cause to delay proceeding further, in restoring the territory."[118]

After receiving Mitchell's letter of 2 May, Monroe addressed his remaining questions at the end of the month. By then Madison was drafting a message to Congress seeking war against Great Britain. Should British troops enter East Florida, the governor was to consider the situation as already covered by the law of 15 January 1811 and use "proper means to defeat it." Further to that end, Campbell was also instructed to give "any assistance, in case of emergency" that Mitchell might require. In issuing that directive, Monroe still assumed that if negotiations with Estrada went well, Mitchell could withdraw U.S. troops from East Florida, subject to the Patriots being protected. If the Patriots refused "to surrender the Country or any part of it to the Spanish authority," however, the governor did not have to compel their obedience. "The United States are responsible for their conduct only," Monroe added, "not for that of the Inhabitants of East Florida." The secretary of state did not believe that to be an injustice to Spain, having reminded Mitchell in his previous letter that nothing was owed for the conduct of the Patriots to Spain, "from whom the United States have received many wrongs which are still unredressed." Otherwise, the governor should continue negotiations with

Estrada, "holding in the meantime the ground occupied." That course, Monroe declared, was "justifiable and proper" in the "present state of our affairs with Great Britain."[119]

On 23 June, five days after the declaration of war against Great Britain, Foster called on Madison to pay his respects before returning home. Both men lamented the outbreak of war, and Foster asked whether the United States would treat Spain as a neutral. Madison remarked that he believed "secret articles might exist between Spain & England" which would require the former "to make common cause" with the latter "in the war against America." Foster denied this and, "having allusion to Florida," warned the president against making "Expeditions" there. Madison rejoined that he "could not be well justified in stopping any expeditions, which might be undertaken at a time when perhaps alone they could be successful." From this, Foster concluded that Madison had "decided to take Florida if he could."[120] He was not wrong. The administration was already following the course Monroe had outlined to Mitchell on 2 May, and on 19 June Representative Troup had called for a committee to frame a bill permitting the president to occupy East and West Florida "without delay." Three days later, Monroe sent the committee copies of the instructions that had been given to Mathews and Mitchell as well as a copy of a draft treaty he had presented in Madrid in 1805 that would have transferred East Florida to the United States in exchange for unsettled spoliations. He also claimed that Spain had been willing to make the transfer but had asked for more territory than the United States had wanted to concede. Since Spain had not agreed to any such thing, either Monroe's memory was faulty or he was trying to persuade the legislators that to occupy East Florida now involved no more than merely taking what Spain had once been willing to give. If the latter, the tactic failed. The House passed the bill the administration desired on 26 June, but one week later the Senate defeated it by two votes.[121]

This setback required the administration to think carefully about its next move. The decision of the Senate meant the president had no explicit sanction for allowing the handful of U.S. troops under Lieut. Col. Smith to remain in East Florida—unless Mitchell could continue to direct them under the law of 15 January 1811. But according to that law, Mitchell could do so only if a foreign force had landed in East Florida or the province had been surrendered by the "local authority"—and the administration had no evidence that either condition obtained. Indeed, it was manifestly unrealistic to expect that the second condition would now occur at all, and if the administration continued to maintain its troops in East Florida, it would be extending the war to Spain—which it did not want to do. Consequently, unless British troops should enter East Florida in the very near future and in some considerable number, the logic of the law compelled Madison to withdraw U.S. forces from the province. Reinforcing that logic were considerations arising from the unhealthy summer in East Florida and the difficulties of making adequate provision for troops in that environment.[122]

Yet a decision to withdraw from East Florida would leave the province open to reinforcement by Spain or to occupation by the British, to say nothing of exposing the borders of southern and western states to attack by "several powerful Indian Tribes" that would fall under British influence. Rumors were already circulating in newspapers that St. Augustine had been reinforced, though it was not clear whether the troops in question were British or Spanish. Even so, Mitchell could only maintain the American position in the province if the troops were British. If they were Spanish, however, the administration could hardly object to their presence and Mitchell could only hold his ground for as long as Spain refused to grant amnesty to the Patriots. These circumstances provided the basis for new instructions, in which Mitchell was reminded to obtain from the Spanish commandant "the best conditions in his power" for the Patriots and not to consider that goal "abandoned." Moreover, the administration still believed it must enforce the law of 15 January 1811, and it intended to do so "as soon as adequate means can be provided, after the contingency occurs on which it depends." And even if the contingency did not occur, unexpected developments in the war might lead to "a new view of the subject . . . and induce Congress at the next session to authorize the President to take possession of the Country." In other words, although the administration chose to assume that Mitchell could ultimately negotiate an amnesty for the Patriots, the governor was to conduct his business in ways that did not expose the American claim to East Florida to the dangers created by the Senate decision of 6 July.[123]

Over the summer of 1812 Mitchell was able to meet some of these conditions. He had already made unsuccessful overtures to Estrada as well as to his successor, Kindelán, who had arrived at St. Augustine on 11 June, regarding whether the Patriots could be granted amnesty before an American withdrawal. The governor had also been able to prolong the business by accusing the Spanish of negotiating in bad faith whenever their forces launched counterattacks and raids on the American forces in the vicinity of St. Augustine. Neither Estrada nor Kindelán was moved by Mitchell's expressions of outrage on these occasions, but more alarming for the Americans was Kindelán's demonstration of his ability to reinforce the province by sea when he brought with him two companies of Cuban troops, one of which consisted of free black volunteer militiamen. This raised the troop strength of the Castillo de San Marcos to between eight hundred and nine hundred men, making it impossible for the Patriots to complete their revolution by taking the fort.[124] One response to their worsening military prospects was for McIntosh to summon a constitutional convention on 10 July whose fifteen members spent the next two weeks drafting both a declaration of independence from Spain and a constitution, a more considered process than had been possible on Amelia Island in March. McIntosh was also elected "Director of the Territory of East Florida," and on 30 July he petitioned Monroe for its admission to the Union, coupled with a plea for more military assistance to spare his supporters from the horrors of slave rebellion and racial war.[125] Crawford also argued to Monroe that the administration should acknowledge this new entity under the law of 15 January 1811, but Madison refused.[126] Regardless of whatever sympathy the president might feel for suffering fellow southerners, McIntosh's convention could no more be considered an effective government for East Florida than Mathews's Patriots at Fernandina had been.

This political and military stalemate produced an escalation of the conflict in East Florida. Mitchell had no desire to abandon the province, but he needed reinforcements to hold his ground. As much as he would have preferred to receive them from the United States, there was no chance of that after July, so he had to call in militia volunteers from Georgia and deploy them to assist the Americans already there as best he could. Over the summer, some 500 Georgians entered East Florida, the largest single detachment of them being a body of 250 men under the command of Col. Daniel Newnan. Kindelán countered by enlisting the aid of the Seminole Indians and the black population that resided in the Indian townships, and he also recruited for auxiliaries among the free black population of St. Augustine. That the Spanish might resort to the Indians had been anticipated by the Patriots, and Mathews had already made three visits to the Seminole leaders, Chief Payne and Chief Bowlegs, trying to secure their neutrality during the Patriot campaign. Kindelán prevailed here, in part because he could exploit divisions among the Indians—Payne favored neutrality while Bowlegs spoke for younger warriors who wanted to resist the Americans—but mainly because the Indian diplomacy of Mathews and McIntosh relied more on threats of force than it did on subtlety. The Indians also took alarm at the news spread by the Spanish about the plans the Patriots were making for the division of their tribal lands after they had completed the conquest of East Florida.[127]

The entry of Indians and blacks into the conflict transformed it into a guerrilla war, characterized by ambushes, raiding parties, and the destruction of livestock and property on an extended scale. The Patriots also contributed their share to the devastation by living off the land and destroying property as a means of coercing local settlers into joining their cause, or of punishing them if they did not. But the Spanish tactics were successful to the extent that they drove the Patriots away from St. Augustine by early August, leading Smith and Newnan to plan a response by raiding the Seminole towns in the Alachua country to the west of the St. Johns River, burning their crops, capturing their livestock, and disrupting their trading activities. Smith, however, could spare no regulars for the campaign, which fell to Newnan and his Georgians to execute in September. It was not a military triumph. Although the Indians decided to seek peace negotiations after its conclusion, Newnan withdrew from the Indian country in October after enduring three inconclusive battles and several days of sniping.[128] The outcome so dismayed Mitchell, who had returned to Georgia in August to recover from illness, that he immediately mobilized a mounted expedition for East Florida. The Georgia Assembly, at its November session, sanctioned the force, and then went further by authorizing Mitchell to invade East Florida himself before dropping the idea in favor of a resolution insisting that the administration seize the province.[129] Georgians were not alone in their concern about the threat posed by Kindelán's use of Indians and blacks. In November, political leaders in Tennessee also took alarm and began to organize volunteer militia forces to enter East Florida.[130]

The administration could hardly tolerate these threats to its control over national policy. After the Senate rejection of the bill to occupy Florida on 6 July, Monroe had made an indirect approach to Onís through the Spanish vice-consul in Alexandria, Pablo Chacón. Madison had never formally recognized the Spanish minister and had little wish to do so now, but after learning that the Cortes in Cádiz had promulgated a new constitution—the *Constitución doceañista*—for Spain in March, it seemed worthwhile to explore whether Onís had received any new credentials or powers to negotiate.[131] If so, Monroe hinted, the administration would be interested in holding discussions on boundaries and spoliations, and it certainly wanted to know whether Onís could influence events in East Florida. Onís was irritated by the clumsiness of this tactic—it was, after all, the height of hypocrisy to suggest negotiations over a province from which the United States should have already withdrawn—but he made a measured response. He had received copies of the correspondence between Kindelán and Mitchell, and he forwarded them to Cádiz in the hope that amnesty for the Patriots would hasten an American withdrawal. As to the extent of his powers, he realized the credentials he had received from the Supreme Central Junta in 1809 might be considered superceded, so he told Monroe he had come to the United States with full authority to settle all outstanding disputes and would receive new powers once the administration had invited him to Washington.[132] Realizing that such an invitation would commit him to acknowledging the Regency and the Cortes as the government of Spain without any guarantee of a settlement, Madison dropped the idea. Onís, he concluded, was merely trying "to bring himself into importance & to gain time."[133]

Instead, the president decided to wait on events in East Florida and seek authority for another attempt to occupy it at the next session of Congress. He had, moreover, recently read some intercepted letters between St. Augustine and Havana which revealed that the Castillo de San Marcos was short on food and confirmed that Kindelán had incited the Indians to arms. That last action alone, Madison remarked, would justify Kindelán's expulsion "if nothing else w[oul]d do it."[134] In the next legislative session, too, the votes of two new senators from the lately admitted state of Louisiana also promised to overcome the two-vote margin that had prevented the occupation of Florida in July. In the interim, the administration relieved Mitchell of his assignment in East Florida to allow him to return to his executive duties in Georgia and replaced him in October with Maj. Gen. Thomas Pinckney of South Carolina, the elder Federalist statesman who had negotiated the Treaty of San Lorenzo in 1795. Additional troops were also dispatched from Tennessee to New Orleans in readiness for action on the Gulf Coast.[135] And when the news about the plans in Georgia and Tennessee for further military intervention in East Florida reached the capital by the first week in December, the president was ready to act. He drafted a message to Congress rehearsing all the old grievances against Spain, pointing out that East Florida was in imminent danger of being occupied by Great Britain while claiming that Spain had violated its neutral obligations toward the United States by arming and inciting "different Tribes of Savages to a merciless war agst. the U.S." and "introducing at the same time into their garrisons troops of a character & colour well calculated to [excite?] revolt among that [portion?] of the Contiguous [population?] of the U.S." On those grounds, he sought authority for "an immediate occupancy" of all Spanish territory east of the Perdido River.[136] Whether Madison then decided to withhold this message to allow state delegations in Congress to appear to take the initiative or whether the state delegations pre-empted the president's move is unclear, but before Madison had completed his draft, Senator Joseph Anderson of Tennessee called for a committee to consider legislation for the same purpose on 10 December.[137]

The Senate, however, proved to be no more cooperative than it had been in July. Anderson's motion was amended to require the submission of evidence that Great Britain intended to occupy Florida and that East Floridians desired to enter the Union. Senators also called for papers relating to the history of recent negotiations with Spain as well as information on Spanish troop strength along the Gulf Coast. The State Department took nearly a month to select and copy the documents needed in response, and the case Monroe constructed on the basis of their contents was not entirely persuasive. As for Great Britain occupying East Florida, Monroe could say little more than that "the intention and the act would become known at the same time," coupled with the assertion that because Spain had ceased to have an independent existence, the Regency at Cádiz was "essentially" already under the control of London. That East Floridians desired to join the Union he adduced from the willingness of the Patriots to cede the province to Mathews while Spanish troop numbers between St. Augustine and Mobile were estimated at 1,650 men. The secretary of state also forwarded copies of the correspondence between Kindelán and Mitchell, but he did so to make the case that negotiations had reached an impasse, and he reinforced the point by referring to provisions in the new Spanish constitution that prohibited the king of Spain from alienating his territories. On that basis he argued that the prospect of obtaining the "peaceable possession" of East Florida as compensation for spoliations was gone forever. Nor was there "the slightest cause" to hope that Spain would indemnify the United States "by the payment of money." Monroe then concluded his case with a recapitulation of the arguments that had been outlined in the "No Transfer" resolution and legislation of January 1811.[138]

The debate on Anderson's motion and bill did not begin until 1 February 1813, but the next day the Senate, by a three-vote margin, struck out the clause authorizing the occupation of East Florida, leaving the administration with the possibility of taking no more territory than that remaining unoccupied in West Florida to the Perdido after October 1810—that is, Mobile. Debate over the issue was not extensive, and it was dominated by the Rhode Island Federalist William Hunter, who observed that the documentation of the administration's case was "more remarkable for its deficiency than its contents." Ignoring Monroe's observations about the significance of the new Spanish constitution, Hunter declared that the administration's case was no better than it had been in July and that for the Senate to reverse its position would be to invite retaliation from, if not war with, Spain—a war that could not be justified and would not be worth its costs. There was also no evidence that East Floridians, other than Mathews's Patriots, desired to join the Union, and whatever the benefits were of seizing the province, "with its wide waste of sands, its dismal swamps, [and] its mixed mongrel population," they would not accrue to the merchants who had suffered the spoliations. That would leave the nation with a war undertaken on behalf of the state of Georgia; indeed, Hunter insinuated, the fact that the president himself had not asked Congress for authority to wage it could suggest that Madison did not even support it. That the war against Great Britain had not gone well either only added to Hunter's case, and not even a proposal to authorize the seizure of East Florida in the event of Spain commencing hostilities against the United States was able to command a majority. The amended bill passed Congress on 9 February, and Madison signed it three days later.[139]

With respect to East Florida, that outcome left the administration in an even weaker position than it had been in July 1812. Little time was lost in proceeding to the occupation of Mobile, which was completed on 15 April 1813 by forces from New Orleans under Maj. Gen. James Wilkinson, but that still left Madison without any means, diplomatic or military, either to vindicate the claim to East Florida or to control its border with Georgia.[140] At that juncture, though, the president was rescued by the fluctuations of international politics. In the first week of March 1813, news reached Washington of the proposal of Alexander I of Russia, made to American minister John Quincy Adams in St. Petersburg in September 1812, that he mediate in the war with Great Britain. Madison scarcely hesitated before accepting it and then set about thinking how it might be turned to American advantage.[141] At the same time, Onís conveyed to the State Department a copy of a decree issued by the Cortes on 15 December 1812 for a general pardon for the Patriots, provided they thereafter conducted themselves as "good & loyal Spaniards & [obeyed] the legitimate authorities constituted by the National Government of the Spanish Monarchy established in the Peninsula."[142] Despite its considerable anger at the administration for its interventions in Florida, the Cortes had little trouble reaching this decision. Its priorities were to remain at peace with the United States to ensure the flow of grain and other supplies to the Iberian Peninsula, and to get the Americans out of East Florida. If an amnesty was required to deprive Madison of any pretext for remaining there, the Cortes was willing to oblige.

Rather more complicated was news conveyed by Tobias Lear in April. Lear had been expelled from his post as American consul in Algiers in August 1812 when the dey of that Ottoman Regency decided to go to war with the United States. Returning home via Gibraltar and Cádiz, Lear brought with him copies of a report made by Spanish Secretary of State

Pedro Labrador on 31 December 1812, which held the administration and its agents responsible for many of the disturbances taking place in the Spanish-American colonies, particularly in East Florida, West Florida, and Texas.[143] Lear also reported that "the Spanish Government had sold their right to the Floridas to the British, and had actually received two Millions sterling on that account."[144] No firm evidence for this claim was provided, but Madison and Monroe were more than ready to believe it and reacted accordingly. Among the instructions they issued to the American commissioners to St. Petersburg was one requiring them to introduce into mediation the American claims to East and West Florida, clearly with a view toward persuading Great Britain to accept them as part of a peace settlement.[145] Gallatin, who was to be one of the commissioners and who had never shared his colleagues' concerns about Florida, opposed this, pointing out that it was a "Southern" scheme that still risked war with Spain and would "disgust every man north of Washington."[146] Madison and Monroe held firm, though, in the hope that mediation would bring peace on advantageous terms in 1813, including the possibility that the United States would emerge from the war with one less challenge to its territorial pretensions on the Gulf Coast.

To make "proper explanations" for the "very erroneous impressions" likely to arise from the Spanish reaction to the occupation of Mobile and to complement the negotiations in Russia, Madison also decided to send Anthony Morris of Philadelphia, a long-standing friend of Dolley Payne Madison, to the Cádiz Regency as an informal diplomatic agent. If nothing else, this decision was a belated admission that the "expiring" little committee he had so casually dismissed in 1810 would have to be a factor in his future considerations.[147] Even so, the president was not so much anticipating that he might have to acknowledge the Regency as he was seeking confirmation of the report that Great Britain had acquired Florida. Should Great Britain have done so, Morris was advised that "it will leave little doubt of its policy or of the obligation imposed by it on the United States." For that reason, Morris's mission was expected to be short, and he was told his "communications with the Regency should be oral and not written" because "when written . . . they cannot be official." Nevertheless, the administration also hoped that the Russian mediation would have some effect in Cádiz and that Spain might yet be persuaded to settle its differences with the United States along the lines it had previously proposed—that the United States receive all Spanish territory east of the Mississippi River in return for indemnities owed or be allowed to hold such territory "in trust subject to future negotiation & adjustment." If Spain agreed, Morris could suggest that the Regency might order Kindelán to deliver East Florida to the United States "either in discharge of the claims to indemnity or in trust." The effect of such an agreement, though "informal," would be the same "as if it were done by treaty."[148]

But even before these diplomatic preparations had been completed, the administration sent the Spanish pardon for the Patriots to Pinckney for negotiations with Kindelán. The governor had, in fact, already received the proclamation from the Cortes and released it on 15 March 1813, giving the Patriots a period of four months in which they could either leave East Florida or present themselves in St. Augustine for a pardon. On that basis, Pinckney, on 7 April, agreed to the withdrawal of all American troops from the province and promised to evacuate St. Johns by 29 April and Amelia Island one week later. He did make a plea for a longer withdrawal period for those who wished to remain to harvest the crops they had planted, but Kindelán refused, and the terms of the agreement were implemented.[149] Many of the Patriots were angry, declaring they had been betrayed, and they remonstrated bitterly with both Pinckney and the administration about the injustice of being abandoned to their fate. A small number of them continued to resist Spanish authority in East Florida for another year, and McIntosh even made a rapid journey to Washington later in the summer in a desperate effort to persuade the president not to withdraw American forces from the province. Neither he nor his followers received any support.[150] The administration knew it had already paid too high a price for indulging the hope that a revolution in East Florida could be the means of adding the province to the Union.

4

TEXAS

There is no wish here to insist on the Rio del Norte as one of the
boundaries.

—John Graham to William Shaler, 21 June 1810

Shortly before Claiborne arrived in Washington in June 1810 for
the meeting with Madison that would set in motion the events leading
to the annexation of West Florida, the secretary of state, on 24 May, called
the Connecticut merchant William Shaler to the capital.[1] The president
had met Shaler earlier in the year, when he and his brother, Nathaniel, also
a merchant, came to Washington in February to patent a "System of Sig-
nals for Vessels." Over a dinner held on 24 February, Madison learned
something of William's career.[2] It had been, as Shaler himself was to remark, an "errant" and "wandering" one, marked by fluctuating fortunes
that were unusual even for merchants in the tumultuous age of the
Napoleonic Wars.[3] Orphaned by the age of thirteen and with no formal education, Shaler had early gone to sea and by the time he was thirty had
seen much of South and Central America, including Buenos Aires,
Guatemala, Montevideo, San Blas, and Valparaiso. The authorities in that
last port had briefly imprisoned him, and the experience stimulated what
was to become a lifelong interest in the subject of political liberty in the dominions of Spain.[4] It may have also inspired him to produce an English
translation of the writings of the Chilean Jesuit Juan Ignacio Molina repudiating European criticisms of American backwardness, which Madison

had received a copy of from one of Shaler's business associates, Nathaniel Ingraham of New York.[5] Shaler was also one of the first Americans to display an interest in the Pacific, and between 1803 and 1805 he visited California, Hawaii, and China, publishing an account of that voyage in the *American Register* in 1808.[6] Since then, he had incurred some heavy losses as a result of Napoleon's confiscation of American vessels seized in Spanish ports, but by 1810 he was in the process of reorganizing his affairs and contemplating a new business venture in China.[7]

The secretary of state did not explain why he had summoned Shaler, but the decision was almost certainly a response to early news of the emerging crises in Spain and its American empire, including reports that officials in Cuba had just reduced duties on American ships and goods and rumors that independent governments both there and in Mexico might shortly be established.[8] By 29 May Shaler was in the capital, where he was told that "the establishment of the Spanish colonies into independent states" was "more or less in prospect" and then asked to undertake confidential missions to Cuba and Mexico.[9] He agreed and went to New York to arrange a voyage to Havana. For his travels Shaler received three sets of instructions and two commissions, one as an agent for American commerce and the other as an agent for seamen, the latter position being the most likely to be acceptable to Spanish colonial officials, who were notoriously reluctant to admit representatives of foreign powers into their jurisdictions.[10] But the real goals of his mission were broader than the promotion of trade or the protection of stranded sailors. His more important duties were to spread American goodwill in Cuba and Mexico in the event of their breaking away from either Bourbon or Bonapartist rule and to acquire information about their population, wealth, trade, and fiscal and military resources. Shaler was to engage in diplomacy as well, notably by determining whether opinions in Havana were in favor of Cuba joining the United States. While there, he was also to seek a passport for Mexico, preferably to admit him to Veracruz, from where he should go to "the place where the local authority of Mexico may reside." Should his conversations with that authority turn to the unsettled western boundaries of the Louisiana Purchase, Shaler was to inform the successor regime in Mexico that the United States would negotiate the matter in "a spirit of amity and equity." By that the administration meant it would not insist on the Rio Grande as the boundary between Mexico and the United States. The administration also disavowed any desire to interfere in Mexico's affairs or in its relations with Europe, but it assumed, in turn, that the Mexicans would agree to both East and West Florida being incorporated into the Union and would accept that there could be "no idea" of placing Cuba, "in the event of its separation from Spain, in a dependence on any other foreign power."[11]

Shaler reached Havana on 1 August 1810. He lost no time in presenting his credentials as an agent for commerce and seamen to the captain-general, the marqués de Someruelos, who stated that he lacked the authority to recognize Shaler in any capacity.[12] This was certainly true, though whether Someruelos actually believed that Shaler was who he purported to be is uncertain. The captain-general sent a report of his arrival to Onís in Philadelphia, from which the minister concluded that Shaler was a Bonapartist agent, one of several men he believed France had recruited for the purpose of subverting Bourbon rule throughout Spanish America.[13] Such suspicions, or misunderstandings, were widely held by Spanish officials, who often had difficulty determining whether the Americans who approached them were acting on behalf of their own government or whether they were merely cat's-paws in Napoleon's schemes to take over Spain and its empire for himself and his family. And since the United States was generally more hostile to Great Britain as Spain's ally than it was to France as Spain's enemy, it was all too easy for beleaguered Bourbon administrators to conclude that Madison and Napoleon shared the same goals. Shaler could not have been entirely surprised by this setback. Even before he had left New York he had the impression that Someruelos was "a mere tool suffering himself to be carried along by the current of events" and that the old Spanish imperial system would survive in an attenuated form until France could dispose of the Cádiz Regency once and for all.[14] The agent therefore delayed informing Someruelos of his wish to travel to Mexico until the circumstances seemed more promising.

In the interval, Shaler turned his attention to gathering information and making contact with prominent figures in Havana society. Perhaps because he was a merchant himself, he gravitated toward his Cuban counterparts and struck up friendships with Francesco Arango y Parreño and Antonio de Valle Hernandez, members of the *consulado* (merchant's guild), who like many Spanish-American merchants and creoles had showed some interest in the possibility that Cuba might establish a greater degree of autonomy from Spain. Shaler also met planters who were willing to entertain him socially, and by such means he was able to observe something of Cuba beyond the limits of Havana. On these occasions the agent cautiously raised the subject of the political future of Cuba, hinting to his hosts that they might consider the advantages of American-style republicanism, or "rational liberty" as Shaler called it, of which he personally was an ardent devotee. But Shaler may not have fully appreciated that merchants and planters carried relatively little weight in Cuba, which was still predominantly a garrison colony with a strong military ethos, and the results of these discussions were disappointing.[15] Shaler found that his Cuban friends did not rate the prospects for their independence very highly and that although they were interested in ideas about free trade and expanding their commerce with the United States, they could scarcely conceive of their being economically and politically independent of Mexico. Nor did they believe that Spanish Americans might become republicans—in part because they were not convinced the United States itself was proof that republican government was practicable—and it was their sense that if they ever did become independent from Spain, they would probably offer a crown to a member of the Portuguese royal family, which had been relocated to Brazil under British protection.[16]

Nevertheless, Shaler was able to use these occasions to gather information, and he began compiling sets of data and thumbnail sketches about the leading "characters" of Cuba. Usually these amounted to a few lines about their family backgrounds, their official positions, and their political beliefs—at least as far as Shaler was able to ascertain them—and he was to fill many pages in his letter books and dispatches with this sort of material. Much of it was rather random in nature, but Shaler was probably trying to get some sense of where the loyalties of the Cuban elite would fall when the anticipated break with Spain occurred. Would their sympathies lie with France, Great Britain, or the United States in a post-Bourbon new world order?[17] Shaler supplemented this sort of information with copies of newspapers, Spanish decrees and other official documents, and whatever scraps of news and rumors he could collect about events elsewhere in Spanish America, particularly Mexico, from where by October 1810 he had heard accounts, albeit contradictory ones, of the beginning of a revolt led by the creole priest Miguel Hidalgo y Costilla.[18] Naturally, he welcomed that development, assuming that if the revolt were successful, it would leave Cuba standing alone in "the wreck of the Spanish Monarchy," and that if the Mexican rebels got control of a seaport, he could then immediately start on the second, and more important, leg of his mission.[19] And in order to improve his knowledge of the Mexican situation, Shaler, early in 1811, commenced corresponding with Claiborne in New Orleans.[20]

The circumstances for pressing Someruelos for a passport to Veracruz never arose, however. By April 1811 Shaler was aware that Hidalgo had been defeated, though against that news he tried to offset other accounts, invariably vague in nature, of continuing resistance to the reassertion of full Bourbon control on the mainland. Even so, the situation in Mexico was so uncertain that he realized it might be many months yet before he could enter the province by any normal channel.[21] As he waited it out, he continued his conversations with his Cuban friends and became quite worried about how they might react in the event of Great Britain attempting to occupy the island, either to relocate the Cádiz Regency there or to use it as a base in a war against the United States.[22] For their part, Cubans were less alarmed about the British than they were about the French, and they also fretted over the possibility that the Cortes in Cádiz might give serious consideration to ending slavery and the slave trade. Throughout 1811 the authorities stepped up efforts to insulate the island from external influence—they expelled French nationals and suppressed news about unwelcome developments in the Cortes—and eventually Shaler himself became a victim of their concerns.[23] In November 1811 he was arrested while on a visit to the countryside and taken back to Havana where Someruelos ordered him to depart after telling him his reputation as a "french partizsan" without "any visible business" on the island had "at least an equivocal appearance."[24] The agent felt that this treatment was unjust, but there was little he could do. He left Havana on 11 December for New Orleans, where he arrived ten days later. Seeking news about Mexico, he called on Claiborne, but the governor could tell him nothing beyond suggesting that he might go to Natchitoches on the far western frontier of Orleans Territory to await developments there. Shaler decided he would do so unless the administration informed him it had other plans.[25]

While waiting for news from Washington, Shaler summarized the results of his stay in Cuba. For sixteen months he had written regularly to the secretary of state, but he was well aware that he had accomplished less than the administration might have liked, particularly in the matter of providing information on the wealth and military resources of Cuba and Mexico. He explained his failure to do so in terms of the "jealousy" of the Cuban authorities making it "imprudent and foolish" for him to have appeared to have been too interested in such topics.[26] He then attempted to repair that omission by writing four extended essays on Cuba and Spanish America between January and March of 1812. The first and second of these essays Shaler devoted to the subject of the "Revolution in So. America," starting with an assessment of the importance of the rebellion in Mexico to the United States and warning against the dangers of allowing Great Britain to extend its influence there. Just as Madison had done, Shaler had read reports about Lord Wellesley's offer in June 1811 to mediate disputes between Spain and its American colonies in return for "valuable considerations to guarantee the integrity of the Spanish Monarchy on this continent." He had little doubt that Great Britain would pursue this policy and that it would eventually be able to "controul the policy of Mexico" in order to direct its resources against the United States. To prevent that development, he advocated that the United States intervene on behalf of the Mexican rebels, by supplying them with arms and sending in "an Auxiliary Army of 5000 regular troops" and "as many volunteers" to establish a "free and independent Mexico," which from "gratitude and common interest" would then become the friend of the United States.[27]

The second essay developed the same points with reference to Cuba, with Shaler dwelling on the strategic significance of its location, which might tempt France and Great Britain to occupy it and control access to the Mississippi River. Once so positioned and being able to exercise an equivalent influence in Mexico, those nations would then be able to "wrest from us our late acquisitions of Louisiana and Florida" and possibly even affect "a division of our Union" and blast all "our prospects of future happiness and political grandeur." American possession of, or influence over, Cuba was therefore essential to prevent those outcomes and to secure the Union "forever." Shaler reinforced this case by providing as much positive information as he had been able to collect on its population and agricultural resources, the former totaling about 600,000 inhabitants and the latter consisting mainly of exports of coffee and sugar but also "innumerable herds of cattle, horses, mules and swine" in the interior. The island was not self-sufficient in flour, but Shaler believed an enterprising government would be able to make it so as well as be able to produce "all the necessaries of life equal to its own consumption." He also claimed the forests of Cuba could "furnish an unlimited supply of as fine timber for naval construction as any in the world" and that the ports of Havana and Santiago de Cuba had the potential to become "great naval depots." Thus, he argued, "Cuba has with strict propriety obtained the expressive appellation of Key to the Spanish continental provinces."[28]

As for the Cubans themselves, Shaler analyzed them in his third and fourth essays, the first of which he left untitled and the second he headed "Notes on Manners and Society in Havana." Here his impressions were much more mixed. Under their present rulers, Cubans posed no threat to the United States because of their "torpid character and weak government," but Shaler feared that events beyond their control would eventually force them to confront the question of their independence, and he doubted they had "the means necessary to form a respectable political corps" to maintain it "without foreign aid." Yet with a greater degree of assurance than he had felt while he was in Havana, Shaler was prepared to predict that Cubans, or at least his friends in the merchant community, would not allow the island "to pass into the hands of any other European power without a bloody struggle." In that event, they would have to seek the assistance of the United States, especially in case of an American war with Great Britain, and he estimated their militias might "bring 40,000 men into the field," which in the climate of the island would be "sufficient for defensive war." Should that scenario come to pass, Shaler believed it would matter little whether Cuba then became part of Mexico, or was "incorporated into our Union," or became an independent state. The main point of American policy must be to destroy Cuba's dependence on any European nation. That would allow its people time to overcome the obstacles to their development imposed on them by centuries of misrule by Spain and the Roman Catholic Church. Colonial status had kept Cubans in a state of "degrading dependence" that had corrupted their morals—Shaler particularly deplored their fondness for "gambling and dissipation"—but as they increased their contacts with the United States, the agent was hopeful they would make progress and "very soon take the rank among men that nature has so well qualified them to hold."[29]

Shaler discussed these ideas with Claiborne, who enthusiastically endorsed some of them in his own letters to Washington.[30] He also gave the governor copies of his essays with instructions he should mail them to the Secretary of the Navy.[31] Why he chose to send these summaries to Paul Hamilton rather than to Monroe is not entirely clear, but he had never met Monroe and felt the lack of a personal acquaintance placed him at something of a disadvantage.[32] He also knew Monroe's appointment in the place of Robert Smith had been the subject of considerable political controversy, and he may have feared that those circumstances would make Monroe suspicious of, if not hostile to, any mission or ideas that had originated with his predecessor. Hamilton, on the other hand, he knew well, even to the point of being willing to entrust him with the supervision of the education of a nephew who was under Shaler's care.[33] But in the end, it did not matter anyway. No evidence survives to suggest that any of Shaler's four essays ever reached their destination, probably because of failures in the mails between New Orleans and Washington.[34] In that sense, Shaler's mission to Cuba was even less successful than he ever had grounds to suspect.

One reason Shaler headed for New Orleans after his expulsion from Havana was the news that a Mexican revolutionary, "Colonel Bernard," had passed through the city en route to Washington to seek assistance and recognition from the United States.[35] The revolutionary in question was José Bernardo Maximilian Gutiérrez de Lara, a moderately prosperous merchant and blacksmith from Revilla in Nuevo Santander, who along with his brother, Father José Antonio Gutiérrez de Lara, had been among the earliest supporters of the Hidalgo rebellion.[36] The two brothers had remained faithful to the cause even after the defeat and execution of Hidalgo over the spring and summer of 1811, but in order to reach the United States from Texas, Bernardo Gutiérrez had to cross the Neutral Ground between the Sabine and Calcasieu rivers, where Royalist forces, while seeking to kill him, robbed him of his papers. He managed, nevertheless, to reach Natchitoches and the U.S. military post of Fort Claiborne in September 1811, where he provided American officials, including Lieut. Col. Zebulon Montgomery Pike, Capt. Walter Overton, and the agent to the Caddo Indians, John Sibley, with outdated, if not somewhat exaggerated, accounts of the strength of revolutionary sentiment in Mexico, particularly in Texas. Pike and Sibley passed these accounts on to officials in Washington, where they had arrived before Gutiérrez himself reached the capital on 11 December.[37]

Gutiérrez was to remain in Washington until the first week of January 1812. He met with most members of the administration, including Madison, who received him with "great courtesy." They conversed very little, however, because the president could not understand Spanish.[38] Neither the secretary of state nor his chief clerk was quite so handicapped, though, and it was with them, as well as with Secretary of War Eustis, that the Mexican was to spend most of his time. To Eustis, Gutiérrez provided a lengthy explanation for his mission. To justify his requests for arms, ammunition, troops, and trade from the United States, he outlined the three-hundred-year history of the oppression of Mexico by Spain, emphasizing the subordination of the Mexican economy to the selfish demands of the metropolis. He also provided an account of the rebellion in Mexico, where the leadership of the cause had passed to General Ignacio Lopez Rayón in the region around Mexico City.[39] Gutiérrez described recent developments in Texas, closer to his native province, where he had left a fellow rebel, Col. José Menchaca, at San Antonio de Béxar to organize the local Indians and civilian population to reinstate a republican regime that had been set up in January 1811 by Juan Bautista de las Casas and then overthrown four months later by Juan Manuel Sambrano. The United States could assist that endeavor, he suggested, by expanding trade between Louisiana and Texas in such items as horses, mules, silver, and wool. And if Mexico and the United States generally increased their trade, he believed both nations would become less dependent on Europe and better placed to resist "if any country comes from Europe to rule Mexico."[40]

The administration was neither unprepared for nor unsympathetic to Gutiérrez's mission. To the extent Madison had been able to follow developments in Mexico in 1811, he sensed that the Royalist victory over Hidalgo would be a short-lived one and that it would only be a matter of time before Mexico's creoles renewed their quest for greater freedom from

Spain.[41] In accordance with that view, the president, in his annual message of November 1811, had called on Congress to prepare itself to respond to the "momentous" events that portended the emergence of a new order "in the southern portion of our own hemisphere," the effects of which would "extend into our neighbourhood." The House of Representatives reciprocated these sentiments on 10 December, the day before Gutiérrez reached Washington, in a resolution promising to establish relations with the provinces of Spanish America once they had "attained the condition of nations by the just exercize of their rights."[42] As a consequence, the arrival of a Mexican in the capital occasioned a good deal of curiosity and interest. Despite the loss of his credentials in the Neutral Ground, the administration was quite willing to talk with Gutiérrez as an authentic spokesman for the revolution in Mexico, though eventually Monroe had to tell him he would have to return home "to fetch the documents necessary to undertake the purchase of arms" and to report the "friendly disposition" of the United States to favor the establishment of a republic in Mexico.[43]

More awkward matters arose in other conversations with Eustis. The secretary of war inquired about American troops entering Texas to take possession of the province "to the banks of the Rio Grande," in accordance with the administration's understanding of the western limits of the Louisiana Purchase. Gutiérrez was reluctant to sanction so extensive an American claim and proposed instead that "a certain portion of land" be left "as a neutral tract" between Mexico and the United States. Since this was no more than what the United States had been seeking, in principle, from Spain since 1804, Eustis could agree readily enough, though he did get Gutiérrez to understand that it would be difficult for the United States to send troops to Texas at all unless it did so to enforce rights claimed under the 1803 treaty. To send them there for other reasons, the secretary believed, might provide both France and Spain with cause for war with the United States, a risk the administration was unwilling to take as it prepared for conflict with Great Britain.[44] But there was little point in pursuing that problem at this stage. Even with the information Gutiérrez had provided, the administration still knew very little about the progress of the Mexican revolution, especially in the region around Mexico City.[45] Moreover, that information had ceased even to reflect accurately the state of affairs in Texas, from where news arrived on 13 December that Menchaca, the revolutionary colleague of Gutiérrez, had abandoned the republican cause and returned to the service of Spain. That development could only consolidate Royalist control over Texas at San Antonio de Béxar. Under those circumstances, the administration decided the best course of action would be to pay Gutiérrez's expenses to return him home so that he might continue working to advance the revolution in Mexico.[46]

Gutiérrez had difficulty believing that Menchaca had betrayed him, but he accepted the administration's offer, and after making visits to Baltimore and Philadelphia he departed for New Orleans at the end of February. He arrived there on 23 March and contacted Claiborne, to whom he presented a letter from John Graham asking that the governor "expedite" his return to Mexico. Uncertain about how he might do this, Claiborne introduced Gutiérrez to Shaler, who immediately offered to share lodgings with him, and together they agreed to go to Natchitoches. They left New Orleans on 8 April and reached their destination twenty days later.[47] Gutiérrez took up residence at an inn in Natchitoches; Shaler was accommodated outside the town in Fort Claiborne as a member of "the family of Captain Overton." Throughout this period and for several months thereafter, Shaler paid the costs of travel and lodgings for Gutiérrez, for which he later asked the State Department for reimbursement to the amount of $458.15.[48] The agent assumed these costs not merely because Claiborne requested that he do so but also for the more obvious reason that he had been instructed to seek out the leaders of the Mexican rebellion, and he almost certainly hoped to avail himself later of Gutiérrez's assistance to enter Mexico. At all stages in these transactions, though, Shaler wrote regularly to the State Department to inform the administration of his actions and to obtain its consent for them. He remained concerned that he had heard nothing from Washington since his arrival in New Orleans and feared that Madison had abandoned both him and his mission. On 2 May, however, Monroe finally wrote to him to acknowledge the receipt of some of his letters, informing him at the same time that the president approved of his conduct and wished him "to proceed immediately to Mexico in fulfillment of [his] original instructions."[49]

How Gutiérrez and Shaler passed the summer of 1812 in Natchitoches is a subject of some controversy.[50] The Mexican was no stranger to the town, having spent time there in the fall of 1811, but after he had learned of Menchaca's defection, it must have been clear to him he would have to make an effort to revive the revolutionary cause in Texas. He began doing so within days of his arrival by contacting the Caddo Indians in the region of San Antonio de Béxar, telling them to end their "hostilities against the Spanish" as they harmed the local soldiers and civilians and to await his orders "as to what they were to do in future."[51] One week later, on 15 May, Gutiérrez recorded in his diary that he had met with a "French gentleman." Shaler, in his letters to Monroe, identified the man as a French agent named Jean-Jacques Paillette, and he reported that Paillette had offered the Mexican the services of four thousand men and $100,000 for the purchase of arms. That sum seems implausibly large, but Gutiérrez almost certainly received some money at this time from a source other than Shaler since by the end of May he had arranged for the printing of proclamations to be sent into Mexico.[52] He also made contact with a French agent in New Orleans, Pierre Girard, who may have begun distributing for him recruiting notices for a filibustering force to be known as the "Republican Army of the North." Americans who wished to join this force were urged to assemble outside the limits of the United States, in the Neutral Ground, to avoid prosecution under the 1794 Neutrality Act. The reward for their services was unspecified, but the recruiting handbills stated that it would be "equally reciprocal" with the incentives to be offered to Mexicans.[53] The pace of these activities seemed so rapid that by mid-June Shaler mentioned that as many as three separate armed expeditions might enter Mexico from the surrounding regions, including one headed by John Adair of Kentucky. Shaler assumed Adair was interested in replaying in Texas a coup similar to the one George Mathews had just staged in East Florida.[54]

The knowledge that Gutiérrez was planning a filibuster and that Americans of Adair's prominence might be involved in it troubled Shaler. His first impressions of Gutiérrez had been positive. The Mexican had struck him as a "prudent" and "honest" man who was suitably grateful for any assistance he received. But even before they had left for Natchitoches, Shaler and Claiborne had both wondered whether Gutiérrez was prudent enough to avoid involvement with French agents. Shaler's doubts on these matters only increased in Natchitoches, and he confronted Gutiérrez with them on more than one occasion. Gutiérrez freely admitted that he was seeking the assistance of Americans for his cause, and when Shaler warned him that the members of the administration, no matter how much they might wish for Mexican independence, would not approve any "unauthorized proceedings by men unknown, not under their control, and in no way possessing their confidence," he responded with the observation that if Americans should offer him their services, "all the world would regard him as a fool not to profit by the circumstance."[55] Nor did Gutiérrez deny that he had talked with French agents, but the more mysterious nature of those contacts only led Shaler to report to Washington his fear that Gutiérrez would tolerate French interference in Mexican affairs. Unresolved anxieties on that point eventually led Shaler to conclude Gutiérrez was deceiving him, though he continued to cooperate with him on matters of mutual interest, including the drafting of a letter to be sent to Rayón in which they both attempted to inform the general of recent developments in Texas and Washington and to explain to him Madison's policies toward Great Britain and Mexico. Shaler even advanced Gutiérrez a further sum of $100 to help him distribute printed proclamations in Mexico, probably because he wished to use Gutiérrez's couriers to get his own message into Mexico and because he hoped these same couriers would be able to send to Natchitoches within the month "an exact account of the state of the revolution in the interior of Mexico." But as he had done earlier, Shaler took pains to explain these decisions to Washington, believing they were consistent with the ultimate purposes of his instructions.[56]

Shaler's problem was not that he opposed some form of American assistance to the Mexican rebels. Nor did he fail to appreciate that auxiliaries like the Caddo Indians might play a useful role in bringing down the Spanish regime in San Antonio de Béxar and that this, in turn, would open up the Internal Provinces of Mexico to American trade. In May 1812 he even suggested that the War Department relocate the garrison at Natchitoches on the banks of the Sabine River and immediately reinforce it with five hundred men, and later by an additional five thousand troops, in order to make contact with republican forces in Mexico, where he still assumed that Great Britain intended to install the Cádiz Regency. If nothing else, he argued, such measures would protect Louisiana itself from invasion in the impending war with Great Britain. But these matters aside, Shaler could not accept that the administration would be willing to leave vital questions relating to war and peace on the southwestern frontier to the decisions of private individuals operating outside the law. And certainly not to individuals like Gutiérrez, in whom he was losing all confidence and whom he was coming to regard as a man of many weaknesses, given to "the most ridiculous flights of vanity." Gutiérrez, he reported, had not been happy with the letter Shaler had sent to Rayón, in which he had suggested that the general send his own delegation to Washington to seek assistance and recognition. From those circumstances the agent could only deduce that Gutiérrez's plans were designed more to bring "immortal glory" to himself than they were to advance the cause of Mexican republicanism in general.[57]

Shaler therefore found himself in a dilemma. Its difficulties were compounded by his awareness that an armed expedition against Mexico would almost certainly be launched after July 1812 and that he was powerless to stop it. He lacked the means to do that, and it was not his task to enforce the neutrality legislation anyway. For that reason he reported on developments relating to the filibuster to both the administration in Washington and to Claiborne in New Orleans on the assumption that the enforcement of the law was their responsibility. Nor could he involve himself any more closely in Gutiérrez's plans, at least not without taking the risk of appearing to be either a spy seeking to obstruct them or a willing participant in what he knew to be an illegal enterprise.[58] And despite his misgivings about Gutiérrez's character, Shaler's own commitment to spreading republicanism in Mexico remained strong enough to prevent him from wishing the filibuster would fail. He regarded the Spanish regime as weak and vulnerable, and if a filibuster were to be "well conducted," it could result in the establishment of a republic in Texas. If that happened, Shaler thought it possible that the time would then be ripe for him to make his own entry into Mexico to carry out his instructions, provided it was safe for him to do so. He had, as he remarked to Monroe, no desire "to be shot at as the target of party malevolence" in the course of such proceedings.[59]

Any action against the filibuster, therefore, would have to come from New Orleans, where Claiborne was otherwise engaged in overseeing the transition of his territory into statehood in the Union. The governor certainly knew, by the first week of July 1812 if not earlier, that a filibuster was being planned, but as he had already issued standing instructions to the "Civil Authority at Natchitoches" to enforce the neutrality legislation, he hoped further action *"for the present"* would not be necessary, particularly as he had been informed the filibuster would not take place unless war were declared against Great Britain. And as late as the last week in June, Claiborne believed there would be no war, predicting that all the deliberations and talk in Washington would "end in a War of Words" only.[60] Once he learned Congress had declared war, Claiborne was immediately preoccupied by the problems of defending Louisiana east of the Sabine River, but on 5 August he returned his attention to Texas by requesting that Brig. Gen. James Wilkinson at New Orleans assist the civil authorities in suppressing any filibuster. The general had few resources to do so. Indeed, he had only 1,680 regular troops to defend a front of more than six hundred miles between Natchitoches and Fort Stoddert and, like Claiborne, he worried that Louisiana was more vulnerable to the east than it was from the west.[61] Compounding Claiborne's difficulties at this juncture was the resignation of John C. Carr, the parish judge at Natchitoches. Carr probably sympathized with the aims of the filibuster and may well have lacked the nerve to arrest bands of armed men who could all too easily either resist him or disappear into the no-man's-land of the Neutral Ground, but Claiborne was irked by the resignation. He angrily rejected it on 7 August, ordering Carr to remain in office because "a project to invade the Spanish Province of Tehus, was stil [*sic*] in agitation." Three days later, Claiborne reported that he believed the filibuster had not yet commenced, and on 11 August he issued a proclamation warning Americans not to join it and reminding them of the penalties they could suffer if they did so.[62]

By the time Shaler received the proclamation, it was too late. A filibustering force of about three hundred men had set out from the Neutral Ground for Nacogdoches on 8 August. Shaler regretted that the proclamation had not been issued a month earlier, as it might have "quashed" the expedition "before anything was done, or any person of character injuriously committed in it."[63] Yet although he continued to disapprove of the filibuster "as contrary to law and good policy," he was less upset by its departure than Claiborne, who never condoned it and always feared that armies of lawless men headed by desperate characters could only threaten both the security of Louisiana and the integrity of the Union.[64] Shaler doubted this would be the case, in part because Gutiérrez had been able to recruit U.S. Army lieutenant Augustus W. Magee as the military leader of the filibuster. Magee's motives for joining the filibuster were mixed. He had, apparently, hoped for promotion and service in the war against Great Britain but had been disappointed, and feeling "personally slighted" in his profession, he resigned his commission on 22 June.[65] Thereafter, he sought to turn his experience in conducting operations on the Louisiana-Texas border to personal advantage, and Shaler, who had met him at Natchitoches, believed that Magee was a "man of honor" motivated only by a desire for "military fame" who would never countenance schemes that jeopardized the Union. But he hoped, too, that Magee would be able to control Gutiérrez by preventing him from running into "the extravagances of revolutionary injustice and tyranny" until such time as he could be replaced by a Mexican creole leader of "more merit and capacity."[66] Accordingly, once Shaler had learned the United States was at war with Great Britain, he came to regard the filibuster with "indifference," as he still expected there would be war between Spain and the United States, after which he intended "to avail [himself] of its consequences to pursue [his] route" into Mexico.[67]

Shaler decided against accompanying the filibuster into Texas, however. He was indisposed by illness at the time, and regarding himself essentially as a diplomat to the future republic of Mexico, he thought it improper to enter the country in the presence of a band of rebels and adventurers. Finding himself again at something of a loose end, he passed the time by composing yet another essay on the future of Spanish America. This document was far more ambitious than any of the four pieces he had earlier written in New Orleans. Its title alone—"Reflections on the Means of Restoring the Political Ballance and Procuring a General Peace to the World"—gives some indication of its reach and reveals as well that Shaler was a relentless autodidact who sought to synthesize every aspect of his thinking into a coherent and harmonious whole.[68] The starting point for this essay was Shaler's assumption that Napoleon would eventually succeed in the conquest of Spain and Portugal and that Great Britain could do no more than "retard the catastrophe" for a time. Once France had uncontested control of Europe, not even Russia could resist her "overwhelming power," which would then be directed to "organizing the Turkish Empire and turning its immense resources to the accomplishment of her views of Universal dominion." That development threatened to destroy what little was left of the balance of power among nations that was essential for the preservation of peace and the maintenance of civilization itself. Only two nations, Great Britain and the United States, would thereafter have the capacity to respond to these circumstances, and Shaler sought to explain how they might do so.[69]

Since Great Britain and the United States were now at war, it was obviously necessary for them to make peace. Whether that would result from the United States winning its war against Great Britain or whether Great Britain would rid itself of its current "infatuated ministry and imbecille prince" in favor of a more reasonable government that would offer the United States acceptable peace terms was unclear. Very probably Shaler believed these two developments could take place concurrently. But the basis for a peace with Great Britain required that the United States receive "the provinces of the Canadas; Nova Scotia; the Island of Cuba; and the Floridas with their respective dependencies." That arrangement would secure for the United States "their natural boundaries, and the intire command of the navigation of all their great rivers: and it is believed that it would place the confederate States in intire independence of France and oblige her to conclude a general peace on principles consistent with the future safety and independence of all parties." Optimistically, Shaler chose to assume that Great Britain would make no "insurmountable" objections to such terms, with the possible exception of ceding Nova Scotia, which might be regarded "as necessary to the prosperity of the British fisheries." But once at peace, the United States and Great Britain could form a "Union in friendship" and act together to lead other nations to end their wars so that they could all unite in "a grand confederation on principles best calculated to ensure their own happiness and the peace of the world."

As for how that peace concerned the rest of the Americas and the Spanish empire, Shaler envisaged that Great Britain should be compensated for its losses to the United States by the addition of Brazil, Puerto Rico, Santo Domingo, and the Philippines to its empire. These possessions were of "the greatest value" in themselves, and the Philippines would secure "the British Empire in the East" as well as allow it to command "the most important commerce with Mexico, Peru, and Chili" in the Pacific Ocean. The remaining Spanish-American provinces could then be united into "Sovereign independent states, under such forms of government as their respective inhabitants shall elect, and their independence forever guarantied [*sic*] by the contracting parties." Here Shaler stipulated that all the Spanish provinces north of the isthmus of Darien should form a single state. The provinces south of Darien could be merged into three separate states, centering on Quito, Peru, and Buenos Aires, respectively.[70] If the scope of such proposals now seems both hopelessly visionary and futuristic in nature, it should be remembered that Shaler's ultimate purpose was to restore a stable international balance of power as a way of ensuring peace among nations, and the idea that international peace might be preserved by the formation of leagues, or confederations, of nations was a very old one in the history of European political thought. Even more recent jurists such as Vattel in his *Law of Nations* retained something of this thinking in his description of the concert of Europe as "a sort of republic" held in balance by its various treaties of alliance and commerce.[71] It is difficult to be certain about the sources of Shaler's ideas, though, as he left no clues about the nature and extent of his reading. Nevertheless, it was with such grand schemes that he spent his time while waiting for the results of Gutiérrez and Magee's invasion of Texas.

What Madison and Monroe thought of this essay when it reached Washington is unrecorded. Madison had never believed that leagues, or confederations, of nations were the best way to preserve international peace, and since Shaler's "Reflections" were predicated on several sequences of events that never came to pass, it is more than likely they were completely ignored.[72] News about the filibuster, though, was another matter. Just as the president was leaving the capital on 1 September for a delayed vacation at Montpelier, he received a letter from a distant relative in Tennessee apparently indicating that recruiting for an expedition into Mexico was taking place in that state. Madison immediately forwarded the letter to Monroe, adding that it should serve "as a momento" to the letter he was to write to Governor Willie Blount in Knoxville "on the subject of the illegal enterprize on foot in [his] State." Madison's directive would suggest that the administration was already alarmed about the news Shaler was sending from Natchitoches.[73] Moreover, Monroe had written to Shaler even before he received Madison's reminder, alluding to the filibuster and ordering the agent "to discountenance the measure, so far as the expression of your opinion may avail." Two days later, on 3 September, Monroe sent more strongly worded instructions to the governors of both Tennessee and the Louisiana-Missouri Territory, requiring them to take all necessary measures against "the illegal enterprize on foot."[74]

Those exchanges indicated that the administration did not regard Shaler as being responsible for the filibuster or believe he would be able to stop it. But Madison and Monroe did want the filibuster suppressed, and not merely because it was illegal. It also needlessly complicated the possibilities for a negotiated settlement with either Spain or Mexico over the western boundaries of Louisiana and other related matters. On 19 June, the day after war was declared against Great Britain, Lieut. Col. Pike had passed through Washington en route from Natchitoches to Canada, where he would eventually be killed at the Battle of York in April 1813. As he did so, he met up with Dr. John Hamilton Robinson, a companion from his days as an explorer when they had both become lost while reconnoitering the region around Santa Fe in 1807 and had been arrested by Spanish troops, who delivered them into the custody of the commandant-general of the Internal Provinces of Mexico, Nemesio Salcedo y Salcedo, at Chihuahua. Together, Pike and Robinson provided the administration with their assessment of future developments in Mexico and the best way to respond to them. Like Madison, Monroe, and Shaler, they assumed that Mexico would become independent and even that some of its eastern Internal Provinces would join the Union. The most serious obstacle to that prospect, though, was Salcedo, whom they regarded as a "crafty" and formidable opponent of both the United States and Mexican independence. The commandant-general of the Internal Provinces, moreover, owed his position and his loyalties not to any viceroy in Mexico City but to the king in Spain, and Pike and Robinson believed that Salcedo would preserve Chihuahua as an autonomous outpost of Bourbon power for as long as possible and regardless of what might occur elsewhere in Mexico. Furthermore, many of the remnants from Hidalgo's cause had retreated to the Internal Provinces, where they were now engaged in "predatory warfare" against Salcedo's government. Pike and Robinson reckoned Salcedo and the administration had a common interest in suppressing such warfare—which would, if left unchecked, destroy the Neutral Ground that since 1806 had been essential for the preservation of peace between the United States and Spain—and they suggested that Monroe send an emissary to Chihuahua for negotiations on that basis.[75]

Madison and Monroe agreed. After all, the prospect that Pike and

Robinson had depicted of Mexico fragmenting into revolutionary and loyalist regions as it broke away from Spain was anything but appealing, and
they would have hardly needed Shaler's warnings that such circumstances
might provide further temptations for Great Britain to meddle in Mexican
affairs. Accordingly, on 1 July Monroe dispatched Robinson as a special
agent to Salcedo to encourage him to suppress the "banditti" that were as-
sembling and operating in his territories—and these "banditti" necessarily included the filibuster headed by Gutiérrez and Magee—and to tell him
that the United States would support such a policy with a view toward
leaving the western boundaries of Louisiana "the subject of an amicable
negotiation hereafter, at a period which may be convenient to the parties
concerned."[76] Consequently, when Monroe wrote to Shaler on 1 September, he informed him of the mission recently commenced by Robinson, and the secretary of state also assumed that the two agents would be
able to meet in Natchitoches to coordinate their missions into Mexico.
Monroe stressed that Robinson's assignment was in no way intended to
undercut Shaler's and that Shaler should cooperate with Robinson in "cultivating a good understanding between the United States and the Governments & people of the Provinces, to which you are respectively sent."[77]

These initiatives met with no success. On receiving Monroe's directions
to prevent recruiting for filibusters in Tennessee, Governor Willie Blount
reported that he had consulted with members of the General Assembly as
well as the U.S. marshal for Western Tennessee but could find "not the
shadow of truth" in the claim that any such activities were taking place.[78]
That finding might have been considered odd inasmuch as Gutiérrez had
passed through Tennessee in November 1811 and recorded in his diary that
members of the state's political elite, including the governor, had received
him and his cause with great enthusiasm and had offered him their services.[79] Moreover, newspapers in Tennessee had reported at length on
events in Mexico and in ways that gave their readers every encouragement
and all necessary information for joining the filibuster.[80] As for Monroe's
letter to Benjamin Howard in St. Louis, it probably never reached its destination, as there is no record of the governor having received it or of his
making any response. And when Shaler read Monroe's letter suggesting he
"discountenance" the filibuster and assist Robinson, there was still nothing he could do. He had no quarrel with Robinson's assignment and

promised him "every aid in [his] power," but the assignment itself was pointless because the doctor was marching "too far in the rear of events." Long before Robinson might reach Chihuahua, Shaler predicted that the filibuster would succeed in its goals by sweeping "the crazy remains of Spanish government from the Internal Provinces, and open[ing] Mexico to the political influence of the U.S. and to the talents and enterprize of [its] Citizens."[81] Only Magee took Robinson seriously, threatening to arrest him at Trinidad de Salcedo, Texas, in mid-October in order to prevent him from reaching Salcedo. On reflection, Magee decided not to arrest him and let the agent proceed, provided that he exchange his U.S. passport for documents issued under the authority of the Revolutionary Army of the North and promise not to furnish the commandant-general with information that might harm its prospects.[82]

Shaler was optimistic because the filibuster, in its early stages, did seem destined for success. On 12 August, only four days after its departure from the Neutral Ground, it had taken Nacogdoches, and the following day Trinidad de Salcedo, capturing at the same time substantial amounts of money, stores, and trade goods that would sustain it for months to come.[83] Success also bolstered its numbers, which quickly doubled to about six hundred men and grew steadily thereafter, with significant numbers of the new recruits coming from the local Mexican and Indian populations.[84] One of the more important new adherents to the cause, Shaler reported, was Samuel Davenport, an American citizen who had become a Spanish subject in order to hold the position of Spanish Indian agent in the Eastern Internal Provinces at Nacogdoches. He now became quartermaster-general for the filibuster.[85] All that seemed necessary thereafter to secure Texas for republicanism was the capture of the presidios at La Bahía del Espíritu Santo (Goliad) and San Antonio de Béxar, and the filibuster occupied the former by the second week in November. Once in La Bahía, however, the filibuster was besieged by revitalized Spanish forces under the command of Simón de Herrara, governor of Nuevo León, and Manuel María de Salcedo y Quiroga, governor of Texas and nephew of Nemesio Salcedo. For almost the next four months, until the third week of February 1813, they succeeded in blocking the progress of the filibuster by combinations of outright defiance, skirmishing, and occasional battles, as well as with the assistance of bad weather.[86]

The effect of this setback was to throw both Gutiérrez and Magee into a state of panic. The former, fearful of the consequences of Spanish vengeance if the filibuster should fail, implored Shaler to come and join him, urging him to bring U.S. troops with him, in return for which he was willing to accept that the territory between Nacogdoches and La Bahía del Espíritu Santo might be annexed to the United States.[87] Magee suffered from profound shock at having met with any resistance at all, and he, too, wished for Shaler to bring U.S. troops in order to annex Texas as far west as the Rio Grande.[88] At one point he even considered surrendering to the Spanish, only to be prevented from doing so by other officers in the filibuster, who then suggested that Shaler or the administration should replace Magee with another American, possibly John Adair, who was reported as having traveled to Natchez, Mississippi Territory, with a view toward coming to Texas. The episode fatally weakened Magee's authority, and shortly thereafter he fell ill. He died of undetermined causes on 6 February 1813 and was replaced in the military command by the filibustering veteran from West Florida, Samuel Kemper.[89] Shaler, who had hoped to be well advanced into Texas by November and who had requested that the State Department send him a proper passport for diplomatic purposes, responded variously to these developments.[90] Gutiérrez he ignored, but Magee he tried to encourage to give battle to the Spaniards and go on to seize San Antonio de Béxar, reassuring him that if he did so it would be merely a matter of time before Congress declared war on Spain over the situation in East Florida and his overall situation improved. When that failed, Shaler could only reprimand him for cowardice, remarking that if he could not defeat his opponents, he had "no just claim on the confidence of the people . . . and should never have undertaken such an enterprize" in the first place.[91] His reaction to Kemper was essentially negative. He did not deny that Kemper was a man of "courage," but he dismissed him for having no education and for being "of doubtful capacity for chief command." As for the notion that the administration might designate Adair to command the filibuster, he merely replied that it could take no position on the matter.[92]

Nevertheless, Shaler could not remain unaffected by the pall that had fallen on the affairs of the filibuster. His own moods often alternated between great enthusiasm and optimism, on the one hand, and extreme melancholy, on the other, and by Christmas 1812 the news from Texas had plunged him into a bout of depression that was not to lift until the spring of 1813.[93] While in that frame of mind, Shaler seriously considered abandoning his mission and returning to Washington. As he reported to Monroe, "The feebleness of the councils of the volunteers has raised in my mind strong doubts about their success, unless they should be very much favor'd by circumstances." In the event of the filibuster failing, he continued, "it appears that any longer stay on this frontier" on his part would be "without any object of public utility, for then, there will be no possible chance of my proceeding to my destination."[94] More than two months later, in late February 1813, his attitude had not changed when he reminded the State Department that the filibuster remained "in a very critical situation from the want of an able commander, and vigorous councils." Belatedly, he confessed he had made an error of judgment in placing his hopes in Magee. The lieutenant, he recalled, was "certainly a very promising young man," but it had become all too clear he did not possess the "superiority of mind" necessary to "bind together" the "disparate materials" of the Revolutionary Army of the North and inspire it with "the confidence requisite to success in all enterprizes of any difficulty."[95]

From Shaler's vantage point, the situation did not begin to improve until after 19 February 1813 when Herrara and Salcedo abandoned their siege of La Bahía del Espíritu Santo and retreated to San Antonio de Béxar. That allowed the filibuster to regroup its forces, recruit a few more Indians and Mexicans, and march on San Antonio de Béxar on 20 March. Nine days later, the filibuster defeated the Royalist army just outside the city at the Battle of Salado Creek, and on 1 April Herrara and Salcedo offered to surrender to the American forces headed by Kemper while the Mexicans under Gutiérrez waited at the Alamo nearby. Kemper, however, insisted the Mexicans should receive the surrender, and it was Gutiérrez who finally plucked Salcedo's sword from the ground where the governor had thrust it in what was to be his final act of defiance against the rebellion.[96] Upon hearing of these developments, Shaler's spirits soared, and he predicted that the Mexican republicans, provided they conducted their affairs "with only a little address," would be in a position "to form a treaty of friendship and intercourse with the U.S. as soon as circumstances will permit." And once San Antonio de Béxar itself had been taken, the success of the revolution in Texas would be certain and "its effects on the general revolution in Mexico must be incalculably great." Nothing then, he hoped, would prevent him from "proceeding on [his] Journey" but the fear that he might still be regarded as "a partisan in the revolution, and thereby committing the government." Those obstacles, he trusted, would be removed "by the submission of San Antonio."[97]

This optimism was shattered by the news that on 3 April the Mexicans in the filibuster, in reprisal for the execution of participants in the unsuccessful Las Casas rebellion of 1811, had murdered Herrera and Salcedo, along with several other Spanish officers, possibly on orders issued by Gutiérrez.[98] In the two weeks thereafter Gutiérrez and his Mexican supporters then proclaimed Texan independence from Spain, on 6 April, and promulgated a constitution, on 17 April, stipulating that Texas was to be an integral part of a future Mexican republic. The "illustrious liberator" Gutiérrez was authorized to appoint a junta to form a provisional government for the protection of the nation, the rights of man, and the Roman Catholic religion. The junta was also to name a president protector as its highest officer, and it did so by selecting Gutiérrez.[99] These transactions horrified Shaler. His problem was not that the Mexicans had declared their independence or denied that the United States had any claim to Texas under the Louisiana Purchase. The difficulty Shaler had was with the "black act" of murdering the Spanish officers along with the drafting of the "absurd revolutionary farce" that passed for a constitution. That document, Shaler complained, had no other purpose than to permit Gutiérrez to loot the treasury and live "in the style of an Eastern Basha, while everything around him is penury and want."[100]

This reaction crystallized all the misgivings Shaler had developed about the Mexican since the summer of 1812 in Natchitoches, but it also revealed that Gutiérrez's conception of what a republic might be diverged widely from Shaler's notions of "rational liberty." There is no reason to doubt that Gutiérrez, as a patriotic Mexican creole, sincerely wished to establish a republic free of Spanish and monarchical rule that would protect both personal and economic liberty and at the same time open up Texas to free trade and immigration from the United States. The provisions of the Texan declaration of independence, the 17 April constitution, and Gutiérrez's proclamation of the following day putting it into effect all make that abundantly clear.[101] But it is also clear that Gutiérrez saw far fewer necessary connections between the forms of the state and the protection of economic and personal liberty than Shaler did. Under the new frame of government, the junta and the president protector were assured of complete control over all affairs of state, including diplomacy, war, financial and judicial matters, and the election of delegates to a future Mexican congress. There was no provision for religious liberty—the Roman Catholic religion was to remain "unchanged in the way it is now established"—and the Spanish system of local government for San Antonio de Béxar also remained unaltered. Other towns in Texas were to be placed under a military officer to be named by the president protector.[102] And in drawing up these provisions Gutiérrez does not appear to have consulted very closely with the Americans in the filibuster, many of whom were already deeply disturbed by the murders of Herrara and Salcedo and were beginning to make preparations to return to the United States.[103]

At that point, Shaler, in his rage, redefined the fundamental issue in the Mexican rebellion not as independence from Spain but as a stark choice between the alternatives of barbarism and despotism, on the one hand, and humanity and liberty, on the other. Thereafter, he never deviated from that conviction and its corollary that the revolution had to be redeemed for liberty if his mission was to have any purpose or prospect for success. As chance would have it, an instrument of redemption came to hand in the person of José Álvarez de Toledo y Dubois, a rebellious Cuban-born former deputy to the Spanish Cortes from Santo Domingo, who arrived in Natchitoches in the first week of April. Gutiérrez reacted to this news with alarm. He had met Toledo in Philadelphia and Washington over the previous winter, when he became convinced that the Cuban was as "passionately devoted to the cause of the liberty of Mexico" as he was, and the two men had opened a correspondence on the understanding that Toledo would come to Mexico later in 1812.[104] Gutiérrez had even taken some of Toledo's writings with him for distribution in Texas, but Toledo had been tardy in honoring his commitment and by the time he arrived, both Gutiérrez and Shaler had received intelligence to the effect that he was not what he claimed to be. That information was provided by Nathaniel Cogswell, a lawyer from the District of Maine, who had known Toledo when they were both in Philadelphia, boarding with the aging American revolutionary Ira Allen of Vermont. Cogswell had also come to the Louisiana-Texas frontier—he was one of a number of New Englanders who did so at this time, most of them traveling companions of Toledo—and the gist of his charge was that Toledo, far from being a devotee of Spanish-American independence, was the agent of various members of the Cortes and the Regency in Cádiz, among them being the marqués de Villa Franca and the duque de Infantado, whom Cogswell described as "inveterate foes of the Patriot cause." Toledo had come to Texas, Cogswell warned, to place himself at the head of the filibuster in order to lay the groundwork for its "utter ruin."[105]

Cogswell provided a number of details in support of his allegations. Among them was an anecdote recounting the circumstances of a visit he and Toledo had made in the fall of 1812 to Baltimore, where they learned that the Venezuelan revolutionary Francisco de Miranda had recently surrendered the short-lived republic he had helped establish in 1811 to a vastly inferior Royalist force. The local supporters of the Spanish-American cause were "thunderstruck," but Toledo seemed hardly affected at all, largely because, Cogswell claimed, he had been in regular contact with Miranda and must have had advance warning of his presumably treacherous intentions.[106] Though such evidence might seem to be insubstantial, it is clear from what is now known about Toledo's career that Cogswell may not have been so far off the mark. The Cuban did hold a commission from some American members of the Cortes to liberate the northern regions of the Internal Provinces, a detail he almost certainly omitted to impart to Gutiérrez on the occasion of their meetings in Philadelphia and Washington.[107] Cogswell also quoted Toledo's dismissal of Gutiérrez as "an ignorant and simple fellow" whom he believed he could displace as leader of the Mexican republicans with little difficulty. Having just established his own republic and having less need of Toledo's support than he had supposed in 1812, Gutiérrez was more than willing to give credence to Cogswell's charges. The account of Toledo's alleged connections with that "dangerous and forgotten man Genl. Miranda" particularly resonated with him as proof that the Cuban was "inimical to the cause of the patriots" and that his object was "treachery."[108] Consequently, when Toledo arrived in Nacogdoches from Natchitoches and offered to serve as second in command in the filibuster, Gutiérrez ordered him out of Texas.

Shaler took the opposite view. Although he pleaded briefly with Gutiérrez to accept Toledo's services, he had long been looking for "a creole of more merit and capacity" to lead the Mexicans, and he quickly concluded that Toledo could be that man.[109] Indeed, he appears to have regarded Toledo as the very embodiment of all that Spanish-American republicans might become once they had cast off the shackles of their colonial past. Shaler discovered he could converse with Toledo more easily in French than he had ever been able to communicate with Gutiérrez in either English or Spanish. He found Toledo's political views much more congenial than those of Gutiérrez, and Toledo brought him up to date on larger developments in the Spanish-American world. From Toledo Shaler received a copy of a statistical and political memoir on the four Eastern Internal Provinces that had been presented to the Cortes by the delegate from Cohuila, Miguel Ramos de Arispe, and the agent eagerly sent off a fifty-page translation to Washington "for the information of the government."[110] Toledo may also have given Shaler a copy of the Spanish Constitution of March 1812, upon which he sketched four pages of notes critiquing its contents. Needless to say, Shaler did not like what he read. The efforts of the Cortes to combine liberal reforms with the essential elements of the old order—the crown, the nobility, the clergy, and the people—displeased him, leading him to remark that "a Republic would very properly abolish them, and declare perfect equality."[111] Toledo, who had resented very greatly the condescension and hostility that Spanish-American delegates to the Cortes had received from metropolitan Spaniards in Cádiz, doubtless encouraged these sentiments, and together the two men began to discuss ways in which the command of the Revolutionary Army of the North might be transferred from Gutiérrez to Toledo.

To accomplish this, Shaler had to coordinate activities on three interconnected fronts. Cogswell had continued to broadcast his charges against Toledo, ultimately going so far as to link Shaler with Toledo's cause by informing Gutiérrez that the agent had told him Gutiérrez's throat should be cut before Toledo replaced him.[112] At the end of June 1813, Cogswell, Shaler, Toledo, and several of their supporters finally met at a point on the road between Natchitoches and Nacogdoches, but on that occasion Cogswell failed to demonstrate that his charges against Toledo could be substantiated. Those present at the meeting then drew up a declaration denouncing Cogswell as "a base and treacherous calumniator," and Shaler gathered up affidavits from members of Toledo's party to forward to Washington as proof that the allegations against Toledo were ground-less.[113] Shaler also sent members of Toledo's party into San Antonio de Béxar to undermine support for Gutiérrez in both the city and the fili-buster.[114] They did so by establishing a printing press whose publications, the *Gaceta de Texas* and *El Mexicano,* faulted Gutiérrez for not being suf-ficiently attached to "rational liberty" while also accusing him of plotting to introduce an army of mulattoes from Haiti and pirates from Barataria into Texas.[115] Shaler sent evidence of these activities to the administration in Washington as well, pointing out that Gutiérrez was losing control of affairs in San Antonio de Béxar, that desertions from the filibuster were on the rise, and that the Mexican rebels had not only missed opportunities to bring down Spanish rule in the Eastern Internal Provinces but also ne-glected to take proper precautions against the growing signs of a Royalist counteroffensive.[116]

This last matter was cause for considerable concern in San Antonio de Béxar as tensions between Americans and Mexicans in the filibuster in-creased throughout April and May of 1813. These were further exacerbated by the approach of an advance guard of Royalist troops under Col. Igna-cio Elizondo from the Presidio del Norte on the Rio Grande in June.[117] Elizondo was a bitter enemy of Gutiérrez and his cause. He had been in-strumental in the capture of Hildago in March 1811; he was responsible for the subsequent death of Gutiérrez's colleague José Menchaca; and he had also promised to send Gutiérrez to "Hell" where his hair would be "pulled out," his body "burnt," and his ashes "scattered."[118] He attempted to make good on that promise by exploiting the situation in San Antonio de Béxar with an offer to spare the Americans if they would betray Gutiérrez and his Mexicans. Some of the Americans were tempted to do so, and they quarreled at length with the Mexicans over the advisability of making a re-treat. With the assistance of Col. Henry Perry of Virginia, Gutiérrez man-aged to rally enough support to stage a surprise attack on Elizondo at the Battle of Alazán on 20 June, but not even that was sufficient to overcome the effect of Shaler's campaign on behalf of Toledo.[119] By the end of June most of the Americans in San Antonio de Béxar were convinced of the need for a change, and they resolved to accept Toledo. One of them conveyed the news to Shaler thus: "Old *Granny Bernardo* is now in the dumps and is now traversing the room behind me while I write this, one minute drumming on the window glass with his fingers and the other catching flies and *pinching off their heads.*"[120] Gutiérrez warned the Americans against Toledo, but aware that his position had become untenable, he quit and withdrew to Louisiana.

On receiving this news, Shaler prepared to set out for Texas on 20 July, where he intended to assist Toledo in taking over the filibuster by supporting his plans to "annul Bernardo's absurd government," to form a new junta "by the free suffrages of the people," and to "march immediately to the rio grande."[121] That he expected to operate as a minister to this new government he indicated by sending a confidential letter to Washington in which he ordered the dress uniform of a naval captain, complete with gold epaulettes, eagles, and buttons, and adorned with tassels on the hat.[122] Indeed, so enthusiastic did he become about the prospects for the Mexican revolution that two days before his departure Shaler penned yet another paper speculating about the future of Mexico and its relationship with the United States. On this occasion he drew on the essay he had published in the 1808 *American Register,* using its findings to modify some of the proposals he had sent to Monroe in August 1812. Shaler assumed as he always had that Mexico would become independent and that a free Mexico would include Texas, but he now argued that as Mexico had never been able to build up much in the way of its own maritime commerce and navigation, it would be better for it to cede the province of Alta California to the United States in order to keep it and its resources out of the hands of the expanding Pacific powers of Great Britain and Russia. In this context, he worried about Russia more than he did about Great Britain, fearing that Alexander I would demand California as a condition for any alliance with the Cádiz Regency against Napoleon. In making these suggestions, Shaler assumed that the United States would eventually be able to communicate easily with the Pacific through the Columbia and Missouri rivers and on that basis build up a fur trade and an "important nursery for Seamen." That would permit the United States "completely to develop the resources of the western portion of our Empire" and to lay the foundation for a Pacific trade "which at no distant day may become equal to that we enjoy on the Atlantic." Those developments, he concluded, would give the United States "a preponderance" of power on the Pacific "that no European power could ever shake."[123] And by arguing thus, Shaler became the first American to make the case that the United States should acquire California from an independent Mexican nation.

Following the dispatch of Robinson to Chihuahua and the failure of its efforts to prevent filibustering in the fall of 1812, the administration ceased to pay much attention to developments in Texas. It would be months before the outcome of Robinson's mission could be known anyway, and in the interval it was the events of the war with Great Britain and the stalemate in East Florida that preoccupied the president and his colleagues. Madison and Monroe continued to assume that Claiborne would take whatever measures he could to preserve American neutrality with Spain by preventing conflicts along the Louisiana-Texas border, and Secretary of War Eustis strongly discouraged hints he had received from Wilkinson in New Orleans that he might assist the Mexican rebels by entering Texas "to extend our occupances to our Western limits the Rio Grande." The general was expressly directed to remain at his post, where he was to confine himself to cooperating with Claiborne to defend the Gulf Coast and to do nothing that risked hostilities with Spain.[124] And when Shaler reported the news of the early successes of the filibuster in the fall of 1812 along with his request for a passport to enter Mexico, the State Department merely sent him the passport and arranged for him to receive a regular subscription to the *National Intelligencer* in Natchitoches so he could be kept abreast of current events.[125]

However, when news of the events in Texas in the spring of 1813 finally reached Washington in the first week of June, the administration responded sharply by telling Shaler he had departed from his instructions and ordering him to remain at Natchitoches and not to enter Mexico at all. The problem here was not the success of the filibuster in taking San Antonio de Béxar—that event was generally celebrated by Republican newspapers in the eastern states as an important blow for liberty—so much as it was the nature and implications of that development for the administration's policy of obtaining a negotiated settlement of the western boundary of Louisiana.[126] The news that Gutiérrez's supporters had murdered the Spanish officers who had surrendered San Antonio de Béxar greatly shocked the secretary of state, who lamented that American citizens had become "engaged in the contest between the two parties in Mexico."[127] But the fact that the nephew of Nemesio Salcedo had been one of the victims of this massacre could only have led Madison and Monroe to wonder about the outcome of Robinson's mission. To that point, they had heard almost nothing from, or of, Robinson other than a brief note the agent had written on 12 April 1813 on his return to Natchitoches from Chihuahua. On that occasion Robinson had stated that he was not yet prepared to entrust any account of his mission to the mails until he was further inside U.S. territory.[128] Shaler also mentioned, however, that Robinson had passed through Natchitoches in April, and although he made no mention of the results of the mission to Salcedo, he did report that Robinson had met Toledo and that together they were planning an expedition into Mexico, the details of which would be given to Monroe when Robinson reached Washington.[129] Only one conclusion was possible from these remarks—that the mission to Salcedo had failed and Robinson and Toledo were now planning their own filibuster. The administration did not even wait to receive Robinson's report, which was not written until 26 July.[130] One month before that date, on 25 June, Monroe sent the doctor a curt letter terminating his employment as a government agent.[131]

Shaler's information about Toledo would have been no less disturbing. Like Gutiérrez, Monroe was familiar with Toledo, having met him in Washington in December 1811 when the Cuban had proposed to him the formation of an Antillean confederation comprising Cuba, Puerto Rico, and Santo Domingo to resist British encroachments on the Spanish-American empire.[132] The secretary of state had liked the idea and had given Toledo a letter of introduction to Shaler, who was then still believed to be in Havana. Toledo, however, never went to Havana. His arrival in Philadelphia from Cádiz in September 1811 had attracted a good deal of publicity and not a little hostile attention, most of the latter from Onís, who worried about the seditious implications of Toledo's publication of his criticisms of the Cortes and its reluctance to treat with its Spanish-American delegates on the basis of equality.[133] The minister warned the Cuban that he would be watching and reporting on all his movements.[134] Thoroughly alarmed at this, Toledo hesitated to take passage for Cuba, fearing that Onís might have him arrested, or even assassinated, the moment he set foot on a Spanish vessel or on Spanish soil. Without any further explanations to Monroe, Toledo, after March 1812, dropped all idea of going to Cuba and turned his attention to Mexico instead.[135] He wrote at length to Gutiérrez about his plans to join him, only to learn by October 1812 that the filibuster had already entered Mexico and would, presumably, be well advanced in its progress long before he could even reach the Louisiana-Texas border. Possibly feeling betrayed by this development, Toledo then returned to Onís, to whom he confessed about his dealings with Gutiérrez and from whom he requested funds to go to Texas, where he promised to act in ways that would ensure that the province remained under Royalist control.[136]

Onís had little money to spare for such activities, and the question of whether Toledo's offer of his services was sincere or not must have seemed as uncertain to him then as it has to historians ever since. With the hindsight derived from the knowledge that Toledo unequivocally returned to the allegiance of Ferdinand VII in 1816, it is tempting to conclude that he had made his choice to do so by October 1812, but the situation was probably more complicated than that.[137] At heart, Toledo, despite his angry arguments in 1811 for Spanish Americans to separate themselves from the unjust rule of the Cortes and the Cádiz Regency, may well have remained something of a Spanish-American liberal who believed that the proper relationship between Spain and its American kingdoms should be one of equality, provided Spain could regain its freedom from Napoleon and provided Spanish America did not come under the control of revolutionaries whose ideas of independence, or "emancipation," required the repudiation of the loyalty all good Spaniards still owed to their monarch. In 1812 that vision was not necessarily an impossible one, and by attempting to deal with both Gutiérrez and Onís as he did, Toledo probably believed he could help bring it about. In that sense, he was more of an opportunist governing himself by circumstances than he was a traitor to a cause.[138]

Be that as it may, however, within three days of Toledo re-establishing contact with Onís, Madison was warned that he had been talking with the Spanish minister and was enjoying his confidence to the extent of being able to acquire knowledge of the sentiments of both the Cortes and the Regency about the expediency of Spain's going to war with the United States over the American presence in East Florida.[139] Exactly how much credit Madison gave to this news at the time is hard to tell, but that Toledo was talking to Onís at all must have seemed alarming. The president passed the information on to Monroe, who could hardly have forgotten it when he read Shaler's letters of May 1813, along with other accounts that contained descriptions of Toledo arriving on the frontier wearing a Spanish uniform and in the company of a French agent.[140] That the French agent was none other than Paillette, whom Shaler had denounced in the spring of 1812 as a bad character who had corrupted Gutiérrez, must also have been puzzling, if not troubling.[141] By May 1813, though, Shaler was so enraged at Gutiérrez that he failed to attach much significance to Toledo's contacts with Paillette, but it is unlikely Monroe would have felt that Toledo deserved the benefit of further doubt about his intentions, given his past record and the company he had recently been keeping. In any event, the administration now had clear and unequivocal evidence that Shaler was departing from his instructions by trying to manage the filibuster. And were he to be successful, he would also deliver the Texan revolt into the hands of a potentially dangerous and unscrupulous character. That Shaler was justifying these decisions by filling his letters with fulsome tributes to Toledo's talents, virtues, and "enlightened mind" could have done little to recommend the agent's judgment to his superiors.[142]

The administration therefore acted. On 5 June 1813 Monroe sent Shaler a reprimand, reminding him that Madison wished him to "observe strictly" his instructions and "not to interfere" in the affairs of Mexico or "to encourage any armaments of any kind against the existing government." The United States, he pointed out, was at peace with Spain, and it wished "to preserve that relation with whatever government may exist there." That, Monroe added, was "the spirit of the instructions" given to Shaler at the start of his mission, and "they have never since been altered." The agent was then ordered not to go to San Antonio de Béxar but to remain at Natchitoches to await further instructions.[143] By the time Shaler received that letter, however, he had already reached Nacogdoches. He retraced his steps immediately, apologizing as he did so for displeasing the president but adding that his motives had always been good. His actions had been intended to allow him "to keep a vigilant eye on what was passing," and his defense of Toledo was an entirely "personal" matter arising from his resentment at the attacks made by Cogswell. He also defended himself against Monroe's implied charge that he might have violated the 1794 Neutrality Act by claiming that all preparations for the filibuster had taken place on "the desolate banks of the Sabine" and outside the limits of the United States. The volunteers had gone out "either singly, or in small bands, usually armed as hunters," and if any of their supplies had been purchased within the United States, they were "furnished in the common way of trade." It was not, in fact, a very repentant letter, and Shaler concluded it with the hope that Toledo would yet be successful and thus wipe away the stain from the Texan revolution that had resulted from the "atrocious conduct" of Gutiérrez.[144]

Shaler was fortunate Monroe acted as promptly as he did. As the agent returned to Natchitoches, Toledo arrived in San Antonio de Béxar, where he was accepted as commander of the filibuster on 4 August. He had little time to reorganize the force before he had to prevent Elizondo's army from being reinforced by 1,600 additional troops under the new commanding general of the Eastern Internal Provinces, Joaquín de Arredondo y Mioño. He failed to do so, and on 18 August at the Battle of Medina, Arredondo decisively routed the filibuster.[145] When the news reached Shaler, he realized the disaster was "fatal" and "conclusive of the revolution in the neighboring provinces perhaps forever."[146] There was, therefore, little point in his remaining at Natchitoches, and he decided to return to Washington, where he arrived on 19 December 1813. Two days later, he met Monroe for the first time. He was pleasantly surprised, and perhaps more than a little relieved, when the secretary of state received him with "friendly politeness," and the reason for that, Shaler was to learn, was that the administration was far more upset with Robinson than it was with him. As for Shaler's role in Texas, Monroe reminded him that the administration was "friendly to Mexican independence but would never countenance private expeditions," and he concluded their discussion by asking Shaler if he understood that the United States "could not take any part in that business." Ruefully, the agent recorded in his diary that he "knew it well."[147]

5

TOWARD THE TRANSCONTINENTAL TREATY

In leaving the Boundary from the source of the Sabine, West and North, to be settled by Commissaries, any adjustment there will be avoided, which might affect our claims on Columbia River, and on the Pacific.

—James Monroe to George W. Erving, 30 May 1816

After the failure of the filibuster into Texas in August 1813, there were few developments of any immediate consequence in the borderlands, and Madison sent no more agents into Spanish-American territory. Both Gutiérrez and Toledo retreated to the United States, from where they tried to organize further insurrectionary activities against the Spanish regime in Mexico. In New Orleans Gutiérrez became involved in the independence movement briefly headed by the Congress of Chilpancingo, while Toledo, from Nashville, tried to rally the remnants of the Republican Army of the North and come to agreements with John Hamilton Robinson and a recently arrived French agent, Jean-Joseph Amable Humbert, about launching another expedition into Texas.[1] Little was to come of these schemes, and the administration, having anticipated that Robinson would resort to filibustering, made several efforts to have him arrested, albeit without success.[2] At about the same time, in November 1813, Anthony Morris arrived in Cádiz to commence the informal mission on which Madison had dispatched him in June. He was able to report on "reliable authority" that Spain had not sold or transferred the Floridas to Great Britain and that the current members of the Spanish Regency were con-

siderably more hostile toward their British ally than those who had held office at the end of 1812. To that extent, Morris allowed himself to hope the
Spanish government might become slightly more favorably disposed toward the United States than it had been in the past.[3]

Even so, there was little chance Morris would be able to make an agree-
ment about Florida. Not only was there an epidemic in Cádiz that disrupted almost all government business, but also there was no permanent
minister of foreign affairs in office with whom any business might be done.
Moreover, news of Napoleon's crushing loss at the Battle of Leipzig in
October 1813 had just arrived, and the Cortes was planning to relocate to
Madrid, which had recently been abandoned by King Joseph and the
French army following their defeat at the Battle of Vitoria in June. These
developments, as Morris put it, quite altered the "tone" in Cádiz, and
while the Regency had no objection to his having informal conversations
with minor officials and ministers, the president's agent was also the re-

cipient of a good deal of Spanish resentment toward the United States for the ways in which its "democratic Government" under "the Frenchified señors Jefferson and Madison" had sent agents into Florida and Texas to foment rebellions as part of their "inalterable intention" to "weaken and finally to annihilate the Spanish Government in America." Morris even heard talk that Spain would attempt to recover its former colony of Louisiana, which along with Florida and Texas might be reorganized into a new jurisdiction whose integrity would be guaranteed by "the United Powers of Spain, England, Russia, and Sweden." This new entity could be governed as "a limited monarchy," and if successful, it not only would protect Mexico against further "enterprises" from the United States but, "like Hercules in infancy," might even "strangle the serpent of democratic usurpation" in North America altogether.[4]

These prospects seemed alarming. They suggested not merely that Spain would not discuss American territorial claims in the borderlands but that it would reassert the position it had taken immediately after the purchase of Louisiana in 1803, namely that the United States had no valid claim to any part of the territory at all and that Spain might expect its European allies, especially Great Britain, to support this contention. For that reason, Morris suggested it would be "prudent Policy" for the United States to maintain a permanent and "respectable force" near to Florida to counteract any "attempts by the British in that quarter." Later, he even went further by proposing to the Regency, as his instructions allowed, that it permit the United States to occupy the Gulf Coast on a temporary basis to help maintain order on the frontiers and keep British naval vessels out of the coastal ports. But before any of these developments might take place, the Regency would require from the United States "a formal recognition" of its authority. It was now inevitable, Morris pointed out, that all European governments would soon acknowledge the Regency as the only legitimate source of power in Spain, and the implication of that observation was that it would only be a matter of time before the United States had to follow suit by recognizing and receiving Onís.[5]

The American position on the Gulf Coast was not quite so weak as Morris supposed—victories over the Creek Indians during the winter of 1813–14 gave the United States a much more secure control over the hinterland of western Georgia and the Mississippi Territory than he could have

predicted—but even so, Madison had little desire to resume formal dealings with Spain.[6] In his annual message to Congress in December 1813 he
made no statement about any aspect of relations with Spain, and for the
next several weeks he was more than fully preoccupied with other matters, particularly the failure of the Russian mediation, the winter offensive
against the New York frontier by British troops from Upper Canada, and
an unexpected British offer to open negotiations on "principles of perfect
reciprocity" that were "not inconsistent with the established maxims of
public law, and with the maritime rights of the British empire." In January 1814, he decided to accept the British offer by sending a new diplomatic commission to Europe, to which he attached William Shaler—now
forgiven for his recent indiscretions with Toledo—as a bearer of dispatches
with additional instructions to gather any information that might affect
American interests in the post-Napoleonic order that was slowly beginning to emerge.[7] Consequently, the president saw no reason to make decisions about Spanish problems. The future shape of Europe was still too
uncertain to permit new policy to be plotted with any confidence. But
Madison's hopes that he might be granted the luxury of time in this matter were to be denied. Even Napoleon realized Spain was lost, and in December 1813 he signed a treaty at Valencia with Ferdinand VII returning
him to his throne. The restored monarch arrived in Madrid in May 1814,
shortly after the European allies had occupied Paris, overturned Napoleon,
and reinstated the French Bourbon dynasty in the person of Louis XVIII.[8]

These developments, understandably enough, were far more pleasing
to Onís than they were to Madison, though the minister worried that the
administration would continue to pursue an aggressive policy against
Florida, partly to gratify its own ambitions but mainly as a last desperate
attempt to aid France by provoking a war with Spain that might force both
Great Britain and Spain to divert resources away from Europe to the Gulf
Coast.[9] To forestall that possibility Onís commenced, in December 1813,
yet another campaign to persuade the administration to accept his credentials.[10] The secretary of state was in no hurry to receive these documents, and as in the past he kept the minister at a distance by doing no
more than having informal conversations with vice-consul Chacón from
Alexandria. Even as late as mid-March 1814 Monroe continued to assert
that the "contest" in Spain was "not yet terminated" and that until such

time as "the government of Spain [was] established in some permanent and independent form," there could be no harm in "a little further delay" before Madrid and Washington resumed diplomatic relations.[11] Frustrated, Onís tried to insist he should be recognized, and he wrote to the Spanish foreign ministry to ensure that he received new credentials from Ferdinand VII so that those he held from the Regency could not be rejected for being out of date.

As these delaying tactics were being played out, how did the administration assess developments in Europe following the restoration of the French and Spanish Bourbons? Much would depend, as Madison pointed out in May 1814, on the character of Ferdinand VII and how far he would consider himself bound by the Constitution of 1812 and other reforms introduced by the Cortes while it sat in Cádiz. Also relevant here would be the attitude of other European powers, particularly Great Britain and Russia, toward Spanish-American questions, especially the extent to which they might support, or even assist, Ferdinand VII in suppressing the ongoing rebellions in his South American colonies. On this last score, the president was inclined to suspect the worst of Great Britain, and he also assumed that its government would probably succeed in persuading other European nations that the long-standing claims of the United States against Spain were unjustifiable.[12] Matters did not seem to be any better with respect to Ferdinand VII, and throughout the summer of 1814 American newspapers printed accounts of how the monarch, *el rey deseado,* whose throne the Cortes had labored so strenuously to preserve, had repudiated not only the Constitution of 1812 but also many of the other reforms that had been implemented by both that body and the ministers of the former King Joseph.[13] Indeed, Ferdinand VII did not merely refuse to assemble another session of the Cortes—he abolished it altogether, imprisoned many of its members, and then proceeded to restore the Inquisition as well as several unpopular taxes.[14]

One of the more interesting pieces of information Madison received during the summer of 1814 was a long letter from his former chargé d'affaires in Madrid, George W. Erving, written in Paris, where he had established contacts with some of the more liberal members of the French and Spanish aristocracies who had supported the reforms of both King Joseph and the Cortes in the belief that only fundamental change imposed by enlightened rulers could rescue Spain from the legacies of its despotic and priest-ridden past. Erving, needless to say, was appalled by the conduct of Ferdinand VII, and he wondered "under what strange infatuation, or by what perverse councils" the king could expect his subjects and his colonies to submit to "his leaden sway of ignorance & bigotry." But at this point in their history Erving seriously doubted that the Spaniards would consent to be driven "back to the darkness of the 14th century." Noting the appearance of disaffection against the regime in Catalonia as well as in the northern and southern provinces of Spain along with his report of "some new facts with respect to the abdication of Charles the 4th" that promised to call into question the validity of Ferdinand's title to the throne, the diplomat predicted the restored monarch could soon be overthrown. "Charles may reassume his throne, (on terms)," he wrote, "and Ferdinand die in a cloister if not on a scaffold." These possibilities, coupled with the likelihood that the United States could expect "no harmonious intercourse" with Madrid anyway until it had regained control over its American colonies, led Erving to advise the president to continue a policy of delay. "The present state of things cannot be permanent," he believed, and "we are yet to wait for the final result."[15]

Madison was unable to wait on such predictions. As both the diplomatic environment in Europe and the military situation in the war with Great Britain continued to evolve throughout the summer of 1814 in ways that were unfavorable to the United States, the president concluded that it would be prudent to accept the Bourbon restoration in Spain. After all, if the impending peace talks with Great Britain were to fail and the war to continue into the foreseeable future, it would surely be better for the United States to return to normal and ostensibly friendly relations with Madrid rather than risk the prospect of seeing Spain, as a British ally, enter the American conflict. And there was also the possibility that Great Britain might insist on U.S. recognition of Ferdinand VII as a precondition for a peace treaty anyway.[16] Consequently, in August 1814 Madison decided to send Erving back to Madrid as a fully accredited minister plenipotentiary.[17] He was even prepared to allow Monroe to state that Ferdinand VII was now securely established on his throne by popular consent, though it is unlikely, perhaps, that the president truly believed that statement. The implementation of the decision, however, was delayed by the disruptions to government in Washington that resulted from the British destruction of the capital on 23 August, and the instructions for Erving's mission were not completed until the first week of October.

The contents of these instructions revealed that the administration, at this juncture, had no strategy for settling its differences with Spain. Monroe, in fact, did not even bother to restate the issues in contention, assuming that Erving, by virtue of his previous experience in Madrid, was already thoroughly familiar with them. Should he be able to engage the Spanish government in discussions about them, though, he was to be guided by the instructions Madison had written in 1804 for Monroe's unsuccessful negotiation in Aranjuez in 1805. On that occasion, the Spanish government had not merely rejected American demands for a settlement of the disputed boundaries of Louisiana along with the unpaid spoliation claims from the 1802 Convention but had done so without even presenting any counterproposals.[18] Madison had no reason to suppose the Spanish position would be any different now, and Erving's main task was simply to keep Spain out of the war with Great Britain. Noting that the connection between that country and Spain was "becoming more intimate than it has been," the new minister was to explain the causes of the war with Great Britain in order to persuade Madrid to accept American views about maritime rights, and above all else, he was to request that Spain give "express orders" to its colonial officials "to prevent the landing of British troops in Florida."[19] In short, Spain should remain as neutral in the Anglo-American war as the United States asserted it had been in the contest between the Regency and King Joseph in the Iberian Peninsula.

Since Spain would be bound to disagree with this last claim, Erving was also "to place that subject in a proper point of view" for Madrid and to remind it, if necessary, that Ferdinand VII himself had recently concluded that neither the Cortes nor the Regency had been legally constituted authorities. That argument, however, also raised the question of whether the United States would regard itself as obliged to recognize Onís as a minister in return for Madrid accepting the credentials of Erving. Madison hoped not, trusting that Ferdinand's views about the illegality of the actions of all those who had attempted to govern Spain during his imprisonment in France would also extend to the appointment of Onís. If the logic of that position failed to carry the day, Erving was to point out that the Spanish minister had "made himself personally objectionable" to the president, who would prefer to see "another person" in his place.[20] But why did Madison decide Onís was "objectionable?" Certainly, there had never been any personal warmth between them in their brief encounters in the years after 1809, with the president regarding the minister as an untrustworthy spokesman for a doomed cause and the minister dismissing the president as a weak and compliant tool of Napoleon.[21] The president also worried that Onís had fed Cádiz a constant stream of misinformation about the United States and its policies, but the sources of his concern were, in fact, more specific and more deeply rooted than that. Onís's offense, for which Madison never forgave him, was the letter he had written in February 1810 to the captain-general in Caracas, in which the minister had advocated that Great Britain and Spain should send armed forces to the Gulf Coast to divide the Union into "two or three republics" and leave them "in a state of perfect Nullity."[22] If those views had been bad in 1810, how much worse were they in 1814, when there seemed to be a far greater possibility they might be put into effect?

Events were to prove that the administration's fears about a "more intimate" connection between Great Britain and Spain centering on Florida were by no means groundless. Late in 1814, as part of their campaign to invade the Gulf Coast, British forces entered Pensacola, where they had been invited by Governor Gonzáles Manrique to provide protection against a possible attack by American forces under Maj. Gen. Andrew Jackson, fresh from his victories over the Creek Indians. The British also attempted, albeit unsuccessfully, to seize Mobile before they launched their disastrous assault against New Orleans on 8 January 1815.[23] From Philadelphia, Onís dutifully reported these developments to Madrid, torn by conflicting sentiments as he did so. Aware that Jackson had prepared a strong defense at New Orleans, he feared that the British campaign could end "badly," but he hoped, nevertheless, for a great British victory that might set in motion a chain of calamities for the United States, including national bankruptcy, slave rebellions, continuing Indian wars, and the loss of its western territories as well as the navigation of the Mississippi River. Such misfortunes, the minister believed, were no more than the republic deserved for its "Machiavellian" conduct toward Spain, and they might indeed reduce it to the "absolute nullity" he had dreamt of in 1810.[24]

The British defeat at New Orleans brought an end to these hopes, but an even more serious blow to Spanish interests was the Treaty of Ghent, signed on 24 December 1814 and ratified by Great Britain one week later. By ratifying the treaty before sending it across the Atlantic, the ministry of Lord Liverpool indicated that it would not continue the war for any reason—and certainly not for an agenda to serve Spanish interests. Onís was hardly blind to the implications of this decision, though he could not complain about them too loudly given the extent of the British losses at New Orleans.[25] The end of the war also allowed Madison to continue evading Onís, with the result being a series of procedural disputes that prevented the resumption of negotiations for fifteen months. Madrid contributed to the delay as well. Although Erving had received his instructions to go to Madrid in November 1814, he was unable to do so. The new Spanish foreign minister turned out to be none other than Pedro Cevallos, to whom Erving had taken a very considerable dislike during his earlier sojourn in Spain, and Cevallos would not issue a passport to Erving until Madison had received Onís. That news hardly surprised Erving, who informed the president that Ferdinand VII had fallen under the influence of a "bigoted and cunning" confessor and that nothing good could be expected from his foreign minister anyway. Consequently, Erving had no choice but to wait and see if Cevallos should change his mind or if the administration would send him fresh instructions. He was, however, sufficiently annoyed by the slight to suggest that the administration would not be treating Spain too harshly if it should send him to Mexico instead of Madrid, presumably to settle the disputed boundaries of Louisiana with a rebel regime in the New World.[26]

This last proposal was, if nothing else, impractical. There was at this time little approaching a successful rebel government in Mexico that might be recognized by the United States, and Madison persevered with his campaign to have Onís replaced. It was, he protested to Monroe in March 1815, "impossible" that Spain could "persist with the extravagance of saying, I will receive *no* Minister from you, unless you receive a particular Minister from me, and him too a man confessedly guilty of an attempt to create Civil War & dismemberment in your Country."[27] Shortly thereafter, Madison did sound out his cabinet colleagues to see if they thought it advisable to accept Onís, though as he did so he could scarcely conceal his concern that should the minister be received and knowledge of his "indecorous & *criminal* conduct toward the U.S." become public, it would "not make an impression in our favor, unless great considerations of national interest called for a disregard of all minor ones."[28] European developments then prevented the administration from pursuing this course. In May 1815 the news that Napoleon had escaped from his confinement on Elba and returned to Paris in March reached the United States. That event would have widespread repercussions, and as Madison noted it would "also materially affect Spain & Spanish America, and be highly interesting to us in that point of view." The president therefore decided to do nothing. "Our general policy," he wrote, "seems clearly to be, for the moment, in preserving a posture, which will leave us free to chuse the course, recommended by further information, and best according with our neutral rights and national interests."[29]

Yet the pressure of events would again force Madison into making decisions sooner than he might have anticipated. On the basis of letters received from Morris, who had remained at his post despite Madison's wish that he relinquish his duties to Erving, the administration learned that Spain had received the news of the Treaty of Ghent (and thus the end of the war with Great Britain) with "great surprise" and that it would probably adopt a more moderate attitude toward the United States, which could be reflected in new credentials and new instructions that might be sent to Onís.[30] That news seemed encouraging, and it prompted the secretary of the Treasury, Alexander James Dallas, to consider whether the United States might now speak to Madrid in "a language of defiance." On reflection, though, Dallas concluded that a "conciliatory" course that met Spain "more than half way" might be preferable. "We can deal better with Spain detached from England," he wrote to the president, who had retired briefly to Montpelier, "than by protracting the direction of our existing differences, until the two powers become again united for some common object." And even if it should prove necessary to take "strong measures" with regard to Florida, he added, "the more we have done to make them unnecessary, the more certain we may be of the support of the nation, and of Congress."[31]

Eventually, Madison reached the same conclusion. His first move was to ask Dallas to have a meeting with Onís, on which occasion the Treasury secretary learned that although the minister had been sent new credentials in January 1815, he had been given no instructions, which meant he lacked authority to enter into negotiations.[32] Onís, however, insisted he be received, and by mid-July the president conceded, albeit reluctantly, that it was probably only a matter of time before his request would have to be granted.[33] To get around the deadlock that had arisen over which government should make the first move, Monroe opted to make a direct approach to Cevallos by stating that the United States would recognize Onís if he was given new credentials and if Ferdinand VII asked the president to accept his minister as a personal favor rather than as an obligation that Spain might impose as a precondition for negotiations.[34] This last request did not mean that the prospect of Onís as an accredited envoy in Washington had become more palatable to Madison, but it did go some way toward alleviating his concern that the reason why Spain had persisted in its demand that the United States take the first step was to extract from him some sort of admission of wrongdoing and the equivalent of an apology for his not having treated Onís more generously when he had arrived in the United States in 1809.[35]

While waiting for Cevallos's response, Onís, as Madison put it, discharged "an incessant fire" of communications at the State Department.[36] These were largely demands that the administration take positive steps to enforce the 1794 Neutrality Act against filibustering and privateering groups that were organizing, mostly in Louisiana, either for further expeditions against Mexico or for the purpose of aiding rebels in Spain's South American possessions.[37] Both Gutiérrez and Toledo were involved in the former projects, which were being undertaken on behalf of the Mexican Congress movement and its delegate to the United States, Juan Manuel de Herrara. On this occasion they were backed by a loose "association" of New Orleans lawyers, merchants, and other adventurers, including the Laffite brothers and the pirates of Barataria.[38] The administration took these matters seriously, understanding full well that unless it could prevent American territory from being used as a base for hostile acts against Mexico, future negotiations with Madrid would be jeopardized. The same concern also applied to the question of whether South American rebel vessels could use American ports. On the problem of the filibusters, the State Department instructed the U.S. attorney in New Orleans, John Dick, to take all legal steps to prevent them, and Madison reinforced that decision by releasing a proclamation, dated 1 September 1815, enjoining all civil and military officials to search out and bring to punishment "all persons engaged or concerned in such enterprises" and to seize "all arms, military stores, vessels or other means provided or providing for the same."[39] The question of rebel vessels using American ports was rather more complicated as the administration, in the longer run, had no desire to discourage the cause of Spanish-American independence but did not wish for that sentiment to prejudice the settlement of its own disputes with Spain. The solution Madison reached was to reaffirm the policy of strict neutrality between the royalist and rebel forces similar to that which he had pursued between 1808 and 1814 with regard to the opposing forces in the Iberian Peninsula itself.[40]

In Madrid, Cevallos indulged in some quibbling over the stipulations Madison and Monroe had imposed for the reception of Onís. In fact, he largely ignored the July letter sent by the secretary of state and chose to respond instead to some earlier correspondence he had received from Onís on the same subject. While Cevallos agreed that the king could not force the president to receive an "objectionable" minister, he pointed out, sarcastically, that Ferdinand VII had no way of acquiring official knowledge that his American minister was so "objectionable." Nor would the king go so far as to request any personal accommodation. The most he was prepared to say was that the reception of Onís "would be agreeable to him" as he was confident the minister would "contribute on his part to the ties of Friendship and good understanding" he wished to preserve with the United States. As proof of his good faith in the matter Cevallos then announced that he had sent a passport to Erving in Paris to permit him to travel to Madrid.[41] The barriers to the resumption of full diplomatic relations were slowly being lowered, but some problems still remained. One was Erving himself, who, having heard nothing from Washington for several months, had concluded that Madison would continue a policy of delay with regard to Spain. Accordingly, he left for home in July 1815 to deal with some private business matters, and he arrived in New York in October.[42] The other problem was whether Madison would accept Cevallos's letter. As Monroe pointed out to Onís, when the president read the letter, it was "not such in all respects" as he had expected or was even entitled to expect. Nevertheless, the president decided not to prolong the dispute, and he directed Monroe to complete the formalities for receiving Onís.[43] The minister finally presented his credentials on 19 December 1815.

After six years of waiting for this moment, Onís opened his diplomatic campaign almost immediately. On 30 December 1815 he sent Monroe a note announcing that relations had now been restored to the status quo ante of May 1808. On that basis he requested the return of those portions of West Florida occupied in 1810 and 1813, called for the arrest and punishment of Gutiérrez, Humbert, Herrara, Toledo, and Robinson as well as any others of their acquaintance who had been engaged in filibustering, and demanded that the United States close its ports to vessels from Spain's rebellious South American colonies.[44] Three weeks later Monroe responded by objecting that Onís had ignored American grievances against Spain, all of them long-standing and unsettled before 1808. Monroe restated their substance—the unratified Convention of 1802 and the unpaid spoliation claims, the withdrawal of the right of deposit at New Orleans in 1802, and the disputed boundaries of Louisiana—to which he added more recent complaints about the use British troops had made of Floridian territory in the events culminating in their attack on New Orleans. The secretary of state also denied American responsibility for the filibusters, claiming they were "inconsiderable" in number and beyond the reach of American law. Finally, he rejected the demand for the closure of American ports by defending the policy of neutrality in the South American wars for independence.[45]

Just over one month later, on 22 February 1816, Onís repeated his demands with regard to the issues of filibustering and the closure of American ports. He also rejected American claims that West Florida and Texas had been part of Louisiana and denied that Ferdinand VII could be fairly held accountable for British behavior in Florida in 1814–15. After including a good deal of documentation in support of his contentions, especially those relating to the facility with which the filibusters had organized many of their activities on American soil, he pointed out that if the administration did not wish to settle with him in Washington, it should consider doing so in Madrid by giving Erving, who had not yet returned to Spain, adequate powers to do so.[46] The administration decided to take the minister at his word. Sensing it would make no progress on the basis of the ground staked out by Onís, it ignored him for nearly the next four months.

As Erving told Monroe, everything he had received from the minister could be dismissed as "the froth & scum of Cevallos's mushy brain." The Spanish, he maintained, had said "all that they have to say" and their "bolt is shot; hereafter their communications will be but reiterations."[47] In the interval the administration concentrated on drawing up a statement of its own approach to the problems with Spain that Erving could take back to Madrid in the spring of 1816.

The considerations underlying Erving's new instructions both extended and modified those that had governed American policy toward Spain before 1808. The substance of the disputes to be settled remained the same— the 1802 convention and the unpaid "French" spoliations as well as the need for clear and negotiated boundaries for Louisiana that at the very least acknowledged that West Florida to the Perdido River had been purchased in 1803. If the United States could attain its goals on these issues, other matters, including the withdrawal of the deposit at New Orleans in 1802 and the British incursions into Florida in 1814, could be treated as being of less concern. In 1816, moreover, no deadline was set for their accomplishment, nor was there any need to decide on whether money might be paid to either France or Spain to facilitate a settlement. With the war in Europe now over and Spain facing difficult and distracting problems both at home and in South America, the administration also assumed it would be under no particular pressure to make undue or hasty concessions. Admittedly, Morris was still reporting rumors that Spain might cede Florida to Great Britain, but Erving believed that these could be safely disregarded. After all, he pointed out, Great Britain would probably not have good reasons "to throw the gauntlet in our face" so soon after the end of the War of 1812, nor would Spain have any strong motives to place Great Britain in a position where it could threaten its control of such important colonies as Cuba and Mexico.[48]

Nevertheless, the administration was under no illusion that a settlement would be easy. Madison and Monroe were well aware that there remained an enormous legacy of hostility to overcome in Madrid for all the events that had occurred between 1795 and 1815, and they knew Madrid would be dilatory, if not obstructive, in negotiating. And there was still the question of what price the United States would pay for a treaty. If money was no longer a major consideration, territory certainly would be. On this last subject, Madison decided to go further than either he or Jefferson had been prepared to go before 1808, even to the extent of accepting a clear western boundary on the Sabine River—with no intervening "neutral ground" between American and Spanish territory—as opposed to a line in the more remote regions of the Colorado River or the Bay of St. Bernard. Certainly, Erving was also directed to try for a better western boundary than the Sabine, but he could ultimately concede if it proved "indispensably necessary" to obtain a treaty.[49] Here it might be assumed that the idea of a neutral ground had ceased to have much appeal, practical experience after 1806 having demonstrated that such a zone only became a no-man's-land that facilitated rather than inhibited criminality and filibustering. In that context, a mere line on the map promised to be a more effective barrier against future conflict between Americans and Spaniards than a physical space that actually separated them.[50] But in reaching that conclusion, Madison made an additional stipulation. Assuming that Spain would ultimately acknowledge the 1803 American title to West Florida, accept American spoliation claims, and cede East Florida to the United States in return for its relinquishing most, if not all, of the claim to Texas, Erving was instructed not to settle the northern and western boundaries between Spanish and American territories in ways that would jeopardize "our claims on Columbia River, and on the Pacific."[51] In other words, provided the United States came into undisputed possession of all Spanish territory east of the Mississippi, the administration was prepared to abandon Texas in a boundary settlement that confirmed by treaty that the United States had valid claims in the Pacific Northwest.

That Spain's colonial territories on the west coast of North America might pose foreign policy problems for the United States had been apparent at least as early as 1790, when the crisis at Nootka Sound had threatened to embroil the republic in a European war.[52] The crisis was averted when Spain, in order to avoid conflict with Great Britain, agreed to abandon its exclusive claims in the Pacific Ocean, thereafter leaving the region open to commercial and colonizing ventures by Great Britain and other powers. The British government lost no time in consolidating its triumph over Spain by dispatching Royal Navy Captain George Vancouver to the Pacific Northwest with instructions to survey the coastline and ascertain whether there was any navigable passage between the North Pacific and North Atlantic oceans. In the course of doing so, he encountered, in April 1792, the American merchant vessel *Columbia,* commanded by Robert Gray of Boston, who was seeking sealskins and other furs for a trade that would take him across the Pacific to Hawaii and, ultimately, to China. After the meeting of the two captains, it became apparent that Gray, in the course of his voyage, had discovered the mouth of the Columbia River and that Vancouver had missed it. On the basis of "this casual discovery, this accident of the fur trade," as one historian has described it, the claim of the United States to possessing territorial rights in the Pacific Northwest was born.[53]

No American was more aware of the potential significance of this discovery than Jefferson. Indeed, from the earliest days of American independence in 1783 Jefferson had worried that British traders from Montreal would push westward to the Pacific coast to monopolize the trade of the region and become inconvenient neighbors for the United States, even though the republic had scarcely extended its own western boundary to the Mississippi. In 1793, in his last days as secretary of state, Jefferson had also tried to encourage the French botanist (and secret agent) André Michaux to explore the Missouri River to its source in the Rocky Mountains and then seek a route to the Pacific through "a river called Oregan." Nothing came of this, but the success of the Scottish explorer Alexander Mackenzie in reaching the Pacific in 1793 under the employ of the Northwest Company and the subsequent publication of his exploits in 1801 only heightened Jefferson's concerns. As he read Mackenzie's *Voyages from Montreal* in late 1802, Jefferson noted the positive assessment the Scot had made of the feasibility of the Columbia River as a route for commerce between the Atlantic and the Pacific. The response of the third president was crystallized in his decision a few months later to send Captains William Clark and Meriwether Lewis off on a voyage of discovery and scientific exploration to establish an American path to the Pacific.[54]

The assumptions embodied in the instructions Jefferson wrote for Lewis and Clark in June 1803 reflected the beliefs, widely held by most contemporary explorers and geographers, that the sources of all major North American rivers in the West could be found in fairly close proximity to one another and that they were separated by little more than a single divide that might be easily portaged. Related to these assumptions was the view that the Rocky Mountains consisted of little more than a single ridge, or perhaps a series of relatively narrow ridges, that might be traversed with similar ease.[55] In July 1803, however, Jefferson and Madison learned that Livingston and Monroe in Paris had purchased a title to Louisiana that embraced a vast and scarcely defined amount of the trans-Mississippi West. That development promised to facilitate the passage of Lewis and Clark through the Northwest—at least they no longer needed to worry so much about possible obstruction from the handful of Spanish officials remaining in upper Louisiana—but it also required the administration to undertake further voyages of exploration. As Jefferson pointed out to Lewis, because "the boundaries of interior Louisiana are the *high lands inclosing all the waters which run into the Mississippi or Missouri directly or indirectly,* with a greater breadth on the gulph of Mexico, it becomes interesting to fix with precision by celestial observations the longitude & latitude of the sources of these rivers, and furnishing the points in the contour of our new limits."[56] From those concerns arose the southwestern expeditions headed by William Dunbar, George Hunter, Peter Custis, and Thomas Freeman between 1804 and 1806.

All these enterprises were failures in the sense that they accomplished little toward clarifying the boundaries of Louisiana and provided the United States with no immediately useful information for its disputes with Spain.[57] Lewis and Clark were more successful inasmuch as they completed voyages to and from the Pacific, but their findings hardly confirmed the prevailing wisdom about the nature of the river systems and the mountains in the West or about the presumed ease of traversing them. In fact, the two captains' accounts of the immense size of the Rocky Mountains and the difficulties of passing through their many jagged ridges and passes, to say nothing of the turbulent nature of the rivers, most of which led neither to the Columbia nor to the Pacific, were positively depressing. Yet this news was not widely disseminated in the years immediately after Lewis and Clark's return to Washington in 1806, largely because of a number of difficulties, including the suicide of Lewis himself in 1809, in arranging for the publication of their journals.[58] Consequently, many of the assumptions that had inspired Jefferson to send them on their mission continued to circulate in various ways for several years after the mission's conclusion.

For example, shortly after Jefferson retired from the presidency, U.S.

Navy Master Commandant David Porter sent him a proposal in August 1809 for another voyage of discovery to the Pacific Northwest. Porter knew nothing of the findings of Lewis and Clark, though he had a vague sense they had not been successful in establishing a northwestern route to the Pacific. But rather than conclude that the project itself was "chemerical," Porter chose to believe there still existed "a more easy and direct mode of communication between the Atlantic states and the shores of the Pacific." By that, Porter did not mean a direct ocean passage across the top of the North American continent so much as, he hoped, an as-yet-undiscovered point of entry on the Pacific coast, between either the latitudes of 38 and 48° N or 50 and 58° N, that might lead sufficiently far inland so as "to make the land carriage to some of the great branches of the Mississippi short." If so, he predicted, "the intercourse between India and the Atlantic states could be rendered easy and we should probably by means of regular Caravans (such as are established in Egypt, Persia, Barbary &c) reap all the advantages that could result to Europe from the discovery of a N.W. passage."[59] Porter also sent a copy of this proposal to the Navy Department. He was not entirely sure the fourth president would like it, but he did not "despair of Mr. Madison's patronage" either. The departmental chief clerk sent it to the president, coupled with the prediction that he would not "at this time approve the project."[60] The clerk was right. Madison ignored it, and indeed throughout his entire tenure in the State Department between 1801 and 1809 his correspondence reveals that he had paid little or no attention to Jefferson's enthusiasm for finding a route to the Pacific.

Yet Madison's indifference was not enough to kill American dreams of the Pacific. By 1810 the New York merchant John Jacob Astor had established his Pacific Fur Company to execute a scheme, based very much on presumptions called into question by Lewis and Clark, that envisioned the construction of a trading post at the mouth of the Columbia River that would be connected by a series of inland posts to the Mississippi and Missouri rivers. Astor lobbied hard to obtain some degree of administration sanction for his plans—which he hoped would lead to his gaining total control of the northwestern fur trade and position him to extend it to China—but Madison responded to these overtures with a silence that hinted more of disapproval than support. It was no secret that Astor's plans would lead to rivalry with the interests of the Alaska-based Russian-American Company that had been created by Paul I in 1799, and the difficulties of Anglo-American relations throughout Madison's first term very much dictated a policy of cultivating Russian sympathy on issues of commerce and maritime rights. Even so, Astor was sufficiently encouraged to pursue his plans by the interest shown in them by Treasury Secretary Gallatin, and in the summer of 1811 he established the post of Astoria at the mouth of the Columbia River.[61]

Astoria, however, became a victim of the misfortunes of the War of 1812. Cut off by the conflict from all contact with the east coast of the United States, the Astorians decided to sell the post to their British Northwest Company rivals in October 1813. Two months later, in December 1813, Royal Navy officers from HMS *Racoon* reinforced the American retreat from the region by taking possession of Astoria in the name of George III and running a Union Jack up its flagpole. This was a needlessly dramatic gesture that in the long run proved to be a serious miscalculation because it contributed in no small part to Astoria and the Pacific coast becoming significant factors in American postwar diplomacy with both Great Britain and Spain. In the short term, though, the episode seemed to be of no very great consequence. Astor, when he finally received the news in July 1814, took it with remarkable equanimity.[62] If Madison had any reaction, it has not been recorded, but he may well have felt that his lack of interest in Pacific questions had been vindicated. Certainly, the president had more important issues on his mind in the years between 1812 and 1815.

By an unusual quirk of circumstances, though, it was to be Shaler who reminded the administration of the significance of the Pacific Northwest and Astoria for its boundary disputes with Spain. As the agent hastily wrote out his essay on California for the Navy Department before departing for Texas in July 1813, he recapitulated the arguments he had made in his 1808 account of his earlier voyage between "China and the North-Western Coast of America" about the importance of its resources and their potential for development. Before 1813, Shaler had assumed California would eventually become part of an independent Mexican nation, though he also noted that the Spanish authorities in Mexico City had done little to secure their control over the region and that its conquest by a foreign power would be "absolutely nothing; it would fall without effort to the most inconsiderable force." In 1813, however, Shaler feared that the Cádiz Regency would be compelled to cede California to Russia in return for an alliance against Napoleon and that development would extend the rivalries of "the great maritime powers of Europe" into the Pacific in ways that threatened American interests. Pointing out that the United States needed to expand its own trade with China, that it had a right to the Columbia River "by every right of property ever alledged in such cases," and that "our enterprising citizens [have] begun a settlement at the mouth of that river"—which Shaler, too, still believed lay within easy reach of the Missouri River—he urged the administration to consider the case for obtaining California from an independent Mexico.[63]

Shaler believed Mexico would readily consent to such a cession. After all, he asserted, the Mexicans themselves would probably do little to develop a carrying trade in the Pacific, and their inability to do so would leave them dependent on either Great Britain or Russia in that respect. Thus vulnerable "to the ambition of Europe," the Mexicans, he assumed, would prefer to place their Pacific trade in the hands of Americans, and for that purpose they would cede California to the United States "without difficulty." And as the United States increased its own trade through the Missouri and Columbia rivers and built up the fisheries and a coasting trade in the Pacific Northwest, it would be able "completely to develop the resources of the western portion of our Empire" and thus "lay the foundation for a commerce on the [Pacific] ocean, which at no distant day may become equal to that we enjoy on the Atlantic." That, Shaler claimed, would "give us a preponderance there that no European power could ever shake." As he projected this vision of the future, the agent was warning the administration that Russia was the power most likely to encroach on California in the immediate future, but he also concluded his essay with the observation that "no notice has been taken of either England or France in the foregoing from a belief that their ambition and resources are so well known as to make it quite unnecessary."[64]

Shaler's essay appears to have provoked a reaction in Washington. Navy Secretary William Jones docketed it as "interesting," and it is reasonable to conclude that its contents were discussed at greater length during Shaler's visit to the capital over the winter of 1813–14. When the agent was given his new brief in February 1814 to act as a bearer of dispatches and gatherer of information for the American peace negotiators in Europe, he was specifically directed to turn his attention not only to the problems of Anglo-American relations but also to "Florida, the Spanish provinces in America, and even old Spain, and also the territories of America on the Pacific Ocean."[65] These remarks assumed (implicitly) at least two things. One was that all the issues at stake in the Napoleonic Wars—colonial, maritime, and territorial—might be dealt with in a comprehensive peace settlement not unlike that which had concluded the War of the Spanish Succession at Utrecht in 1713.[66] The other was that Spain itself had been so weakened by the events of 1808–1814 that it was by no means impossible that significant transfers of Spanish-American territory to other European powers would form part of the settlement. That thoughts along these lines had occurred to the administration is strongly suggested by a 22 March 1814 instruction Monroe sent to the American peace commissioners to remind them that "the United States had in their possession at the commencement of the war a post at the mouth of the River Columbia which commanded the river." Here Monroe was anticipating the possibility that Astoria might be conquered and held by the British and that even before the news of its capture had been received in Washington, he was stipulating it be returned. In that manner, well before negotiations to end the war had begun, the administration had rejected the view that Great Britain had "any claim whatever to Territory on the Pacific Ocean."[67]

The Treaty of Ghent in December 1814 provided for the mutual restoration of all territories and places occupied by Great Britain and the United States during the War of 1812. Nothing was done immediately to reclaim Astoria, in part because the U.S. Navy was too preoccupied with a war against Algiers and the problems of policing the Caribbean against pirates operating out of ports in Spain's rebellious American colonies to spare the vessels for an extended cruise into the Pacific. Astor continued to press the administration to restore Astoria to him, but eventually he relinquished this hope and wrote the matter off as a bad business venture. Nevertheless, even as the Navy could not spare vessels for the Pacific, the importance of the region was highlighted again by David Porter, who, in 1815, published a lengthy account of the exploits of his naval squadron there against British cruisers and whalers between 1812 and 1814. And although Porter's Pacific cruise had culminated in the loss of his flagship, the USS *Essex*, at the

Battle of Valparaiso in March 1814, the commodore, four months previously in November 1813, had annexed the island of Nukahiva in the Marquesas group to the United States. He renamed it "Madison's Island," with a capital of "Madisonville," to be defended by "Fort Madison" in Taiohae Bay, which, in order not to appear unduly repetitious, he marked on his map as "Massachusetts Bay."[68]

The president was unmoved by this outburst of imperialism, but Porter followed it up in October 1815 with another letter to Madison about the importance of the Pacific to the United States. On this occasion he abandoned his 1809 arguments about a transcontinental route to the Northwest in favor of advocating a voyage of discovery and exploration into the Pacific itself for the purpose of persuading the rulers of China and Japan to begin opening their ports to outsiders. For the most part, Porter justified this proposal as a contribution to scientific knowledge. There were, he pointed out, vast areas of the Pacific that remained unknown to explorers and geographers, but he was not unmindful of the commercial benefits either. Noting that not even the British had been admitted to China and that only the Dutch had gained access to Japan—and "by the most abject and servile means" too—he proclaimed that "the time may be favorable, and it would be a glory beyond that acquired by any other nation for us, a nation of only forty years standing, to beat down their rooted prejudices, secure to ourselves a valuable trade, and make that people known to the world."[69]

As had been the case in 1809, the president made no reply, but it was becoming increasingly difficult to deny that the United States needed a policy for the Pacific. Almost twenty years later, in 1835, Gallatin, who was in Washington briefly in the spring of 1816, would recall for Astor that it was at this very time he gained the impression that Madison was now prepared to respond more actively to developments in the Pacific than he had in the past.[70] The instructions written for Erving on 30 May 1816 confirm the accuracy of Gallatin's memory on this point. Three weeks later there was a new crisis in the Pacific. Reports reached the capital that Spanish officials in Peru had seized twenty-six American whaling vessels because they lacked a sea letter according to the Spanish interpretation of article 12 of the 1795 treaty. The administration disputed this view, but more importantly both the secretary of state and the Treasury secretary informed the president that insurance, mercantile, and whaling interests were demanding not only restitution but also that a frigate be sent into the Pacific to compel respect for the American flag.[71] Madison did not disagree, and as he consented to the advice of his colleagues he suggested that the frigate should also "visit the mouth of Columbia as belonging to the United States" but without using any force, in order to avoid the risk of a conflict with Great Britain. As it happened, the frigate designated for this purpose, the USS *Congress,* had to be diverted to the Caribbean in order to respond to a later incident in which a Spanish squadron had fired on an American naval vessel, the USS *Firebrand,* off Veracruz. But as Madison reviewed these matters, he requested that the members of his cabinet "undergo a liberal consultation" on "the critical state of our affairs with Spain." "Little more is wanting," he concluded, "if there be not enough already, to call for some final explanation from her."[72]

If Madison hoped the return of Erving to Madrid would expedite a settlement with Spain, he was to be disappointed. Even before the envoy had reached his destination, the news was bad. Writing from Paris in June 1816, Erving reported that the state of Spain's "domestick affairs is most unfavorable" and that he could not indulge in any "hopes of success." In Spain, he continued, there was "a total disaffection amongst all classes—even to the priesthood; universal misery in the government[;] total ineptitude & penury; certainly a dismal perspective." Lest the administration should be tempted to conclude that this state of affairs might incline Madrid to accept American demands, Erving warned that "a government which must needs be wholly engrossed with the care of its own preservation to which we cannot contribute can scarcely be expected to occupy itself, seriously in political arrangements of remote advantage." In short, the government of Spain had "not improved since the time of Charles the 4th either in its morality or its good sense," and Erving feared that a government that could look only to "its necessities or its apprehensions" would not act reasonably or responsibly. Indeed, all the "respectable opinions" Erving had consulted in Paris were agreed that it was "impossible that the system should stand for six months."[73]

Accordingly, Erving's dealings with Cevallos were short and unproductive, with his dispatches and private letters from Madrid amounting to little more than amplifications of the impressions he had reported from Paris.

Ferdinand VII he denounced as bad-tempered, jealous, suspicious, and vindictive. Worse, he had taken to bypassing his ministers and secretaries and ruling instead through an unofficial *camarilla* (clique) consisting of court favorites and the Russian ambassador, Count Dimitri Pavlovich Tatishchev. Cevallos was no better. Erving conceded that the foreign secretary was "just intelligent enough" to prepare for the "evil day" he knew would soon befall Spain, but he was also corrupt, selfish, servile, and weak, his character having "deteriorated" since the American minister had last encountered it a decade ago. At their only meeting of any length in September 1816, Erving proposed that Spain and the United States settle their differences within three weeks, only to hear Cevallos reply that "he could not give me three hours in three weeks." The two diplomats restated and rebuffed the positions of their respective governments on the issues at stake, but at the end of the meeting Cevallos suggested the negotiation be transferred back to Washington to get rid of "the weight and trouble of it here." Erving hardly bothered to contest the request.[74]

Possibly Erving was the wrong man for Madison to have sent to Madrid, since he could scarcely conceal his anger and contempt for what he saw at the Spanish court. It is unlikely, however, that a more conciliatory diplomat could have done better. As the minister himself pointed out, "Too much mildness swells [the Spaniards] into pride & self-importance, and produces a mulish obstinancy; by a contrary course as their situation is desperate, there is danger of putting them to defying consequences."[75] But the reality was that Spain, to the extent it was concerned with American questions, was still too preoccupied with the rebellions in South America—which it assumed could be suppressed—to pay enough attention to thinking about a settlement with the United States, as Madison and Monroe were about to find out.[76] When the negotiations resumed in Washington in January 1817, Onís had already suggested, in conversation, that Spain could relinquish both East and West Florida in return for the United States surrendering its claim to any territory west of the Mississippi. Since this transaction would require the United States to abandon its claim not only to Texas but also to the entire Louisiana Purchase, including the state of Louisiana, which had been admitted to the Union in 1812, Monroe rejected it. He inquired, instead, whether Onís would negotiate on other matters, such as the 1802 convention and spoliations.[77]

The minister, however, presented written proposals for the mutual exchange of territory, insisting there had to be a true reciprocity on territorial questions and revealing at the same time that he lacked instructions to make any specific concessions. Nor would Spain negotiate on other matters until the boundaries of Louisiana had been settled first. Monroe could do little more than express regret that the Spanish minister had yet to receive adequate instructions from his government.[78]

The immediate consequence of this situation was that Madison would complete his second term in March 1817 without having achieved a settlement of any of the disputes with Spain. Nevertheless, during the president's last months in Washington, discussions on matters other than the boundaries of Louisiana continued, largely in the form of Onís's demands that the administration take further steps to suppress filibustering expeditions against Mexico and to close American ports to all vessels, including those belonging to pirates, sailing to and from Spain's rebellious colonies.[79] At first, no progress was made, with Madison on one occasion directing Monroe to give Onís no more than "the ordinary answer," namely that "the law of Nations, and our position in relation to the contest between Spain and Spanish America will of course govern the reply to these representations."[80] By the end of 1816, however, Madison conceded that "the ordinary answer" would no longer suffice. His change of mind may have owed a little to a belated awareness of the ease with which anti-Spanish forces had continued to avail themselves of American resources and territory for their enterprises as well as to a better understanding of the practical difficulties U.S. officials had encountered in enforcing the 1794 Neutrality Law. It was also obvious that Spain would continue to exploit these problems to delay negotiations. But it was probably the *Firebrand* incident of August 1816 that did the most to alter the president's thinking here.

On that occasion, Spanish warships, in an effort to thwart a filibuster against Galveston headed by Louis Aury and backed by the "associates" in New Orleans, had attacked and briefly detained the USS *Firebrand,* formerly a pirate vessel that had been captured and refitted by the U.S. Navy, as it provided convoy protection for the anti-Spanish insurgents. This was not the first occasion on which Commodore Daniel Patterson, the ranking Navy officer at New Orleans, had permitted the vessel to be used for such improper purposes, which were unquestionably contrary to administration policy.[81] In response, Madison, in mid-October, personally drafted new instructions for U.S. Navy vessels in the Caribbean to police the sea more vigorously against piracy and to enforce more stringently the policy of neutrality between Spain and its rebellious colonies.[82] He reinforced that decision in December by requesting new legislation either to detain armed vessels that had been equipped in American ports or to require the owners of such vessels to provide "adequate securities against the abuse of their armaments."[83] This proposal was not entirely popular. Some legislators thought it conceded too much to pressure from Spain; others feared that it failed to demonstrate a proper republican sympathy for the cause of Spanish-American independence. But the legislation was passed, with fines of up to $10,000 and up to ten years imprisonment for violations, and Madison signed it on his last day in office, 3 March 1817.[84]

When Madison left the presidency the next day, his feelings about what he might have contributed toward an ultimate settlement of the disputes between Spain and the United States were undoubtedly mixed. Although he always realized that the diplomacy would be protracted (and he had personally contributed to its protraction by his reluctance to deal with Onís), he could not resist a final complaint about the "habitual mean cunning" of the Spanish government, which, "after drawing the negotiations to Madrid, has now sent them back to Onís with powers, without instructions." That would suggest, at least, some sense of personal disappointment. But, as always, Madison preferred to strike a more optimistic tone. The Spaniards "foolishly forget," he continued, "that, with respect to territorial questions at least, we are in possession of that portion of our claims, which is immediately wanted."[85] By that statement, the president meant to indicate that Congress had recently undertaken a reorganization of the Mississippi Territory that would provide for the inclusion of portions of West Florida as far east as the Perdido River in both the new state of Mississippi and the new territory of Alabama.[86] With the addition of a second state on the Gulf Coast comprising some of the territories acquired between 1803 and 1813, it would become increasingly difficult for Spain to adhere to the notion that its boundary disputes with the United States could be solved by a mutual exchange of their claims on the eastern and western banks of the Mississippi. Nor did Madison anticipate that Spain's most powerful ally, Great Britain, would come to its rescue. "The British

Cabinet," he noted, "seems as well disposed as is consistent with its jealousies, and the prejudices it has worked up in the nation agst. us." As for the remaining matters, he concluded, "delay is our ally, and even Guarantee for everything."[87]

After 4 March 1817 Madison became a spectator to the events that led to the final settlement with Spain. For information about the course of the negotiations between Onís and Monroe's successor in the State Department, John Quincy Adams, he was, inevitably, dependent on what he could read in the newspapers and on accounts provided by his correspondents and by visitors to Montpelier. His most frequent correspondent was his own successor, Monroe, who regularly sent him copies of the documents on Spanish affairs that he communicated to Congress, on the assumption that they would be "interesting" to him, "having so long been a party to them."[88] In doing so, Monroe may well have been seeking advice about, and confirmation of, his own decisions as much as he was conveying information, though on occasion Madison confessed he did not always read all the Spanish material he received.[89] Such admissions need not be read as proof that Madison had lost interest in the disputes with Spain. He had invested far too much of his own public life in these matters to be indifferent to their outcomes. But now that he was out of office, Madison no longer felt the compulsion to attend to state papers in the manner that he had while in Washington between 1801 and 1817. Nor did he need to. There was little about the substance of American relations with Spain between 1817 and 1821 that he was not already thoroughly familiar with, and the policies of the Monroe administration did not significantly depart from those he had contemplated or pursued himself. Madison also knew that Madrid would continue to be difficult, and he had developed over the years a deeply ingrained dislike of the condescending and dilatory ways in which its representatives conducted their business. As he once joked to Jefferson after the latter had recovered from a serious illness, he could not bring himself to say "with the Spaniards I kiss your hands, but I say with all my heart, God preserve you much[o]s añ[o]s."[90]

Negotiations and policy implementation on the larger agenda that the Madison administration had staked out in May 1816 did not properly get under way until the end of 1817. At that time Adams and Monroe dispatched a naval vessel, the USS *Ontario,* to the Pacific to reclaim Astoria, and in December Adams also commenced negotiations with Onís.[91] For the greater part of the next six months, these negotiations were stalled over the by-now-very-old debate about whether the United States had any valid title to West Florida and Texas. Onís asserted that as the United States had no title at all to the former, Spain could hardly be expected to cede it unless the United States was prepared to make an equivalent cession of its own territory west of the Mississippi (that is, Louisiana). Adams rejected this out of hand and did so with an abrupt demand that Onís cease his "procrastination" and agree to discuss the boundaries that the United States had proposed as long ago as 1805.[92] Notes were also exchanged on other issues, including the 1802 convention, the exclusion of Spanish-American rebel vessels from American ports, and the restraining of filibusters by land.[93] On this last matter, events had recently taken a dramatic turn when Amelia Island, between July and September 1817, was occupied by two insurgent groups, one headed by Gregor McGregor, who claimed to act under a commission issued by the Spanish-American rebels in Cartagena, the other led by Aury and his junta based in Galveston. Seizing on these developments as proof that Spain had lost all capacity to govern its province of East Florida, the United States took possession of the island in December 1817.[94]

Monroe defended this decision as necessary to prevent piracy, smuggling, and illegal slave trading in a territory sharing a border with the United States, to say nothing of the fact that the United States also regarded East Florida as a resource for settling the dispute with Spain over the "French spoliation" claims.[95] Madison did not so much challenge the need for action here as raise questions about what he understood to be Monroe's justifications. As he read the president's messages on the subject, it seemed unclear to him whether the United States had occupied Amelia Island as a way of enforcing a territorial claim to East Florida and whether in doing so it might also have violated the rights of the local Indians to their land. As far as the Indians were concerned, Madison pointed out that the United States could claim only "a right of preemption" over Indian land rather than a right of conquest, and he wondered whether such actions lay within the discretion of the executive anyway.[96] Monroe was perplexed by the misunderstanding. He responded that the facts about the "piratical" nature of the rebel establishments made his reasoning "conclusive," and as for the Indians he declared that the more the United States took them "under our protection, compelling them to cultivate the earth, the better it will be for them."[97] But if Madison had been trying to press Monroe into making a more explicit statement about how his actions might affect American territorial claims in Florida—as he himself had done in 1810–11—he decided not to pursue the matter, dropping it with the remark that he did not mean to question the doctrines in Monroe's messages "under qualifications which were probably entertained without being specified."[98]

Madison showed more interest in the question of whether the United States should acknowledge the independence of Spain's South American colonies. This question was more complicated for Monroe and Adams than it had been for Madison and Monroe. Before 1816 there had been little good evidence that any of the Spanish-American colonies would be able to establish their independence on a permanent basis, but beginning with Buenos Aires in July 1816 and extending into New Granada, Venezuela, and Chile in the first six months of 1817, Spanish royalist forces sustained several serious defeats that seemed to make it unlikely that Madrid would ever regain effective control in South America. Madison's policy of a strict neutrality between the contending forces risked being overtaken by events as agents for the rebel regimes lobbied in Washington for recognition and groups in Congress, headed by Henry Clay of Kentucky and others who were not entirely supportive of the administration generally, began to debate the case for diplomatic recognition and the exchange of ministers.[99]

From Montpelier, Madison was able to express himself much more clearly on this issue than he had been able to do while in Washington. He took it for granted that the "real sense" of American public opinion was in favor of Spanish-American independence and that, ideally, it should be administration policy to have "good wishes for its success and every *lawful* manifestation of them." At the same time, however, to translate these sentiments into active policy now carried a much higher risk of war, the more so as Spain was mounting a vigorous diplomatic campaign to prevent European nations, and especially Great Britain and Russia, from recognizing the rebel regimes. That campaign, moreover, had been successful to the extent that Great Britain had agreed to resume its earlier efforts to offer mediation between Madrid and its colonies, while Russia not only endorsed the British policy but through Alexander I also hinted that should the offer of mediation fail "to produce a moral effect on the Colonies," an "application of force" might follow.[100]

Madison took the risk of war with Great Britain seriously in this case, much more so than he ever did based on the occasional rumors that still circulated that war between London and Washington might result from Spain's ceding Florida to Great Britain. The administration attempted to defuse the pressures for recognition of the rebel regimes by sending a three-man commission to South America in December 1817 to make a full assessment of the situation in the region comprising Buenos Aires, Chile, and Peru, and Madison concurred with the wisdom of this "circumspect policy."[101] He also realized that diplomatic success on the issue in Europe had the effect of stiffening Spain in its resolve not to negotiate seriously with the United States until such time as it, too, should undertake not to recognize independent governments in South America. If there was an element of paradox in the British position as Madison understood it, it arose from his awareness that while Great Britain appeared to be in favor of upholding Spain's outmoded pretensions and monopolistic practices in the New World, its commercial policies were gradually leading it in the direction of the removal of trade barriers and the opening of markets, preferably for its own advantage. That led him to suggest that the best policy for the United States to follow would be to try to persuade other European nations, especially France and Russia, to adopt "our liberal and provident view in favor of S[outh] America." "The great worth of its emancipation," he argued, "would then be completed per Saltum; for Great Britain could not hold back if so disposed, and Spain would have no choice but acquiescence."[102]

One reason why American policy did not develop along these lines was the intensification of the dispute over boundaries in the summer of 1818 following Andrew Jackson's seizure of Pensacola and St. Marks in May. Jackson had entered Spanish territory in the course of pursuing Creek Indians who had attacked American settlers, and when he also found two British subjects, Robert Ambrister and Alexander Arbuthnot, in the Indian towns, he executed them on suspicion of their having encouraged a war against the United States. After much debate, the administration realized that to disavow Jackson, as Onís demanded, and possibly even consider reparations for his conduct, would retard the negotiations with Spain for some considerable time. Accordingly, it chose to blame Spain for the crisis by faulting it for not restraining the Indians from hostilities, as it was required to do under article 5 of the 1795 treaty.[103] Onís, however, had little desire to rupture negotiations over Jackson's behavior, and in July he and Adams, with the French minister Hyde de Neuville often acting as an intermediary, began to modify their positions on boundaries.[104] Putting Florida aside for the moment, Onís, who had received instructions that would allow him to cede the Floridas in return for a permanent boundary line west of the Mississippi coupled with American promises not to aid or recognize the rebels in South America, hinted that Spain was now ready to proceed with negotiations on that basis.[105]

Adams reciprocated by offering to move the American boundary claim away from the Rio Grande to the Bay of St. Bernard and then suggesting that a line drawn from the source of the Red River might be extended to the Pacific coast.[106] He thus began to build on the strategy that Monroe had first outlined to Erving in May 1816 and that the president and Adams had further discussed in February 1818, though no hint had been given to Onís at that time about the ultimate direction of the administration's thinking.[107] In July 1818, however, Adams decided it was opportune to introduce the question of a line to the Pacific, partly in response to the shift in Madrid's position, partly as a way of maintaining the pressure on Spain at the same time, and partly because he could now safely do so after having recently learned that Great Britain would not contest the American decision to reclaim Astoria or deny that the United States had valid claims in the Oregon country.[108] Doubtless the secretary of state was assuming that if Spain could be persuaded to concede a boundary on the Pacific, his hand would also be greatly strengthened in any future dealings with Great Britain in that region.

Throughout the crisis created by Jackson, Monroe took pains to explain the considerations that guided his conduct to both Jefferson and Madison. He stressed that he had not authorized the general, either directly or indirectly, to enter Florida as a way of enforcing American territorial claims, while also making it clear that he understood that the matter had to be handled in ways that did not put the United States at a disadvantage in negotiations with Spain or expose the president to the charge that he had illegally committed an act of war.[109] It is unlikely, though, that Madison ever thought that Jackson had prior administration consent to enter Florida, as Jackson was to claim, and he would not have had very much difficulty believing that the general was capable of acting in impulsive and embarrassing ways.[110] But at no time in 1818 was Madison ever indiscreet enough to commit to paper any thoughts that he might have had about either Jackson's conduct or that of the administration. The most he was to venture to observe (to Richard Rush, who was located at a considerable distance in London) was that the president had "some delicate and thorny points on hand, but his sound judgment may be relied on to dispose of them in the best manner they will admit."[111]

The decisions of Adams and Onís to modify their positions on the western boundary of Louisiana proved to be the decisive step in breaking the deadlock over American and Spanish territorial claims. Thereafter, progress in the negotiations, to a large extent, came down to Onís having to persuade Madrid to grant him enough latitude to make whatever concessions were necessary on Florida and the other issues in dispute in order for him to obtain northern and western boundary lines that would protect Mexico by keeping American settlers and traders as far away as possible from Texas and Santa Fe. The minister had long been seeking greater flexibility in his instructions, and his priorities were reinforced by those officials in the *Estado* (Foreign Office) who realized that it was in Spain's interest to abandon its claims east of the Mississippi—to a European power such as Russia if not necessarily to the United States—in order to obtain more sustainable boundaries to the west of the river.[112] It was simply to take a very long time before the king and the *Consejo de Estado* (Council of State) were to see the matter in the same light, even after the indifferent and obstructive Cevallos had been replaced by more astute diplomats, including José García de León y Pizarro and Carlos Martínez de Yrujo, who could share this analysis of Spain's borderland predicament. In that context, one of the more beneficial consequences of Jackson's invasion of Florida as far as the United States was concerned was that it accelerated decision making in Madrid, especially among the more rigid members of the camarilla, about where Spain's priorities in North America really lay.

Once that point had been reached, the negotiations proceeded relatively rapidly. By the beginning of 1819, it had been agreed the United States would restore Pensacola and St. Marks to Spain, provided that Madrid sent responsible officers to take delivery of them and that it was understood the administration would not censure or disavow Jackson for his actions. Indeed, not only was Jackson not censured, but his incursion into Florida was positively vindicated by Adams in a lengthy diplomatic note that was designed much more for consumption in Congress and publication in Europe than it was for the persuasion of Onís.[113] For its part, Spain offered to exchange the long-delayed ratifications of the convention of 1802, and the United States agreed to assume the claims of its citizens for the "French spoliations" up to the amount of $5 million, subject to restrictions on the right of Ferdinand VII to make grants of land in East Florida that might otherwise reduce the financial value of the province to the United States.

Fixing the details of the boundaries was more complicated. Spain finally agreed to cede all its territories east of the Mississippi but jibbed right to the end at doing so in a way that would acknowledge that the United States had purchased a valid title to West Florida extending to the Perdido in 1803. Nor was Spain immediately willing to accept that the United States had any claim to Texas or to offer a boundary to the Pacific, but by mid-February 1819, after the United States had retracted its western boundary to the Sabine River and after Onís had received unrestricted powers to make the best treaty he thought fit, he and Adams were able to settle on western and northern lines that ran from the Sabine up to the Red and Arkansas rivers and then westward along the line of 42° N to the Pacific, at a point that left the remaining Spanish territory in the Northwest well to the south of the Columbia River. The details of these matters were then included in a treaty that was signed on 22 February 1819 and ratified unanimously by the Senate two days later.[114]

Madison viewed these developments calmly. Monroe sent him a summary report on them in early February 1819, focusing mainly on the Florida problem and Jackson's behavior there but hinting at the end of his letter that there was "some prospect of an accommodation with Mr. Onis, immediately and essentially on the conditions offer'd some time since and published."[115] As Madison had been experiencing delays in receiving his newspapers, he responded that he was not entirely up to date on recent events, but he expressed his approval of both Monroe's handling of Jackson and Adams's vindication of his invasion of Florida to the extent these rendered the general's conduct "invulnerable to complaints from abroad" while at the same time not irritating "the scruples of his friends & admirers" at home.[116] To Jefferson he later remarked that "the legality & expediency" of Jackson's actions should be judged "essentially on all the circumstances." Madison never doubted Jackson's patriotism and reiterated that "if he s[houl]d have erred in any point, the error ought not to be separated from that merit & that no-one could thoroughly appreciate the transactions without putting himself precisely in his situation."[117] These observations hardly concealed that Madison had some reservations about Jackson's actions, but he may well have agreed with Monroe that there was sufficient justification for them "in the injuries we have rec'd from the criminal aggressors in Florida, & nothing to palliate their conduct in any claims of Spain on us."[118] And on the likelihood of a final treaty Madison wrote only that "it will be a most happy termination of the business if Onis could make good the prospect of the desired accommodation of our affairs [with] Spain."[119]

The signing of the Transcontinental Treaty should have marked the final settlement of all outstanding disputes between Spain and the United States, dating back to the delayed ratification of the 1802 convention and including, more importantly, the disagreements over the boundaries of Louisiana after 1803. For Spain, the treaty was probably the best it could have obtained under the circumstances. Onís certainly thought so, mindful as he was that by 1818 Spain had already lost effective control over most of its possessions east of the Mississippi, that it was also losing ground in its efforts to maintain control over its South American colonies, and that its European allies, Great Britain in particular, were affording it far less diplomatic support and material aid on these issues than Madrid had initially counted on. Onís was, therefore, more than ready to sacrifice both East and West Florida in return for seeing the United States abandon its claim to Texas, even if that also meant conceding to the Americans a boundary line that extended to the Pacific.[120] But Spain did not have any settlements on the Pacific north of San Francisco anyway, and it would have stood little chance of vindicating its historical claim to the entire Pacific coastline against likely future encroachments from Great Britain and Russia regardless of whether the United States had manifested its interest in the same region or not. In ceding territory on the Pacific to the United States, Spain sacrificed little that was of real value to itself.[121]

For the United States, the treaty was, obviously, a substantial triumph. Not only had the republic rid itself of a troublesome neighbor on its southern border, but it had also fulfilled and even exceeded the visions of what the Union might become when its leaders, in the Model Treaty of 1776 and the Louisiana Purchase treaty of 1803, asserted the claims that it was to be the successor state to both the French and the British empires in North America. Nearly two decades of patient, and often frustrating, diplomacy had vindicated those assertions, with the result that the United States had finally obtained secure control of both the Mississippi River and all other points to the east on the Gulf Coast.[122] If the cost of those gains included the sacrifice of Texas, that mattered relatively little.[123] Neither Jefferson nor Madison nor Monroe had ever believed that Texas, in itself, was worth very much, and the Rio Grande had never featured prominently in their visions for the nation's commercial future; rather, Texas was seen as a useful bargaining chip to obtain other more important objectives. Not even Shaler in his most optimistic moments in Texas had ever tried to claim very much for the value of the province either. And by 1816, Madison, who had never shared Jefferson's early enthusiasm for the Pacific Northwest, had also come to realize that this region was of far greater potential importance to the United States than Texas.

Although the matter seemed settled by 1819, the United States was to be denied a complete sense of triumph over Spain for a further two years. Madrid failed to ratify the Transcontinental Treaty within the six-month period stipulated in its final article. Its reasons for not doing so were primarily concerns about the possibility that the United States would now be free to recognize the independence of the rebellious Spanish-American colonies and that it would continue to assist anti-Spanish insurgents in the New World one way or another. Spain had long wanted to extract treaty guarantees on these issues from the United States, but Adams and Monroe would not agree, and Onís, once he had the authority to do so, had declined to insist on the point in order to conclude the treaty. Of secondary importance in Madrid's decision not to ratify were problems arising from the restrictions in article 8 of the treaty on the ability of Ferdinand VII to make land grants in the territories to be ceded to the United States. No such grants made after 24 January 1818 were to be considered valid, but developments after February 1819 revealed that three substantial and controversial awards the king had made in East Florida to his favorite courtiers—the duque de Alagón, the conde de Puñonrostro, and Pedro de Vargas—bore later dates.[124]

Spain consequently delayed the ratification process while it tried to organize another expeditionary force to regain control over Buenos Aires and sent diplomatic envoys to Washington to seek explanations about its concerns. The delay exposed the administration to some pressure after December 1819 either to declare the treaty void or to take possession of Florida anyway and possibly even seize Texas as well as an indemnity for Spain's refusal to accept a treaty properly negotiated by its representative according to the law of nations. Monroe, however, resisted the pressure in favor of a conciliatory approach that would allow Madrid more time to ratify, and he was encouraged to do so by the foreign ministers of all the major European powers, who agreed with the American position that Spain was obliged to ratify the treaty and should do so.[125] When Madison heard the news, he could only remark that "no folly in the Spanish Govt. can now create surprise," but he also approved of the "moderation" in Monroe's decision to solve the problem by diplomacy rather than by force. He, too, was glad to see that on this occasion the "greatest powers" in Europe seemed "predisposed to do justice to us in this respect."[126]

In Madrid, the American minister, John Forsyth of Georgia, who had replaced Erving in February 1819, was quite unable to persuade Spain to ratify, in part because his diplomatic language and style were so tactless that the foreign ministry seldom bothered to reply to his notes. That particular difficulty was resolved after March 1820 when a liberal revolution in Spain compelled Ferdinand VII to accept the restoration of the Cádiz Constitution of 1812, and the reassembled Cortes in October 1820 directed the king both to ratify the treaty and to nullify the controversial land grants in East Florida. Somewhat reluctantly, he did so, and by December 1820 Monroe was able to report to Madison that he had unofficial accounts from Europe that Spain had finally ratified the treaty. Madison responded that the news was "very agreeable" and hoped the ratification would "arrive without clogs on it."[127] Official news of the unconditional Spanish ratification of the treaty reached Washington by February 1821, and it was again submitted to the Senate for advice and consent, which the Senate gave on 19 February. Three days later, on the second anniversary of the signature of the treaty in 1819, Spain and the United States finally exchanged their instruments of ratification.[128] The quarrel with Spain was at an end.

Shortly after the Transcontinental Treaty had been signed in 1819, Madison received a letter from his former cabinet colleague William Eustis, who regretted that the acquisition of Florida and the settlement of the disputes with Spain had been "reserved to grace the presidency of Mr. Monroe" rather than, as Eustis had wished, that of his predecessor.[129] Madison passed over the compliment his colleague had attempted to pay him, and subsequent generations of historians have seldom bothered to consider whether there might have been any point to Eustis's remark. Possibly Madison did regret that the procrastinating diplomacy of Spain had deprived his administration of the accomplishments reached by Monroe and Adams in 1819, and the formidable authority of Adams's diary has always led historians to grant them the credit for solving the disputes with Spain in ways that seemed to elude Jefferson and Madison.[130] In fact, it proved to be far easier for the Monroe administration to settle the problems with Spain after the conclusion of the Napoleonic Wars than it had been for previous administrations to cope with them during those conflicts. And American success after 1815 owed as much to changes in the geopolitical situation of the United States with respect to the European powers as it did to any differences in the diplomatic skills displayed by its political leaders. Between 1776 and 1815 the governments of France—royalist, republican, and imperial—were prepared to support, in varying degrees, American pretensions to independence and territorial expansion as part of their struggle against Great Britain, but never at the cost of completely alienating their allies in Madrid, be they members of the house of Bourbon or the family of Napoleon Bonaparte. After 1815, however, the restored French Bourbons displayed far less interest in American territorial disputes, and Great Britain was by no means very willing to protect Spanish concerns in these matters either.[131] That situation left Spain to confront the United States with less support from its allies than it needed, and in that confrontation most of the advantages lay with the latter.

But regardless of how favorably or unfavorably historians might assess Madison's skills as a diplomatist and as a chief executive, and without denying that John Quincy Adams was unquestionably more experienced and comfortable with foreign policy matters than the fourth president, it should, nevertheless, be apparent that Madison contributed far more to the early territorial expansion of the United States than has been realized. If his knowledge and understanding of Spanish-American affairs was necessarily less extensive than his familiarity with the problems of Anglo-American and Franco-American relations, Madison, nonetheless, throughout his public life and well before the purchase of Louisiana in 1803, had given a good deal of thought to the problems that arose from the presence of Spain on the Gulf Coast and in the American southwest to the extent that he always realized these problems were unlikely to be solved short of the United States obtaining significant territorial concessions in these regions. And while historians have always understood that the Louisiana Purchase and the subsequent disputes over Florida were a direct consequence of the so-called Mississippi Question of 1784–95, Madison was one of the first American political leaders to realize that even the Mississippi Question itself could not be settled without addressing the problem of Florida as well. He was to pursue that insight consistently, and by 1813 he had effectively taken possession of all of West Florida that the United States claimed it had received title to in 1803.

This is not to say, of course, that Madison's pursuit of this goal was flawless. He achieved success in West Florida by means of conquest and occupation rather than by the diplomacy he would have preferred to employ. Madison also made a serious, albeit understandable, error of judgment in 1810 by assuming that the impending fall of Spain to France would permit him to fill the vacuum about to be created by the collapse of Spanish power on the Gulf Coast with relatively little difficulty. What he failed to provide for was the likelihood that the settlers in West Florida itself might not see matters in the same way and that they would, in a moment of panic, take matters into their own hands by declaring their independence. That action compelled the president to seize the territory by force, if for no other reason than to preserve the very claim that had been staked out in 1803 in the Louisiana Purchase treaty. And Madison was, perhaps, fortunate that there proved to be a large enough number of American settlers in West Florida and the surrounding regions to sustain his actions in 1810, or at least to acquiesce in them, without the province falling into the internal quarrels and dangers of civil war that were to characterize the independence movements of many other parts of the Spanish-American empire after 1810.[132]

East Florida, on the other hand, escaped Madison's grasp. This was not because the American claim to the province was any weaker or any more disputable than the claim to West Florida. It was merely a different claim. Rather, the problem was that there were never enough American settlers or sympathizers in the province to give sufficient reality to the claim made by George Mathews in January 1811 that the local population could stage a successful rebellion without outside assistance. Mathews then compounded that error in judgment by refusing to acknowledge that he had ever made it at all and engaging thereafter, for his own reasons as much as any other, in a series of ill-conceived campaigns that had little chance of success, especially against a determined and reasonably well-organized resistance in an environment that hardly favored conventional military operations. It would be too easy to conclude that Madison should never have been persuaded by Mathews's opinions in the first place—recalling again that in 1810–11 the prospects for the survival of Spanish authority seemed poor in the extreme—but it is certainly fair to say, even without the advantages of hindsight, that the president and his colleagues might have exercised stricter supervision over their agent and his activities than they did. In truth, what the episode in East Florida really revealed was that Madison, as the War of 1812 would subsequently confirm, was not a very efficient administrator.[133] The result was that Mathews was left too free to create a state of affairs in the province that was beyond the power of any diplomacy to remedy until such time as Spain was willing to concede East Florida voluntarily.

The situation in Texas resembled that in East Florida inasmuch as there were far too few republican sympathizers among any of its peoples to sustain a successful revolt against Spain. Neither of the two republics that were established in San Antonio de Béxar in 1811 and 1813 could survive for more than five months before they succumbed to royalist counteroffensives. Because the United States had far less interest in acquiring Texas for its own sake than in exploiting it as a diplomatic bargaining chip with Madrid, that situation was never a major factor in any of Madison's calculations—or in those of Jefferson and Monroe. What is more important is that Madison, by 1816, had come to appreciate the significance of the Pacific Northwest for the future of the United States and that he was prepared to envision a diplomatic strategy that would eventually allow the republic to relinquish Texas altogether in order to obtain clear titles to both Florida and the Pacific coast at the same time. To point to Madison's contribution here in ways that have been hitherto neglected by historians does not, of course, detract from the accomplishment of Adams in 1818 and 1819 in negotiating the boundary settlement with Spain that then positioned the United States to expand across much of the remainder of North America throughout the nineteenth century. The tactics of that particular diplomatic campaign were those of Adams and Monroe, not Madison. But one reason why Madison's contribution has been overlooked here can be found in the decision of the Monroe administration, in sending selections from the diplomatic correspondence with Spain to the Senate in February 1819, to omit much of the evidence that illuminated the processes whereby the United States abandoned its claim to Texas. The reality was that the claim to Texas had been dropped long before either Congress or the public had any real awareness it had been done, and in the general sense of euphoria that greeted the other provisions of the 1819 treaty, no one seemed particularly disposed to complain about that fact.[134]

That situation changed somewhat between 1819 and 1821 when critics of the administration, and particularly Henry Clay, attacked both Adams and Monroe for conceding too much to Spain by relinquishing Texas. The matter also took on a new significance because it was being debated at the same time that congressional politics began to polarize along sectional lines during the arguments over the admission of Missouri to the Union as a slave state.[135] To Monroe, and possibly to Madison as well, the appearance of sectional cleavages over slavery only served to confirm the wisdom of their decision to drop the claim to Texas, though their willingness to contemplate doing so as early as 1816 was almost certainly not related to that consideration.[136] Yet by a somewhat cruel, if not perverse, twist of fate, it was to be Adams rather than Madison or Monroe who received most of the blame for that decision. In the years after 1821 ever greater amounts of misinformation were circulated about the role of Adams in settling the western boundary of Louisiana at the Sabine River, much of which was willfully disseminated by Andrew Jackson and his supporters as part of a more prolonged campaign to "re-annex" Texas at various points between 1829 and 1845.[137] In the confusion and misunderstandings thus created lay the sources of further American expansionism—and eventually a civil war.[138]

NOTES

Introduction

1. For introductions to the sizable body of theoretical literature on this point, see Derek Gregory, *Geographical Imaginations* (Cambridge, MA, 1994); David Harvey, *Justice, Nature, and the Geography of Difference* (Cambridge, MA, 1996); and Henri Lefebvre, *The Production of Space*, trans. Donald Nicholson-Smith (Cambridge, MA, 1991). For the concept of borders as "an archaic spatial feature," see Charles S. Maier, *Among Empires: American Ascendancy and Its Predecessors* (Cambridge, MA, 2006), 80.

2. For two studies that stress the significance of borders as reflections of state power, see Maier, *Among Empires*, 78–111; and Alan Taylor, *The Divided Ground: Indians, Settlers, and the Northern Borderland of the American Revolution* (New York, 2006), 7–10.

3. One example of the heated polemic generated by this problem is Patrick J. Buchanan, *State of Emergency: The Third World Invasion and Conquest of America* (New York, 2006).

4. The most succinct expression of this view remains Leonard D. White's observation that Madison "would have been much more at home as president of the University of Virginia . . . than he was as President of the United States" (see *The Jeffersonians: A Study in Administrative History* [New York, 1951], 36). With the exception of Irving Brant's six-volume biography *James Madison* (Indianapolis, IN, 1941–61), every full-length study of Madison's life and times has grappled with this problem, even if only by means of providing relatively compressed treatments of Madison's years in Washington between 1801 and 1817 in contrast with extended discussions of Madison's public career between 1776 and 1800.

5. For studies that emphasize the larger continuities rather than the discontinuities in Madison's career, see J. C. A. Stagg, "The Coming of the War of 1812: The View from the Presidency," *Quarterly Journal of the Library of Congress* 37 (1980): 223–41; Stagg, *Mr. Madison's War: Politics, Diplomacy and Warfare in the Early American Republic, 1783–1830* (Princeton, NJ, 1983), xi–xii, 3–7; Lance Banning, *The Sacred Fire of*

Liberty: James Madison and the Founding of the Federal Republic (Ithaca, NY, 1995), 1–13; Gordon S. Wood, "Is There a 'James Madison Problem'?" in Wood, *Revolutionary Characters: What Made the Founders Different* (New York, 2006), 141–72; and Michael Schwarz, "The Great Divergence Reconsidered: Hamilton, Madison, and U.S.-British Relations, 1783–89," *Journal of the Early Republic* 27 (2007): 407–36. For a more general discussion, see Alan Gibson, "The Madisonian Madison and the Question of Consistency: The Significance and Challenge of Recent Research," *Review of Politics* 64 (2002): 311–38.

6. One extended presentation of this interpretation may be found in the two volumes by Bradford Perkins, *Prologue to War: England and the United States, 1805–1812* (Berkeley, CA, 1961) and *Castlereagh and Adams: England and the United States, 1812–1823* (Berkeley, CA, 1964).

7. For the most important statement of this case, see Isaac J. Cox, *The West Florida Controversy, 1798–1813: A Study in American Diplomacy* (Baltimore, MD, 1918), 660–68. See also Hubart B. Fuller, *The Purchase of Florida: Its History and Diplomacy* (Cleveland, OH, 1906), 325–30.

8. For a discussion of how early presidents used executive agents to undertake occasional tasks that could not otherwise be carried out within the existing framework of government, see Henry M. Wriston, *Executive Agents in American Foreign Relations* (Baltimore, MD, 1929).

9. For the leading expositions of these claims, some of which were developed as criticisms of the 1976 report of the Church committee investigating the covert operations of the Central Intelligence Agency, see Charles D. Ameringer, *U.S. Foreign Intelligence: The Secret Side of American History* (Lexington, MA, 1990), 31; John J. Carter, *Covert Operations as a Tool of American Foreign Policy in American History from 1800 to 1920: Foreign Policy in the Shadows* (New York, 2000), 29–42; William J. Daugherty, *Executive Secrets: Covert Action and the Presidency* (Lexington, KY, 2004), 24, 31; Alexander DeConde, *Presidential Machismo: Executive Authority, Military Intervention, and Foreign Relations* (Boston, MA, 2000), 28–29; Richard W. Gronet, "The United States and the Invasion of Texas, 1810–1814," *The Americas* 25 (1969): 281–306; Stephen F. Knott, *Secret and Sanctioned: Covert Operations and the American Presidency* (New York, 1996), 87–107, 111; Edward F. Sayle, "The Historical Underpinnings of the U.S. Intelligence Community," *International Journal of Intelligence and Counterintelligence* 1 (1986): 10–11; and Joseph B. Smith, *The Plot to Steal Florida: James Madison's Phony War* (New York, 1983).

10. For some preliminary findings in that re-examination, see the following essays by the author: "Madison and the Collapse of the Spanish-American Empire: The West Florida Crisis of 1810," in *The Papers of James Madison: Presidential Series* (5 vols. to date, ed. Robert A. Rutland et al.; Charlottesville, VA, 1984–), 2: 305–20; and "Madison and the Problem of Mexican Independence: The Gutiérrez-Magee Raid of August 1812," in ibid., 5: 235–45. See also (by the author) "The Madison Administration and Mexico: Reinterpreting the Gutiérrez-Magee Raid of 1812–1813," *William and Mary Quarterly*, 3d ser., vol. 59 (2002): 449–80; "James Madison and George Mathews:

The East Florida Revolution of 1812 Reconsidered," *Diplomatic History* 30 (2006): 23–55; and "George Mathews and John McKee: Revolutionizing East Florida, Mobile, and Pensacola in 1812," *Florida Historical Quarterly* 85 (2007): 269–96. Most of these essays center on the question of how accurate it is to claim that Madison deliberately sought to subvert Spanish rule in the borderlands.

11. For an exploration of the significance of this formulation, see Jeremy Adelman and Stephen Aron, "From Borderlands to Borders: Empires, Nation-States, and the Peoples in Between in North American History," *American Historical Review* 104 (1999): 813–41. For its application in a specific region, see Aron, *American Confluence: The Missouri Frontier from Borderland to Border State* (Bloomington, IN, 2006).

12. The literature on the expansionist theme in American foreign policy is too vast to be listed here, but for some examples involving Spain, see Wanjohi Waciuma, *Intervention in Spanish Floridas, 1801–1813: A Study in Jeffersonian Foreign Policy* (Boston, MA, 1976); Elena Sánchez-Fabrés Mirat, *Situación Histórica de las Floridas en la segunda Mitad de Siglio XVIII (1783–1819)* (Madrid, 1977), and Ramiro Guerra y Sánchez, *The Territorial Expansion of the United States at the Expense of Spain*, trans. Fernando E. Pérez Peña (Lanham, MD, 2003). For a more comprehensive listing of the secondary literature relating to expansionism in the Spanish borderlands, see the works cited in the articles in n. 10 of this chapter. The best introduction to the racial arguments that justified American expansion is Reginald Horsman, *Race and Manifest Destiny: The Origins of American Racial Anglo-Saxonism* (Cambridge, MA, 1981), 9–61, 81–138, 189–207.

13. The leading studies of Manifest Destiny as an ideology are Albert K. Weinberg, *Manifest Destiny: A Study of Nationalist Expansion in American History* (Baltimore, MD, 1935) and Anders Stephanson, *Manifest Destiny: American Expansionism and the Empire of Right* (New York, 1995). For the argument that it was Jane McManus Storm Cazneau rather than John L. O'Sullivan who coined the term, see Linda S. Hudson, *Mistress of Manifest Destiny: A Biography of Jane McManus Storm Cazneau, 1807–1878* (Austin, TX, 2001). The classic exposition of early-nineteenth-century American expansionism as incipient Manifest Destiny is Julius W. Pratt, *Expansionists of 1812* (New York, 1925). For two more recent statements of the same case, see Frank L. Owsley, Jr., and Gene A. Smith, *Filibusters and Expansionists: Jeffersonian Manifest Destiny, 1800–1821* (Tuscaloosa, AL, 1997), 7–31 and Alexander DeConde, *This Affair of Louisiana* (New York, 1976), 241–55.

14. A recent study that is properly sensitive to these matters is Peter J. Kastor, *The Nation's Crucible: The Louisiana Purchase and the Creation of America* (New Haven, CT, 2004), 40, 244.

15. Robert Kagan, in *Dangerous Nation: America's Place in the World from Its Earliest Days to the Dawn of the Twentieth Century* (New York, 2006), has attempted to explain American expansionism as the product of a "liberal republican" mindset that drove American attitudes from the earliest days of colonization. The argument is not entirely free from difficulties, only one of which is that historians of the early republic have long doubted the utility of such reified categories as "liberalism" and "republi-

canism" as explanatory devices for what are, without question, some very complicated historical problems (see Daniel T. Rodgers, "Republicanism: The Career of a Concept," *Journal of American History* 79 [1992]: 11–38). Moreover, any explanation of U.S. foreign policy that rests too heavily on a single-factor analysis is bound to produce overdetermined interpretations that shortchange complexity and contingency in the decision-making process. Kagan, in fact, devotes little space to explaining how political leaders make policy decisions—as opposed to the ideological justifications given for them—and he pays even less attention to the problem of the early-nineteenth-century borderlands.

16. The "great nation of futurity" was O'Sullivan's definition of the universal democratic republicanism, discussed in an 1839 issue of the *Democratic Review,* that gave meaning to the term *Manifest Destiny* coined in 1845 (see Robert D. Sampson, *John L. O'Sullivan and His Times* [Kent, OH, 2003], 194–95). For brief introductions to the ideology of continentalism, see John Carl Parish, *The Emergence of the Idea of Manifest Destiny* (Los Angeles, CA, 1932); and Richard W. Van Alstyne, *The Rising American Empire* (Chicago, IL, 1960).

17. For a discussion of how continental expansionism contributed to the ideology of exceptionalism, see John Murrin, "The Jeffersonian Triumph and American Exceptionalism," *Journal of the Early Republic* 20 (2000): 1–25. See also Eliga H. Gould, "The Making of an Atlantic State System: Britain and the United States, 1795–1825," in Julie Flavell and Stephen Conway, eds., *Britain and America Go to War: The Impact of War and Warfare in Anglo-America, 1754–1815* (Gainesville, FL, 2004), 241–65.

18. See Henry Adams, *The History of the United States during the Administrations of Thomas Jefferson and James Madison* (9 vols.; New York, 1889–91).

19. For analyses of Adams's literary style and rhetoric, see Jacob C. Levenson, *The Mind and Art of Henry Adams* (Stanford, CA, 1957), 117–89; and William Dusinberre, *Henry Adams: The Myth of Failure* (Charlottesville, VA, 1980), 86–161. Also worth consulting here is Merrill D. Peterson, "Henry Adams on Jefferson the President," *Virginia Quarterly Review* 39 (1963): 187–201.

20. For Adams's assessments of the merits of the claims to West Florida and Texas, see *History of the United States,* 2: 246–47, 296.

21. The point of Adams's emphasis on the absence of a clear relationship between the ends and means of American policy was to underline his larger argument that Jefferson and Madison were, more often than not, simply powerless before the impersonal forces that shaped the destinies of nations. As he remarked to one of his correspondents, the third and fourth presidents were like "mere grass-hoppers, kicking and gesticulating, on the middle of the Mississippi river. There is no possibility of reconciling their theories with their acts, or their extraordinary foreign policy with dignity. They were carried along on a stream which floated them after a fashion without much regard to themselves" (Adams to Samuel J. Tilden, 24 January 1883, in Jacob C. Levenson et al., eds., *The Letters of Henry Adams* [6 vols.; Cambridge, MA, 1982–88], 2: 491).

22. For the view that expansion was a vehicle for Indian-hating, see Richard Drinnon, "The Metaphysics of Empire-Building in the Age of Jefferson and Monroe,"

Massachusetts Review 16 (1975): 668–88. For the related view that expansion was a means of assimilating and "civilizing" the Indians, see Peter Onuf, *Jefferson's Empire: The Language of American Nationhood* (Charlottesville, VA, 2000), 18–52. For a variety of arguments that expansion was necessary to preserve democratic republicanism for the ages, see Julian P. Boyd, "Thomas Jefferson's 'Empire of Liberty,'" *Virginia Quarterly Review* 24 (1948): 538–54; Drew McCoy, *The Elusive Republic: Political Economy in Jeffersonian America* (Chapel Hill, NC, 1980), 185–208; Richard Slotkin, *The Fatal Environment: The Myth of the Frontier in the Age of Industrialization* (New York, 1985), 68–78; Patricia Nelson Limerick, *The Legacy of Conquest: The Unbroken Past of the American West* (New York, 1987), 58, 71, 94; and Onuf, "The Expanding Union," in David Thomas Koenig, ed., *Devising Liberty: Preserving and Creating Freedom in the New American Republic* (Stanford, CA, 1995), 50–80. For the notion that expansion was a "safety valve" that would defuse tensions arising from class and slavery, see Henry Nash Smith, *Virgin Land: The American Land as Symbol and Myth* (Cambridge, MA, 1950), 234–45; William W. Freehling, *The Road to Disunion: Secessionists at Bay, 1776–1854* (New York, 1990), 121–31, 155–57; and Freehling, "The Complex Career of Slaveholder Expansionism," in *The Reintegration of American History: Slavery and the Civil War* (New York, 1994), 158–75. For the best explanation of expansionism as a response to demographic pressures on land supply, see Alan Taylor, "Land and Liberty on the Post-Revolutionary Frontier" in Koenig, *Devising Liberty*, 81–108.

23. Throughout the dispute, Spain usually argued that the Louisiana Purchase did not convey to the United States any claim to West Florida and Texas, but in 1818 the Spanish minister went so far as to maintain that France itself had never had good title to any part of Louisiana, however the province was defined. He dismissed the charters issued by Louis XIV as the acts of a "disordered imagination" and adduced them as proof of France's acknowledgment that its Louisiana settlements had been made on territory that had always belonged to Spain (see Luis de Onís to John Quincy Adams, 5 January 1818, Notes from Foreign Legations to the Department of State, Spain, RG 59, National Archives). The United States refused to take this argument seriously (see Adams to Onís, 16 January 1818, Notes from the Department of State to Foreign Ministers and Consuls in the United States, RG 59, National Archives).

24. The Spanish position on the extent of Louisiana was that France, by dismembering Louisiana in November 1762 prior to transferring the territory to the west of the Mississippi River to Spain and transferring Florida to Great Britain, had abandoned the view that the boundaries of the province were the River Perdido in the east and the Rio Grande in the west. Napoleon could not, therefore, have regained, either in theory or in practice, the full extent of the original French claim to Louisiana in 1800. For Adams's endorsement of this position, albeit one that was based on a selective and out-of-context reading of a single French document, see *History of the United States*, 2: 5–7. For further discussion of this matter, see chapter 1 at p. 41 and n. 103.

25. For the general rules governing the interpretation of treaties that guided both Jefferson and Madison, see Emmerich de Vattel, *The Law of Nations; or, The Princi-*

ples of Natural Law, Applied to the Conduct and to the Affairs of Nations and of Sovereigns, trans. Charles G. Fenwick (Washington, DC, 1916 [orig. 1758]), 199–221. Throughout the boundary dispute with Spain, Madison would invoke Vattel's principles to ridicule the view that the United States had no right to interpret the meaning of a treaty to which it was a signatory, especially when France and Spain appealed to meanings of the treaty that were not embodied in its text. As he remarked in 1805, "France assigned to us Louisiana as described in the conveyance to her from Spain. Our title to the written description is therefore good against both, notwithstanding any separate explanation or covenant between them, unless it be shewn that notice thereof was given to the United States before their bona fide purchase was made." With respect to France, he noted that "it will scarcely be pretended that any such notice was given." (Madison to John Armstrong, 6 June 1805, Diplomatic Instructions of the Department of State, RG 59, National Archives.) Eleven years later Madison reiterated that it was simply not true, as Spain had maintained, that "France & Spain alone who were parties to the treaties can interpret the respective intentions recorded in them." "To this," he added, "must be opposed the meaning, deducible by the legal rules of interpretation, and the fact that the U.S. were bona fide purchasers without notice of any other interpretation, altho' Spain was not ignorant of our views, of purchasing, and even referred us to France as alone having the right to sell." (Madison to James Monroe, 13 July 1816, Miscellaneous Letters of the Department of State, RG 59, National Archives.)

26. *City of Washington Gazette,* 9 and 11 January 1819.

27. Americans understood the boundaries of Antoine Crozat's 1712 grant to be "fixed by the Illinois river and the lake of that name on the North; by Carolina on the East, the gulph of Mexico on the South, and New Mexico on the West" (see Thomas Hutchins, *An Historical Narrative and Topographical Description of Louisiana and West Florida* [Philadelphia, PA, 1784], 7).

28. Charles Francis Adams, ed., *The Memoirs of John Quincy Adams, Comprising Portions of His Diary from 1795–1848* (12 vols.; Philadelphia, PA, 1874), 4: 219–20 (entry for 15 January 1819). Treasury secretary William Harris Crawford told John Quincy Adams that the author of the article was John Armstrong of New York, former U.S. minister to France and Madison's secretary of war in 1813–14. Adams was disinclined to believe that Armstrong would have spoken so disrespectfully of his late brother-in-law, Livingston, in a newspaper publication—the author had mocked him as "this old Polonius"—but Crawford responded that this was "no objection" to his attribution. It might be added that Crawford's information, by virtue of his close association with the editor of the *City of Washington Gazette,* Jonathan Elliot, was probably accurate.

29. For brief discussions of Henry Adams's intense dislike of his grandfather and his affection for his grandmother, Louisa Catherine Adams, see Michael O'Brien, *Henry Adams and the Southern Question* (Athens, GA, 2005), 23–28, 108–113; and Gary Wills, *Henry Adams and the Making of America* (Boston, MA, 2005), 4, 15, 31. As a historian, Henry Adams dealt with the family problem in a characteristically backhanded way. He disapproved of the Transcontinental Treaty on a number of grounds, one of

them being that it was proof of how far his grandfather, by delivering Florida to the slaveholding oligarchy that was later to destroy the Union, was willing to go in order to advance his presidential ambitions. Yet the *History* took almost no explicit cognizance of that transaction, beyond noting that the terms on which the treaty ceded Florida to the United States in 1819 were irrefutable proof that the Monroe administration had admitted that the Spanish policies of its predecessors were indeed fraudulent usurpations (see Adams, *History of the United States,* 6: 235–44). In that sense, John Quincy Adams had exposed the dishonesty of a bad policy that was to have serious consequences for the future of the Union, but his grandson would not give him any credit for that. After the *History* had been published, Henry Adams also sabotaged the efforts of his brother, Brooks Adams, to publish a favorable biography of their grandfather, again partly on the grounds that the acquisition of Florida had been a discreditable act (see Paul C. Nagel, *Descent from Glory: Four Generations of the John Adams Family* [New York, 1983], 351–58).

30. Bolton's initial statement of this case can be found in *The Spanish Borderlands: A Chronicle of Old Florida and the Southwest* (New Haven, CT, 1921), but the best short exposition of what he believed should constitute the study of American history is his essay "The Epic of Greater America," *American Historical Review* 38 (1933): 448–74. A useful discussion of the relationship between the thinking of "Bolton of the Borderlands" and "Bolton of the Americas" can be found in Samuel Truett, "Epics of Greater America: Herbert Eugene Bolton's Quest for a Transnational American History," in Christopher Schmidt-Nowara and John M. Nieto-Phillips, eds., *Interpreting Spanish Colonialism: Empires, Nations, and Legends* (Albuquerque, NM, 2005), 213–48.

31. See the appreciations of Bolton by John Francis Bannon, *Herbert Eugene Bolton: The Historian and the Man* (Tucson, AZ, 1978); and David J. Weber, "Turner, the Boltonians, and the Borderlands," *American Historical Review* 91 (1986): 66–81. For a convenient listing and discussion of much of the relevant scholarship up until the 1970s, see the essays and critical bibliographies on Alabama, Florida, Louisiana, and Mississippi edited by William S. Coker in the *Latin American Research Review* 7 (1972): 3–94. For a comparable survey for Texas, see Gerald E. Poyo and Gilberto M. Hinojosa, "Spanish Texas and Borderlands Historiography in Transition: Implications for United States History," *Journal of American History* 75 (1988): 393–416.

32. Among the best recent borderland studies are Ramón A. Gutiérrez, *When Jesus Came the Corn Mothers Went Away: Marriage, Sexuality, and Power in New Mexico, 1500–1846* (Stanford, CA, 1991); James F. Brooks, *Captives and Cousins: Slavery, Kinship, and Community in the Southwest Borderlands* (Chapel Hill, NC, 2002); Steven W. Hackel, *Children of Coyote, Missionaries of St. Francis: Indian-Spanish Relations in Colonial California, 1769–1850* (Chapel Hill, NC, 2005); Andrés Reséndez, *Changing National Identities at the Frontier: Texas and New Mexico, 1800–1850* (New York, 2005); and Juliana Barr, *Peace Came in the Form of a Woman: Indians and Spaniards in the Texas Borderlands* (Chapel Hill, NC, 2007). By far the best synthesis and updating of Spanish borderland studies since the 1970s is David J. Weber, *The Spanish Frontier in North America* (New Haven, CT, 1992). See also John L. Larson and Michael A. Mor-

rison, eds., "Community and Culture in the Borderlands: Essays from a SHEAR Symposium," *Journal of the Early Republic* 18 (1998): 71–139. For an attempt to formulate a more general theory for borderland regions, see Michiel Baud and Willem Van Schendel, "Toward a Comparative History of Borderlands," *Journal of World History* 8 (1997): 211–42.

33. For the concept of transnational history, see Ian Tyrrell, "American Exceptionalism in an Age of International History," *American Historical Review* 96 (1991): 1031–55; David Thelen, "The Nation and Beyond: Transnational Perspectives on United States History," *Journal of American History* 86 (1993): 965–75; Nina Schiller, Linda Basch, and Christina Blanc-Szanton, *Towards a Transnational Perspective on Migration: Race, Class, Ethnicity, and Nationalism Reconsidered* (New York, 1992), 1–7; Schiller et al., *Nations Unbound: Transnational Projects, Postcolonial Predicaments, and the Deterritorialization of Nation States* (Amsterdam, 1994), 1–19; and Samuel Truett and Elliott Young, "Making Transnational History: Nations, Regions, and Borderlands," in Truett and Young, eds., *Continental Crossroads: Remapping U.S.-Mexico Borderlands History* (Durham, NC, 2004), 1–32. For the view that the emergence of the United States itself might be understood as the outcome of contingent developments in a globalizing world after 1500, see Thomas Bender, *A Nation among Nations: America's Place in World History* (New York, 2006).

34. For Wallerstein's approach, which divided the world into core and peripheral regions (principally Europe and its colonies) in order to demonstrate how the concentration of power and resources in the core led to underdevelopment and weakness in the peripheries, see his three-volume work, *The Modern World-System:* vol. 1, *Capitalist Agriculture and the Origins of the European World-Economy in the Sixteenth Century* (New York, 1974); vol. 2, *Mercantilism and the Consolidation of the European World-Economy, 1600–1750* (New York, 1980); and vol. 3, *The Second Era of Great Expansion of the Capitalist World-Economy, 1730–1840s* (New York, 1989). Studies relevant to the Spanish borderlands that reflect the influence of this approach include Peggy K. Liss, *Atlantic Empires: The Network of Trade and Revolution, 1713–1826* (Baltimore, MD, 1983); Thomas D. Hall, *Social Change in the American Southwest, 1350–1880* (Lawrence, KS, 1989); Richard D. White, *The Roots of Dependency: Subsistence, Environment, and Social Change among the Choctaws, Pawnee, and Navajos* (Lincoln, NE, 1983); and Donna J. Guy and Thomas E. Sheridan, eds., *Contested Ground: Comparative Frontiers on the Northern and Southern Edges of the Spanish Empire* (Tucson, AZ, 1998).

35. For Bailyn's contributions, see his "The Idea of Atlantic History," *Itinerario* 20 (1996): 19–44; "Atlantic Dimensions," in *To Begin the World Anew: The Genius and Ambiguities of the American Founders* (New York, 2003), 131–49; and *Atlantic History: Concept and Contours* (Cambridge, MA, 2005). Developments at Johns Hopkins are described in Greene, "Beyond Power: Paradigm Subversion and Reformulation, and the Re-creation of the Early Modern Atlantic World," in *Interpreting Early America: Historiographical Essays* (Charlottesville, VA, 1996), 17–42; "Comparing Early Modern American Worlds: Some Reflections on the Promise of a Hemispheric Perspective," *History Compass* 1 (2003), at http://www.blackwell-synergy.com/doi/full/10.1111/

1478–0542.026; and "Early Modern Southeastern North America and the Broader Atlantic and American Worlds," *Journal of Southern History* 73 (2007): 525–38. Anthologies and historiographies of the subject now abound, but see the following: Silvia Marzagalli, "Sur les origines de l' 'Atlantic History': Paradigme interprétatif de l'histoire des espaces atlantiques à l'époque moderne," *Dix-huitième siècle* 33 (2001): 17–31; Horst Pietschmann, "Atlantic History—History between European History and Global History" in Pietschmann, ed., *Atlantic History: History of the Atlantic System, 1580–1830* (Göttingen, 2002), 11–54; Donna Gabaccia, "A Long Atlantic in a Wider World," *Atlantic Studies* 1 (2004): 1–27; and Ian K. Steele, "Bernard Bailyn's American Atlantic," *History and Theory* 46 (2007): 48–58. See also Christine Daniels and Michael V. Kennedy, eds., *Negotiated Empires: Centers and Peripheries in the Americas, 1500–1820* (New York, 2002); and Jorge Cañizares-Esguerra and Erik R. Seeman, eds., *The Atlantic in Global History, 1500–2000* (Upper Saddle River, NJ, 2007). Discussions of the varieties of "Atlantic history," especially the concepts of a "British Atlantic" and a "black Atlantic," are also proliferating very rapidly. For only a few examples, see "Conference: The Nature of Atlantic History," *Itinerario* 23, no. 2 (1999): 48–173; David Armitage and Michael J. Braddick, eds., *The British Atlantic World, 1500–1800* (Basingstoke, UK, 2002); Alison Games, "Atlantic History: Definitions, Challenges, and Opportunities," *American Historical Review* 111 (2006): 741–57; Stephen J. Hornsby, *British Atlantic, American Frontier: Spaces of Power in Early Modern British America* (Hanover, NH, 2005); Elizabeth Mancke and Carole Shammas, eds., *The Creation of the British Atlantic World* (Baltimore, MD, 2005); Daniel Walker Howe, *American History in an Atlantic Context* (Oxford, UK, 1993); and William O'Reilly, "Genealogies of Atlantic History," *Atlantic Studies* 1 (2004): 66–84. For the "black Atlantic," see particularly Paul Gilroy, *The Black Atlantic: Modernity and Double Consciousness* (Cambridge, MA, 1995) and John Thornton, *Africa and Africans in the Making of the Atlantic World, 1400–1800*, 2d ed. (New York, 1998). See also Ira Berlin, "From Creole to African: Atlantic Creoles and the Origins of African-American Identity in Mainland North America," *William and Mary Quarterly*, 3d ser., vol. 53 (1996): 251–88; Philip D. Morgan, ed., "African and American Atlantic Worlds," special issue, *William and Mary Quarterly*, 3d ser., vol. 56 (1999): 241–414; and Peter Kolchin, ed., "Slaveries in the Atlantic World," special issue, *William and Mary Quarterly*, 3d ser., vol. 59 (2002): 551–696.

36. Meinig, *The Shaping of America: A Geographical Perspective on 500 Years of History*, vol. 1, *Atlantic America, 1492–1800* (New Haven, CT, 1986), especially pp. 3–65, 257–454; and vol. 2, *Continental America, 1800–1867* (New Haven, CT, 1993), especially pp. 3–218. Recent developments in the study of cartography have also emphasized the extent to which advances in mapmaking contributed to the formation of national identities and, in the case of Americans, to the desire to encroach on the borderland possessions of European powers in North America (see, for example, Martin Brückner, *The Geographical Revolution in Early America: Maps, Literacy, and National Identity* [Chapel Hill, NC, 2006]; and John Rennie Short, *Representing the Republic: Mapping the United States, 1600–1900* [London, 2001]).

37. It should be mentioned that the "transnational" and Atlantic paradigms, despite their popularity, have come in for serious criticism on a variety of grounds, among them being doubts about the consistency and stability of the definitions they employ, about whether the relationships among the states and regions that bordered the Atlantic basin can be comprehended as a coherent system as opposed to a complex of subsystems (to say nothing of the fact that by the early nineteenth century many "Atlantic" nations—including the United States—were also developing substantial interests in the Indian and Pacific oceans), and about whether it is even practicable for historians to attempt to master all the languages and archives that would permit them to produce a truly "Pan-Atlantic" history of the Atlantic (see, for example, "Conversation: On Transnational History," *American Historical Review* 111 [2006]: 1441–64; Peter A. Coclanis, "*Drang Nach Osten:* Bernard Bailyn, the World-Island, and the Idea of Atlantic History," *Journal of World History* 13 [2002]: 169–82; "Forum: Beyond the Atlantic," *William and Mary Quarterly,* 3d ser., vol. 63 [2006]: 675–742; Jorge Cañizares-Esguerra, "Some Caveats about the 'Atlantic' Paradigm," *History Compass* 1 [2003], at http://www.blackwell-synergy.com/doi/full/10.1111/1478-0542.004; and Trevor Burnard, "Only Connect: The Rise and Rise (and Fall) of Atlantic History," *Historically Speaking* 7 [July–August 2006]: 19–21). Other skeptics include John H. Elliott; see his *Do the Americas Have a Common History? An Address* (Providence, RI, 1997) and more particularly his *Empires of the Atlantic World: Britain and Spain in America, 1492–1830* (New Haven, CT, 2006), xiii–xx, 403–11. To get around these difficulties, some scholars have proposed the concept of an "interregional arena" rather than conceive of various parts of the globe as either a total system or merely a particular region (see Sugata Bose, *A Hundred Horizons: The Indian Ocean in the Age of Global Empire* [Cambridge, MA, 2006], 6), while others, most recently, have coined the phrase *entangled empires,* particularly to describe the colonial rivalries between Great Britain and Spain (see the essays in "Entangled Empires in the Atlantic World," *American Historical Review* 112 [2007]: 710–99).

38. All of these definitions and points have been made in the literature cited at nn. 30–35 of this chapter. A recent statement of the same ideas with respect to the northern border of the United States is Joshua M. Smith, *Borderland Smuggling: Patriots, Loyalists, and Illicit Trade in the Northeast, 1783–1820* (Gainesville, FL, 2006).

39. For the argument that Atlantic history, properly understood, is necessarily a "history without borders," see Douglas R. Egerton et al., *The Atlantic World: A History, 1400–1888* (Wheeling, IL, 2007), 1–6.

40. For a more general discussion of this issue, see Michael McGerr, "The Price of the 'New Transnational History,'" *American Historical Review* 96 (1991): 1056–67. It might also be noted that many of the writings on transnationalism display hints of ideological bias against the study of the nation-state and its history. Not only is such history seen to be too parochial and restrictive, it is also deemed to have undesirable political consequences by encouraging beliefs in the "exceptionalist" nature of the nations in question (see, for example, David Thelen, "Making History and Making the United States," *Journal of American Studies* 32 [1998]: 373–97). Yet it is surely pos-

sible, as McGerr has observed, to write the history of a nation-state without succumbing either to the sins of a blind and chauvinistic nationalism or to notions of exceptionalism, however that term might be defined. In that sense, it should be possible to study the national history of the United States as a "nation among nations." The description of contested borders as "rough edges" is taken from Baud and Van Schendel, "Toward a Comparative History of Borderlands," 214.

41. This argument, of course, draws on the two meanings of *errand*—one referring to a subordinate sent to perform a task for a superior and the other referring to the purpose of the task itself (see Perry Miller, *Errand into the Wilderness* [Cambridge, MA, 1956], 1–15).

42. For a discussion of the difficulty of combining these two perspectives, see James A. Hijiya, "Why the West Is Lost," *William and Mary Quarterly*, 3d ser., vol. 51 (1994): 276–92. As Hijiya observes, "It seems impossible for historians, even the best ones, to write both the history of the nation-state and the history of non-Anglos. . . . To someone studying the nation-state, non-Anglos seem peripheral; to someone scrutinizing non-Anglos, the nation-state seems peripheral. Thus United States history and Western U.S. history exist in separate and incompatible universes. The insights achieved by historians of Native Americans or Mexicans remain inside the ghettoes of Indian or Borderlands history instead of escaping to transform American history" (285).

43. For an effort to generalize about these matters in order to construct a model of the decision maker as "an intuitive social scientist," see Yaacov Y. I. Vertzberger, *The World in Their Minds: Information Processing, Cognition, and Perception in Foreign Policy Decisionmaking* (Stanford, CA, 1990), especially pp. 111–91. Another essay that discusses the potential of diplomatic, or transnational, histories to integrate a variety of approaches to history is Melvyn P. Leffler, "New Approaches, Old Interpretations, and Prospective Reconfigurations," *Diplomatic History* 19 (1995): 173–96.

Chapter 1. A Troublesome Neighbor

1. Most notably, Henry Adams in his *History of the United States*, 2: 245–49, 3: 22–23. For more recent explorations of this theme, see Alexander DeConde, *This Affair of Louisiana* (New York, 1976), 209–55; Roger G. Kennedy, *Mr. Jefferson's Lost Cause: Land, Farmers, Slavery, and the Louisiana Purchase* (New York, 2003), 11–16, 235–44; Allan Kulikoff, *Tobacco and Slaves: The Development of Southern Cultures in the Chesapeake, 1680–1800* (Chapel Hill, NC, 1986), 421–35; Adam Rothman, *Slave Country: American Expansionism and the Origins of the Deep South* (Cambridge, MA, 2005), 1–35; Robert W. Tucker and David C. Hendrickson, *Empire of Liberty: The Statecraft of Thomas Jefferson* (New York, 1990), 157–58; and Frank L. Owsley, Jr., and Gene A. Smith, *Filibusters and Expansionists: Jeffersonian Manifest Destiny, 1800–1821* (Tuscaloosa, AL, 1997), 7–31.

2. A. de Clercq, *Recueil des traités de la France* (23 vols.; Paris, 1864–1917), 1: 411–13, 2: 59–62.

3. See Max Savelle, *The Origins of American Diplomacy: The International History of Anglo-America, 1492–1763* (New York, 1967). More specifically on Franco-Spanish rivalry before 1763, see Henry Folmer, *Franco-Spanish Rivalry in North America* (Glendale, CA, 1953); James Pritchard, *In Search of Empire: The French in the Americas, 1670–1730* (Cambridge, UK, 2004); and Robert S. Weddle, *The French Thorn: Rival Explorers in the Spanish Sea, 1682–1762* (College Station, TX, 1991).

4. For Franklin's "Proposed Articles of Confederation," ca. 21 July 1775, see Leonard W. Labaree et al., eds., *The Papers of Benjamin Franklin* (39 vols. to date; New Haven, CT, 1959–), 22: 125. See also John Adams, diary entry for September 1775, in Lyman H. Butterfield et al., eds., *Diary and Autobiography of John Adams* (4 vols. to date; Cambridge, MA, 1961–), 3: 327; and Adams to the Boston Committee of Correspondence, September 1774, in Robert J. Taylor et al., eds., *The Papers of John Adams* (13 vols. to date; Cambridge, MA, 1977–), 2: 178–79.

5. For the first and final drafts of the Model Treaty, see Worthington C. Ford et al., eds., *Journals of the Continental Congress, 1774–1789* (34 vols.; Washington, DC, 1904–37), 5: 579ff, 770ff. For a more general discussion, see William C. Stinchcombe, "John Adams and the Model Treaty," in Lawrence S. Kaplan, ed., *The American Revolution and "A Candid World"* (Kent, OH, 1977), 69–84.

6. For a brief discussion of the contemporary meanings of the terms *union* and *confederated republic,* see Hendrickson, "The First Union: Nationalism versus Internationalism in the American Revolution," in Eliga H. Gould and Peter S. Onuf, eds., *Empire and Nation: The American Revolution in the Atlantic World* (Baltimore, MD, 2005), 35–53.

7. Ford et al., *Journals of the Continental Congress,* 5: 554. This phrasing was ultimately embodied in article 9 of the ratified Articles of Confederation (see Murray G. Lawson, "Canada and the Articles of Confederation," *American Historical Review* 58 [1952]: 39–54).

8. The invitation from Congress to the Assembly of West Florida fell into the hands of the British governor, who suppressed it (see Cecil Johnson, *British West Florida* [New Haven, CT, 1943], 204–5; and J. Barton Starr, *Tories, Dons, and Rebels: The American Revolution in British West Florida* [Gainesville, FL, 1976], 45–46). In East Florida there was no assembly before 1781 (see Charles L. Mowat, *East Florida as a British Province, 1763–1784* [Berkeley, CA, 1943], 34, 42, 178).

9. Ford et al., *Journals of the Continental Congress,* 5: 554. For the belief that Great Britain would shortly be at war with Spain, see Richard Henry Lee to Patrick Henry, 3 December 1776, in Paul H. Smith, ed., *Letters of Delegates to Congress, 1774–1789* (26 vols.; Washington, DC, 1976–2000), 5: 565.

10. For Vattel's thinking, see *The Law of Nations; or, The Principles of Natural Law, Applied to the Conduct and to the Affairs of Nations and of Sovereigns,* trans. Charles G. Fenwick (Washington, DC, 1916 [orig. 1758]), 251. For further evidence of the influence of this strand of discourse in the Revolutionary period, see David Armitage, "The Declaration of Independence and International Law," *William and Mary Quarterly,* 3d ser., vol. 59 (2002): 49; Peter Onuf and Nicholas Onuf, *Federal Union, Modern*

World: The Law of Nations in an Age of Revolutions, 1776–1814 (Madison, WI, 1993), 4–6, 11–19; Nicholas Onuf, *The Republican Legacy in International Thought* (Cambridge, UK, 1998), 58–84; and Daniel Deudney, *Bounding Power: Republican Security Theory from the Polis to the Global Village* (Princeton, NJ, 2007), 136–60.

11. For the instructions of 24 September 1776 to Benjamin Franklin, Silas Deane, and Arthur Lee, see Ford et al., *Journals of the Continental Congress,* 5: 816; for those of 30 December 1776, see ibid., 6: 1057.

12. Under the terms of the treaty France renounced all territorial ambitions in North America, including any claim to Canada, in favor of prospective acquisitions in the Caribbean. Nothing was stipulated about Florida, but for a secret article reserving the rights of the king of Spain, see Ford et al., *Journals of the Continental Congress,* 11: 454.

13. For the proceedings relating to the definition of peace terms that culminated in the instructions of 14 August 1779, see Ford et al., *Journals of the Continental Congress,* 13: 239–44, 329, 330, 339ff; 14: 831ff, 883, 885, 920–66. Gérard's successor, the Chevalier de la Luzerne, also tried to persuade Congress it had no valid claims to territory extending to the Mississippi, to the right to navigate the river, or to Florida, but he failed to make much impression, adding that these claims had "put down deep roots since the peace of 1763" (see La Luzerne to the comte de Vergennes, 11 February 1780, in Mary A. Guinta et al., eds., *The Emerging Nation: A Documentary History of the Foreign Relations of the United States under the Articles of Confederation, 1780–1789* [3 vols.; Washington, DC, 1996], 1: 33).

14. For an account of Madison's first days in Congress, see Brant, *James Madison: The Nationalist, 1780–1787* (Indianapolis, IN, 1946), 11–21.

15. For Madison's commonplace book, see *The Papers of James Madison* (17 vols., ed. William T. Hutchinson, William M. E. Rachal, et al.; Chicago, IL, and Charlottesville, VA, 1962–91), 1: 22.

16. While secretary of state and president, Madison relied on translations of Spanish documents made by State Department clerks. Contemporaries, including the Mexican rebel José Bernardo Maximiliano Gutiérrez de Lara who met Madison in 1811, recalled that he knew no Spanish (see Elizabeth H. West, ed., "Diary of José Bernardo Gutiérrez de Lara, 1811–1812," *American Historical Review* 34 [1928–29]: 73). It is possible, though, that he may have tried occasionally to decipher Spanish documents on the basis of his knowledge of French and Latin (see, for example, Madison to John Graham, 11 August 1816, where he complained about the difficulties he was experiencing in reading a Spanish script, Miscellaneous Letters of the Department of State, RG 59, National Archives). In the "Report on Books for Congress" that he drew up in January 1783, however, Madison listed several works on the Spanish exploration and settlement of America, including the Abbé Raynal's *Philosophical and Political History of the Settlements and Trade of the Europeans in the East and West Indies,* which had gone into a six-volume translation by 1776 (see *Papers of James Madison,* 6: 96–107).

17. Robertson's three-volume *History of America* (London, 1777) and his *History of the Reign of the Emperor Charles V* (3 vols.; London, 1769) were included in Madison's 1783 booklist (see *Papers of James Madison,* 6: 78, 101). The views summarized here

could be found in book 7 of any edition of Robertson's *History of America* as well as in books 6 and 7 of any edition of Raynal's *Philosophical and Political History*—from which source they also influenced Adam Smith's *An Inquiry into the Nature and Causes of the Wealth of Nations*, ed. Edwin Cannan (New York, 1937), 238–39, 399, 479, 534–35, 575–78, 975. For discussions of Robertson's philosophy of history, see Robert A. Humphreys, *William Robertson and His "History of America"* (London, 1954); Nicholas Phillipson, "Providence and Progress: An Introduction to the Historical Thought of William Robertson," in Stewart J. Brown, ed., *William Robertson and the Expansion of Empire* (Cambridge, UK, 1997), 55–73; and J. G. A. Pocock, *Barbarism and Religion: Narratives of Civil Government* (Cambridge, UK, 1999), 268–305. For Madison's exposure to Robertson at Princeton, see Ralph Ketcham, "The Mind of James Madison" (Ph.D. diss.; Syracuse University, 1956), 5.

18. David A. Brading, *The First America: The Spanish Monarchy, Creole Patriots, and the Liberal State, 1492–1867* (Cambridge, UK, 1991), 432–41; and Jorge Cañizares-Esguerra, *How to Write the History of the New World: Histories, Epistemologies, and Identities in the Eighteenth-Century Atlantic World* (Stanford, CA, 2001), 38–44, 53–55, 120–26, 169–82. For introductions to the Bourbon reforms in Spain and its empire, see Richard Herr, *The Eighteenth-Century Revolution in Spain* (Princeton, NJ, 1958), 3–200; and John Lynch, *Bourbon Spain, 1700–1808* (London, 1989), 336–74.

19. Madison seems to have held a certain regard for Charles III and was fond of repeating a story, apparently told to him by John Jay, that the king was "chiefly *proud* of two things: 1. He had never broken his word or treaty with any sovereign. 2. He had *pissed* every day for 30 years against a particular oak" ([Jesse Burton Harrison], "Notes of conversations with Mr Madison in 1827," Burton Norvell Harrison Family Papers, Library of Congress).

20. Patrick Henry to Bernardo de Gálvez, 14 January 1778, in H. R. McIlwaine, ed., *Official Letters of the Governors of the State of Virginia* (3 vols.; Richmond, VA, 1926), 1: 228.

21. Light Townsend Cummins, *Spanish Observers of the American Revolution, 1775–1783* (Baton Rouge, LA, 1991), 84–88. On 31 October 1778 Congress decided that military operations on the Mississippi in relation to Florida were not practicable at that time (see Ford et al., *Journals of the Continental Congress*, 12: 1083–84).

22. Ford et al., *Journals of the Continental Congress*, 12: 1116–21 (resolution of 10 November 1778). See also Henry to Henry Laurens, 23 November 1778, in McIlwaine, *Official Letters of the Governors of the State of Virginia*, 1: 328.

23. Madison to Edmund Randolph, 3 October 1780, *Papers of James Madison*, 2: 109.

24. Ford et al., *Journals of the Continental Congress*, 18: 900–902.

25. Barbé-Marbois to Vergennes, 21 October 1780, in Giunta et al., *Emerging Nation*, 1: 126. For Madison's meetings with Barbé-Marbois, see *Papers of James Madison*, 2: 117–26.

26. For the report, see *Papers of James Madison*, 2: 127–34.

27. Ibid. For arguments about the right of "innocent passage," see Vattel, *Law of Nations*, 119. Madison continued to press this point whenever it seemed appropriate.

In 1792, for example, while assisting Jefferson in his preparations for negotiations with Spain over the Mississippi, he forwarded a note relating an anecdote he had heard from Philip Barbour—who had resided in West Florida—about how the Spanish authorities in New Orleans had attempted to deny Great Britain the advantages of navigating the river after 1763 by refusing British vessels the right to use the banks of the Mississippi and the port of New Orleans itself. Eventually, the British sent a frigate to enforce the claim to use the port (see "Memorandum on New Orleans," [ca. 1 March 1792], *Papers of James Madison*, 14: 242).

28. *Papers of James Madison*, 2: 133–34.

29. For a discussion of how Madison's decision to go to war with Great Britain in 1812 was influenced by the growth of British trade on the Great Lakes and the St. Lawrence River, see J. C. A. Stagg, *Mr. Madison's War: Politics, Diplomacy and Warfare in the Early American Republic, 1783–1830* (Princeton, NJ, 1983), 3–47.

30. For the argument that Madison in the early 1780s is best understood as a Virginian continentalist, see Lance Banning, *The Sacred Fire of Liberty: James Madison and the Founding of the Federal Republic* (Ithaca, NY, 1995), 42. For extended discussions of the development of continentalist thinking, see David J. Calabro, "Consensus for Empire: American Expansionist Thought and Policy, 1763–1789" (Ph.D. diss.; University of Virginia, 1982), especially pp. 96–133; and Richard W. Van Alstyne, *Genesis of American Nationalism* (Waltham, MA, 1970), 3–57. For an analysis of how Americans constructed continentalism in geographical and scientific terms, see James D. Drake, "Appropriating a Continent: Geographical Categories, Scientific Metaphors, and the Construction of Nationalism in British North America and Mexico," *Journal of World History* 15 (2004): 323–58.

31. The best exposition of Franklin's thinking on these matters remains Gerald Stourzh, *Benjamin Franklin and American Foreign Policy*, 2d ed. (Chicago, IL, 1969), 33–82. For the views of Coxe, Douglass, Jefferys, Kennedy, Logan, Mitchell, Neal, Oldmixon, Shirley, and Young, see Van Alstyne, *Genesis of American Nationalism*. Madison was also to place the writings of Coxe, Douglass, Jefferys, Neal, and Oldmixon on the list of books he recommended to Congress for purchase in January 1783 (see *Papers of James Madison*, 6: 62–115). Similarities between the political economy and strategic thinking of Franklin and Madison have been noted by Walter Lafeber (see his "Foreign Policies of a New Nation: Franklin, Madison, and the 'Dream of a New Land to Fulfill with People in Self-Control,'" in William Appleman Williams, ed., *From Colony to Empire: Essays in the History of American Foreign Relations* [New York, 1972], 101–37); and Drew McCoy, *The Elusive Republic: Political Economy in Jeffersonian America* (Chapel Hill, NC, 1980), 49–67, 121–32.

32. Jay to Samuel Huntington, 25 April 1781, in Francis Wharton, ed., *Revolutionary Diplomatic Correspondence of the United States* (6 vols.; Washington, DC, 1889), 4: 384.

33. For debate on these matters, lasting from 18 November 1780 through 28 May 1781, see Ford et al., *Journals of the Continental Congress*, 18: 1070–71, 19: 151–53, 20: 551–54.

34. Madison to Joseph Jones, 25 November 1780, *Papers of James Madison*, 2: 202–3.

35. Madison to Jones, 5 December 1780, and to Edmund Pendleton, 5 December 1780, ibid., 2: 224–26.

36. For Madison's 1 February 1781 resolution on new instructions for Jay, see *Papers of James Madison*, 2: 302–3. So opposed was Madison to this retreat that when it was reported in an 1815 edition of David Ramsey's *History of the American Revolution* that he, along with other members of the Virginia delegation, had been responsible for it, Madison wrote to the newspapers to correct the error (see Madison to Hezekiah Niles, 8 January 1822, printed in the Baltimore *Weekly Register*, 26 January 1822). Madison also took pains to point the error out to Jared Sparks (see Herbert B. Adams, ed., *The Life and Writings of Jared Sparks* [2 vols.; Boston, MA, 1893], 2: 34–35).

37. Pendleton to Madison, 23 July 1781, *Papers of James Madison*, 3: 179.

38. Madison had described Spain's desire to regain Gibraltar as a "hobby horse" in his 23 January 1781 letter to Pendleton (see *Papers of James Madison*, 2: 297).

39. Ibid.; and Madison to Pendleton, 18 September 1781, *Papers of James Madison*, 3: 318.

40. For Madison's 7 January 1782 report on instructions for the American peace commissioners, see *Papers of James Madison*, 4: 7–13.

41. For Madison's 22 April 1782 report on Jay's negotiations in Spain, see *Papers of James Madison*, 4: 168–69; and Madison to Pendleton, 5 August 1782, *Papers of James Madison*, 5: 20.

42. See Madison's report of 22 April as cited in preceding note.

43. See Madison's 6 August 1782 comments on instructions for Jay, *Papers of James Madison*, 5: 23–24.

44. The best discussion remains Richard B. Morris, *The Peacemakers: The Great Powers and American Independence* (New York, 1965), 282–437.

45. Madison to Randolph, 18 March 1783, *Papers of James Madison*, 6: 355.

46. Morris, *The Peacemakers*, 441–49.

47. See Madison to Philip Mazzei, 7 July 1781, *Papers of James Madison*, 3: 179; and Virginia Delegates to de Gálvez, 4 May 1783, *Papers of James Madison*, 7: 8. For a positive assessment of Spain's contributions to American independence, see Thomas E. Chávez, *Spain and the Independence of the United States: An Intrinsic Gift* (Albuquerque, NM, 2002).

48. See Madison's "Notes on Debates in Congress," 12–15, 18, 19, 22 March 1783, *Papers of James Madison*, 6: 328–32, 351, 359–65, 376–77.

49. "Notes on Debates in Congress," 23 January 1783, *Papers of James Madison*, 6: 116.

50. For the details, see Samuel Flagg Bemis, *Pinckney's Treaty: America's Advantage from Europe's Distress, 1783–1800,* 2d ed. (New Haven, CT, 1960), 1–59.

51. Madison to James Monroe, 18 December 1784, *Papers of James Madison*, 8: 188–90.

52. For the background, see Patricia Watlington, *The Partisan Spirit: Kentucky Politics, 1779–1792* (New York, 1972), 3–78.

53. For the Vermont problem, see Chilton Williamson, *Vermont in Quandary, 1763–1825* (Montpelier, VT, 1949), 90–164; and Peter S. Onuf, *The Origins of the Federal Republic: Jurisdictional Controversies in the United States, 1775–1787* (Philadelphia, PA, 1983), 127–45.

54. Madison to Monroe, 21 June 1786, *Papers of James Madison*, 9: 82. While the altered relationship between Spain and the United States might be sufficient to account for the marked shift in Madison's attitude here, it is also possible that while reading in the volumes of Charles Joseph Panckoucke's *Encyclopédie méthodique* sent to him by Jefferson from Paris in the 1780s, Madison came across an article titled "Espagne," by Nicolas Masson de Morvilliers. Its contents were a stinging indictment of Spanish backwardness and the baneful influence of the clergy and the Inquisition on its government. The publication caused a considerable furor throughout Spain and Europe (see Herr, *Eighteenth-Century Revolution in Spain*, 220–30). That being said, though, at no time after 1783 did Madison's views about Spain and Spaniards, or Spanish Americans for that matter, ever reflect the extremes of anti-Spanish and anti-Catholic sentiment that were embodied in the Black Legend about the history of Spain's involvement in the New World.

55. Madison to Lafayette, 20 March 1785, *Papers of James Madison*, 8: 251–53. For a discussion of how Vattel justified the European balance of power in terms of natural law, see David G. Lang, *Foreign Policy in the Early Republic: The Law of Nations and the Balance of Power* (Baton Rouge, LA, 1985), 1–66.

56. Madison to Thomas Jefferson, 20 August 1784, *Papers of James Madison*, 8: 166.

57. Madison to Monroe, 8 January 1785, ibid., 8: 220.

58. Madison to Jefferson, 7 September 1784, and to Lafayette, 20 March 1785, ibid., 8: 113, 251–53.

59. Madison to Jefferson, 20 August 1784, ibid., 8: 109–10.

60. See two articles by Gilbert Din: "The Immigration Policy of Governor Estaban Miró in Spanish Louisiana" *Southwestern Historical Quarterly* 73 (1969): 155–75; and "Spain's Immigration Policy in Louisiana and the American Penetration, 1792–1803," *Southwestern Historical Quarterly* 76 (1973): 355–76. See also Max Savelle, *George Morgan: Colony Builder* (New York, 1932), 200–228.

61. Madison to Monroe, 5 November 1788; to John Brown, 31 January 1789; to George Washington, 26 March 1789; and to Jefferson, 29 March 1789, *Papers of James Madison*, 11: 333, 426–27; 12: 28–30, 39.

62. The literature on these subjects is extensive, but see the following: Jane M. Berry, "The Indian Policy of Spain in the Southwest, 1783–1795," *Mississippi Valley Historical Review* 3 (1917): 462–77; Randolph C. Downes, "Creek-American Relations, 1782–1790," *Georgia Historical Quarterly* 21 (1937): 142–84; Jack D. L. Holmes, *Gayoso: The Life of a Spanish Governor in the Mississippi Valley, 1789–1799* (Baton Rouge, LA, 1965), 136–73; Arthur P. Whitaker, "Spain and the Cherokee Indians, 1783–98," *North Carolina Historical Review* 4 (1927): 252–69; Whitaker, *The Mississippi Question, 1795–1803: A Study in Trade, Politics, and Diplomacy* (Gloucester, MA, 1962), 3–78; and Whitaker, *The Spanish-American Frontier, 1783–1795* (Gloucester, MA, 1962),

1–61. For a more recent study with a greater emphasis on the role of the Indians, see Charles A. Weeks, *Paths to a Middle Ground: The Diplomacy of Natchez, Boufouka, Nogales, and San Fernando de Barrancas, 1791–1795* (Tuscaloosa, AL, 2005), 1–141.

63. Edmund C. Burnett, ed., "Papers Relating to Bourbon County, Georgia, 1785–86," *American Historical Review* 15 (1909): 66–111.

64. Madison to Monroe, 21 June 1785, *Papers of James Madison*, 8: 306–7.

65. Whitaker, *Spanish-American Frontier*, 68–74.

66. Ford et al., *Journals of the Continental Congress*, 29: 494, 562–629, 658, 829–30; 30: 323, 400–401; 31: 469–83, 510, 537, 552, 574–99, 613–97; 32: 184–88. For secondary accounts, see Bemis, *Pinckney's Treaty*, 60–90; and Joseph L. Davis, *Sectionalism in American Politics, 1774–1787* (Madison, WI, 1977), 109–26.

67. Madison to Monroe, 21 June 1786, *Papers of James Madison*, 9: 83–84.

68. See Madison to Jefferson, 12 August 1786, ibid, 9: 96–97. For further discussion of Madison's expectations about the development of the southwestern frontier, see Drew McCoy, "James Madison and Visions of American Nationality in the Confederation Period: A Regional Perspective," in Richard Beeman et al., eds., *Beyond Confederation: Origins of the Constitution and American National Identity* (Chapel Hill, NC, 1987), 226–58. For an overview of Virginian thinking on the same subject, see L. Scott Philyaw, *Virginia's Western Visions: Political and Cultural Expansion on the Early American Frontier* (Knoxville, TN, 2004).

69. Madison to Jefferson, 19 March 1787, *Papers of James Madison*, 9: 319–20.

70. As Madison recalled nearly fifty years later in his autobiography, his "main object" in returning to Congress was to stop "the project of Mr Jay for shutting the Mississippi which threatened an alienation" of Kentucky and Virginia "from any increase of federal power" (see Douglass Adair, ed., "James Madison's Autobiography," *William and Mary Quarterly*, 3d ser., vol. 2 [1945]: 202).

71. See Madison's 13 March 1787 notes on his conversation with Gardoqui, *Papers of James Madison*, 9: 309–11.

72. Ford et al., *Journals of the Continental Congress*, 32: 389–92; and Madison, "Notes on Debates," 18–19 April 1787, *Papers of James Madison*, 9: 389–92.

73. For Madison's criticisms of the Federal Constitution, see his 24 October 1787 letter to Jefferson, *Papers of James Madison*, 10: 206–19. For a discussion of how the disputes with Spain shaped the treaty clause, see Jack N. Rakove, "Solving a Constitutional Puzzle: The Treaty-Making Clause as a Case Study," *Perspectives in American History, New Series* 1 (1984): 267–81.

74. For Washington's questions on Spain, ca. 25 July 1789, see *Papers of James Madison*, 12: 310–12.

75. For Jefferson's views on Spanish questions, see his 20 June 1787 letter to Madison, *Papers of James Madison*, 10: 64–65.

76. For the background, see the discussions in William R. Manning, "The Nootka Sound Controversy," in *Annual Report of the American Historical Association for the Year 1904* (Washington, DC, 1905), 283–361; and Warren L. Cook, *Flood Tide of Empire: Spain and the Pacific Northwest, 1543–1819* (New Haven, CT, 1973), 200–249.

77. Manning, "Nootka Sound Controversy," 412–23.

78. Jefferson to Washington, 12 July 1790, in Julian P. Boyd et al., eds., *The Papers of Thomas Jefferson* (33 vols. to date; Princeton, NJ, 1950–), 17: 108.

79. See Jefferson, "Outline of Policy Contingent on a War between England and Spain," 12 July 1790, ibid., 17: 109–10.

80. Jefferson to William Carmichael, 2 August 1790, ibid., 17: 111–17.

81. See the correspondence between Madison and George Nicholas between 31 December 1790 and 9 February 1794, *Papers of James Madison*, 13: 338–40; 14: 75–76, 473; 15: 136–38, 254–55.

82. See the works cited in n. 62 of this chapter, particularly Whitaker, *Spanish-American Frontier*, 153–57, 163–70. See also William S. Coker and Thomas D. Watson, *Indian Traders of the Southeastern Spanish Borderlands: Panton, Leslie & Company and John Forbes & Company, 1783–1847* (Pensacola, FL, 1986), 157–81.

83. For these developments, see Richard K. Murdoch, *The Georgia-Florida Frontier, 1793–1796: Spanish Reaction to French Intrigue and American Designs* (Berkeley, CA, 1951); and Frederick Jackson Turner, "The Origin of Genet's Projected Attack on Louisiana and the Floridas," *American Historical Review* 3 (1898): 650–71.

84. For the negotiation of the 1795 Treaty of San Lorenzo, see Bemis, *Pinckney's Treaty*, 198–314; and Whitaker, *Spanish-American Frontier*, 171–222. See also Raymond A. Young, "Pinckney's Treaty—A New Perspective," *Hispanic American Historical Review* 43 (1963): 526–35.

85. For the terms of the treaty, see Hunter Miller, compiler, *Treaties and Other International Acts of the United States of America* (8 vols.; Washington, DC, 1931–48), 2: 318–38.

86. Madison to Monroe, 26 February 1796, and to Jefferson, 29 February and 6 March 1796, *Papers of James Madison*, 16: 232, 238, 246–47.

87. For the background, see E. Wilson Lyon, *Louisiana in French Diplomacy, 1759–1804*, 2d ed. (Norman, OK, 1974), 79–98.

88. On the Blount Conspiracy, see Whitaker, *Mississippi Question*, 104–15.

89. See Hamilton's letters to Lafayette, 6 January 1799, and to James McHenry, 27 June 1799, in Harold C. Syrett et al., eds., *The Papers of Alexander Hamilton* (27 vols.; New York, 1961–87), 22: 404–5, 23: 227. For further discussion, see John Lamberton Harper, *American Machiavelli: Alexander Hamilton and the Origins of U.S. Foreign Policy* (Cambridge, UK, 2004), 208–12, 227–33, 239–42.

90. Madison to Monroe, 5 January 1798, and to Jefferson, 12 February 1798, *Papers of James Madison*, 17: 74, 78.

91. Madison to Hamilton, 26 May 1801, in *The Papers of James Madison: Secretary of State Series* (8 vols. to date, ed. Robert Brugger et al.; Charlottesville, VA, 1986–), 1: 228–29.

92. Miller, *Treaties of the United States*, 2: 457–82.

93. Lyon, *Louisiana in French Diplomacy*, 101–26. See also the works cited in n. 3 of this chapter. On some eighteenth-century French maps, Florida was marked as "Presqu' Isle de la Louisiane" (see Weddle, *French Thorn*, 324–25).

94. The best discussion remains that of Richard R. Stenberg, "The Western Boundary of Louisiana, 1762–1763," *Southwestern Historical Quarterly* 35 (1931): 95–108. Only later, after 1808, did Spain address this problem, when the authorities in Mexico City directed Father José Antonio Pichardo to compile a report, three thousand folio pages in length, denying that France had ever had any valid title to Texas (see Charles Wilson Hackett, ed., *Pichardo's Treatise on the Limits of Louisiana and Texas* [4 vols.; Austin, TX, 1931], 1: xi–xx).

95. David J. Weber, *The Spanish Frontier in North America* (New Haven, CT, 1992), 275–76.

96. Alexandre Berthier to Charles-Maurice de Talleyrand-Périgord, 25 and 30 Fructidor, An VIII, Archives du Ministère des Affaires Étrangères: Correspondence Politique, Supplement VII (Louisiane et Florides—1792 à 1803) (copy in Library of Congress). For an essay that argues for the centrality of Napoleon's intention to regain West Florida to the Perdido River in the retrocession of Louisiana, see Ronald Caldwell, "Bonaparte's Efforts to Obtain Florida, 1799–1803," in *The Consortium on Revolutionary Europe, 1750–1850: Selected Papers, 1994* (Tallahassee, FL, 1994), 517–25.

97. Talleyrand, "Rapport au Premier Consul," Frimaire An XI, Archives du Ministère des Affaires Étrangères: Correspondence Politique, Espagne, vol. 630 (transcript in Henry Adams Collection of French State Papers, Library of Congress). Talleyrand pointed out that the recovery of West Florida to the Apalachicola River as part of Louisiana would be sufficient because it would give France the port of Pensacola and more than half of the population of the two Floridas. The issue, he argued, was not whether France should regain its status as an American colonial power but whether, in seeking both East and West Florida, it was risking the acquisition of more territory than it could profitably administer. The essence of imperial strength did not consist in accumulating distant and extended territories but in settling and developing such territories. Even as matters stood by the end of 1802, Talleyrand believed that France had already acquired more American territory than its commerce could sustain.

98. Madison to Charles Pinckney, 25 September 1801, and to Robert R. Livingston, 28 September 1801, *Papers of James Madison: Secretary of State Series*, 2: 131–32, 142–45.

99. See Jefferson to Dupont de Nemours, 1 February 1803, Thomas Jefferson Papers, Library of Congress.

100. Opinions about the economic potential of Florida, as reflected in contemporary travel accounts, promotional literature, and surveyors' reports, were sharply divided between those who saw the region as a veritable Garden of Eden and those who dismissed it as a wasteland (see Robert Olwell, "Florida, Kew, and the British Imperial Meridian in the 1760s," in Elizabeth Mancke and Carole Shammas, eds., *The Creation of the British Atlantic World* [Baltimore, MD, 2005], 272–76). The American surveyor Andrew Ellicott, who ran the boundary line between Spanish and American territory after the Pinckney Treaty of 1795, was much more inclined to the latter view—see *The Journal of Andrew Ellicott* (Philadelphia, PA, 1803), 198–300—and his views probably influenced those of Jefferson and Madison. As Jefferson told Dupont

in explaining why the United States sought Florida, "The country . . . which we wish to purchase . . . is a barren sand 600. miles from east to west, & from 30. to 40. & 50. miles from north to south, formed by the deposition of the sands by the Gulf Stream in its circular course round the Mexican Gulf, and which . . . has made from its last depositions the sand bank of East Florida. In West Florida, indeed, there are on the borders of the rivers some rich bottoms, formed by the mud brought from the upper country . . . [but] the spaces between river and river are mere banks of sand; and in East Florida there are neither rivers, nor consequently any bottoms. We cannot then make anything by a sale of the lands to individuals. So it is peace alone which makes it an object with us" (Jefferson to Dupont, 1 February 1803, Jefferson Papers). This account was later confirmed for Madison by Harry Toulmin, who after taking a trip across East and West Florida informed the secretary of state that the land between Mobile and Pensacola was "poor, pine barrens and unsettled"; that the land between Pensacola and the Apalachicola River was "the poorest land in the world, not producing even pine, but mean stunted black jacks"; and that the land between St. Marks and St. Johns was "a poor unsettled country" (Toulmin to Madison, 6 December 1807, James Madison Papers, Library of Congress). Even after Florida had been safely acquired for the United States, Madison seems to have remained somewhat agnostic, at best, about its future promise (see his 30 January 1821 letter to Peter Chazette in response to Chazette's pamphlet promoting the growth of tropical products in East Florida, Madison Papers).

101. See Lyon, *Louisiana in French Diplomacy*, 167–88.

102. For these instructions of 2 March 1803, see *Papers of James Madison: Secretary of State Series*, 4: 364–78.

103. Livingston to Madison, 20 May 1803; Monroe to Madison, 23 May 1803; Livingston and Monroe to Madison, 7 June 1803; and Monroe to Madison, 7 June 1803, *Papers of James Madison: Secretary of State Series*, 5: 19–20, 25, 69, 72–75, 104–5. The idea of inserting the 1800 retrocession clause in the 1803 treaty as a way of acquiring West Florida along with Louisiana and New Orleans originated with Livingston. The first French draft of the article of cession, dated 22 April 1803, stipulated merely that France would cede Louisiana and the island of New Orleans as they had been acquired from Spain in October 1800, but after Livingston had seen the text of the retrocession treaty he pressed for the inclusion of its third article in the purchase agreement. He even sought a clause that would bind both France and Spain to uphold his interpretation, but Barbé-Marbois persuaded him to accept instead a more general assurance that "should the occasion arise, the first consul would afford [the United States] all the assistance in his power." Monroe was slower to reach the same conclusion but eventually agreed that the insertion of the retrocession clause in the treaty would suffice to sanction the American claim to West Florida (see Francis Paul Renaut, *La Question de la Louisiane, 1796–1806* [Paris, 1918], 154–57, 219–21; George Dangerfield, *Chancellor Robert R. Livingston of New York, 1746–1813* [New York, 1960], 367–68; and Barbé-Marbois, *The History of Louisiana, particularly the Cession of that Colony to the United States of America* [Philadelphia, PA, 1830], 298). Or, to put the matter more simply, the

French offered to sell what they had acquired from Spain by 1803; the Americans, con-
strained by their instructions, agreed to purchase what the French had claimed in 1800,
and the French did not object. Napoleon then consented to the wording of the purchase
agreement. It required no great intelligence to predict that this solution would cause future difficulties, but the often-told story that Napoleon deliberately chose to insert an
ambiguous definition of Louisiana in the 1803 treaty so that he could later exploit those
difficulties is not exactly correct.

104. Jefferson to Madison, 24 August 1803, *Papers of James Madison: Secretary of
State Series,* 5: 340–41; and Jefferson to John Breckinridge, 25 August 1803, Jefferson
Papers. By 7 September 1803 Jefferson had completed an essay titled "An Examination
into the Boundaries of Louisiana," accompanied by a chronology of French activities
in the Mississippi Valley and on the Gulf Coast between 1673 and 1783. His argument
was based on an awareness that it had been France's intention in 1800 to reassert its
claims in these regions as they had been defined before the end of the Seven Years' War
and that were Spain to fail to deliver the country between the Iberville and Perdido
rivers to the United States, "this would not be delivering Louisiana with the extent that
it had when France possessed it & before it had even been dismembered: nor with the
extent it *now* has in the hands of Spain, since it has been restored to it's antient & integral form" ([Jefferson], *Documents Relating to the Purchase and Exploration of
Louisiana* [Boston, MA, 1904], 11–21, 23–40).

105. Henry Adams, for one, ignored the "Examination" altogether. Tucker and Hendrickson dismiss it as no better than "a directed verdict" (see *Empire of Liberty,* 142).

106. For discussions that grasp the full dimensions of Jefferson's thinking, see
Richard W. Van Alstyne, "The Significance of the Mississippi Valley in American Diplomatic History, 1686–1890," *Mississippi Valley Historical Review* 36 (1949): 215–38;
and Donald Jackson, *Thomas Jefferson and the Stony Mountains: Exploring the West
from Monticello* (Urbana, IL, 1981), 297–301.

107. Carlos Martínez de Yrujo to Madison, 4 September 1803, *Papers of James Madison: Secretary of State Series,* 5: 378–79; and Madison to Monroe, 26 December 1803,
ibid., 6: 213.

108. For the so-called Mobile Act, see Richard Peters et al., compilers, *The Public
Statutes at Large of the United States of America* (17 vols.; Boston, MA, 1848–73), 2:
251–54; and Yrujo to Madison, 7 March 1804, *Papers of James Madison: Secretary of
State Series,* 6: 557–62.

109. Madison to Yrujo, 19 March 1804, *Papers of James Madison: Secretary of State
Series,* 6: 604–5. The consequences of the rupture between Madison and Yrujo were
to plague American relations with Spain for several years. The minister's conduct made
him no longer welcome in Washington social circles, but the administration hesitated
to declare him persona non grata as it did not wish to end all negotiations with Spain.
Madison tried to induce Yrujo to depart voluntarily while also hinting that Spain might
recall him. These tactics failed to produce the desired result and the minister's recall
was formally requested in April 1805. Charles IV evaded the issue by doing no more
than granting Yrujo permission to depart at his own discretion. In the interim, the

minister took to attacking the administration in the newspapers under the pseudonym "Graviora Manent." Madison regarded this as a breach of Yrujo's diplomatic status and was outraged when the minister claimed the First Amendment rights of an American citizen in his defense. Indeed, so angry was Madison at these developments that he eventually sent a sixty-three-page letter to the American legation in Madrid protesting Yrujo's actions. (See Madison to Pinckney, 10 April 1804, ibid., 7: 30; Madison to Monroe, 26 October 1804, ibid., 8: 223–24; Monroe and Pinckney to Cevallos, 13 April 1805, and Cevallos to Monroe and Pinckney, 16 April 1805, both enclosed in Monroe and Pinckney to Madison, 16 April 1805, Diplomatic Dispatches of the Department of State, Spain, RG 59, National Archives. See also Madison to George W. Erving, 20 January 1807, Diplomatic Instructions of the Department of State, RG 59, National Archives.)

110. Madison to Livingston, 31 January 1804; to Pinckney, 6 February 1804; to Monroe, 8 March 1804; and to Pinckney, 10 April 1804, *Papers of James Madison: Secretary of State Series,* 6: 407–13, 438, 441, 565; 7: 28–31. The administration's dissatisfaction with Pinckney arose from a number of factors, including his disregard of instructions that he should wait in Madrid until Monroe's arrival in Europe before trying to settle the disputes with Spain. Pinckney, however, pressed on and almost caused a rupture with Spain before Monroe arrived (see Madison to Monroe, 9 November 1804, ibid., 8: 269–71; also Jefferson to Monroe, 8 January 1804, Jefferson Papers).

111. Madison to Monroe, 15 April 1804, *Papers of James Madison: Secretary of State Series,* 7: 51–61. For a map depicting Madison's intentions, see Thomas Maitland Marshall, *A History of the Western Boundary of the Louisiana Purchase* (Berkeley, CA, 1914), opposite p. 31.

112. The idea that $1 million might be paid for East Florida in conjunction with the settlement of the boundary disputes was discussed in an 18 February 1804 cabinet meeting (see "The Anas," in Paul L. Ford, ed., *The Writings of Thomas Jefferson* [10 vols; New York, 1892], 1: 304–5).

113. The August 1802 convention, which had established a commission to settle spoliations committed by Spanish vessels against American merchantmen during the Quasi-War with France, had been submitted to the Senate in January 1803 and rejected because it had failed to provide for claims against French vessels operating from Spanish ports. The Senate subsequently reconsidered the matter and ratified the convention in January 1804, by which time a new ratification was required from Spain. Angered by the Mobile Act of February 1804, Spain refused. For the text of the convention and its history, see Miller, *Treaties of the United States,* 2: 492–97.

114. It is misleading to assume that the United States was merely engaging in an act of extortion by seeking East Florida in this manner. According to its reading of the law of nations, the administration could have argued that it was entitled to seize the province as a reprisal for Spain's failure to prevent French abuse of its territory during the Quasi-War, and the weight of at least two notable authorities—Hugo Grotius and Vattel—could be adduced in support of that position (see Grotius, *De Jure Bellis AC Pacis Libri Tres,* trans. Francis W. Kelsey [Oxford, 1925 (orig. 1646)], 267–68; and

Vattel, *Law of Nations,* especially p. 228, where the Swiss jurist declared that in an un-resolved dispute between nations when one party "has taken possession of what be-longs to another, if it refuses to pay a debt, to repair an injury, or to make due satisfaction," the other "may seize something belonging to that Nation and may turn the object to its own advantage to the extent of what is due to it, together with inter-est and damages, or it may hold the object as security until full satisfaction has been made"). The United States was to adhere to this position until the negotiation of the Transcontinental Treaty in 1819.

115. After the signing of the Louisiana Purchase treaty in 1803, France became in-creasingly reluctant to enforce Jefferson's understanding of the retrocession clause on Spain, with the result being, as Livingston pointed out to Madison, that the grounds for the American claim to West Florida became "uncertain" and were likely to become subject to negotiations carrying a higher price. By the end of 1804, Livingston's suc-cessor in Paris, John Armstrong of New York, had reported that France was "treading back all their steps" on West Florida and had "decidedly expressed" against the view that it had been part of Louisiana. From Madrid, Pinckney summed up these devel-opments in a witticism that would have been worthy of Henry Adams when he re-marked that "France wants to be paid three times for [Louisiana]—Once, as she has already by us—secondly by Spain (as she now is) to save West Florida to her & place the Western Limit at Natchitoches & if this succeeds at some future period to sell the Floridas to us on something like the scheme already proposed through our friend Mr [Livingston] & for a price not unlike that given for Louisiana & France to receive the money." (See Livingston to Madison, 20 June 1804, *Papers of James Madison: Secre-tary of State Series,* 7: 343–4. See also Livingston to Madison, 21 November 1804, ibid., 8: 312–13; Monroe to Madison, 27 November 1804, ibid., 8: 329–33; Armstrong to Madison, 24 December 1804, ibid., 8: 417–19; and Pinckney to Madison, 26 April 1805, Diplomatic Dispatches, Spain).

116. Madison to Jefferson, 27 March 1805, Jefferson Papers. It was for this reason that Gallatin was always reluctant to press the claim to West Florida too vigorously at a time when the military strength of the United States could not support its preten-sions. As he put it to Madison, "To go to war for the western boundary of Louisiana, or even for the country between Mississippi and Perdido, after having omitted in our treaty of purchase to bind France to a certain construction of limits, will never do" (see Gallatin to Madison, 6 August 1805, Madison Papers).

117. For the claims commission, see Miller, *Treaties of the United States,* 2: 516–23.

118. See the letters of Monroe and Pinckney under the following dates: 2 February, 21 March, 16 April, 3, 16, 23, 25 May 1805, all in Diplomatic Dispatches, Spain. On 26 May 1805 Monroe forwarded to Madison a private journal he had kept throughout the negotiation (William Cabell Rives Collection of James Madison Papers, Library of Congress), and Pinckney sent Madison a long letter written in the form of a journal between 3 March and 22 May. Both Monroe's journal and Pinckney's letter are in Diplomatic Dispatches, Spain.

119. Madison to Jefferson, 2 August and 14 September 1805, Jefferson Papers; and

Madison to Albert Gallatin, 2 and 8 August 1805, in Carl E. Prince and Helen Fineman, eds., *The Papers of Albert Gallatin*, microfilm ed. (Philadelphia, PA, 1969), roll 11.

120. Jefferson to Madison, 4 August 1805, Madison Papers; and 7 August 1805, Rives Collection of Madison Papers.

121. Madison to Jefferson, 20 August, 1 and 30 September 1805, Jefferson Papers.

122. Jefferson to Madison, 17 August 1805, Rives Collection of Madison Papers; 25 and 27 August 1805, Madison Papers; and 11 October 1805, Rives Collection of Madison Papers.

123. Armstrong to Madison, 10 September, 3 October 1805, 9 March 1806, Diplomatic Dispatches of the Department of State, France, RG 59, National Archives. For a more detailed discussion, see Clifford L. Egan, "The United States, France, and West Florida, 1803–1807," *Florida Historical Quarterly* 47 (1969): 227–52.

124. Jefferson to Madison, 23 October 1805, Rives Collection of Madison Papers.

125. In a 12 November 1805 cabinet meeting, Gallatin voiced opposition to the idea of purchasing Florida "under an apprehension of war, lest we should be thought in fact to purchase peace," but he was overruled by the president and his colleagues (see "The Anas," in Ford, *Writings of Thomas Jefferson,* 1: 308). For other expressions of Gallatin's reservations, see his 21 November and 3 December 1805 letters to Jefferson, and his 1 March 1806 memorandum to Madison, all in Prince and Fineman, *Papers of Albert Gallatin,* roll 11.

126. For the Congressional debate, see Joseph Gales, compiler, *The Debates and Proceedings of the Congress of the United States* (42 vols.; Washington, DC, 1834–1856), 9th Cong., 1st sess., 946–55, 956–93, 1117–44. The claim that Madison had said "France wanted money & must have it" was not actually reported in the debates, though it was strongly implied, and it appears to have been the result of Randolph's interpretation of a conversation he had with the secretary of state. Madison resented the attribution of the remark and drew up a memorandum headed "For the public if found expedient," in which he wrote that it was "due to the Station &c to state that without undertaking to recollect the particular expressions made by me on the occasion, or remarking on the facility of misconceptions incident to transient conversations" that he should deny it was "within the view of the Ex. or of myself, to apply in whole or in part, monies which might be appropriated by Congress" for any purpose other than "a bona fide purchase for a valuable consideration in territory; or to purchase any territory from, or pay the price thereof, to any other, than the nation owning the territory & conveying the legal title thereto" (Madison Papers). Madison did not publish this statement, but when the Washington, DC, *National Intelligencer* began printing the congressional proceedings after 4 April 1806, it took pains, on 11 April and 5 May, to deny that the appropriation of $2 million was "a bribing of France to bully Spain" as well as to refute the report that "a distinguished member of the executive government" had "made application to the Secretary of the Treasury for money to aid in the negociation for the purchase of the Floridas, previous to any appropriation having been made for this purpose by Congress."

127. See Madison to Armstrong and Bowdoin, 13 March 1806, and to Bowdoin, 18

March 1806, both in Diplomatic Instructions. For maps of Madison's proposals for a neutral zone in the west, see Marshall, *A History of the Western Boundary of the Louisiana Purchase*, 42–49.

128. Armstrong to Madison, 4 May and 9 August 1806, Diplomatic Dispatches, France; Bowdoin to Madison, 22 August and 3 October 1806, Diplomatic Dispatches, Spain; and Erving to Madison, 17 June, 13 July, 27 and 28 August, 6 December 1806, ibid.

129. Bowdoin to Madison, 23 July 1806, 1 May and 2 October 1807, Diplomatic Dispatches, Spain; Erving to Madison, 13 July 1806, ibid. See also C. Edward Skeen, *John Armstrong: A Biography* (Syracuse, NY, 1981), 80–87.

130. See Armstrong to Madison, 16 October 1806, Diplomatic Dispatches, France; and William Lee to Madison, 14 December 1806, Consular Dispatches of the Department of State, Bordeaux, RG 59, National Archives. For Napoleon's German campaign of 1806, see Paul W. Schroeder, *The Transformation of European Politics, 1763–1848* (Oxford, UK, 1994), 301–10.

131. W. C. C. Claiborne to Madison, 8 October 1806, Territorial Papers of the Department of State, Orleans, RG 59, National Archives; and draft instructions to James Wilkinson, 8 November 1806, in the hands of Jefferson, Gallatin, and Madison, Jefferson Papers. For the establishment of the Neutral Ground, see J. Villasana Haggard, "The Neutral Ground between Louisiana and Texas, 1806–1821," *Louisiana Historical Quarterly* 28 (1945): 1028–47; and Jack D. L. Holmes, "Showdown on the Sabine: General James Wilkinson vs. Lieutenant-Colonel Simón de Herrara," *Louisiana Studies* 3 (1964): 46–76.

132. Madison to Armstrong and Bowdoin, 15 July 1807, Diplomatic Instructions. There was to be one further attempt to negotiate a financial arrangement as a way of settling the borders of Louisiana, proposed by Joseph Bonaparte as King of Spain in 1811 in return for the sum of $6 million. Madison would have none of it, pointing out that any treaty made while Spain was in a state of civil war and without a legitimate sovereign government could give the United States "neither right, nor possession" of the territories it claimed and would not "place us an inch nearer our object" (see Joel Barlow to Madison, 30 December 1811, and Madison to Barlow, 24 February 1812, in *The Papers of James Madison: Presidential Series* [5 vols. to date, ed. Robert A. Rutland et al.; Charlottesville, VA, 1984–], 4: 97–104, 199–202).

133. See Armstrong to Madison, 15 February 1808, Diplomatic Dispatches, France. Or, as the minister summarized it rather cryptically, "*With the one hand, they offer us the blessings of equal alliance against Great Britain and with the other they menace us with war if we do not accept this kindness, and with satisfaction, they pick our pockets with all imaginable diffidence, dexterity and impudence.*" Armstrong's advice to the administration, especially if it intended to resist British policy anyway, was "to avail ourselves of the circumstance as to draw from it the advantage of which it may be productive, viz: *accession of the Floridas and settlement of a western boundary.* In either case, do not suspend a moment the seizure of the Floridas."

134. See Madison to Armstrong, 2 May 1808, Diplomatic Instructions.

135. Erving to Madison, 15, 18, 21, 25 March, 14 May 1808, Diplomatic Dispatches, Spain. For events in Spain, see Gabriel H. Lovett, *Napoleon and the Birth of Modern Spain* (2 vols.; New York, 1965), 1: 85–179.

136. For warnings about Napoleon's possible intervention in Spain, see Erving to Madison, 29 October, 3 and 20 November 1807, Diplomatic Dispatches, Spain; and Armstrong to Madison, 15 November and 1 December 1807, 13 January 1808, Diplomatic Dispatches, France.

137. See Madison to Armstrong, 22 July and 9 September 1808, Diplomatic Instructions; also Madison to Jefferson, 29 July 1808, Jefferson Papers. For background to the British interest in emancipating Spanish America, see John Lynch, "British Policy and Spanish America, 1783–1808," *Journal of Latin American Studies* 1 (1969): 1–30; and Gabriel Paquette, "The Intellectual Context of British Diplomatic Recognition of the South American Republics, c. 1800–1830," *Journal of Transatlantic Studies* 2 (2004): 75–95.

138. These consequences were pointed out to Madison by the American minister in London, William Pinkney, in his letters of 7 September and 25 December 1808, Diplomatic Dispatches of the Department of State, Great Britain, RG 59, National Archives.

139. Madison to Jefferson, 7 August [1808], Jefferson Papers (the letter is misdated 1807). See also Lovett, *Napoleon and the Birth of Modern Spain*, 1: 181–230.

140. Madison to Gallatin, 19 August 1808, in Prince and Fineman, *Papers of Albert Gallatin,* roll 17. The intensity of Madison's language here was provoked by its being his response to a suggestion coming from the Federalist Party in Boston to the effect that the administration should end the Embargo, recognize the Supreme Central Junta in Spain, and then attempt to trade with Europe, in defiance of Napoleon's Continental System, through Spain. Nevertheless, Madison was often to express similar sentiments on later occasions (see, for example, his 22 October 1809 letter to Caesar A. Rodney, in which he remarked, "Whatever noise may be made on the occasion, the thing cannot admit of doubt with men who consult their judgments, not their sympathies with Spain," *Papers of James Madison: Presidential Series,* 2: 26).

141. See Madison to Armstrong, 9 September 1808, Diplomatic Instructions; also Pinkney to Madison, 2 August 1808, Madison Papers.

142. For Erving's reports from Spain, see his letters to Madison under the following dates: 22 June, 11 August (two letters), 10, 13, 20, 22, 27, 29 September, 6 October, 8 and 11 November, 1 and 31 December 1808, 9 and 12 January, 14 February 1809, all in Diplomatic Dispatches, Spain. See also his letters of 14 March, 14, 28, 30 May, 14 June, 9 July, 3 and 25 August, 19 September, 28 November 1809, ibid.

143. See Madison to Pinkney, 23 October 1809, *Papers of James Madison: Presidential Series,* 2: 28; also Robert Smith to Erving, 1 November 1809, Diplomatic Instructions. Madison would also have been doubtful about the claim made by Onís that he had the power to settle the disputes between Spain and the United States. When the State Department translated Onís's credentials, they contained no description of his powers. Madison would have regarded this as a tactic to entice him into recognizing the Supreme Central Junta without his knowing what position it would be likely to take

in any negotiations (see Erving's 9 July 1809 dispatch to Robert Smith, accompanied by John Graham's translation of Onís's credentials, Diplomatic Dispatches, Spain).

144. See Erving to Robert Smith, 28 November 1809, Diplomatic Dispatches, Spain.

145. Madison to Jefferson, 28 March 1809, and Jefferson to Madison, 31 March 1809, *Papers of James Madison: Presidential Series*, 1: 84, 93. In 1809 Erving had also facilitated an agreement between Joseph Yznardi and Richard Hackley over which of them should hold a consular office in Spain they had been disputing, for which he was censured by the administration. In reporting the matter to Jefferson, Madison included it as "among the faux pas" of Erving (see Madison to Jefferson, 9 April 1809, ibid., 1: 107).

146. Madison to Jefferson, 24 April 1809, ibid., 1: 135–36.

147. See Erving to Robert Smith, 25 January, 7 and 9 February 1810; and to John Graham, 2 March 1810, Diplomatic Dispatches, Spain. For the French siege of Cádiz, which was to last until August 1812, see Lovett, *Napoleon and the Birth of Modern Spain*, 1: 355–414.

148. See the accounts printed in the Washington, DC, *National Intelligencer*, 13 and 18 June 1810. For a discussion of the developments in Caracas, see P. Michael McKinley, *Pre-revolutionary Caracas: Politics, Economy, and Society, 1777–1811* (Cambridge, UK, 1985), 146–58.

Chapter 2. West Florida

1. Claiborne to Madison, 17 December 1809, in *The Papers of James Madison: Presidential Series* (5 vols. to date, ed. Robert A. Rutland et al.; Charlottesville, VA, 1984–), 2: 136–37.

2. For Claiborne's career as territorial governor, see Joseph T. Hatfield, *William Claiborne: Jeffersonian Centurion in the American Southwest* (Lafayette, LA, 1976), 118–236; and Peter J. Kastor, *The Nation's Crucible: The Louisiana Purchase and the Creation of America* (New Haven, CT, 2004), 55–75.

3. See the biographical sketches of Casa Calvo and Morales in Jared W. Bradley, ed., *Interim Appointment: W. C. C. Claiborne Letter Book, 1804–1805* (Baton Rouge, LA, 2002), 484–98. See also Claiborne to Madison, 20 October 1804, Territorial Papers of the Department of State, Orleans, RG 59, National Archives.

4. Claiborne to Madison, 24 January 1804, in *The Papers of James Madison: Secretary of State Series* (8 vols. to date, ed. Robert Brugger et al.; Charlottesville, VA, 1986–), 6: 377.

5. Claiborne and Wilkinson to Madison, 27 December 1803, ibid., 6: 233.

6. Claiborne to Vicente Folch, 2 June 1804, in Dunbar Rowland, ed., *Official Letter Books of W. C. C. Claiborne* (6 vols.; Jackson, MS, 1917), 2: 185–86.

7. For the extent to which federal officials near the borderlands had to engage in "diplomacy" with Spain, see Peter J. Kastor, "Motives of Peculiar Urgency: Local Diplomacy in Louisiana, 1803–1821," *William and Mary Quarterly*, 3d ser., vol. 58 (2001): 819–48.

8. Madison to Claiborne, 20 February and 28 August 1804, *Papers of James Madi-*

son: Secretary of State Series, 6: 496–97, 7: 643; and 7 January 1805, Domestic Letters of the Department of State, RG 59, National Archives.

9. Claiborne to Madison, 25 July 1804, *Papers of James Madison: Secretary of State Series,* 7: 520–21; and 5 and 19 January 1805, Territorial Papers, Orleans. For additional material on this dispute, see Bradley, *Interim Appointment,* 145–57.

10. Claiborne to Madison, 30 May 1804, *Papers of James Madison: Secretary of State Series,* 7: 266; and 6 August 1805 and 26 June 1806, Territorial Papers, Orleans.

11. See the orders issued by Charles de Grande Pré to all syndics in New Feliciana, West Florida, 23 April 1805, Philip Hicky and Family Papers, Louisiana State University. See also Andrew McMichael, "The 'Kemper Rebellion': Filibustering and Resident Anglo-American Loyalty in Spanish West Florida," *Louisiana History* 43 (2002): 136–41.

12. Claiborne to Madison, 5 November 1804, *Papers of James Madison: Secretary of State Series,* 8: 260–61; and 21 April, 19 May, 3, 5, 6, 7, 10 August 1805, Territorial Papers, Orleans. For Clark's oppositional politics, see Hatfield, *William Claiborne,* 157–62.

13. See Claiborne to Madison, 5 August 1805, Territorial Papers, Orleans.

14. No written record of Madison's inquiry has been found, but see Jacob Wagner's 24 September 1805 response to it, James Madison Papers, Library of Congress.

15. Claiborne to Madison, 27 June, 25 July (two letters), 11 December 1804, *Papers of James Madison: Secretary of State Series,* 7: 379, 520–22; 8: 369–70. Also Claiborne to Madison, 5 and 21 April, 5 June, 23 August 1805, 21 January 1806, Territorial Papers, Orleans.

16. As Claiborne remarked in his 27 July 1804 letter to Madison, the activities of the Spanish officers in Orleans ensured that the territory "will for some time be subjected more or less to foreign influence" (see *Papers of James Madison: Secretary of State Series,* 7: 529).

17. Claiborne to Madison, 23 November 1804, ibid., 8: 315–17. For a study of Folch's career in the borderlands, see David H. White, *Vicente Folch, Governor in Spanish Florida, 1787–1811* (Washington, DC, 1981).

18. Claiborne to Madison, 5 November 1804, *Papers of James Madison: Secretary of State Series,* 8: 260–61; and 19 and 21 April, 24 and 31 October, 5 November 1805, 15 March 1806, all in Territorial Papers, Orleans.

19. For the commercial dependence of New Orleans on West Florida, see Daniel Clark to Madison, 13 December 1803, *Papers of James Madison: Secretary of State Series,* 6: 166. For Spain's Indian policy and the relationship with John Forbes and Company, see William S. Coker and Thomas D. Watson, *Indian Traders of the Southeastern Spanish Borderlands: Panton, Leslie & Company and John Forbes & Company, 1783–1847* (Pensacola, FL, 1986), 73–92, 182–242.

20. For such requests, see Madison to Claiborne, 28 August 1804, *Papers of James Madison: Secretary of State Series,* 7: 643; and 18 March 1805, Domestic Letters.

21. Claiborne to Madison, 5 July, 9 August 1805, 6 March 1806, Territorial Papers, Orleans.

22. See, for example, Claiborne to Folch, 7 March 1804; Folch to Claiborne, 15 March 1804; Claiborne to Morales, 22 October 1805; and Claiborne to Folch, 31 October 1805, in Rowland, *Claiborne Letter Books,* 2: 19, 38; 3: 205–6, 221–22. See also Claiborne to Madison, 24 and 31 October 1805, 18 March 1806, 21 April 1807, Territorial Papers, Orleans; Edmund Pendleton Gaines to Henry Dearborn, 17 April 1807, in Clarence E. Carter et al., eds., *The Territorial Papers of the United States* (28 vols.; Washington, DC, 1934–75), *Mississippi,* 5: 546–48; and Harry Toulmin to Madison, 25 February 1809, Madison Papers.

23. Toulmin to Madison, 6 July and 11 October 1805, in Walter Lowrie and Matthew St. Clair Clarke, compilers, *American State Papers: Documents, Legislative and Executive, of the Congress of the United States* (38 vols.; Washington, DC, 1832–61), *Foreign Relations,* 2: 682–83; and Claiborne to Madison, 24 and 31 October, 9 December 1805, Territorial Papers, Orleans.

24. The petition came from a convention of delegates representing several settlements east of the Pearl River in the Mississippi Territory (see Carter et al., *Territorial Papers: Mississippi,* 6: 26–30).

25. See Joseph Gales, compiler, *The Debates and Proceedings of the Congress of the United States* (42 vols.; Washington, DC, 1834–1856; hereafter *Annals of Congress*), 11th Cong., 2d sess., 1257, 1443, 1761. See also Madison to the House of Representatives, 9 February 1810, *American State Papers: Foreign Relations,* 3: 341; and Washington, DC, *National Intelligencer,* 20 June 1810. In reporting the failure of these petitions, the Mississippi territorial delegate, George Poindexter, complained bitterly in his 2 May 1810 circular letter to his constituents that the United States had allowed "a contemptible commandant, deriving his powers from a dethroned prince, to tax a portion of our citizens in the very country over which we have actually exercized the right of legislation" (see Natchez *Weekly Chronicle,* 25 June 1810).

26. These remarks are based on the essays "A Sketch of Pensacola" and "Of West Florida," printed in the *National Intelligencer,* 16 July 1810 and 31 January 1811. For Innerarity's description, see his 21 January 1811 letter to John McKee ("West Florida and Its Attempt on Mobile, 1810–1811," *American Historical Review* 2 [1897]: 705). See also Toulmin to Madison, 20 January 1816, Letters Received by the Secretary of War, Registered Series, T-20 (9), RG 107, National Archives. For descriptions of the frontier economy, see Daniel H. Usner, Jr., *Indians, Settlers, and Slaves in a Frontier Exchange Economy: The Lower Mississippi Valley before 1783* (Chapel Hill, NC, 1992), 145–286; and Robin F. A. Fabel, *The Economy of British West Florida, 1763–1783* (Tuscaloosa, AL, 1988), 49–74, 198–210.

27. See the accounts from the *National Intelligencer* cited in the preceding note; and also Adam Rothman, *Slave Country: American Expansionism and the Origins of the Deep South* (Cambridge, MA, 2005), 54, 70. For more general accounts of the economic development of the region, see David J. Libby, *Slavery and Frontier Mississippi, 1720–1835* (Jackson, MS, 2004), 17–59; and Christopher Morris, *Becoming Southern: The Evolution of a Way of Life, Warren County and Vicksburg, Mississippi, 1770–1860* (New York, 1995), 3–41.

28. Folch to Claiborne, 11 February 1808, in Rowland, *Claiborne Letter Books,* 4:

157–59; and Claiborne to Madison, 17 February 1808 and enclosures, Territorial Papers, Orleans. The enclosed correspondence between Folch and Claiborne revealed that the former, in effect, wished to establish Baton Rouge, Mobile, and Pensacola as depots for American produce for re-export to Havana and other Spanish ports. Resorting to an argument whose irony would not have been lost on Madison, Folch asserted that West Floridians, because of their close proximity to Louisiana, should not be treated as foreigners under American law. For a memorandum, probably originally drafted by Folch, describing how the American enforcement of the Embargo on the inland waterways had reduced West Florida to "the most lamentable situation," see the enclosures sent by the captain-general in Havana to Cevallos on 18 June 1808 (Estado, legajo 5549, Archivo Histórico Nacional, Madrid [copy in Library of Congress]).

29. John Adair to Madison, 9 January 1809, Madison Papers.

30. See Claiborne to William Wykoff, Jr., 14 June 1810, Territorial Papers, Orleans. This letter, as secretary of state Robert Smith pointed out when he forwarded a copy of it to Mississippi territorial governor David Holmes on 21 July 1810, was written "under the sanction of the president" (ibid.). For Madison's knowledge of the expulsion of French nationals from Cuba, see the 31 August 1808 letter sent to the State Department by Claiborne (Territorial Papers, Orleans).

31. See Robert Smith to Pinkney, 13 June 1810, Diplomatic Instructions of the Department of State, RG 59, National Archives.

32. See n. 30 of this chapter. For a discussion of the role of conventions in bridging and legitimizing interregnums in republican theory, see Gordon S. Wood, *The Creation of the American Republic, 1776–1787* (Chapel Hill, NC, 1969), 306–43.

33. For accounts of these developments, see Stanley Clisby Arthur, *The Story of the West Florida Rebellion* (St. Francisville, LA, 1935), 31–33, 37–38; David A. Bice, *The Original Lone Star Republic: Scoundrels, Statesmen and Schemers of the 1810 West Florida Rebellion* (Clanton, AL, 2004), 131–51; and Isaac J. Cox, *The West Florida Controversy, 1798–1813: A Study in American Diplomacy* (Baltimore, MD, 1918), 333–46.

34. Arthur, *Story of the West Florida Rebellion*, 38–42. For Fulton's 20 April 1810 letter to Madison, see *Papers of James Madison: Presidential Series*, 2: 320–21. See also William Barrow et al. to Philip Hicky et al., 3 July 1810, and Hickey et al. to Tomaso Estevan, 5 July 1810, Philip Hicky and Family Papers.

35. For earlier events in West Florida, see Cox, *West Florida Controversy*, 314–25. For the larger developments in the Spanish-American world, see John H. Elliott, *Empires of the Atlantic World: Britain and Spain in America, 1492–1830* (New Haven, CT, 2006), 369–83; John Lynch, *The Spanish American Revolutions, 1808–1826* (New York, 1973), 51–57, 133, 189–95, 233; and Jaime E. Rodríguez O., *The Independence of Spanish America* (New York, 1998), 107–68.

36. McMichael, "Kemper Rebellion," 133–65. Claiborne also dismissed the Kemper revolt as "nothing more than a riot" (see his 21 April 1805 letter to Madison, Territorial Papers, Orleans).

37. See Charles de Grand Pré to Philip Hicky, 13 October 1806, Philip Hicky and Family Papers. Some sense of the cooperation between Spanish officials and American settlers can be gained from the legal and commercial documents assembled by the

WPA of Louisiana, *Archives of the Spanish Government of West Florida* (18 vols.; Baton Rouge, LA, 1939), especially vols. 15 and 18.

38. The best discussion of the degrees of satisfaction and dissatisfaction with Spanish rule is Andrew McMichael, *Atlantic Loyalties: Americans in Spanish West Florida, 1785–1810* (Athens, GA, 2008), 67–107, 127–48. McMichael argues, convincingly, that American settlers were generally content under Spanish rule, while noting an increase in discontent over crime, land policy, and the administration of justice in the Feliciana district after 1807. For an extreme example of American dissatisfaction with Spanish land policy, see the account written by deputy surveyor Ira C. Kneeland of his dealings with two prominent settlers, Robert Percy and William Herries, who apparently resented paying fees for land surveys and had endeavored to "render the surveying business unpopular by making it an American topic of conversation." It was, Kneeland noted, their object "to Carry every point with the Government, for which purpose they descend to the most base meanness, deceit and Hypocrisy." Aside from them, Kneeland remarked that he had "no violent enemies" but they were, he added, "sufficient and have many tools & pimps to support them" (Kneeland to Vicente Pintardo, 10 August 1808, Papers of Vicente Sebastián Pintardo, Library of Congress).

39. Arthur, *Story of the West Florida Rebellion,* 33–34, 40–41, 43. As a report on 2 July 1810 in the *Louisiana Gazette and New Orleans Daily Advertiser* made clear, political opinions about the future of West Florida were divided, and even those Americans who favored joining the Union had "never raised a voice against Spain" or the Spanish resistance to the French invasion. Their conduct, instead, was governed by "principles of self-preservation, the first law of nature." For similar observations, see also Holmes to Robert Smith, 11 July 1810, Territorial Papers of the Department of State, Mississippi, RG 59, National Archives.

40. The draft "constitution" was first published in the Natchez *Weekly Chronicle* on 17 July 1810, after which it was reprinted in several newspapers (see the *Louisiana Gazette and New Orleans Daily Advertiser* of 25 July 1810). To call the document a constitution may be something of a misnomer; it might be more accurate to say that it combined aspects of a political manifesto with a skeletal legal code or constitution. When Claiborne read it, he believed that it had "originated with Individuals not very friendly to the U. States." He continued, "It has been attributed to Mr Skipwith;—But I can trace in the Instrument the hand of Daniel Clark, and his object, (I presume) is, to strengthen his Title to several hundred thousand Acres of Land in West Florida, which subsequent to the Cession of Louisiana, he purchased of the Spanish Indendant Morales" (see Claiborne to Robert Smith, 28 August 1810, Territorial Papers, Orleans).

41. There is little doubt there was some general knowledge that Wykoff had received a letter from Claiborne, but none of this knowledge accurately reflected the letter's contents. As Fulwar Skipwith, later to become the first president of the short-lived republic of West Florida, recalled, "Colo Wykoff, a neighbor of mine [received a letter] from the House of the President & urging him to mount his horse, if necessary, to travel among & to stimulate the Inhabitants of Florida to declare themselves Independent; & that he Govr. C——ne or the Government, I am not certain which, would defray the expenses." On this basis, Skipwith concluded that "both Govr. C——ne & the President" were

"highly delighted at seeing us led on" and that the president was "pre-determined to oc-cupy this Country, after we should subvert the Spanish Authorities" (see Skipwith to John Graham, 14 January 1811, West Florida Papers, Library of Congress). Knowledge of Claiborne's letter also reached the newspapers, and the British chargé d'affaires in Washington was to send to London an account taken from a published 2 February 1811 letter very similar to that Skipwith reported to Graham. The source of that letter was said to be "a gentleman of the first respectability to a friend in Washington," and it was published as evidence that Madison had instigated the West Florida independence move-ment "as a pretext for seizing the country" (see John Philip Morier to Lord Richard Wellesley, 9 May 1811, Public Record Office: Foreign Office, ser. 5, vol. 74 [copy in Li-brary of Congress]). If it is assumed that Wykoff did not deliberately misrepresent the in-structions he had received from Claiborne, the most likely explanation for the mis-understandings about Madison's intentions for West Florida is that the local settlers simply assumed that any talk of a convention necessarily implied that the province was about to declare its independence. Further information on this subject might have been obtained from the letters exchanged between Claiborne and Wykoff, but the latter, act-ing on the advice of the former, may have destroyed their correspondence (see Clai-borne to Wykoff, 26 March 1811, in Rowland, *Claiborne Letter Books,* 5: 189–90).

42. Barrow to John Bedford, 4 June and 5 August 1810, enclosed in Bedford's 4 July and 26 August 1810 letters to Madison, *Papers of James Madison: Presidential Se-ries,* 2: 400, 509.

43. See Barrow to Bedford, 5 August 1810, ibid. See also the *Louisiana Gazette and New Orleans Daily Advertiser,* 6 August 1810.

44. For these proceedings, see the Journal of the West Florida Convention, entries for 25, 26, 27 July 1810, West Florida Papers.

45. See Holmes to Robert Smith, 8 August 1810, Territorial Papers, Mississippi.

46. See Journal of the West Florida Convention, entry for 13 August 1810, record-ing the receipt of a 30 July 1810 address from DeLassus.

47. Ibid., entries for 14, 15, 22 August. For the 22 August ordinance, see *Ordinances adopted by the Convention of West-Florida* (Natchez, 1810), 3–5, 30–32.

48. *Ordinances adopted by the Convention of West-Florida,* 5–26. For discussions of how Spanish colonial government was dependent on the administrative and review functions of its courts, see John Lynch, *Spanish Colonial Administration, 1782–1810: The Intendant System in the Viceroyalty of the Rio de la Plata* (New York, 1958), 237–71; and Charles R. Cutter, *The Legal Culture of Northern New Spain, 1700–1810* (Albu-querque, NM, 1995), 47–148.

49. *Ordinances adopted by the Convention of West-Florida,* 24–30.

50. See Journal of the West Florida Convention, entry for 22 August 1810. As a deputy surveyor Lopéz was directly affected by the proposed reforms in land policy, and he informed his superior, Surveyor General Pintardo, with a touch of sarcasm, that the delegates were forming a government "by which you are requested to regu-late certain things to suit the public good" (Lopéz to Pintardo, 20 August 1810, Pa-pers of Vicente Sebastián Pintardo).

51. For DeLassus's 21 August address to the assembled Spanish officials, see *Archives*

of the Spanish Government of West Florida, 18: 76–80; and also his "Report on the Events of 14 August 1810," ibid., 18: 81–82.

52. See Journal of the West Florida Convention, entry for 22 August 1810. In Philadelphia, Onís, consumed by his fears that the convention would declare West Florida independent, missed the significance of the changes implemented by the 22 August ordinance and adduced them as evidence that the delegates would remain loyal to Spain. As he reported to Madrid, "So has terminated the revolution of West Florida—without violence, without shedding a drop of blood" (Onís to Eusibio Bardaxi y Azura, 30 September 1810, Estado, legajo 5636).

53. See Holmes to Robert Smith, 21 August 1810, Territorial Papers, Mississippi.

54. Johnson to Holmes, 14 August 1810, enclosed in Holmes to Smith, 21 August 1810, ibid.

55. Ibid.

56. See Journal of the West Florida Convention, entries for 24, 25, 27, 28, 29 August 1810.

57. Ibid., entry for 22 September 1810.

58. Ibid., entries for 22, 25, 26 September 1810. For the account of the fate of De-Lassus, see the letter by R. Davidson to Abner L. Duncan, 26 September 1810, printed in the *National Intelligencer,* 19 October 1810.

59. See the preamble to the 26 September 1810 declaration of independence, Journal of the West Florida Convention.

60. See John Rhea to Holmes, 22 September 1810, Journal of the West Florida Convention, entry for 22 September 1810.

61. Rhea to Holmes, 26 September 1810, enclosed in Holmes to Robert Smith, 3 October 1810, Territorial Papers, Mississippi.

62. Rhea to Robert Smith, 10 October 1810, enclosed in Holmes to Smith, 17 October 1810, ibid.

63. See Madison to Robert Smith, 17 July 1810, the contents of which indicate that the president had read a 20 June 1810 letter from Holmes to the State Department reporting on recent developments in West Florida (see *Papers of James Madison: Presidential Series,* 2: 419–21).

64. Holmes to Robert Smith, 31 July, 8 and 21 August 1810, Territorial Papers, Mississippi. The first of these letters was forwarded to Madison by John Graham on 24 August 1810 (see *Papers of James Madison: Presidential Series,* 2: 505). See also Thomas Robertson to Smith, 26 August 1810, forwarded to Madison on 21 September 1810 (*Papers of James Madison: Presidential Series,* 2: 549–50).

65. Madison to Eustis, 30 August 1810 (*Papers of James Madison: Presidential Series,* 2: 517). As late as 29 October 1810 Madison continued to refer to the "expiring Authority at Cadiz" as a factor in influencing the outcomes in West Florida (see his letter of that date to John Armstrong, ibid., 2: 598).

66. Madison to Gallatin, 22 August 1810, and to Eustis, 30 August 1810, ibid., 2: 502, 517.

67. In replying to Madison's 30 August request about how he might extend U.S. au-

thority over West Florida, Eustis stated that it was difficult "to determine what part should be taken by Government" as it was impossible "to divine what course" events might take. He supposed, nevertheless, that if the West Floridians did seek U.S. intervention, "protection of some kind will necessarily be implied" but to what extent he was uncertain (see Eustis to Madison, 7 September 1810, ibid., 2: 531). Navy Secretary Paul Hamilton was no more helpful, remarking merely that he assumed that the administration would "soon be called to the exercize of much circumspection and no little firmness" (see Hamilton to Madison, 20 September 1810, ibid., 2: 546).

68. See Holmes to Robert Smith, 26 September 1810, Territorial Papers, Mississippi, where Holmes mentioned he had enclosed an account by Abner Duncan of the capture of the fort at Baton Rouge. That enclosure cannot now be located, but it clearly provided the basis for the item that appeared in the 19 October 1810 issue of the *National Intelligencer*.

69. Madison to Jefferson, 19 October 1810, *Papers of James Madison: Presidential Series,* 2: 585.

70. Ibid., 585–86. For Lowry's mission, see Robert Smith to Madison, [23 July 1810], ibid., 2: 390; and Madison to Smith, 17 and 26 July 1810, ibid., 2: 420, 439–40, including nn. 2–3.

71. Accounts of the dealings of the Caracas junta with British officials appeared in the *Louisiana Gazette and New Orleans Daily Advertiser,* 10 August 1810, and the *National Intelligencer,* 15 and 26 October, 7 November 1810. See also Lowry to Robert Smith, 6 September 1810 (two letters), Consular Dispatches of the Department of State, La Guaira, RG 59, National Archives. See also Peggy K. Liss, *Atlantic Empires: The Network of Trade and Revolution, 1713–1826* (Baltimore, MD, 1983), 202.

72. Joseph Gales, Jr., "Recollections of the Civil History of the War of 1812," *Historical Magazine,* 3d ser., vol. 3 (1874–75): 157.

73. Ibid.

74. Madison to Jefferson, 19 October 1810, *Papers of James Madison: Presidential Series,* 2: 585.

75. See Holmes to Robert Smith and enclosures, 3 October 1810, Territorial Papers, Mississippi.

76. For the cabinet meeting, see Gales, "Recollections of the Civil History of the War of 1812," 157. Gales recorded that the cabinet meeting was held on 25 October 1810, the same day that he believed Holmes's 3 October letter arrived in the capital. In fact, Holmes's letter arrived on 22 October, but its docket became separated from the letter and is now misfiled in January 1811 in Territorial Papers, Mississippi.

77. For the editing of the proclamation, see the text in *Papers of James Madison: Presidential Series,* 2: 595–96, including nn. 1–3.

78. See Gales, "Recollections of the Civil History of the War of 1812," 157.

79. In his 10 October 1810 letter to Robert Smith, Rhea had stated that unless the administration responded promptly to West Florida's request for admission to the Union, the delegates would be obliged because of their "weak and unprotected situation . . . to look to some foreign Government for support" (see n. 62 of this chapter).

80. Madison to Pinkney, 30 October 1810, *Papers of James Madison: Presidential Series,* 2: 605.

81. That this possibility had occurred to the administration was revealed by Robert Smith in a conversation with the French minister, Louis-Marie Turreau, who had complained to the State Department about the prominent role taken by Americans in the West Florida revolution. Smith responded that he assumed neither Napoleon nor King Joseph could object to the United States taking steps to prevent West Florida from falling into the hands of Great Britain and that the American occupation, being only provisional, should be seen as a request that the question of the status of the province be taken up again in negotiations "as soon as circumstances will permit" (see Turreau to the duc de Cadore, 6 December 1810, Archives du Ministère des Affaires Étrangères: Correspondence Politique, États-Unis, vol. 63 [copy in Library of Congress]). The message was reinforced by American diplomats in Paris, who stated that it was not the intention of the United States "to impair the just claims of other nations" to West Florida and that the republic stood "ready at all times should such claims be supposed to exist to meet & discuss them in the same candid & equitable manner as they would have had not this change of occupancy been effected" (see Jonathan Russell to the duc de Cadore, 18 December 1810, ibid.).

82. Emmerich de Vattel, *The Law of Nations; or, The Principles of Natural Law, Applied to the Conduct and to the Affairs of Nations and of Sovereigns,* trans. Charles G. Fenwick (Washington, DC, 1916 [orig. 1758]), 163.

83. The 10 October request from the West Florida convention for immediate admission to the Union was docketed by John Graham with this remark, to which Graham added "the U.S. asserting a prior right of sovereignty" (see n. 62 of this chapter).

84. *Papers of James Madison: Presidential Series,* 2: 595.

85. Robert Smith to Claiborne, 27 October 1810, Domestic Letters. In its 29 December 1810 issue the *National Intelligencer* reported events from West Florida under the heading of "East Louisiana Affairs." In a letter to Folch, Claiborne explained that the United States deplored "the assumption of the Sovereign power by an association of Individuals" in West Florida, which had imposed upon the republic "the necessity of resorting to the most prompt & effectual means for the preservation of the rights & tranquility of the United States" by taking possession of the province to the Perdido. These "weighty and just considerations," Claiborne hoped, would persuade Folch not to attribute his actions to any "unfriendly disposition" toward Spain. "The limits of Louisiana," he added, would remain "the subject of 'fair and friendly discussion' between our respective Governments" (see Claiborne to Folch, 20 December 1810, Papeles Procedentes de Cuba, Archivo General de Indias, Seville, legajo 1569 [copy in Library of Congress]).

86. For these developments, see Journal of the West Florida Convention, where the delegates, on 25 October 1810, considered a draft constitution, which they adopted two days later (see the entries for 25, 26, 27 October 1810). The constitution established a bicameral legislature—with representatives to be chosen annually and senators to be elected triennially—which was to elect a governor biennially. The province was divided

into five districts—Baton Rouge, New Feliciana, St. Helena, St. Ferdinand (formerly Chifoncté), and Mobile—with each district having three representatives and one senator, with the exception of New Feliciana, which was allocated four representatives. The new legislature met at St. Francisville on 19 November 1810 and three days later elected Fulwar Skipwith as governor (see Arthur, *Story of the West Florida Rebellion,* 127–29). For Skipwith's background and career before 1809, see Henry Bartholomew Cox, *The Parisian American: Fulwar Skipwith of Virginia* (Washington, DC, 1964).

87. The convention had appointed Skipwith as an associate judge of the superior court established by the 22 August ordinance on 24 August. DeLassus vetoed the selection three days later. The convention, nevertheless, had insisted on the appointment, arguing that the importance of having "a gentleman of [Skipwith's] capacity and good character in that station" justified the delegates "in deviating a little from ancient forms" (see Journal of the West Florida Convention, entries for 24, 27, 28 August 1810). When Onís learned of Skipwith's selection, he lost no time in deducing, on the basis of Skipwith being Jefferson's "nephew" and of his long service at the court of Napoleon, that Skipwith had gone to Monticello, where he had received the instructions from Napoleon that Madison had followed in engineering the West Florida revolt for the purpose of annexing the province (see Onís to Bardaxi, 12 January 1811, Estado, legajo 5637). Skipwith was not exactly Jefferson's nephew, but his father, Henry Skipwith, was Jefferson's brother-in-law, by virtue of Henry's marriage into the Wayles family of Virginia.

88. See n. 41 of this chapter.

89. See Claiborne to Robert Smith, 12 December 1810, Territorial Papers, Orleans.

90. For Skipwith's unsent letters to Madison of 5 and 9 December 1810, see West Florida Papers. The West Florida Senate appears to have held no meetings after 9 December 1810. There are no records of deliberations in the House of Representatives after 6 December 1810.

91. Few of Skipwith's personal letters have survived, but he protested bitterly to friends in Washington, particularly John Graham and John Mason, over the way he had been treated by the administration. As he told Graham on 23 December 1810, he had hoped to receive from either him or Mason "a hint in *confidence,* of the course which, individually, you might wish to see the Patriotic Americans in their struggle to throw off the Spanish yoke; but in this I have been disappointed, & for reasons, doubtless satisfactory to yourself" (West Florida Papers). Mason remonstrated against the injustice of these protests, recalling later that in a June 1811 letter Skipwith had written to him that "I might have saved you from being embroiled in that affair." Mason replied, "You are really mistaken, I was not informed of its bearings until it had advanced too far" (see Mason to Skipwith, 15 January 1813, Causten-Pickett Papers, Library of Congress).

92. See Turreau to the duc de Cadore, 1 November 1810, Correspondence Politique, États-Unis, vol. 63. At this juncture, the State Department had relatively few dealings with the British chargé d'affaires, John Philip Morier, for the reason that the British ministry had yet to replace Francis James Jackson, whom Madison had declared persona non grata in October 1809, with a fully accredited minister. For his part,

Morier tended to avoid contact with the administration, in whose statements on West Florida he placed no confidence anyway (see Morier to Wellesley, 16 February 1811, Public Record Office: Foreign Office, ser. 5, vol. 74).

93. *National Intelligencer,* 1 December 1810.

94. For the message of 5 December 1810, see *Papers of James Madison: Presidential Series,* 3: 49–54.

95. This matter has been the source of some confusion ever since Isaac J. Cox pointed out, in 1918, that the administration could not have received Holmes's 17 October letter in time to have made the decisions it did by 27 October (see Cox, *West Florida Controversy,* 416n31). That letter, in fact, was not received until 8 November 1810. (For an account of which letters and their enclosures from Holmes were received before 17 October, see *Papers of James Madison: Presidential Series,* 3: 55n4). Cox assumed no more than that the president "had some reason for concealing the existence of the earlier communications" of 26 September and 3 October from Holmes. Later generations of historians have concluded that the reason must have been to conceal evidence of the administration's presumed involvement in fomenting the West Florida revolt (see, for example, Joseph B. Smith, *The Plot to Steal Florida: James Madison's Phony War* [New York, 1983], 66–67). This is unlikely inasmuch as Holmes's earlier letters hardly contained evidence that the administration was encouraging the West Florida convention to issue a declaration of independence, and their contents revealed no awareness of Claiborne's 14 June 1810 letter to Wykoff, in which the president had explicitly tried to prevent the convention from taking any such step. A more plausible explanation for the confusion is simple clerical inadvertence arising from the fact that Holmes's 17 October letter contained another copy of the West Florida declaration of independence, which the convention had earlier sent to Holmes to be forwarded to Washington. In copying extracts from various letters for inclusion in the president's annual message, State Department clerks probably assumed that many of the documents they were copying had also been included in Holmes's later letter of 17 October. In any event, it makes little sense to assume the administration was trying to conceal evidence of a policy it had never espoused at all.

96. See *Annals of Congress,* 11th Cong., 3d sess., 16, 17, 25, 37ff, 43, 65, 103, 107. See also *National Intelligencer,* 22 and 29 December 1810.

97. *Annals of Congress,* 11th Cong., 3d sess., 382, 465, 474–77, 482–86, 493–508, 514, 515, 525–42, 555, 577, 858, 860, and 936. The West Florida parishes between the Mississippi and Pearl rivers were later added to the state of Louisiana in April 1812 (see Cox, *West Florida Controversy,* 605).

98. See n. 30 of this chapter.

99. Robert Smith to William Harris Crawford, 20 June 1810, Domestic Letters. A copy of the instructions enclosed for the agent Crawford was to select was also sent to Governor Holmes for his information, and they were printed by Clarence E. Carter, who identified them as instructions intended for Wykoff (see Carter et al., *Territorial Papers: Orleans,* 9: 883–84, 885). For a discussion of the confusion created by this misattribution, see *Papers of James Madison: Presidential Series,* 2: 420–21, including n. 4.

100. [Crawford] to Smith, 27 July 1810, Miscellaneous Mss, Robert Smith, Library of Congress (Crawford omitted to sign this letter before sealing it). See also Crawford to Smith, 20 September 1810, Miscellaneous Letters of the Department of State, RG 59, National Archives; and Smith to Crawford, 2 October 1810, Domestic Letters.

101. Crawford to Robert Smith, 1 November 1810, Miscellaneous Letters. See also Reuben Kemper to John Rhea, 28 October 1810, West Florida Papers.

102. See Joseph Pulaski Kennedy to [Zenon Orso], 7 June 1810, Papeles Procedentes de Cuba, legajo 1568B. In this letter Kennedy pointed out that "as for the king of Spain it is out of the question," adding that West Floridians now had to choose between "the Emperor of the French or his brother Joseph." Assuming that no true "American" could opt for the latter, Kennedy requested a meeting at Saw Mill Creek, at the residence of a Mr. Powell, "where everything can be explained and fixed upon." A copy of this letter reached one of the Spanish officers at Mobile, Caetano Perez, who had it translated by James Innerarity. The Spanish authorities then arrested both Orso and Powell (see Kennedy to Perez, 19 July 1810, ibid., in which Kennedy denied that either Orso or Powell were agents of the Mobile Society). In an attempt to mollify the Spanish authorities, Kennedy agreed to leave the region and not return before October 1810.

103. See Kennedy to Perez, 19 July 1810, ibid.

104. Francisco Maximilian de St. Maxent to Richard Sparks, 25 June 1810, copy, Territorial Papers, Mississippi; and Sparks to St. Maxent, [no date, but post 25 June 1810], Papeles Procedentes de Cuba, legajo 1568B. Sparks forwarded this news to the War Department on 12 July 1810—see Carter et al., *Territorial Papers: Mississippi*, 6: 79–82—from where it was then sent to Madison on 7 August 1810 (see *Papers of James Madison: Presidential Series*, 2: 466).

105. Toulmin to Madison, 28 July 1810, *Papers of James Madison: Presidential Series*, 2: 447–53. Kennedy later conveyed the same news, as he passed into Georgia, to the U.S. agent for the Creek Indians, Benjamin Hawkins, only to be reproved by Hawkins who told him that he would be obliged to report it to the administration. Kennedy then declared that there was "No Burrism" in the Mobile Society and that he had informed Hawkins of its plans for him to communicate them to Washington, "hoping the object might be accomplished without the contemplated interposition of the associated" (see Hawkins to Eustis, 21 August 1810, Letters Received, Registered Series, H-186 [5]).

106. Madison to Gallatin, 22 August 1810, *Papers of James Madison: Presidential Series*, 2: 501–2.

107. Madison to Eustis, 10 August 1810, and to Graham, 10 August 1810, ibid., 2: 473–74. After Madison returned to Washington in October, he evidently directed the Secretary of State to meet with the Spanish consul in Baltimore, Juan Bautisa Bernabeu, to convey the message that the president would not only "discountenance" any attempt on Mobile "but he would punish to the full extent of the law any individual offering violence or committing any hostile act against the vessels or territory of Spain" (see Onís to Bardaxi, 12 October 1810, Estado, legajo 5636).

108. Madison to Toulmin, 5 September 1810, *Papers of James Madison: Presidential Series,* 2: 525.

109. Madison to Eustis, 30 August and 7 September 1810, ibid., 2: 516, 529–30; Madison to Graham, 24 August 1810, and Graham to Madison, 29 August 1810, ibid., 2: 504, 515–16.

110. See Journal of the West Florida Convention, entry at 24 October 1810.

111. Toulmin to Madison, 31 October 1810, *Papers of James Madison: Presidential Series,* 2: 606–8. This sense of "panic" seems to have inhibited a filibuster. As Joseph Pulaski Kennedy reported, it made it impossible for Kemper "or any other person to do anything in any amicable way to induce [the people of Mobile] to become freemen, and to assume to themselves that form of government, which secures *to each individual* his natural rights." Kennedy also mentioned that the Spanish officers at Mobile were "determined to dispute every inch of ground" and had prepared the town and the fort "for the worst" (see Journal of the West Florida Convention, entry for 3 November 1810).

112. Toulmin to Madison, [6 November 1810], *Papers of James Madison: Presidential Series,* 3: 3.

113. Toulmin's address to the grand jury of Washington County, Mississippi Territory, was first printed in the Natchez *Weekly Chronicle* on 8 October 1810 and was reprinted in the *National Intelligencer* on 7 and 13 November 1810, where it was accompanied by editorial praise for Toulmin as a "a zealous and enlightened judge."

114. See n. 111 of this chapter.

115. See Robert Smith to Holmes, 21 December 1810, Miscellaneous Mss, Robert Smith.

116. Toulmin to Madison, 22 and 28 November 1810, *Papers of James Madison: Presidential Series,* 3: 22–23, 36–38. For an account of these events from Gaines's perspective, see James W. Silver, *Edmund Pendleton Gaines: Frontier General* (Baton Rouge, LA, 1949), 23–27.

117. See James Innerarity to Toulmin, 22 November 1810, "West Florida and Its Attempt on Mobile," 703. Why Folch changed his mind at this point is an interesting question. Aside from the motives mentioned by Innerarity, it is possible that Innerarity himself suggested the idea to Folch, acting, if he did so, on a hint he had received from Brig. Gen. James Wilkinson that this would be the best way to avoid bloodshed (see Wilkinson to Innerarity, 27 October 1810, Papales Procedentes de Cuba, legajo 2375, reproduced in William S. Coker, compiler, *The Papers of Panton, Leslie, and Company,* microfilm ed., roll 18).

118. Toulmin to Madison, 28 November 1810, *Papers of James Madison: Presidential Series,* 3: 37.

119. It would have been far more difficult for a filibustering force to take Mobile than it had been to overpower the small fort at Baton Rouge. According to the U.S. Army commander at Fort Stoddert, the Spanish fort at Mobile was garrisoned by a force of somewhere between eighty to one hundred men who controlled thirty-six pieces of heavy artillery and was surrounded by a deep ditch and an "18 feet thick" wall "built

of brick" (see Sparks to Claiborne, 21 December 1810, in Rowland, *Claiborne Letter Books,* 5: 74).

120. For these events, see Cox, *West Florida Controversy,* 422–27, 477–86.

121. Toulmin to Madison, 6 and 12 December 1810, 10 January 1811, 13 February 1812, *Papers of James Madison: Presidential Series,* 3: 56–57, 68–69, 110–16; 4: 180–84.

122. Folch to Robert Smith, 2 December 1810; to John McKee, 2 December 1810; and to Eustis, 5 December 1810, all in *American State Papers: Foreign Relations,* 3: 398–99.

Chapter 3. East Florida

1. See McKee to Folch, 17 January 1811, Papeles Procedentes de Cuba, Archivo General de Indias, Seville, legajo 1569 (copy in Library of Congress).

2. See Morier to Robert Smith, 15 and 22 December 1810, in Walter Lowrie and Matthew St. Clair Clarke, compilers, *American State Papers: Documents, Legislative and Executive, of the Congress of the United States* (38 vols.; Washington, DC, 1832–61), *Foreign Relations,* 3: 399–400. Under the pseudonym "Verus," Luis de Onís also published an attack on the occupation of West Florida. For the most part, his pamphlet was a statement against the case that West Florida had been part of Louisiana and that it was, therefore, a violent crime for the United States to have seized it. Onís also hinted that Madison was probably responsible for organizing the convention that declared the province to be independent (see [Onís], *The Passage of the President's Message, which relates to the Forcible Occupation of West Florida* [n.p.; 1810], especially p. 17).

3. Madison to Congress, 3 January 1811, in *The Papers of James Madison: Presidential Series* (5 vols. to date, ed. Robert A. Rutland et al.; Charlottesville, VA, 1984–), 3: 93–95.

4. Joseph Gales, compiler, *The Debates and Proceedings of the Congress of the United States* (42 vols.; Washington, DC, 1834–1856; hereafter *Annals of Congress*), 11th Cong., 3d sess., 378–80, 1118–42.

5. Madison to Congress, 10 January 1811, *Papers of James Madison: Presidential Series,* 3: 108. For a discussion of how the threat of disunion resonated emotionally and politically in Madison's thinking, see Rogan Kersh, *Dreams of a More Perfect Union* (Ithaca, NY, 2001), 66–96.

6. *Annals of Congress,* 11th Cong., 3d sess., 1142–48. For a more extended discussion, see John A. Logan, Jr., *No Transfer: An American Security Principle* (New Haven, CT, 1961), 111–22.

7. Robert Smith to Madison, [17 January 1811], *Papers of James Madison: Presidential Series,* 3: 122–23.

8. McKee to James Innerarity, 17 January 1811, *Florida Historical Quarterly* 16 (1937): 130; and McKee to Robert Smith, 28 January 1811, Miscellaneous Treasury Accounts of the General Accounting Office, account no. 26,533, RG 217, National Archives.

9. For McKee's removal as Choctaw agent, see Henry Dearborn to McKee, 21 May 180[2], John McKee Papers, Library of Congress. The standard authorities on the Blount conspiracy—William Masterson, *William Blount* (Baton Rouge, LA, 1954); and Buckner F. Melton, *The First Impeachment: The Constitution's Framers and the Case of Senator William Blount* (Macon, GA, 1998)—make no mention of McKee, but the contents of a surviving folder of his correspondence with Blount in the McKee Papers leaves little doubt that the agent was closely involved in every aspect of Blount's affairs.

10. Robert S. Cotterill, *The Southern Indians: The Story of the Civilized Tribes before Removal* (Norman, OK, 1954), 119, 148. McKee's dealings with the Choctaw had also led him into a degree of involvement in the Burr conspiracy (see Thomas Perkins Abernethy, *The Burr Conspiracy* [New York, 1954], 35, 116–17, 215, 218). For McKee's business relationship with John Forbes and Company, see the "Memorandum for Col. McKee," dated 16 June 1809 at Pensacola (William S. Coker, compiler, *The Papers of Panton, Leslie, and Company,* microfilm ed., roll 17); and McKee's letters to James Innerarity of 2 August, 6 November, 8 and 23 December 1811, McKee Papers.

11. McKee to James Innerarity, 17 January 1811.

12. Ibid.

13. See [Crawford] to Robert Smith, 27 July 1810, Miscellaneous Mss, Robert Smith, Library of Congress. All throughout his life, Mathews was interested in land speculation. He had also been governor of Georgia during the Yazoo land frauds of the 1790s, at which time he "outdid all of his predecessors in signing illegal land warrants" (see C. Peter Magrath, *Yazoo: The Case of Fletcher v. Peck* [Providence, RI, 1966], 7). For further discussion of Mathews's interests in Florida land, see J. C. A. Stagg, "George Mathews and John McKee: Revolutionizing East Florida, Pensacola, and Mobile in 1812," *Florida Historical Quarterly* 85 (2007): 271–73.

14. For Forbes's grants, see *American State Papers: Public Lands,* 4: 163–66. For Forbes's plans for them, see his 1804 *Description of the Spanish Floridas,* ed. William S. Coker (Pensacola, FL, 1979), 19–34. For the problem of Indian indebtedness to Forbes, see William S. Coker and Thomas D. Watson, *Indian Traders of the Southeastern Spanish Borderlands: Panton, Leslie & Company and John Forbes & Company, 1783–1847* (Pensacola, FL, 1986), 243–72; and J. Leitch Wright, Jr., *Britain and the American Frontier, 1783–1815* (Athens, GA, 1975), 137–40.

15. Robert S. Cotterill, "A Chapter of Panton, Leslie, and Company," *Journal of Southern History* 10 (1944): 275–92. For McKee's advocacy of land cessions to the United States as a way to redeem Indian debt, see his 11 June 1802 letter to Dearborn (in Dunbar Rowland, ed., *Official Letter Books of W. C. C. Claiborne* [6 vols.; Jackson, MS, 1917], 1: 158–59). That Madison himself knew about Mathews's dealings with Forbes can be assumed from the fact that the secretary of state forwarded him Crawford's 27 July letter describing the circumstances under which the agent had accepted his assignment (see Smith to Crawford, 2 October 1810, Domestic Letters of the Department of State, RG 59, National Archives).

16. Robert Smith to Mathews and McKee, 26 January 1811, Domestic Letters.

17. Ibid.

18. For the report, see *Papers of James Madison: Presidential Series,* 3: 123–24. For Atkinson's remarks, see his testimony in *United States vs Francisco and Peter Pons,* Miscellaneous Treasury Accounts, no. 73, 347.

19. For Hall, see Mary M. Dupree and G. Dekle Taylor, "Dr. James Hall, 1760–1837," *Journal of the Florida Medical Association* 61 (1974): 626–31. For Seagrove's 2 September 1805 letter to Madison, see James Madison Papers, Library of Congress.

20. George F. J. Clarke to Enrique White, 7 January 1811, East Florida Papers, bundle 198C16, Library of Congress. There is no reason to suppose the claim that Seagrove had received a letter from the State Department is true.

21. Robert Smith to Crawford, 20 June 1810 (and see also chapter 2, n. 99).

22. See n. 18 of this chapter. The extent to which Mathews's claims about Lopez might be regarded as true is difficult to tell. At no time in 1811–12 did he behave in ways that were consistent with Mathews's report.

23. John Forbes reached exactly the same conclusion. He, too, had talked with Arredondo, and they had agreed that East Florida was too weak to stand alone in the world and that if Great Britain did not take over the province, it would be obliged to seek protection elsewhere—i.e., from the United States (see Forbes to Joseph Hibberson, 18 September 1810, Coker, *The Papers of Panton, Leslie, and Company,* roll 17).

24. James G. Cusick, *The Other War of 1812: The Patriot War and the American Invasion of Spanish East Florida* (Gainesville, FL, 2003), 41. For discussions of the failure of the Spanish authorities to encourage sufficient numbers of immigrants to build up the East Florida population after 1783, see Paul E. Hoffman, *Florida's Frontiers* (Bloomington, IN, 2002), 234–48, 252–60; and Abel Poitrineau, "Demography and the Political Destiny of Florida during the Second Spanish Period," *Florida Historical Quarterly* 66 (1988): 420–43.

25. See n. 18 of this chapter.

26. Eustis to Thomas A. Smith, 4 and 26 January 1811, Letters Sent by the Secretary of War Relating to Military Affairs, RG 107, National Archives. Smith acknowledged receipt of these orders on 18 March 1812 (see his letter to Eustis of that date in Letters Received by the Secretary of War, Registered Series, S-161, RG 107, National Archives).

27. Paul Hamilton to Hugh G. Campbell, 26 October, 11, 24, 28, 29 December 1810, 9, 22, 25, 26 January, 25 February, 30 March, 13 and 19 April, 28 August, 2, 12, 21 September 1811, 22 January 1812, Letters Sent by the Secretary of the Navy to Officers, RG 45, National Archives.

28. *Papers of James Madison: Presidential Series,* 2: 612–13.

29. See *Annals of Congress,* 11th Cong., 3d sess., 378–88, 457–61.

30. Mathews to Robert Smith, 25 February 1811, Miscellaneous Letters of the Department of State, RG 59, National Archives.

31. Ibid.

32. Ibid.

33. The cover of Mathews's 25 February letter bears a docket of that date.

34. For Madison's "Memorandum on Robert Smith," [ca. 11 April 1811], see *Papers of James Madison: Presidential Series,* 3: 255–63, 264n3, 265n19.

35. See Ralph Isaacs to Mathews and McKee, 31 March [1811], McKee Papers.

36. McKee to Robert Smith, 27 March and 3 April 1811, Territorial Papers of the Department of State, Florida, RG 59, National Archives. From his vantage point in New Orleans, Claiborne believed that the mission of Mathews and McKee would "do no good." Convinced that Folch's overtures to the administration had been in bad faith, he pointed out that in order to remove the remaining outposts of Spanish power in West Florida, "the Bayonet must at last be the Negociator" (see Claiborne to Hamilton, 18 May 1811, in Rowland, *Claiborne Letter Books,* 5: 247).

37. Monroe to Mathews and McKee and to Claiborne, 29 June 1811, Domestic Letters. That these letters were never sent is suggested by their being copied out of sequence in the letter book many years later with the remark: "Among the loose papers of the Department . . . there are a considerable number of rough drafts of letters of old dates, which it does not appear have been recorded. This to genl. Mathews and Col. McKee is the first belonging to this series." Neither Mathews and McKee nor Claiborne ever acknowledged receiving any letter from the State Department dated 29 June 1811.

38. See McKee to Monroe, 5 June 1811, Territorial Papers, Florida. See also the account printed in the *National Intelligencer,* 29 June 1811.

39. The documents were reprinted in the *Connecticut Mirror,* 24 June 1811, and again in the *National Intelligencer* on 27 and 29 June 1811.

40. *National Intelligencer,* 25 July, 20, 29, 31 August 1811.

41. See Lord Wellesley to Augustus John Foster, 10 April 1811, Public Record Office: Foreign Office (hereafter cited as F.O.), ser. 5, vol. 76.

42. Foster to Wellesley, 5 July and 5 August 1811, ibid.

43. Foster to Wellesley, 18 and 29 September 1811, ibid. See also Onís to Bardaxi, 8 September 1811, Estado, legajo 5637, Archivo Histórico Nacional, Madrid (copy in Library of Congress).

44. McKee to Robert Smith, 10 April and 1 May 1811, Territorial Papers, Florida.

45. On Folch's recall to Havana, see David H. White, *Vicente Folch, Governor in Spanish Florida, 1787–1811* (Washington, DC, 1981), 104–5.

46. See McKee to Monroe, 11 May 1811, McKee Papers; copy of Mathews to Eustis, 13 May 1811, ibid.

47. See Mathews to Monroe, 28 June 1811, Territorial Papers, Florida; and Isaacs to McKee, 28 June 1811, McKee Papers.

48. Mathews to Monroe, 28 June 1811, copy in McKee Papers.

49. For a discussion of the role of blacks, slave and free, as auxiliaries in sustaining Spanish rule in Florida, see Jane Landers, *Black Society in Spanish Florida* (Urbana, IL, 1999), 202–9.

50. See the testimony of James Hall in *United States vs Francisco Xavier Sánchez,* Miscellaneous Treasury Accounts, account no. 74,969.

51. Mathews to Monroe, 28 June 1811, copy in McKee Papers. See also the newspaper accounts in the *Republican and Savannah Evening Ledger,* 23 and 30 May, 1, 4, 27 June, 11, 13, 16, 20 July 1811; and the *National Intelligencer,* 4, 6, 11, 13 July 1811. For

further discussion of the reasons for the absence of discontent with Spanish rule, see Sherry Johnson, "The St. Augustine Hurricane of 1811: Disaster and the Question of Political Unrest on the Florida Frontier," *Florida Historical Quarterly* 84 (2005): 28–56.

52. For the increasing dependence of East Florida on both American and British trade, see James G. Cusick, "Spanish East Florida in the Atlantic Economy of the Late Eighteenth Century," in Jane Landers, ed., *Colonial Plantations and Economy in Florida* (Gainesville, FL, 2000), 168–88; and Christopher Ward, "The Commerce of East Florida during the Embargo, 1806–1812: The Role of Amelia Island," *Florida Historical Quarterly* 68 (1989): 160–79.

53. See Mathews to Monroe, 28 June 1811; also Isaacs to McKee, [postmarked 28 June 1811], McKee Papers. (This last letter has been damaged by fire and its dateline is no longer legible).

54. For McIntosh's recollections of his meetings with Mathews, see *Daily National Intelligencer,* 2 July 1823.

55. McIntosh to William Craig, 23 July 1811, and to Juan José Estrada, 24 July 1811, East Florida Papers, bundle 147D12.

56. Mathews to Monroe, 3 August 1811, Territorial Papers, Florida (marked "copy" by Mathews).

57. See Mathews to McKee, [ca. 7 September 1811], McKee Papers. The dateline on this letter, as well as some of its contents, has been damaged by fire, but the surviving internal evidence is sufficient to establish both its approximate date as well as its purpose. Francis Lennon had been a priest in Francisville, West Florida, from where he fled to Pensacola after the uprising at Baton Rouge in September 1810. He was still in Pensacola in the spring of 1811 when Mathews and McKee met with him and suggested to the State Department that it would be "sound policy as well as justice to invite him to return & to make a provision for his support." Exactly where Lennon's political loyalties lay is unclear—his behavior during the West Florida revolt suggested they were with Spain—but Mathews and McKee, who claimed to have long known him, believed otherwise, remarking that the priest had "uniformly discovered a friendly disposition towards the United States" (see Mathews and McKee to Robert Smith, 24 April 1811, Territorial Papers, Florida).

58. See Mathews to Monroe, 14 October 1811, ibid.

59. Some details of Keene's career, which included his seduction of Luther Martin's fifteen-year-old daughter as well as charges that he violated the Embargo and was guilty of treason against both Spain and the United States, can be found in his apologia, *A Letter of Vindication to His Excellency Colonel Monroe, President of the United States, by Richard Raynal Keene, Colonel in the late Constitutional Service of Spain* (Philadelphia, PA, 1824), 3–47. For his petition for the land grant in East Florida, see the documents attached to Enrique White's 3 November 1809 letter to the marqués de Someruelos, Papeles Procedentes de Cuba, legajo 1567). Keene did not receive any land in Florida, but in 1815 he was awarded a very substantial grant in Texas (see *Letter of Vindication,* 5).

60. It should be stressed that Mathews had grounds for concern here. He believed

that Keene had sought all vacant and unlocated land in Florida and land "ceded or unceded by the Indians," and he knew that Forbes had made little or no progress in developing his own grants. Moreover, Keene was a Spanish subject, but Forbes was contemplating alienating land to Mathews, an American citizen who was notoriously unsympathetic to Spain. It was no great leap of the imagination to suppose that the Spanish authorities would refuse to sanction any business dealings between Forbes and Mathews (or McKee). It was also true that the Spanish intendant, Morales, was looking into land grants to foreigners at this time, as when he wrote to the captain-general in Havana on 14 August 1811, reminding him of the relevant regulations in response to a request for an opinion on "the petition of Don Ricardo Raynal Keene, asking to buy lands" (see Coker, *The Papers of Panton, Leslie, and Company,* roll 18).

61. Mathews's informant signed himself as THEMISTOCLES AT MAGNESIA, and his communication was dated 21 September 1811. While it is probably impossible to identify THEMISTOCLES with absolute certainty, it might be conjectured he was James Hall. According to Plutarch, after his victories over the Persians the Athenian leader had lived out his final days in banishment at Magnesia, where he was subjected to pressures from both the Greeks and the Persians to choose sides when they renewed their wars (see *Plutarch's Lives,* ed. John Dryden [6 vols.; London, 1758], 1: 280–321). Those circumstances seem to mirror how Hall felt about his own expulsion from East Florida in September 1810 (see Dupree and Taylor, "Dr. James Hall," 630–31).

62. McKee to Mathews, 18 September 1811, McKee Papers. McKee reported that Hampton had told him "in the most positive terms" that Madison had revoked the commissions issued to the two agents. McKee was reluctant to credit the news and he hoped that the general had "only heard at Washington that the President finding the object of our mission not likely to be effected had spoken of our probable recall which [Hampton] in his great zeal for the public interest has anticipated to the commanding officer here" (at Fort Stoddert).

63. Foster to Wellesley, 5 November 1811, F.O., ser. 5, vol. 77.

64. The surviving text of Mathews's 3 August 1811 letter is clearly marked "copy." Crawford's 5 November 1811 note to Monroe forwarding it to the State Department is docketed as covering "two letters from Govr Mathews 3d Augt 14th Octr 1811" (Miscellaneous Letters).

65. *National Intelligencer,* 31 October 1811. Details of the story were confirmed in consular dispatches received by the State Department (see Richard Hackley to Monroe, 10 and 27 September 1811, Consular Dispatches of the Department of State, Cádiz, RG 59, National Archives; and William Shaler to Monroe, 17 September 1811, Consular Dispatches of the Department of State, Havana, RG 59, National Archives). For British mediation efforts with Spain, see John Rydjord, "British Mediation between Spain and Her Colonies, 1811–1813," *Hispanic American Historical Review* 21 (1941): 29–36; and William W. Kaufmann, *British Policy and the Independence of Latin America, 1804–1828* (New Haven, CT, 1951), 65–76.

66. See Gallatin's "Notes on the President's Message," [ca. 1 November 1811], *Papers of James Madison: Presidential Series,* 3: 537–38.

67. For Madison's statement to this effect, see Foster to Lord Castlereagh, 24 June 1812, F.O., ser. 5, vol. 86 (reprinted in *Papers of James Madison: Presidential Series,* 4: 502).

68. Foster to Lord Wellesley, 5 November 1811, F.O., ser. 5, vol. 77.

69. *American State Papers: Foreign Relations,* 3: 544–45.

70. Madison to Joel Barlow, 17 November 1811, *Papers of James Madison: Presidential Series,* 4: 21.

71. See Hackley to Monroe, 10 September 1811, Consular Dispatches, Cádiz; and Shaler to Monroe, 21 October 1811, Consular Dispatches, Havana.

72. See n. 70 of this chapter.

73. For a more extended discussion of this matter, see J. C. A. Stagg, "James Madison and George Mathews: The East Florida Revolution of 1812 Reconsidered," *Diplomatic History* 30 (2006): 45–47.

74. *National Intelligencer,* 9 December 1811.

75. This point emerges very clearly in letters Mathews wrote to Monroe after November 1811 (see those under the dates of 23 January 1812 [Letters Received, Registered Series, M-344] and 14, 21, 28 March 1812 [Territorial Papers, Florida]). On each of these occasions, Mathews repeated his requests for the reinforcements he had first made on 3 August 1811.

76. The best secondary accounts are by Cusick, *Other War of 1812,* 83–142; and Rembert W. Patrick, *Florida Fiasco: Rampant Rebels on the Georgia-Florida Border, 1810–1815* (Athens, GA, 1954), 70–113.

77. Isaacs to McKee, 14 November 1811, McKee Papers.

78. For the evidence that McIntosh was persuaded by Monroe's 2 November letter to Foster, see his 30 July 1812 letter to the secretary of state (Territorial Papers, Florida).

79. See n. 19 of this chapter.

80. See the testimony of George F. J. Clarke in the case of *United States vs Francisco and Peter Pons.*

81. Mathews to Monroe, 23 January 1812. The letter bears a docket date of 4 August 1812 in the hand of a War Department clerk. For Mathews's earlier meetings with Kindelán, see Richard K. Murdoch, *The Georgia-Florida Frontier, 1793–1796: Spanish Reaction to French Intrigue and American Designs* (Berkeley, CA, 1951), 136–40. The success of any plan to seize the Castillo de Marcos "by surprise" depended on the broken drawbridge at the fort not being repaired.

82. For Mathews's meeting with Mitchell, see Mitchell to John Floyd, 18 March 1812, Governors' Letter Books, 1809–1814, Georgia Department of History and Archives. Here Mitchell expressed his surprise at learning about Mathews's plans and complained that he had not been informed about them earlier. At that point Mitchell had just learned of Mathews's attack on Fernandina on 14 March, and he remarked that it was "scarcely probable" that Mathews's plans, which were "uncertain on the 17th or 18th of February," could be "ripe for execution by the 17th of March." From these circumstances, Mitchell had been initially inclined to suspect that the administration had intended he be "kept in ignorance of the time for the execution of their plans for the

reduction of St. Augustine," but as he learned more about what Mathews had done, he eventually concluded that the agent had both exceeded his orders and misled the administration (see Mitchell to Floyd, 16 April 1812, ibid.).

83. Foster to Castlereagh, 23 April 1812, F.O., ser. 5, vol. 85.

84. See the extract of a letter, copied by John Graham, from McIntosh to George M. Troup, 12 March 1812, Territorial Papers, Florida, where the final paragraph with the reference to McIntosh's children and Estrada's violation of their "contract" has been crossed out by Graham. That Mathews had finally worn McIntosh down seems to have occurred to Madison when he reflected on the matter nearly a year later. The president then expressed surprise, "considering the apparent intelligence & capacity of McIntosh," that he allowed himself "to have been imposed on, by Mathews's pretensions and proceedings, which were so extravagant that it was a reflection on the Govt. to suppose he c[oul]d be pursuing their views" (see Madison to Monroe, 19 August 1813, James Monroe Papers, Library of Congress).

85. See Campbell to Hamilton, 29 February, and copy of Mathews to Campbell, 11 March 1812, Captains' Letters, RG 45, National Archives. In reporting the meeting to the secretary of the Navy, Campbell added that he would have felt "much more justified" in aiding Mathews if he had been "honored with Instructions from you on that head."

86. See the copy of Wylly to McIntosh, 10 March 1812, enclosed in Mathews to Monroe, 14 March 1812, Territorial Papers, Florida.

87. That the information provided by Wylly drove Mathews to act before he was ready is clear, but Rembert Patrick has dismissed the possibility that Wylly and Mathews essentially colluded to justify the agent's actions to Washington on the grounds that the administration was already fully aware of, and in support of, Mathews's plans (see *Florida Fiasco*, 314n37). However, if it is assumed the administration had not condoned Mathews's plans, Wylly's intervention on 10 March takes on a different meaning. There was no more evidence available to Mathews in March 1812 that Great Britain was sending black troops to East Florida than there had been in June or July of 1811 when Mathews had discounted that possibility and rejected it as a reason for attempting to "pre-occupy" East Florida. Given the evidence that John Floyd was to uncover about Wylly's role, along with that of Joseph Hibberson, a British merchant who regularly reported to Foster in Washington, it is more than likely that Wylly's information was intended to force Mathews to reveal his hand. Floyd described Hibberson as a man "capable of Acting the part of an Idiot, or the profound politician," and he suspected that the British minister had anticipated Mathew's actions with the intention of using them as a pretext to demand that the United States relinquish East Florida to Great Britain. Should the administration refuse, Floyd believed that Great Britain would declare war and "use every means in her power to deluge the Southern states with our Domestics." As for Wylly, Floyd remarked that he "knew the *man*" and that it was "more than probable" he communicated the news about black British troops "for he was in the secret" (see Floyd to Crawford, 21 March 1812, Miscellaneous Letters).

88. For extended accounts of Mathews's confrontations with Laval, see Cusick, *Other War of 1812*, 78–92; and Patrick, *Florida Fiasco*, 70–82.

89. See Mathews to McKee, [6 March 1812], McKee Papers. The dateline and the addressee of this letter have been burned, but it is in Mathews's hand and is clearly the letter McKee acknowledged receiving from Mathews on 1 April 1812 (ibid.). Further evidence of Mathews's intention to seize Pensacola after the fall of St. Augustine was provided by Andrew Ellicott to Timothy Pickering, following a visit that Ellicott had made to Georgia (see Ellicott to Pickering, 17 May 1812, Timothy Pickering Papers, Massachusetts Historical Society). For evidence that Mathews was communicating his intentions to McKee before March 1812, see his letter dated ca. 1 October 1811 and Isaacs to McKee, 14 November 1811, McKee Papers. There also survives in this collection a badly burned fragment, very likely dating after November 1811, in which Mathews informed McKee that affairs in East Florida remained in the state they were in when Isaacs last wrote to him. Matters were said to be "in train for a [illegible] but the prospect not immediate."

90. McIntosh to Troup, 12 March 1812.

91. For McIntosh's recollection of this statement from Mathews, see *Daily National Intelligencer,* 2 July 1823. For accounts of the fall of Fernandina, see Cusick, *Other War of 1812,* 102–25; and Patrick, *Florida Fiasco,* 83–98.

92. See Mathews to Monroe, 14 March 1812, Territorial Papers, Florida. On Amelia Island itself, there was little room for doubt about what Mathews was doing, with Campbell observing that there was "no disguise upon his actions" and reporting the agent as saying that if the Spanish fort at Fernandina did not surrender to the gunboats of the U.S. Navy, they would "knock it down upon their ears" (Campbell to Hamilton, 11 April 1812, Captains' Letters).

93. Mathews to Monroe, 21 March 1812, Miscellaneous Letters. As Arredondo informed Estrada, the success of the Patriots would depend largely on how much support they received from the forces of the United States. Most of the rebels were poorly armed, and if the United States withdrew its forces, it would be easy to subjugate them because "all the Planters of [Amelia] Island although few remain loyal to their legitimate Sovereign" (see Arredondo to Estrada, 21 April 1812, East Florida Papers, bundle 147D12).

94. This was provided for in the fourth article of the draft treaty Mathews forwarded on 21 March.

95. Filed in the State Department records is a 21 March letter from Fernando de la Maza Arredondo and Sons to Stephen Girard, informing Girard that Mathews had arranged for the ports of East Florida to remain open to British trade until May 1813 and that Girard, who had cargoes of British goods waiting at Amelia Island, could expect to be able to import them into the United States (see Territorial Papers, Florida).

96. See Forbes to McKee, 28 February 1812, McKee Papers.

97. This was stipulated in the fifth article of the draft treaty, which read, "Whereas the Government at Pensacola and Mobile will probably be excited to great irritation in consequence of this revolution and as they border upon tribes of Indians who might be engaged in acts of hostility their revolution is rendered indispensable for the security of East Florida, and we the inhabitants of the East Florida having prior to this ces-

sion proceeded to raise an army and to appoint officers for the revolution of said places, and having rendered ourselves incompetent to it by yielding up our funds to the U States, the U States doth agree to carry the same into full effect unless in their wisdom it shall be deemed injurious to the province or to the U States."

98. This was provided for in the sixth article of the draft treaty. Presumably Mathews was assuming these requirements could never be met.

99. See Mathews to Monroe, 28 March 1812, Territorial Papers, Florida. See also the copy of Mathews to Campbell, 2 April 1812, enclosed in Campbell to Hamilton, 16 April 1812, Captains' Letters.

100. See Campbell to Hamilton, 16 April 1812, Captains' Letters. Campbell clearly feared for Mathews's sanity, observing that before the start of the revolution on 14 March, the agent had been the most "silent & prudent of men." After that date, he had become "more gay and unreserved than any Man" in St. Marys (ibid.).

101. Mathews to Madison, 16 April 1812, *Papers of James Madison: Presidential Series*, 4: 326–29; and to Monroe, 16 April 1812, Territorial Papers, Florida. For Mathews's remarks about going on to Mexico and Peru, see Campbell's 16 April letter, cited in n. 99 of this chapter.

102. Mathews's 14 March letter has no docket date, though that is by no means an unusual circumstance as State Department clerks were far less consistent than their War Department counterparts in recording the receipt of their correspondence.

103. Hamilton to Campbell, 28 March and 4 April 1812, Letters Sent to Officers. For the embargo of April 1812, see J. C. A. Stagg, *Mr. Madison's War: Politics, Diplomacy and Warfare in the Early American Republic, 1783–1830* (Princeton, NJ, 1983), 95–102.

104. See Monroe to McKee, 2 January 1812, McKee Papers. For McKee's acknowledgment of the letter's receipt on 14 May, see his 20 May letter to Monroe, ibid.

105. See McKee to Mathews, 1 and 10 April 1812, and to James Innerarity, 8 April 1812, ibid.

106. McKee to Monroe, 25 March and 15 April 1812, Territorial Papers, Florida.

107. Foster to Lord Castlereagh, 2 April 1812, F.O., ser. 5, vol. 85.

108. Hawkins to Eustis, 23 March 1812, docketed as received on 4 April 1812 with a clerk's endorsement: "states the substance of a letter from Gnl. Mathews," Letters Received, Registered Series, H-185 (6). After further reflection and receiving more information, Hawkins revised his belief that Mathews had authorization for his actions, and he wrote to the agent to express his concern that he had "greatly exceeded [his] powers." Hawkins continued, "It has been hinted to me that you originated the whole movement of the patriots and that you even attempted to aid them with a part of the troops of the United States in disguise." Furthermore, he protested, it is said that "an agent or spy of Mr. Forbes has been present and made acquainted with every occurrence. If this is true, I think the government will be greatly perplexed by the transaction" (see Hawkins to Mathews, 12 April 1812, Charles L. Grant, ed., *Letters, Journals, and Writings of Benjamin Hawkins* [2 vols.; Savannah, GA, 1980], 2: 606–7).

109. That the administration had to piece together from a variety of sources what had actually happened at Amelia Island is confirmed by Crawford's sending Monroe

an account of the events there that he received on the morning of 5 April from John Floyd. This account, he assured the secretary of state, could be relied on, and it proved that "the affair is worse than I had expected" (see Miscellaneous Letters).

110. See Monroe to Mathews, 4 April 1812, in which he acknowledged the receipt of Mathews's 14 March letter, Domestic Letters; and Monroe to Mitchell, 4 April 1812, Keith Read Collection, courtesy of Hargrett Rare Book and Manuscript Library, University of Georgia Libraries. For further discussion of the significance of the dating of these letters, see Stagg, "James Madison and George Mathews," 48–49, 51–52.

111. Mathews was by no means oblivious to the possible international repercussions of his conduct. When Campbell pointed out to him that Great Britain, as an ally of Spain, would be fully justified in attacking the Patriots in retaliation for their actions, Mathews merely remarked that "it would answer a very good purpose, that of bringing on a war" (see Campbell to Hamilton, 16 April 1812, Captains' Letters).

112. Madison to Jefferson, 24 April 1812, *Papers of James Madison: Presidential Series,* 4: 346.

113. For Madison's message communicating the letters of John Henry, see *Papers of James Madison: Presidential Series,* 4: 235–36. On the Henry affair generally, see Samuel E. Morison, "The Henry-Crillon Affair of 1812," *Proceedings of the Massachusetts Historical Society* 69 (1950): 207–31.

114. It was axiomatic under the law of nations that valid treaties could only be made by effective and legitimate sovereigns (see Emmerich de Vattel, *The Law of Nations; or, The Principles of Natural Law, Applied to the Conduct and to the Affairs of Nations and of Sovereigns,* trans. Charles G. Fenwick (Washington, DC, 1916 [orig. 1758]), 160–61). To get around this difficulty, Georgia representative George M. Troup had suggested to Monroe that the administration might recognize the East Florida revolt on the assumption that all the Patriots could be regarded as Spanish subjects for the purpose of constituting an "existing local authority," but even Troup admitted to doubting whether it would be possible "to keep out of sight" the "agency of . . . ," by which he meant the very public participation of Mathews and the gunboats of the U.S. Navy in the capture of Fernandina (see Troup to [Monroe], undated, but probably a cover letter in which he forwarded the 12 March 1812 letter he had received from McIntosh, cited in n. 84 of this chapter).

115. For the delay occasioned by the need to correct the orders sent to Smith, see Stagg, "James Madison and George Mathews," 52n91. See also Mitchell to Monroe, 2 May 1812, Territorial Papers, Florida.

116. See Mitchell to Monroe, 2 May 1812, Territorial Papers, Florida.

117. Hamilton to Campbell, 8 April 1812, Letters Sent to Officers; also Campbell to Hamilton, 25 April 1812, Captains' Letters. Campbell had continued to cooperate with Mathews "in doubts and fears," and he repeatedly complained of "the unpleasant and unofficerlike situation" in which he felt he had been placed (see his letters of 21 March, 11 and 16 April 1812 to the Secretary of the Navy, ibid.).

118. Monroe to Mitchell, 2 May 1812, Keith Read Collection, courtesy of Hargrett

Rare Book and Manuscript Library, University of Georgia Libraries. Monroe explained the matter more succinctly to the French minister in Washington two days later by remarking that "things having reached this stage, it would be more dangerous to retreat than to go on" (see Louis Sérurier to the duc de Bassano, 4 May 1812, Correspondence Politique, États-Unis, vol. 67).

119. See Monroe to Mitchell, 27 May 1812, Keith Read Collection, courtesy of Hargrett Rare Book and Manuscript Library, University of Georgia Libraries; also Monroe to Mitchell, 2 May 1812 (ibid.).

120. See the source cited in n. 67 of this chapter. Foster was appalled by this prospect, remarking to Monroe at the time that he hoped the United States and Great Britain were not going to war "for a sandbank." It might be argued that Madison's willingness to condone "expeditions" against Florida after the declaration of war amounted to him sanctioning a filibuster, which would have been contrary to the 1794 neutrality legislation. However, the 1794 law applied only to nations with which the United States was at peace—and if Madison believed, as he told Foster, that Spain would join Great Britain in the war, expeditions against Florida in that context would not be illegal.

121. *Annals of Congress,* 12th Cong., 1st sess., 324–26, 1683–94. See also Monroe to [Samuel Latham Mitchill], 22 June 1812, printed and edited by Rembert W. Patrick in the *Florida Historical Quarterly* 23 (1945): 197–201. Patrick identifies the recipient of this letter as Madison, but the letter was intended for a committee in the House of Representatives, and Mitchill was the chair of the House committee on Spanish-American affairs. Moreover, the docket on the letter, returning it to Monroe on 26 June 1812, is in the hand of Mitchill.

122. Monroe to Mitchell, 6 July 1812, Keith Read Collection, courtesy of Hargrett Rare Book and Manuscript Library, University of Georgia Libraries.

123. Ibid.

124. See the accounts in Cusick, *Other War of 1812,* 169–87; and Patrick, *Florida Fiasco,* 134–43.

125. See McIntosh to Monroe, 30 July 1812, enclosing a "Constitution of East Florida," Territorial Papers, Florida. See also Patrick, *Florida Fiasco,* 164–69.

126. Crawford to Monroe, 6 August 1812, Monroe Papers, Library of Congress.

127. Cusick, *Other War of 1812,* 209–19; and Patrick, *Florida Fiasco,* 137–43. For discussions of the role of blacks in the conflict over the summer of 1812, see Kenneth W. Porter, "Negroes and the East Florida Annexation Plot, 1811–1813," *Journal of Negro History* 30 (1945): 9–29; and Landers, *Black Society in Spanish Florida,* 220–28. For the role of the Indians, see Claudio Saunt, *A New Order of Things: Property, Power, and the Transformation of the Creek Indians, 1733–1816* (New York, 1999), 237–39; and Albert H. Wright, *Our Georgia-Florida Frontier: The Okefenokee Swamp, Its History and Cartography* (Ithaca, NY, 1945), 17–18.

128. Cusick, *Other War of 1812,* 219–43; and Patrick, *Florida Fiasco,* 183–210.

129. Cusick, *Other War of 1812,* 243–44, 247–48; and Patrick, *Florida Fiasco,* 214–18.

130. Patrick, *Florida Fiasco,* 225–36.

131. On the Spanish constitution of March 1812, see Lovett, *Napoleon and the Birth of Modern Spain,* 2: 449–90.

132. See Onís to Ignacio de la Pezuela, 19 July, 3, 11, 12, 22, 31 August 1812, Estado, legajo 5638. See also Onís to Monroe, 18 July, 3, 5, 23 August 1812, with the last letter filed with John Graham's translation on 29 August 1812, Notes from Foreign Legations to the Department of State, Spain, RG 59, National Archives. The Regency took alarm at this flurry of correspondence, and on 29 October 1812 it directed Chacón and Onís to terminate it and entertain no further proposals for the cession of Florida.

133. Madison to Monroe, 8 September 1812, *Papers of James Madison: Presidential Series,* 5: 288.

134. Ibid. Letters on conditions in St. Augustine had been forwarded to Madison by Eustis on 5 September 1812 (ibid., 5: 273–74, including n. 6).

135. See the administration's instructions to Thomas Pinckney in the letters sent by Eustis under the dates of 4 and 24 October, 27 November 1812 (Letters Sent by the Secretary of War Relating to Military Affairs). See also Eustis to Willie Blount, 15 September 1812, ibid.

136. News of the developments in Georgia were printed in the *National Intelligencer* on 21 November 1812, and on 4 December Crawford wrote to Mitchell to inform him that the administration and Congress were waiting for the arrival of the Georgia petition in the mail before acting (see Crawford to Mitchell, 4 December 1812, William Harris Crawford Collection, Library of Congress). At the same time, the War Department alerted Pinckney to the need to prepare his troops for the occupation of East Florida (see Eustis to Pinckney, 2 December 1812, and Monroe to Pinckney, 13 January 1813, Letters Sent by the Secretary of War Relating to Military Affairs). For the draft of Madison's message to Congress, ca. 8 December 1812, see *Papers of James Madison: Presidential Series,* 5: 487.

137. See *Annals of Congress,* 12th Cong., 2d sess., 124.

138. Ibid., 124–25. For Monroe's response, see his 14 January 1813 letter to Madison, which the president forwarded to the Senate the same day (*Papers of James Madison: Presidential Series,* 5: 577–82, including nn. 1–8).

139. See *Annals of Congress,* 12th Cong., 2d sess., 126, 127, 130, 131, 132. The text of Hunter's speech was printed in pamphlet form and included in the *Annals of Congress,* 13th Cong., 1st sess., 505–36.

140. For the occupation of Mobile, see Isaac J. Cox, *The West Florida Controversy, 1798–1813: A Study in American Diplomacy* (Baltimore, MD, 1918), 615–20.

141. For the offer of Alexander I, see John Quincy Adams to Monroe, 30 September 1812, Diplomatic Dispatches of the Department of State, Russia, RG 59, National Archives. The administration accepted the offer on 8 March 1813 (see the *Daily National Intelligencer,* 9 March 1813).

142. A copy of the decree is filed in Notes from Foreign Legations, Spain, between the dates of 19 February and 22 March 1813.

143. Two copies of this report survive. One may be found in Department of State:

Spanish Affairs, 1810–1816, Library of Congress, accompanied by a translation by John Graham; the other is in Miscellaneous Letters.

144. See Lear to Madison, 9 April 1813, Madison Papers; and Lear to Monroe, 9 April 1813, Consular Dispatches of the Department of State, Algiers, RG 59, National Archives. The *Daily National Intelligencer* printed the report on 23 April 1813, adding that it did not know whether it was true but that if it were true, the United States regretted it.

145. See Monroe to John Quincy Adams, James Ashton Bayard, and Albert Gallatin, 27 April 1813, Diplomatic Instructions of the Department of State, RG 59, National Archives.

146. Gallatin to Monroe, 2 and 8 May 1813, Monroe Papers, Library of Congress.

147. It is not entirely clear at what point Madison realized Spain would not fall to France. French armies had, in fact, abandoned their siege of Cádiz in August 1812, but as late as February 1813 Madison continued to look for signs that the Regency and their British allies might still lose the contest in the Iberian Peninsula (see Madison to Henry Dearborn, 6 February 1813, *Papers of James Madison: Presidential Series,* 5: 646).

148. Monroe to Anthony Morris, 9 June 1813, copy in James Monroe Museum and Memorial Library, Fredericksburg, Virginia. Morris also made two trips to Washington, between 16 and 19 May and again between 29 June and 1 July, on which occasions he was briefed for his mission by Madison, Monroe, and State Department clerks (see [Morris], "Memos Made at Washington. May & June 1813," Anthony Morris Papers, Historical Society of Pennsylvania).

149. Cusick, *Other War of 1812,* 258–68; and Patrick, *Florida Fiasco,* 254–67. The administration made no public reference to the offer of amnesty until it learned that it had been received at St. Augustine and that Kindelán would implement it. For that reason the amnesty was not reported in the *Daily National Intelligencer* until 26 April 1813, when the editor was able to publish the details from a 10 April 1813 issue of a Savannah newspaper.

150. For the aftermath of the Patriot War, see Cusick, *Other War of 1812,* 268–92; and Patrick, *Florida Fiasco,* 268–83. For McIntosh's visit to Washington, see his 11 September 1813 letter to Mitchell, in which he reported that he had been unable to meet with Madison because of the president's illness over the summer of 1813 but that he did meet with Monroe, who told him, somewhat disingenuously, that Pinckney had been given "discretionary orders" to accommodate the Patriots (East and West Florida 1764 to 1850, Georgia Department of History and Archives).

Chapter 4. Texas

1. See Robert Smith to William Shaler, 24 May 1810, William Shaler Papers, Historical Society of Pennsylvania.

2. The patent, signed by both Nathaniel and William Shaler, is in William Shaler and Family Papers, Library of Congress, as is Madison's dinner invitation, dated 22 February 1810.

3. Shaler to Madison, 23 March 1812, in *The Papers of James Madison: Presidential Series* (5 vols. to date, ed. Robert A. Rutland et al.; Charlottesville, VA, 1984–), 4: 259–60.

4. For Shaler's biography, see Roy F. Nichols, "William Shaler: New England Apostle of Rational Liberty," *New England Quarterly* 9 (1936): 71–75. See also Samuel L. Knapp, *American Biography* (New York, 1833), 296–98; and Richard J. Cleveland, *Voyages and Commercial Enterprises of the Sons of New England* (New York, 1857), 219–21, 400, 402.

5. The translation was Giovanni Ignazio Molina, *A Geographical, Natural, and Civil History of Chili* (2 vols.; Middletown, CT, 1808). For Shaler's role in the translation, see Nathaniel J. Ingraham to Madison, 3 December 1808, Miscellaneous Letters of the Department of State, RG 59, National Archives. For discussions of the significance of the work, see Jorge Cañizares-Esguerra, *How to Write the History of the New World: Histories, Epistemologies, and Identities in the Eighteenth-Century Atlantic World* (Stanford, CA, 2001), 253–54; and Antonello Gerbi, *The Dispute of the New World: The History of a Polemic, 1750–1900*, trans. Jeremy Moyle (Pittsburgh, PA, 1973), 212–17.

6. See "Journal of a Voyage between China and the North-Western Coast of America, Made in 1804," *American Register; or, General Repository of History, Politics, and Science* 3 (1808): 137–75.

7. See Shaler to Edward Carrington, 12 February 1810, Shaler Papers.

8. *National Intelligencer*, 16 and 25 May 1810.

9. See Robert Smith to Shaler, 29 May 1810, Shaler Papers. The remarks about impending Spanish-American independence are from Smith to Shaler, 18 June 1810, ibid.

10. See John Graham to Shaler, 15 June 1810, and Robert Smith to Shaler, 16 and 18 June 1810, ibid.

11. See Smith to Shaler, 18 June 1810, ibid. For the administration's position on the western boundary of Louisiana, see Graham to Shaler, 21 June 1810, ibid.

12. Shaler to Robert Smith, 5 August 1810, Communications from Special Agents of the Department of State, RG 59, National Archives; and Someruelos to Shaler, 7 August 1810, Shaler Papers.

13. See Onís to Bardaxi, 25 March 1811, Estado, legajo 5637, Archivo Histórico Nacional, Madrid (copy in Library of Congress). The impression that Shaler was a French agent may have been reinforced by the fact that although he could read and translate Spanish, he was unable to speak it fluently and conducted most of his conversations with Spanish officials in Cuba in French. For Napoleon's use of agents in Mexico, see John Rydjord, "Napoleon and the Independence of New Spain," in Charles Wilson Hackett, ed., *New Spain and the Anglo-American West: Historical Contributions presented to Herbert Eugene Bolton* (2 vols.; Los Angeles, CA, 1932), 1: 289–312.

14. See Shaler to Robert Smith, 5 June 1810, Consular Dispatches of the Department of State, Havana, RG 59, National Archives.

15. For discussions of society and culture in Cuba, see Allan J. Kuethe, *Cuba, 1753–1815: Crown, Military, and Society* (Knoxville, TN, 1986), 113–38, 174–77; and Sherry Johnson, *The Social Transformation of Eighteenth-Century Cuba* (Gainesville, FL, 2001),

71–96. Shaler may also not have understood that Arango had already tried, and failed, to establish an autonomous junta in Cuba following the confinement of Ferdinand VII in France in 1808 (see Kuethe, *Cuba*, 152–62; and Johnson, *Social Transformation of Eighteenth-Century Cuba*, 175–90).

16. For reports of Shaler's conversations, see his dispatches to Robert Smith, 22 September, 24 October, 19 November 1810, 4 and 23 March 1811, Consular Dispatches, Havana; and those of 9 and 12 August 1810, Communications from Special Agents. The idea that a member of the Portuguese royal family might rule the Spanish-American dominions was vigorously promoted by the sister of Ferdinand VII, Carlota Joaquina, who had married Dom João, the prince regent of Portugal, and whose daughter, in 1810, had married a nephew of Charles IV of Spain. In exile in Rio de Janeiro after 1808, Carlota Joaquina sought to rule Spanish America as regent for her imprisoned brother (see Juliá Mariá Rubio, *La infanta Carlota Joaquina y la política de Espana en America* [Madrid, 1920], 18–19).

17. See, for example, Shaler's "Notes on Different Characters in Havana," filed after his 25 November 1811 dispatch to the State Department, Consular Dispatches, Havana. Similar listings may be found after 18 August 1812 in Communications from Special Agents; and at March 1812 in the entries in the first volume of the Shaler Letter Books (3 vols.; Gilder Lehrman Collection, New York Historical Society). See also Shaler's "A Schedule of the Ecclesiastical Civil and Military State of the Island of Cuba," 28 August 1810, Communications from Special Agents.

18. See the documents enclosed in Shaler to Robert Smith, 28 August 1810, Communications from Special Agents; and Shaler to Smith, 24 October 1810 and 5 April 1811, Consular Dispatches, Havana.

19. See Shaler to Smith, 19 November and 4 December 1810, Consular Dispatches, Havana.

20. Copies of Shaler's correspondence with Claiborne for this period have not survived, but for references to it, see Shaler to Robert Smith, 26 February 1811, ibid.; and Claiborne to Shaler, 3 March 1811, in Dunbar Rowland, ed., *Official Letter Books of W. C. C. Claiborne* (6 vols.; Jackson, MS, 1917), 5: 168.

21. See Shaler to Robert Smith, 25 April, 7 May, 19 July 1811, Consular Dispatches, Havana.

22. See Shaler to the State Department, 14 June 1811, ibid.

23. See Shaler to the State Department, 5 June, 8 July, 23 September 1811, ibid. For the anxiety of Cuban creoles that the Cortes might abolish slavery, see John H. Elliott, *Empires of the Atlantic World: Britain and Spain in America, 1492–1830* (New Haven, CT, 2006), 385, 391. For a more general discussion of the efforts of Cuban planters to insulate the island from changes occurring in the wider Atlantic world, see Matt D. Childs, *The 1812 Aponte Rebellion in Cuba and the Struggle against Atlantic Slavery* (Chapel Hill, NC, 2006), 38–45.

24. See Shaler to Monroe, 13 November 1811, Consular Dispatches, Havana.

25. See Shaler to Monroe, 27 December 1811, ibid.

26. See Shaler to Monroe, 25 November 1811, ibid.

27. Shaler entered copies of these four essays at various points in his first letter book between the dates of 7 January and 23 March 1812. The first, filed after 7 January 1812, may be read in J. C. A. Stagg, ed., "The Political Essays of William Shaler," on the *William and Mary Quarterly* website at http://oieahc.wm.edu/wmq/Apr02/stagg .htm. It seems unlikely that Shaler was aware that disagreements between Spain and Great Britain over whether Mexico should be included in the mediation were among the reasons for its failure (see Rydjord, "British Mediation between Spain and Her Colonies, 1811–1813," *Hispanic American Historical Review* 21 [1941]: 40–42).

28. The second essay was filed after 4 February 1812 in Shaler's letter book (see http://oieahc.wm.edu/wmq/Apr02/stagg.htm).

29. The third, untitled essay was also filed at 4 February 1812 (ibid.), and "Notes on Manners and Society in Havana"—which was an expanded version of some remarks Shaler had included in his consular dispatch of 25 November 1811—was filed at 23 March 1812 (ibid.).

30. Claiborne to Hamilton, 26 December 1811 and 3 January 1812, in Rowland, *Claiborne Letter Books*, 6: 21–22, 28.

31. Claiborne to Hamilton, 23 January and 1 February 1812, ibid., 6: 38, 45.

32. Shaler admitted as much in his 23 March 1812 letter to Madison (see n. 3 of this chapter).

33. See Shaler to Hamilton, 15 July 1812, Shaler Letter Books.

34. For Claiborne's report of three successive failures of the mail between New Orleans and Washington, see his 17 February 1812 letter to Hamilton (Rowland, *Claiborne Letter Books*, 6: 57).

35. See Shaler to Monroe, 13 November 1811, Consular Dispatches, Havana.

36. Biographical material can be found in Donald E. Chipman and Harriett Denise Joseph, *Notable Men and Women of Spanish Texas* (Austin, TX, 1999), 226–49; and in Joseph C. Milligan, "José Bernardo Gutiérrez de Lara, Mexican Frontiersman (Ph.D. diss., Texas Tech University, 1975). See also the older (and undocumented) work by Lorenzo de la Garza, *Dos Hermanos Héroes* (repr., Mexico City, 1939); and Gutiérrez to the Mexican Congress, 1 August 1815, in Charles A. Gulick, ed., *The Papers of Mirabeau Buonaparte Lamar* (6 vols.; Austin, TX, 1921–27), 1: 4–12.

37. Pike to Eustis, 28 October 1811, Letters Received by the Secretary of War, Registered Series, P-131 (6), RG 107, National Archives; and Sibley to Eustis, 24 September 1811, ibid., S-29 (6). Gutiérrez also sent an advance letter from Natchitoches to Washington in which he claimed that Mexican republican forces under Ignacio Lopez Rayón were more than 200,000 strong and that Veracruz had been cut off from Mexico City by a rebel army of 30,000–40,000 men (see Francisco Mariano Sora and Gutiérrez to Monroe, 27 September 1811, Consular Dispatches of the Department of State, Mexico City, RG 59, National Archives).

38. For Gutiérrez's meeting with Madison on 16 December 1811, see Elizabeth H. West, ed., "Diary of José Bernardo Gutiérrez de Lara, 1811–1812," *American Historical Review* 34 (1928–29): 73.

39. Gutiérrez to Eustis, [ca. 11 December 1811], Correspondence Relating to the

Filibustering Expedition against the Spanish Government of Mexico, 1811–1816, RG 59, National Archives. An emphasis on construing the three hundred years of Spanish rule as a form of oppression that violated an essential contract between the crown and its subjects in America was a common trope in the thinking of creole patriots in Spanish America (see Anthony Pagden, *Spanish Imperialism and the Political Imagination: Studies in European and Spanish-American Political Theory* [New Haven, CT, 1990], 120–25. See also Elliott, *Empires of the Atlantic World,* 383).

40. For the January 1811 rebellion in San Antonio de Béxar, see the collection of documents compiled by Frederick C. Chabot, *Texas in 1811: The Las Casas and Sambrano Revolutions* (San Antonio, TX, 1940), and J. Villasana Haggard, "The Counter-Revolution of Bexar, 1811," *Southwestern Historical Quarterly* 43 (1939): 222–35. It should also be noted that Gutiérrez's desire for more trade was a reflection of the fact that trade between the United States and Texas in such items as horses, mules, cattle, hides, tallow, and wool was already increasing as a result of American expansion into Louisiana. Pressures arising from the Embargo of 1807–9 also encouraged settlers in the Eastern Internal Provinces of New Spain to seek trade goods in the United States. However, because such trade was illegal under Spanish law, its expansion necessarily entailed problems of criminality and political dissent for Mexicans, all of which were exacerbated by the barrier of the "no-man's-land" in the Neutral Ground after 1806 (see Odie B. Faulk, *The Last Years of Spanish Texas 1778–1821* [The Hague, 1964], 113–31; C. Norman Guise, "Trade Goods for Texas: An Incident in the History of the Jeffersonian Embargo," *Southwestern Historical Quarterly* 60 [1957]: 507–19; Mattie Austin Hatcher, *The Opening of Texas to Foreign Settlement, 1801–1821* [Austin, TX, 1927], 71–126; and Jack Jackson, *Los Mesteños: Spanish Ranching in Texas, 1721–1821* [College Station, TX, 1986], 450–583).

41. Madison never mentioned the Hidalgo revolt in his correspondence, but in May 1811 the French minister, Louis Sérurier, recorded a conversation with him on the subject. The president was aware Hidalgo had been defeated, remarking that his rebellion had failed because it lacked adequate support from the creole population of Mexico. In the future, Madison believed, the *peninsulares* in Mexico would not be able to count on the creoles and would thus be vulnerable to defeat (see Sérurier to the duc de Cadore, 5 May 1811, Archives du Ministère des Affaires Étrangères: Correspondence Politique, États-Unis, vol. 65 [copy in Library of Congress]).

42. See Madison's 5 November 1811 message to Congress, *Papers of James Madison: Presidential Series,* 4: 4; and Joseph Gales, compiler, *The Debates and Proceedings of the Congress of the United States* (42 vols.; Washington, DC, 1834–1856), 12th Cong., 1st sess., 335, 427–40.

43. West, "Diary of Gutiérrez," 73.

44. Ibid., 71.

45. As Madison had remarked in his 17 November 1811 letter to Joel Barlow, "Mexico, according to our intelligence wch. is difficult & obscure, is still in the struggle between the revolutionary & royal parties" (see *Papers of James Madison: Presidential Series,* 4: 21).

46. West, "Diary of Gutiérrez," 71, 77.

47. Ibid., 281–89. See also Claiborne to Graham, 31 March 1812, and to Shaler, 7 April 1812, in Rowland, *Claiborne Letter Books,* 6: 68–69, 71–72.

48. Four sets of accounts for Shaler's missions to Cuba and Mexico are filed at the end of his correspondence in Communications from Special Agents. The expenses for the accommodation of Gutiérrez and Shaler in Natchitoches are recorded in the third and fourth set of accounts. The total cost for Shaler's mission between June 1810 and December 1813 was $7,026.00, based on a salary of $2,000.00 per year (see Miscellaneous Treasury Accounts of the General Accounting Office, account no. 27,893, RG 217, National Archives).

49. Shaler to Madison, 23 March 1812, *Papers of James Madison: Presidential Series,* 4: 259–60; and Monroe to Shaler, 2 May 1812, where the secretary of state acknowledged receipt of seven letters sent by Shaler between 13 November 1811 and 15 February 1812, Shaler and Family Papers.

50. The controversy centers on the extent to which Shaler was actively assisting Gutiérrez to organize a filibuster into Mexico. For arguments that it is a misunderstanding of Shaler's actions to believe that he was assisting Gutiérrez and that he had authorization from Washington to do so, see J. C. A. Stagg, "The Madison Administration and Mexico: Reinterpreting the Gutiérrez-Magee Raid of 1812–1813," *William and Mary Quarterly,* 3d ser., vol. 59 (2002): 449–80. This is not to deny, however, that Spanish officials could only conclude that by virtue of his accompanying Gutiérrez, Shaler must have been sent by the United States to aid the Mexican rebellion (see Peter Samuel Davenport to Bernadino Montero, 12 May 1812, and Manuel María de Salcedo to Nemesio Salcedo, 3 June 1812, *Bexar Archives,* University of Texas, microfilm edition, roll 51).

51. See West, "Diary of Gutiérrez," 293. The possibility that the Caddo might play a role in Gutiérrez's filibuster was a cause of concern to Sibley, who worried that in the event of a war between Spain and the United States, the Spanish authorities would be able to recruit the Caddo as allies. In response, Sibley's policy was not to encourage the Caddo to support either the filibuster or the United States but to persuade them to remain neutral. Because the Caddo chief Dehahuit had no desire to be caught up in a war between Spain and the United States, Sibley was, by and large, successful, though smaller numbers of other Indians were eventually recruited for the filibuster (see Sibley to Eustis, 14 July and 5 August 1812, Letters Received, Registered Series, S-308 [6] and S-351 [6]). For more detailed studies of Caddo responses to American and European rivalries on the Louisiana-Texas frontier, see Cecile E. Carter, *Caddo Indians: Where We Come From* (Norman, OK, 1995), 245–51; David La Vere, *The Caddo Chiefdoms: Caddo Economics and Politics, 700–1835* (Lincoln, NE, 1998), 127–34; F. Todd Smith, *The Caddo Indians: Tribes at the Convergence of Empires* (College Station, TX, 1995), 84–102; and Smith, *From Dominance to Disappearance: The Indians of Texas and the Near Southwest, 1786–1859* (Lincoln, NE, 2005), 75–77, 89–91.

52. See West, "Diary of Gutiérrez," 293. See also Shaler to Monroe, 17 May 1812, Communications from Special Agents. Shaler's reports about the dealings with Paillette

were confirmed by Sibley (see Sibley to Eustis, 24 June 1812, Letters Received, Registered Series, S-293 [6]).

53. Claiborne forwarded a copy of this recruiting notice, headed "Stipulations to be entered into by a certain number of Volunteers," in his 6 July 1812 letter to Monroe (see Miscellaneous Letters).

54. See Shaler to Monroe, 12 and 23 June 1812, Communications from Special Agents.

55. Claiborne to Graham, 13 and 31 March 1812, in Rowland, *Claiborne Letter Books*, 6: 71–72, 79–80. See also Shaler to Monroe, 23 June 1812, Communications from Special Agents.

56. Shaler to Monroe, 23 and 31 March, 17 and 22 May, 12 and 23 June 1812, Communications from Special Agents.

57. Shaler to Monroe, 17 May, 12 June, 12 July 1812, ibid. The idea of relocating the American garrison on the Sabine River had also been suggested to Claiborne by John C. Carr, the parish judge at Natchitoches (see Carr to Claiborne, 7 January 1812, in Clarence E. Carter et al., eds., *The Territorial Papers of the United States* [28 vols.; Washington, DC, 1934–75], *Orleans*, 9: 975–78).

58. Shaler to Monroe, 23 June 1812, Communications from Special Agents.

59. See Shaler to Monroe, 12 and 15 July 1812, Communications from Special Agents. For a discussion of Shaler's commitment to republicanism in Mexico, see Lyon O. Rathbun, "The Representation of Mexicans and the Transformation of American Political Culture, 1787–1848" (Ph.D. diss.; University of California at Berkeley, 1994), 86–103. A most graphic testament to the vulnerability of the Spanish regime in Texas was provided in the statement of its governor in 1809 that he required at least four thousand troops to defend an area with a European population of little more than three thousand (see Nettie Lee Benson, ed., "A Governor's Report on Texas in 1809," *Southwestern Historical Quarterly* 71 [1968]: 603–15).

60. Claiborne to Monroe, 6 July 1812, Communications from Special Agents; and to Stephen Kingston, 25 June 1812, in Rowland, *Claiborne Letter Books*, 6: 116. For Claiborne's earlier "standing orders" against filibustering, see his letters of 4 and 30 July 1811 to Carr (Carter et al., *Territorial Papers: Orleans*, 9: 943–44; and Rowland, *Claiborne Letter Books*, 5: 319–20). See also his 4 August and 19 November 1811 letters to Monroe, ibid., 5: 328–29, 383.

61. See the copy of Claiborne to Wilkinson, 5 August 1812, enclosed in Wilkinson to Eustis, 10 August 1812, Letters Received, Registered Series, W-303 (6). For Wilkinson's difficulties in defending New Orleans and West Florida, see his letters to Eustis, 13, 22, 28 July 1812, ibid., W-259 (6), W-265 (6), W-267 (6).

62. For Carr's difficulties in executing his "standing orders," see the 4 January 1812 memorial of the merchants of Natchitoches to Claiborne, in which they pointed out that the judge lacked the power to suppress filibusters and "banditti" and that he also lacked the authority to coerce the services of the local militia for any period of time (see Carter et al., *Territorial Papers: Orleans*, 9: 976–78). For Claiborne's rejection of Carr's resignation, see his 7 August 1812 letter and also his 11 August 1812 proclama-

tion (Rowland, *Claiborne Letter Books,* 6: 149, 160, 229–30). The penalties for violating the 1794 Neutrality Act could extend to fines up to $3,000 and three years in prison.

63. See Shaler to Claiborne, 25 August 1812, Shaler Letter Books. The size of the filibustering force fluctuated throughout the year between August 1812 and August 1813, as did the relative numbers of Americans, Mexicans, and Indians in its ranks. It is impossible to determine these numbers with any accuracy, but by August 1813 estimates of its total size ranged from 1,200 to 3,000, and by that stage Indians and Mexicans probably outnumbered Americans by two to one (see, for example, the figures provided by Vito Alessio Robles, *Coahuila y Texas en la epocha colonial* [Mexico City, 1938], 658). From the available sources, historians have been able to identify by name only about fifty Americans and little more than twenty Mexicans. There were also a small number of men from France and Spain in the filibuster (see Henry P. Walker, ed., "William McLane's Narrative of the Magee-Gutiérrez Expedition, 1812–1813," *Southwestern Historical Quarterly* 66 [1963]: 474–75, 577–88; see also Seb S. Wilcox, ed., "Arredondo's Report of the Battle of Medina," ibid., 43 [1939]: 257–58).

64. For Claiborne's criticisms of the filibuster, see his letters of 10 August 1812 to Monroe and 9 July 1813 to Madison, Miscellaneous Letters. See also his 23 October and 29 November 1813 letters to Madison (James Madison Papers, Library of Congress).

65. Magee to Eustis, 22 June 1812, Letters Received by the Office of the Adjutant General, RG 94, National Archives. For a brief sketch, see M. L. Crimmons, "Augustus William Magee, the Second Advance Courier of American Expansion to Texas," *West Texas Historical Association Year Book* 20 (1944): 92–98.

66. See Shaler to Claiborne, 25 August 1812, Shaler Letter Books. See also Shaler to Monroe, 25 and 27 August 1812, Communications from Special Agents. For Magee's previous experience in the Neutral Ground, see the correspondence enclosed in Wade Hampton to Eustis, 1 April 1812, Letters Received, Registered Series, H-213 (6).

67. See Shaler to Monroe, 12 July 1812, Communications from Special Agents. See also Shaler to Claiborne, 27 August 1812, Shaler Letter Books.

68. The essay was enclosed in Shaler's 18 August 1812 letter to Monroe, Communications from Special Agents, though without the title Shaler had provided for it in his letter book copy of the same date (see Shaler Letter Books).

69. For a discussion of the ideology of "maritime whiggery," which made it possible for early modern European thinkers to conceive how maritime nations such as Great Britain and the United States could check the power of much larger, land-based empires, see Daniel Deudney, *Bounding Power: Republican Security Theory from the Polis to the Global Village* (Princeton, NJ, 2007), 114–35.

70. The essay is available on the *William and Mary Quarterly* website at http://oieahc.wm.edu/wmq/Apr02/stagg.htm.

71. Emmerich de Vattel, *The Law of Nations; or, The Principles of Natural Law, Applied to the Conduct and to the Affairs of Nations and of Sovereigns,* trans. Charles G. Fenwick (Washington, DC, 1916 [orig. 1758]), 251, 253. For two introductions to

these ideas, see Sylvester J. Hemleben, *Plans for World Peace through Six Centuries* (Chicago, IL, 1943), 42–95; and Francis H. Hinsley, *Power and the Pursuit of Peace: Theory and Practice in the History of Relations between States* (Cambridge, UK, 1963), 1–80, 153–212. For the "republicanization" of these ideas in an American context, see Peter Onuf and Nicholas Onuf, *Federal Union, Modern World: The Law of Nations in an Age of Revolutions, 1776–1814* (Madison, WI, 1993), 4–6, 11–19, 197–211; and Nicholas Onuf, *The Republican Legacy in International Thought* (Cambridge, UK, 1998), 58–84.

72. For Madison's reservations about confederations of nations, see his 31 January 1792 *National Gazette* essay titled "Universal Peace" (*The Papers of James Madison* [17 vols., ed. William T. Hutchinson, William M. E. Rachal, et al.; Chicago, IL, and Charlottesville, VA, 1962–91], 14: 206–8), where he wrote that the achievement of "universal peace" through confederations of nations could not exist but "in the imaginations of visionary philosophers or in the breasts of benevolent enthusiasts."

73. Madison to Monroe, 1 September 1812, *Papers of James Madison: Presidential Series,* 5: 245. The enclosed letter was from Gilbert Dade Taylor, a grandson of Erasmus Taylor. Monroe probably returned the letter to Madison, who may have decided—as he often did with family correspondence—not to preserve it among his papers. Sibley may have also reinforced Shaler's misgivings about the filibuster, writing that while Americans at Natchitoches would "rejoice to see an authorized body of troops" marching to the aid of Mexico's republicans, "all sober Reflecting persons" regarded the Gutiérrez-Magee raid "with unpleasant fears" (see Sibley to Eustis, 24 June 1812, Letters Received, Registered Series, S-293 [6]).

74. See Monroe to Shaler, 1 September 1812, Shaler Papers; and Monroe to Willie Blount and to Benjamin Howard, 3 September 1812, Domestic Letters of the Department of State, RG 59, National Archives. The letter to Howard was written in response to a 21 June 1812 letter from the territorial governor (not found), which apparently reported that residents of the territory were planning to "visit" Mexico.

75. Pike to Monroe, 19 June 1812, James Monroe Papers, New York Public Library. The letter is in the hand of Robinson and signed by Pike. For biographical details about Robinson, see Harold A. Bierck, Jr., "Dr. John Hamilton Robinson," *Louisiana Historical Quarterly* 25 (1942): 644–69.

76. Monroe to Robinson, 1 July 1812, Correspondence Relating to the Filibustering Expedition against the Spanish Government of Mexico.

77. Monroe to Shaler, 1 September 1812, Shaler Papers.

78. Blount to Monroe, 3 October 1812, Miscellaneous Letters.

79. West, "Diary of Gutiérrez," 65–68.

80. See the accounts of Mexico that appeared in the *Nashville Democratic Clarion and Tennessee Gazette,* 28 and 30 April, 5 May, 3 September 1812. See also the *Nashville Whig,* 23 September 1812, where potential recruits for the filibuster were advised that because war between Spain and the United States was inevitable, their joining its ranks would be "both laudable and legal in itself."

81. See Shaler to Monroe, 5 October 1812, Communications from Special Agents.

82. Robinson to Monroe, 26 July 1813, Correspondence Relating to the Filibustering Expedition against the Spanish Government of Mexico.

83. For these events, see Julia K. Garrett, *Green Flag over Texas: A Story of the Last Years of Spain in Texas* (New York, 1939), 149–62.

84. On 27 December 1812 John Sibley informed the War Department that about two hundred "well Mounted" men from Nuevo Santander had joined the filibuster (Letters Received, Registered Series, S-35 [7]). The source of the Indian recruits is a matter of dispute. Sibley believed they came not from the larger nations such as the Apache, the Comanche, or the Caddo but from smaller groups of "vagabond" Indians who had migrated to the west of the Mississippi River, such as the "Allibamis & Conchattas (Descendents from the Creeks) who live[d] on or near the Coast along the Bay of St Bernard with a few Choctaws, Nabedaches & Nacogdochettas." (See [Sibley] to the Secretary of War, 12 February 1813, Letters Received by the Secretary of War, Unregistered Series, I-1813, RG 107, National Archives. For a brief description of how and when such groups had been driven west of the Mississippi, see Gary Clayton Anderson, *The Indian Southwest, 1580–1830: Ethnogenesis and Reinvention* [Norman, OK, 1999], 188–95.) Evidence from later in 1813, however, suggests that the Indians in the filibuster came from tribes that had long been hostile to Spain, such as the Tonkawas, the Lipan Apache, and the Tawakonis, whose warriors were taken prisoner by the Spanish after the Battle of Medina (see Mattie Austin Hatcher, ed., "Joaquín de Arredondo's Report of the Battle of Medina, August 18, 1813," *Quarterly of the Texas State Historical Association* 11 [1908]: 226; and Smith, *From Dominance to Disappearance*, 98–99).

85. See Shaler to Monroe, 17 September 1812, Communications from Special Agents. See also J. Villasana Haggard, "The House of Barr and Davenport," *Southwestern Historical Quarterly* 49 (1945): 84–88.

86. Garrett, *Green Flag over Texas*, 163–74; and Felix D. Almaráz, Jr., *Tragic Cavalier: Governor Manuel Salcedo of Texas, 1808–1813* (Austin, TX, 1971), 164–68. For recollections by a participant, see Walker, "William McLane's Narrative," 249–51.

87. Gutiérrez to Shaler, 25 November 1812, enclosed in Shaler to Monroe, 25 December 1812, Communications from Special Agents.

88. See Magee to Shaler, 14 November 1812, enclosed in Shaler to Monroe, 29 November 1812, ibid. See also Magee to Shaler, 25 November 1812, enclosed in Shaler to Monroe, 25 December 1812, ibid.

89. See Shaler to Monroe, 10 and 23 January, 26 February, 20 March 1813, Communications from Special Agents. It has never been determined whether Magee died of consumption, committed suicide, or was murdered (see Walker, "William McLane's Narrative," 250).

90. For Shaler's request for a passport, see his 10 November 1812 letter to Monroe, Communications from Special Agents, where he pointed out that his instructions of June 1810 were hardly a proper document to be shown to a new government in Mexico.

91. See Shaler to Magee, 20 December 1812, Shaler Letter Books.

92. See Shaler to Monroe, 26 February 1813, Communications from Special Agents.

93. A biographical sketch of Shaler, published shortly before his death in 1833, described him as a man of "great gravity and full of thought" but with a countenance with "something like melancholy in it . . . that seemed to say . . . that there had been some blow to his heart" (see Knapp, *American Biography,* 298). Shaler was aware of this himself, remarking to his brother on one occasion that "my mind sometimes soars very high, and at others falls very low" (see William Shaler to Nathaniel Shaler, 10 August 1813, Shaler Papers).

94. See Shaler to Monroe, 25 and 27 December 1812, Communications from Special Agents.

95. See Shaler to Graham, 26 February 1813, Shaler Letter Books.

96. See Garrett, *Green Flag over Texas,* 175–79; and Almaráz, *Tragic Cavalier,* 168–71.

97. See Shaler to Monroe, 3 April 1813, Communications from Special Agents.

98. Almaráz, *Tragic Cavalier,* 171–73.

99. Julia K. Garrett, "The First Constitution of Texas, April 17, 1813," *Southwestern Historical Quarterly* 40 (1937): 290–308.

100. See Shaler to Monroe, 14 May 1813, enclosing a copy of the Texan constitution, Communications from Special Agents.

101. Articles 3 and 4 of the Texan constitution guaranteed private property and personal liberty, and article 17 could be read as supporting the view that Americans and Mexicans would be treated equally for whatever services they had provided to the revolution and the new republic. That message was reinforced in Gutiérrez's 18 April proclamation, which stated that one of the purposes of the new government was to encourage the "emigration of free men of all nations" and to remove "barbarous and unnatural laws" that had prohibited "a useful intercourse with adjoining powers that existed only in contraband which was dangerous to the undertaker and bringing disgrace on the existing government." Significant portions of the 6 April declaration of independence were similarly devoted to complaints about how Spain had hindered Mexico's development by selling its trade and resources to court "favorites" and "monopolists" whose greed perverted legitimate commerce with neighboring regions into a "trifling system of smuggling." Gutiérrez also painted a glowing picture of the natural resources of Texas, which promised "felicity" to "the welcome immigrant" and an "honorable subsistence" to all who would leave "their native soil to enjoy unmolested the comforts of freedom with the new independent Patriots of Texas." Copies of these documents may be found in the José Bernardo Maximiliano Gutiérrez de Lara Papers, Center for American History, University of Texas.

102. See articles 2, 5, 7, 8, 9, 10, and 17 of the Texas constitution. These seemingly contradictory elements in Gutiérrez's vision have given rise to some debate as to whether he should be regarded as a true "republican" or whether he betrayed his ideals by "reverting to type" and creating an essentially "Spanish" authoritarian political system (see Garrett, "The First Constitution of Texas," 291; and also Virginia Guedea, "Autonomía e independencia en la provincia de Texas: La junta de gobierno de San Antonio de Béjar,

1813," in Guedea, compiler, *La independencia de México y el proceso autonomista novo-hispano, 1808–1824* [Mexico City, 2001], 164–70). It has been suggested as well that Gutiérrez was an incipient Texan caudillo but that he and his supporters had to operate as "pragmatic rebels" who needed to bridge sharp regional and ideological differences among their followers in order to obtain external support to expel the Spanish (see David E. Narrett, "José Bernardo Gutiérrez de Lara: Caudillo of the Mexican Republic in Texas," *Southwestern Historical Quarterly* 106 [2002]: 195–228). While it is certainly plausible to suspect a potential for caudillism in some of Gutiérrez's actions, it remains unclear whether he could be properly described as a local "strong man" who could command access to both men and resources in significant quantities. His brief career as the ruler of Texas in 1813 suggests he lacked both the means and the temperament to act in ways that characterized the behavior of later Latin American caudillos. And it would not be entirely fair to say that Gutiérrez attempted to govern outside of any sort of constitutional framework; indeed, the notion that a ruler might assume extraordinary powers as a "protector" of the people against anarchy and oppression was by no means unknown to Spanish constitutional thinking (see John Lynch, *Caudillos in Spanish America, 1800–1850* [Oxford, UK, 1992], 4–9, for a discussion of these problems of definition). It also seems clear that the period of Gutiérrez's rule in San Antonio de Béxar embodied many of the tensions experienced by both Spaniards and Spanish Americans as they tried to combine elements of liberalism with an adherence to older Spanish communal and patriarchal values (see David A. Brading, *The First America: The Spanish Monarchy, Creole Patriots, and the Liberal State, 1492–1867* [Cambridge, UK, 1991], 561–82). In a somewhat analogous manner Eric Van Young has also argued that there were many "atavistic" elements in the ideologies that gave rise to, and justified, the Mexican rebellion against Spain (see *The Other Rebellion: Popular Violence, Ideology, and the Mexican Struggle for Independence, 1810–1821* [Stanford, CA, 2001]: 2–36).

103. Walker, "William McLane's Narrative," 464–68.

104. West, "Diary of Gutiérrez," 75–76. Apparently Toledo wrote to Gutiérrez in July 1812 about coming to Texas (see Toledo to Gutiérrez, [October 1812], Department of State: Spanish Affairs, 1810–1816, Library of Congress). See also Harris G. Warren, "José Álvarez de Toledo's Initiation as a Filibuster, 1811–1813," *Hispanic American Historical Review* 20 (1940): 64.

105. Cogswell to "Generals Bernardo de Gutierres and Magee," 29 December 1812, enclosed in Shaler to Monroe, 12 June 1813, Communications from Special Agents. Other members of Toledo's party were Samuel Alden, Henry Adams Bullard, William Prentiss, Joseph B. Wilkinson, and the exiled Spanish revolutionary Juan Bautista Mariano Picornell y Gomila.

106. Ibid. For an account of Miranda's role in the downfall of the first Venezuelan republic, see William Spence Robertson, *The Life of Miranda* (2 vols.; Chapel Hill, NC, 1929), 2: 167–95. Suspicions that Miranda's behavior had in some way been treasonous were widespread.

107. See Narrett, "José Bernardo Gutiérrez de Lara," 206; and Warren, "José Álvarez de Toledo's Initiation as a Filibuster," 57.

108. Gutiérrez to Cogswell, 11 April 1813, Gutiérrez de Lara Papers.

109. See Shaler to Gutiérrez, 28 May 1813, ibid., where the agent dismissed Cogswell's letter as "a tissue of falsehoods and calumny from beginning to end" that was "unworthy of any sincere refutation." For Shaler's earlier remarks about the need to replace Gutiérrez, see his 27 August 1812 letter to Monroe as cited in n. 66 of this chapter.

110. Shaler forwarded the memoir to Samuel Dana, a U.S. senator for Connecticut, on 10 May 1813, Simon Gratz Autograph Collection, Historical Society of Pennsylvania. For a modern translation, see Nettie Lee Benson, ed., *Report That Dr. Miguel Ramos de Arispe . . . Presents to the August Congress on the Natural, Political and Civil Condition of the Provinces of Coahuila, Nuevo León, Nuevo Santander, and Texas of the Four Eastern Provinces of Mexico* (Austin, TX, 1950). When Shaler met with Dana in Washington over the winter of 1813–14, the senator said that he had concluded Shaler was "out with the party in Texas." The agent resented "this insinuation" but contented himself "with satisfying" the senator "to the contrary" (diary entry for 3–4 January 1814, Shaler Letter Books).

111. Four pages of undated notes on the 1812 Constitution can be found in the Shaler Papers.

112. Cogswell to Gutiérrez, 4 July 1813, enclosed in Shaler to Monroe, 10 July 1813, Communications from Special Agents.

113. Shaler to Monroe, 10 July 1813, ibid. Among the affidavits was one claiming that Cogswell had been expelled from Toledo's party for misappropriating its funds. Shaler, however, supplied Toledo with some funds. He advanced Capt. Walter Overton at Fort Claiborne $200 to cover the costs of a horse Overton had offered to Toledo after the latter had declined it for want of money, and he later gave Toledo other sums amounting to $170 (see the third set of Shaler's accounts filed in Communications from Special Agents).

114. Shaler provided details of these transactions in his letters to Monroe between 16 April and 20 June 1813, Communications from Special Agents.

115. Julia K. Garrett, "The First Newspaper of Texas: Gaceta de Texas," *Southwestern Historical Quarterly* 40 (1937): 200–215.

116. See Shaler to Monroe, 10 July 1813, Communications from Special Agents.

117. For these developments, see Carlos E. Casteñeda, *Our Catholic Heritage in Texas* (7 vols.; Austin, TX, 1936–58), 6: 104–8.

118. See Elizondo to Gutiérrez, 19 April 1813, in Chabot, *Texas in 1811*, 162.

119. Walker, "William McLane's Narrative," 469–72.

120. See Samuel D. Forsyth to Shaler, 28 June 1813, Shaler Papers.

121. See Shaler to Monroe, 14 July 1813, Communications from Special Agents.

122. Shaler entrusted this letter to Robinson as he passed through Natchitoches on his return to Washington (see Robinson to Monroe, 21 August 1813, Correspondence Relating to the Filibustering Expedition against the Spanish Government of Mexico).

123. Shaler enclosed the essay in his 18 July 1813 letter to Navy Secretary William Jones, William Jones Papers, Historical Society of Pennsylvania. The text is available on the *William and Mary Quarterly* website at http://oieahc.wm.edu/wmq/Apr02/

stagg.htm. In July 1812 Russia had made a treaty of alliance with Spain against Napoleon, but it contained no article pertaining to California (see Russell H. Bartley, *Imperial Russia and the Struggle for Latin American Independence, 1808–1828* [Austin, TX, 1978], 98–101).

124. Eustis to Wilkinson, 26 August and 21 September 1812, Letters Sent by the Secretary of War Relating to Military Affairs, RG 107, National Archives.

125. See Graham to Shaler, 14 December 1812; and Monroe to Shaler, 5 February 1813, Shaler Papers. Shaler's passport and commission to the authorities in New Spain as the bearer of communications from the United States was signed on 5 February 1813 (ibid.).

126. The capture of San Antonio de Béxar was reported as "glorious news" (see the *Nashville Democratic Clarion and Tennessee Gazette*, 4 June 1813; the *Nashville Whig*, 8 June 1813; and the Philadelphia *Aurora General Advertiser*, 8 June 1813). The Baltimore *Weekly Register*, on 26 June 1813, went further by remarking that "a very extensive region [had] shaken off the royal, and substituted a republican system of government," and that the other provinces of Mexico would follow "the glorious example." "We trust and hope," Hezekiah Niles concluded, "that *Mexico* will be free."

127. See Monroe to Shaler, 5 June 1813, Shaler Papers.

128. Robinson to Monroe, 12 April 1813, Correspondence Relating to the Filibustering Expedition against the Spanish Government of Mexico.

129. See Shaler to Monroe, 2 May 1813, Communications from Special Agents. Even before he encountered Toledo, Robinson had been considering a filibuster. After leaving Chihuahua in January 1813, he met with José Mariano Cevallos of the republican junta of Guanajuato to discuss obtaining arms and aid from the United States, and he also received a request from Juan Dies of Santa Fe for the same purpose (see Bierck, "Dr. John Hamilton Robinson," 654–55).

130. The report is filed in Correspondence Relating to the Filibustering Expedition against the Spanish Government of Mexico. Its contents provided a narrative of Robinson's journey, including accounts of Magee's efforts to obstruct his mission as well as of his meetings with Manuel de Salcedo and Herrara before he reached Nemesio Salcedo in Chihuahua on 11 December 1812. Salcedo was annoyed Robinson had brought him no letter signed by Madison, but he agreed to engage in a correspondence with the agent, which he abruptly terminated on 3 January 1813 after deciding that Robinson was unable to prove he had official sanction for his business. Robinson also provided an assessment of the rebellion in Mexico, believing that Rayón's armies controlled the southern regions of the country and would eventually be able to unite with Gutiérrez's forces. He feared, however, that both Rayón and Gutiérrez would seek French assistance to establish Mexican independence and that Great Britain would assist Spain in both retaining Mexico and regaining Louisiana from the United States. To prevent these outcomes, Robinson argued that the United States should aid the Mexican republicans and take possession of Texas for itself. As Shaler had done in January 1812, Robinson assumed that if Great Britain did try to occupy Mexico, it would be for the purpose of turning its resources against the United States.

131. Monroe to Robinson, 25 June 1813, Domestic Letters. The agent was told to

consider himself discharged from government employment within three months of the date on the letter.

132. See Warren, "José Álvarez de Toledo's Initiation as a Filibuster," 56–61.

133. Toledo provoked attention by printing his criticism of the Cortes in the 17 December 1811 issue of the Philadelphia *Aurora General Advertiser* as a way of publicizing his pamphlet *Manifesto ó satisfaccion pundonorosa, á todos los buenos españoles europeos y á todos los pueblos de la America* (Philadelphia, PA, 1811). For discussions of the inability of the Cortes to handle the issue of equality for Spanish Americans with metropolitan Spaniards, see Timothy E. Anna, "Spain and the Breakdown of the Imperial Ethos: The Problem of Equality," *Hispanic American Historical Review* 62 (1982): 254–72; and Elliott, *Empires of the Atlantic World*, 378–83.

134. See Onís to Bardaxi, 20 March 1812, Estado, legajo 5638.

135. See Warren, "José Álvarez de Toledo's Initiation as a Filibuster," 61–65.

136. See Onís to Pezuela, 7 October 1812, Estado, legajo 5554.

137. Onís feared that Toledo was only trying to extort money from him. For an account of Toledo's 1816 return to the allegiance of Spain, see Warren, "José Álvarez de Toledo's Reconciliation with Spain and Projects for Suppressing Rebellion in the Spanish American Colonies," *Louisiana Historical Quarterly* 23 (1940): 827–63.

138. For a literary analysis of Toledo's writings warning against exaggerating the extent to which the allegiances of Spanish Americans were firmly fixed during the Napoleonic Wars, see Kristin A. Dykstra, "On the Betrayal of Nations: José Álvarez de Toledo's Philadelphia *Manifesto* (1811) and *Justification* (1816)," *New Centennial Review* 4 (2001): 267–305. For a similar argument to the effect that the movement of Spanish Americans toward independence was not necessarily preceded by the formation of anticolonial national identities, see Jeremy Adelman, *Sovereignty and Revolution in the Iberian Atlantic* (Princeton, NJ, 2006), 175–212. Jaime E. Rodríguez O. has also pointed out that when they spoke of "independence," Spanish Americans more often meant "autonomy" and "equality" than they did "emancipation" from metropolitan Spain (see *The Independence of Spanish America* [New York, 1998], 2–6). Toledo would seem to be a case in point as his quarrel was more with the oppressive and unequal treatment Spanish Americans received from the Cortes than with the king, to whom Toledo continued to profess loyalty in his 1811 *Manifesto*.

139. William Duncan to Madison, 8 October 1812, *Papers of James Madison: Presidential Series*, 5: 378–79. Some seventy years ago both Eric J. Bradner and Harris G. Warren claimed that by November 1812 Monroe had also been informed by an anonymous source that Toledo was "an agent and spy of the Spanish government." See Bradner, "José Álvarez de Toledo and the Spanish American Revolution" (M.A. thesis; Northwestern University, 1931), 18–19; and Warren, "José Álvarez de Toledo's Initiation as a Filibuster," 66, referring to an anonymous letter to Monroe dated 10 November 1812 which was then located in the State Department collection titled "Papers Relative to the Revolted Spanish Provinces." That letter, however, was clearly dated 10 November 1816, and it described Toledo's subsequent activities prior to his seeking a pardon from Ferdinand VII. It can now be found, filed at the later date, in

Correspondence Relating to the Filibustering Expedition against the Spanish Government of Mexico.

140. See Shaler to Monroe, 2 and 7 May 1813, Communications from Special Agents. In his reprimand to Shaler on 5 June 1813, Monroe acknowledged receipt of the agent's letters through 7 May. A description of Toledo arriving in Natchez, Mississippi Territory, wearing a "Spanish Uniform" in the company of five officers with four thousand stands of arms and "a great deal of money" was sent by Stephen Minor to Brig. Gen. James Wilkinson on 22 March 1813 and subsequently transmitted to Washington (see Letters Received, Unregistered Series, reproduced in William S. Coker, compiler, *The Papers of Panton, Leslie, and Company,* microfilm ed., roll 18). That this information came from Minor, an American who had entered the Spanish army during the revolution and had served Manuel Luis Gayoso de Lemos y Amorín, the Spanish governor of Louisiana and West Florida, in a number of capacities, including that of his adjutant in Natchez in 1781, would have done little to reassure the administration about the reliability of Toledo's claims to be a revolutionary.

141. Toledo was to defend his contacts with Paillette and other French agents on the grounds that as a loyal subject of Spain, it was necessary for him to be informed about their plans (see Warren, "José Álvarez de Toledo's Reconciliation with Spain," 834).

142. See the sources cited in nn. 113 and 121 of this chapter.

143. See Monroe to Shaler, 5 June 1813, Shaler Papers.

144. See Shaler to Monroe, 7 August 1813, Communications from Special Agents. Shaler did not believe, however, that the filibuster had been illegally fitted out on U.S. soil, and he had told Claiborne in August 1812 that rumors that the U.S. Army had supplied the filibuster were untrue (see Shaler to Claiborne, 25 August 1812, Shaler Letter Books).

145. The best account of events before and after the engagement is Ted Schwarz, *Forgotten Battlefield of the First Texas Revolution: The Battle of Medina, August 18, 1813* (Austin, TX, 1985), 57–115.

146. See Shaler to Monroe, 5 September 1813, Communications from Special Agents.

147. See diary entries for 19–21 December 1813, Shaler Letter Books.

Chapter 5. Toward the Transcontinental Treaty

1. For these developments see Harris G. Warren, *The Sword Was Their Passport: A History of American Filibustering in the Mexican Revolution* (Baton Rouge, LA, 1943), 73–82, 84–95; and Wilbert H. Timmons, *Morelos: Priest, Soldier, Statesman of Mexico* (El Paso, TX, 1963), 112–24, 129–30. The Congress of Chilpancingo declared Mexican independence from Spain in November 1813, but by March 1814 it had been crushed by the viceroy of New Spain, Félix María Calleja. For the activities of Gutiérrez, see his 1 August 1815 letter to the Mexican Congress in Charles A. Gulick, ed., *The Papers of Mirabeau Buonaparte Lamar* (6 vols.; Austin, TX, 1921–27), 1: 20–29.

2. Monroe to Alexander James Dallas, 15 December 1813; to Ninian Edwards and to William Mears, 21 January 1814; to Claiborne and to Tully Robinson, 14 and 17

February 1814; and to Willie Blount, 12 March 1814, all in Domestic Letters of the Department of State, RG 59, National Archives.

3. See Morris to Monroe, 8 November 1813, Diplomatic Dispatches of the Department of State, Spain, RG 59, National Archives.

4. Morris to Monroe, 26 November 1813 and 4 January 1814, Diplomatic Dispatches, Spain. Filed with the second letter are eleven pages of encoded enclosures, partially decoded by John Graham, that contain accounts of the anti-American sentiments reported by Morris. Much of this information was probably conveyed to Morris by Richard Raynal Keene, who after failing in his efforts to obtain land in Florida had gone to Spain, where he ultimately succeeded in obtaining grants to two substantial tracts in Texas, where he planned to settle German and Irish Catholics (see Keene, *Memoria presentada á S. M. C. El Señor Don Fernando VII, sobre el asunto de fomenter la poblacion & cultivo en los Terrenos Baldíos en las provencias internas de México* [Madrid, 1815]). For Morris's contacts with Keene, see his 4 January 1814 and 30 May 1815 letters to Monroe, Diplomatic Dispatches, Spain. Morris was somewhat skeptical about the information he received from Keene, but he conveyed it, nonetheless, to Washington.

5. Morris to Monroe, 4 January and 10 February 1814, Diplomatic Dispatches, Spain.

6. For an account of the Creek War of 1813–14, see Frank L. Owsley, Jr., *Struggle for the Gulf Borderlands: The Creek War and the Battle of New Orleans, 1812–1815* (Gainesville, FL, 1981), 6–94. The peace treaty with the Creek Indians subsequently signed at Fort Jackson in August 1814 also consolidated American control in the hinterland, by transferring more than twenty million acres of Indian land to the United States.

7. See Lord Castlereagh to Monroe, 4 November 1813, and Monroe to Castlereagh, 5 January 1814, in Walter Lowrie and Matthew St. Clair Clarke, compilers, *American State Papers: Documents, Legislative and Executive, of the Congress of the United States* (38 vols.; Washington, DC, 1832–61), *Foreign Relations*, 3: 621–22. See also Monroe to Shaler, 4 February 1814, William Shaler Papers, Historical Society of Pennsylvania.

8. For the restoration of Ferdinand VII, see Gabriel H. Lovett, *Napoleon and the Birth of Modern Spain* (2 vols.; New York, 1965), 2: 544–53, 809–33.

9. See Onís to Antonio Cano Manuel, 31 December 1813, Estado, legajo 5557, Archivo Histórico Nacional, Madrid (copy in Library of Congress).

10. See Onís to Monroe, 22 December 1813, 5 February, 5 March, 2 April 1814, Notes from Foreign Legations to the Department of State, Spain, RG 59, National Archives; also Onís to Manuel, 18 February 1814, Estado, legajo 5639.

11. "Paper delivered to Mr Chacon, Vice Consul of Spain at Alexandria," 19 March 1814, Notes from the Department of State to Foreign Ministers and Consuls in the United States, RG 59, National Archives.

12. Madison to Monroe, 23 May 1814, James Monroe Papers, Library of Congress.

13. For reports of the actions of Ferdinand VII, see the Washington, DC, *Daily National Intelligencer*, 27 July, 9, 15, 17 August, 7 October 1814; and the Baltimore *Weekly Register*, 30 July, 6 and 20 August 1814.

14. For the actions of Ferdinand VII after his restoration, see Timothy E. Anna, *Spain and the Loss of America* (Lincoln, NE, 1983), 115–29.

15. See Erving to Madison, 11 July 1814, George W. Erving Papers, Massachusetts Historical Society.

16. In his 19 March 1814 paper to Chacón, Monroe had warned the vice-consul that Madison would not entertain such a demand from Great Britain (see n. 11 of this chapter).

17. See Monroe to William Harris Crawford, 11 August 1814, Diplomatic Instructions of the Department of State, RG 59, National Archives.

18. See chapter 1 at pp. 34–36.

19. See Monroe to Erving, 6 October 1814, Diplomatic Instructions.

20. Ibid.

21. Madison had met Onís shortly after his arrival in 1809, when he was introduced at the Georgetown races by the British minister, Francis James Jackson, in an attempt to persuade the president to acknowledge the Spanish resistance (see Madison to Caesar A. Rodney, 22 October 1809, in *The Papers of James Madison: Presidential Series* [5 vols. to date, ed. Robert A. Rutland et al.; Charlottesville, VA, 1984–], 2: 26–27). In his two "Verus" pamphlets criticizing American policy toward Spain, Onís was relatively restrained in his language about the president, but his private feelings were far more hostile. Perhaps the most extraordinary manifestation of his suspicions about Madison's Francophile leanings was a story he reported to the effect that the president, at Napoleon's request, had considered erecting a monarchy in the United States for the benefit of the emperor's brother, Jerome Bonaparte, who had married Elizabeth Patterson, the niece of secretary of state Robert Smith (see Onís to Francisco Saavedra, 24 February 1810, Estado, legajo 5555).

22. For the details here, see chapter 3 at pp. 132–33. When Morris met with Madison in Washington in May 1813, the president told him that "the character of Mr O had been very exceptionable and did not merit tho' it had recd toleration." Madison also feared that the policies of his administration "thro' Mr O . . . had been much misrepresented" ([Morris], "Memos Made at Washington. May & June 1813," Anthony Morris Papers, Historical Society of Pennsylvania).

23. Owsley, *Struggle for the Gulf Borderlands,* 95–119.

24. See Onís to the duque de San Carlos, 3, 9, 11, 20, 28 January 1815, Estado, legajo 5640.

25. See Onís to the duque de San Carlos, 4, 7, 13 February 1815, ibid. The conventional wisdom that it was the Battle of New Orleans that saved the Gulf Coast for the United States is something of a misreading of the geopolitical realities in the region, based on the erroneous assumption that had Great Britain won the battle, it would have continued the war in order to impose a punitive peace along the lines envisaged by Onís. For a corrective interpretation, see James A. Carr, "The Battle of New Orleans and the Treaty of Ghent," *Diplomatic History* 3 (1979): 273–82.

26. Erving to Madison, 6 October and 14 December 1814, Erving Papers.

27. See Madison to Monroe, [March 1815], Monroe Papers, Library of Congress.

28. Madison to Monroe, 18 April 1815, ibid.

29. Madison to Monroe, 2 May 1815, ibid.

30. See Morris to Monroe, 6 January [1815], Diplomatic Dispatches, Spain (Morris misdated the letter 1814).

31. Dallas to Madison, 5 May 1815, James Madison Papers, Library of Congress.

32. "Memo of a Conference of Mr. Dallas with the Chevalier De Onis," 24 June 1815, Notes to Foreign Ministers and Consuls; also Madison to Monroe, 26 June 1815, Monroe Papers, Library of Congress.

33. See Onís to Monroe, 18 and 24 June, 4, 5, 6 July 1815, Notes from Foreign Legations, Spain.

34. Monroe to Cevallos, 17 July 1815, Notes to Foreign Ministers and Consuls.

35. For Madison's concerns on this score, see his 18 April 1815 letter to Monroe (Monroe Papers, Library of Congress).

36. Madison to Monroe, 12 September 1815, ibid.

37. Onís to Monroe, 28 July, 7, 18, 22, 28 August 1815, Notes from Foreign Legations, Spain. See also Onís to Cevallos, 1 August, 1 and 10 September 1815, Estado, legajo 5640.

38. Warren, *The Sword Was Their Passport*, 96–104, 110–14, 119–32. The best account of the postwar activities of the Lafitte brothers and the New Orleans "associates" is William C. Davis, *The Pirates Lafitte: The Treacherous World of the Corsairs of the Gulf* (New York, 2005), 259–80.

39. Monroe to John Dick, 1 September 1815, Domestic Letters. For Madison's proclamation, see *American State Papers: Foreign Relations*, 4: 1. The proclamation was backdated while Madison, who was at Montpelier at the time, corresponded with attorney general Richard Rush over how to word it. Rush took as a guiding precedent the executive proclamations issued at the time of the Burr conspiracy, though he was well aware that Burr had harbored "more criminal intentions than assailing the dominions of Spain." Madison modified Rush's drafts to the extent of not explicitly directing state governors to execute federal laws, though he assumed that all state officials would be embraced by the wording of the proclamation (see the correspondence between Madison and Rush under the dates of 20 August 1815 [Archives of the Henry Ford Museum], 2 September 1815 [Richard Rush Papers, Historical Society of Pennsylvania], and 5 September 1815 [Jasper Crane Collection, Princeton University Library]).

40. Madison to Rush, 5 September 1815, Jasper Crane Collection, Princeton University Library. On this occasion, in response to requests from Pedro Gual of Cartagena for U.S. naval convoy protection for arms shipments he was making to Bogotá and New Granada, Madison instructed Rush to deny the request, explaining that it was administration policy to treat the rebels with "kindness" and to indulge them as much as was consistent with a stance of neutrality. "Within that limit," he added, "we give no cause of quarrel to one party, and consult our policy & our principles by cherishing the good will of the other."

41. Cevallos to Monroe, 13 September 1815, enclosed in Onís to Monroe, 3 December 1815, Notes from Foreign Legations, Spain.

42. Erving to Monroe, 11 October 1815, Monroe Papers, Library of Congress.

43. Monroe to Onís, 8 December 1815, Notes to Foreign Ministers and Consuls.

44. Onís to Monroe, 30 December 1815, Notes from Foreign Legations, Spain.

45. Monroe to Onís, 19 January 1816, Notes to Foreign Ministers and Consuls.

46. Onís to Monroe, 22 February 1816, Notes from Foreign Legations, Spain. Monroe did not respond to this letter until 10 June 1816.

47. See Erving to Monroe, 23 February 1816, Monroe Papers, New York Public Library.

48. See Erving to Monroe, 1 April 1816, ibid. For a general discussion of the considerations underlying administration policy at this time, see James E. Lewis, Jr., *The American Union and the Problem of Neighborhood: The United States and the Collapse of the Spanish Empire, 1783–1829* (Chapel Hill, NC, 1998), 85–95.

49. Or, as Richard Rush put it in a memo of a cabinet meeting summoned by Madison on 29 May 1816, "It was determined, (nem con.) that he [Erving] might offer to the Spanish all the territory that we have, or claim, west of the Sabine, in consideration of East Florida being granted to us" (Anthony Brescia, ed., *Letters and Papers of Richard Rush,* microfilm ed. [Wilmington, DE, 1980], roll 4).

50. For a discussion of the ways in which the Neutral Ground had facilitated filibustering, see J. Villasana Haggard, "The Neutral Ground between Louisiana and Texas, 1806–1821," *Louisiana Historical Quarterly* 28 (1945): 1053–73. The strategic significance of the Neutral Ground had, moreover, been somewhat reduced by the decisions of Joaquín Arredondo and Ignacio Elizondo to turn the region into a wasteland after the Battle of Medina (see Julia K. Garrett, *Green Flag over Texas: A Story of the Last Years of Spain in Texas* [New York, 1939], 225–35).

51. Monroe to Erving, 11 March and 30 May 1816, Diplomatic Instructions. These instructions allowed Erving to negotiate the northern and western boundary lines, or, if Cevallos preferred, the lines could be established by a board of commissioners.

52. See chapter 1 at pp. 34–36.

53. Frederick Merk, *The Oregon Question: Essays in Anglo-American Diplomacy and Politics* (Cambridge, MA, 1967), 1–4.

54. The literature on this subject is vast, but for a recent summary of the relationship between commerce, exploration, and scientific knowledge in Jefferson's thought see Alan Taylor, "Jefferson's Pacific: The Science of a Distant Empire," in Douglas Seefeldt et al., eds., *Across the Continent: Jefferson, Lewis and Clark, and the Making of America* (Charlottesville, VA, 2005), 16–44.

55. James P. Ronda, "Dreams and Discoveries: Exploring the American West, 1760–1815," *William and Mary Quarterly,* 3d ser., vol. 56 (1989): 145–53.

56. Jefferson to Meriwether Lewis, 16 November 1803, Thomas Jefferson Papers, Library of Congress.

57. The most convenient summary is that provided by Dan L. Flores, *Jefferson and Southwestern Exploration: The Freeman and Custis Accounts of the Red River Expedition of 1806* (Norman, OK, 1984), 3–90.

58. For a brief discussion, see Gary E. Moulton, ed., *The Journals of the Lewis and Clark Expedition* (14 vols; Lincoln, NE, 1983–2001), 2: 35–42.

59. David Porter to Jefferson, 17 August 1809, in J. Jefferson Looney et al., eds., *The

Papers of Thomas Jefferson: Retirement Series (4 vols. to date; Princeton, NJ, 2004–), 1: 443–49.

60. Charles Goldsborough to Madison, 20 September 1809, *Papers of James Madison: Presidential Series,* 1: 388.

61. For the best summary see James P. Ronda, *Astoria and Empire* (Lincoln, NE, 1990), especially pp. 79–81, 249–51, 262–63, 271–72.

62. Ibid., 243–307.

63. A copy of Shaler's essay on California and other related material can be found on the *William and Mary Quarterly* website at http://oieahc.wm.edu/wmq/Apr02/stagg. htm.

64. Ibid.

65. See Monroe to Shaler, 4 February 1814, Shaler Papers. Monroe offered Shaler the assignment to Europe on 1 February 1814, remarking that the agent's experience and "knowledge of the world . . . may be very useful to this country." Two days later, the secretary of state told Shaler that "if a congress was formed in Europe [he] must attend it, and make [himself] known to the Russian ministers" (diary entries for 1 and 3 February 1814, Shaler Letter Books [3 vols.; Gilder Lehrman Collection, New York Historical Society]).

66. For the settlements at Utrecht, see Kalevi J. Holsti, *Peace and War: Armed Conflicts and International Order, 1648–1989* (Cambridge, UK, 1991), 71–82. There was, in fact, a degree of similarity in the international crises centering on Spain in 1702–13 and 1808–14, to the extent that both involved either the breakup of the Spanish-American empire or its absorption by France (under the line of Philip V or the family of Napoleon Bonaparte). The Congress of Vienna in 1814–15, however, did not address colonial questions or issues of maritime law, but the problems of rearranging the post-Napoleonic world order continued to provoke rivalries among the European powers over the fate of Spain's American empire. (See ibid., 114–37; and Paul W. Schroeder, *The Transformation of European Politics, 1763–1848* [Oxford, UK, 1994], 574–75. See also Rafe Blaufarb, "The Western Question: The Geopolitics of Latin American Independence," *American Historical Review* 112 [2007]: 742–63.)

67. See Monroe to the Envoys Extraordinary and Ministers Plenipotentiary of the U.S. at Gothenburg, 22 March 1814, Diplomatic Instructions.

68. Porter published his account under the title *Journal of a Cruise Made to the Pacific Ocean by Captain David Porter, in the United States Frigate Essex, in the Years 1812, 1813, and 1814* (Philadelphia, PA, 1815). For a description of Porter's activities in the Marquesas, see David F. Long, *Nothing Too Daring: A Biography of Commodore David Porter, 1780–1843* (Annapolis, MD, 1970), 109–41.

69. Porter to Madison, 31 October 1815, Madison Papers.

70. See Gallatin to Astor, 5 August 1835, in Carl E. Prince and Helen Fineman, eds., *The Papers of Albert Gallatin,* microfilm ed. (Philadelphia, PA, 1969), roll 41, where Gallatin mentioned having discussed the reclaiming of Astoria in 1816 and recalling that "Mr. Madison said he would consider the subject, and although he did not commit himself, I thought he had received the proposal favorably."

71. Dallas to Madison, 26 June 1816, Madison Papers; and Monroe to Madison, 27 June 1816, William Cabell Rives Collection of James Madison Papers, Library of Congress. For a discussion of the increase in American whaling activities in the Pacific after 1815 and its significance, see Lance E. Davis, Robert E. Gallman, and Karen Gleiter, *In Pursuit of Leviathan: Technology, Institutions, Productivity, and Profits in American Whaling, 1816–1906* (Chicago, IL, 1997), 17, 37–39.

72. Madison to Monroe, 29 June 1816, Madison Papers.

73. Erving to Madison, 9 June 1816, Erving Papers.

74. For Erving's official correspondence, see his letters to Monroe of 31 August, 22 and 27 September 1816, Diplomatic Dispatches, Spain. These were supplemented by his private letters of 22 September and 11 October 1816, Monroe Papers, New York Public Library. For the influence of the camarilla on the decision making of Ferdinand VII, see Anna, *Spain and the Loss of America*, 125–27, 151–53; and Michael P. Costeloe, *Response to Revolution: Imperial Spain and the Spanish American Revolutions, 1810–1840* (Cambridge, UK, 1986), 14, 81.

75. See Erving to Monroe, 31 August 1816, Diplomatic Dispatches, Spain.

76. The story of Spain's preoccupation with Southern American questions to the exclusion of those involving North America and the United States may be traced in Anna, *Spain and the Loss of America*, 148–220; and in Costeloe, *Response to Revolution*, 59–85.

77. Monroe to Onís, 14 January 1817, Notes to Foreign Ministers and Consuls.

78. Onís to Monroe, 16 January 1817, Notes from Foreign Legations, Spain; and Monroe to Onís, 25 January 1817, Notes to Foreign Ministers and Consuls. Onís followed up his 16 January note by publishing a lengthy pamphlet, again under the pseudonym "Verus," restating the Spanish position on the boundary disputes and criticizing the activities of American agents and officials in the borderlands (see [Onís], *Observations on the Existing Differences between the Government of Spain and the United States* [Philadelphia, PA, 1817]).

79. Onís to Monroe, 30 May, 22 and 25 July, 23 August, 11 September 1816, all in Notes from Foreign Legations, Spain.

80. Madison to Monroe, 13 and 15 July 1816, Miscellaneous Letters of the Department of State, RG 59, National Archives.

81. The episode generated a substantial amount of correspondence, but see the account by Harris G. Warren, "The *Firebrand* Affair: A Forgotten Incident of the Mexican Revolution," *Louisiana Historical Quarterly* 21 (1938): 208–11.

82. See Madison's draft, "Instructions prepared for the Navy Dept," [ca. 19 October 1816], Madison Papers.

83. See Madison's 26 December 1816 message to Congress and the accompanying documents in Joseph Gales, compiler, *The Debates and Proceedings of the Congress of the United States* (42 vols.; Washington, DC, 1834–1856; hereafter *Annals of Congress*), 14th Cong., 2d sess., 1079–85.

84. For the debate in the House of Representatives, see ibid., 477–78, 716–45, 746–56, 763–64, 766–68, 770. See also Richard Peters et al., compilers, *The Public Stat-*

utes at Large of the United States of America (17 vols.; Boston, MA, 1848–73), 3: 370–71.

85. Madison to Jefferson, 15 February 1817, Madison Papers.

86. For the legislation, see Peters et al., *Public Statutes at Large,* 3: 348–49, 371. American control over the hinterland to those parts of West Florida included in the Alabama Territory was also consolidated by the Congressional grant of some ninety thousand acres of land near the confluence of the Tombigbee and Black Warrior rivers to the Society for the Cultivation of the Vine and Olive. Madison signed the necessary legislation on 3 March 1817 (see Rafe Blaufarb, *Bonapartists in the Borderlands: French Exiles and Refugees on the Gulf Coast, 1815–1835* [Tuscaloosa, AL, 2005], 49–57).

87. Madison to Jefferson, 15 February 1817, Madison Papers.

88. Monroe to Madison, 23 November 1818, ibid.

89. See, for example, Madison to Jefferson, 6 March 1819, ibid.

90. Madison to Jefferson, 6 December 1819, ibid.

91. For the decision to reclaim Astoria, see Merk, *Oregon Question,* 17–23. Adams did not commence his State Department duties until September 1817. It probably took him some time to master the details of the past history of the disputes with Spain—he was to complain on one occasion of the difficulty of locating documents in the State Department records, where he found "all in disorder and confusion"—and he and Onís did not agree to resume the negotiations until 16 December 1817, with Onís sending the first note on 29 December 1817 (see Charles Francis Adams, ed., *The Memoirs of John Quincy Adams, Comprising Portions of His Diary from 1795–1848* [12 vols.; Philadelphia, PA, 1874], 4: 7, 26, 100). See also Onís to Adams, 16 and 29 December 1817, Notes from Foreign Legations, Spain.

92. Onís to Adams, 29 December 1817, 5 and 24 January, 10 February, 23 March 1818, Notes from Foreign Legations, Spain; Adams to Onís, 10 January and 12 March 1818, Notes to Foreign Ministers and Consuls.

93. Onís to Adams, 8 January, 7 May, 19 June 1818, Notes from Foreign Legations, Spain.

94. A convenient short narrative of these developments is T. Frederick Davis, *MacGregor's Invasion of Florida, 1817; Together with an Account of his Successors, Irwin, Hubbard and Aury on Amelia Island, East Florida* (Jacksonville, FL, 1928).

95. Monroe revealed the details of his decision to seize Amelia Island in his messages to Congress of 2 December 1817, 13 January, 26 March 1818 (see Stanislaus M. Hamilton, ed., *The Writings of James Monroe* [7 vols.; New York, 1898–1903], 6: 3–40).

96. Madison to Monroe, 9 and 27 December 1817, Monroe Papers, Library of Congress.

97. Monroe to Madison, 22 December 1817, Madison Papers. Madison's misunderstanding may have arisen from too hasty a reading of Monroe's 2 December 1817 message, in which the president boasted of the rapid progress being made in extinguishing Indian title in the Northwest and predicted that "a similar and equally advantageous effect will soon be produced to the South, through the whole extent of the States and Territory, which border on the waters emptying into the Mississippi and the Mobile" (Hamilton, *Writings of James Monroe,* 6: 38–40).

98. Madison to Monroe, 27 December 1817, Monroe Papers, Library of Congress.

99. For summaries of these developments and the American response to them, see Charles C. Griffin, *The United States and the Disruption of the Spanish Empire, 1810–1822* (New York, 1937), 133–60; and Lewis, *The American Union and the Problem of Neighborhood*, 105–15.

100. Madison to Monroe, 18 February and 21 May 1818, Monroe Papers, Library of Congress. Monroe reported his concerns about the attitude of Alexander I to Madison in his letter to him of 28 April 1818 (Madison Papers). For Great Britain's renewed involvement in mediating between Spain and her colonies, see William W. Kaufmann, *British Policy and the Independence of Latin America, 1804–1828* (New Haven, CT, 1951), 108–20.

101. Madison to Monroe, 21 May 1818, Monroe Papers, Library of Congress. The commissioners were Caesar A. Rodney, John Graham, and Theodorick Bland. For the very mixed findings of their report about affairs in South America, see *American State Papers: Foreign Relations*, 4: 217–348.

102. Madison to Monroe, 2 October 1818, Monroe Papers, Library of Congress; and Madison to Monroe, 28 November 1818, Madison Papers.

103. For these developments, see Robert V. Remini, *Andrew Jackson and the Course of American Empire, 1767–1821* (New York, 1977), 341–70.

.104. For the role of the French minister as intermediary, see Françoise Watel, *Jean-Guillaume Hyde de Neuville (1776–1857): Conspirateur et diplomate* (Paris, 1997), 134–44.

105. For the instructions sent to Onís, dated 25 April 1818, see Philip C. Brooks, *Diplomacy and the Borderlands: The Adams-Onís Treaty of 1819* (Berkeley, CA, 1939), 134. The shift in Madrid's position was prompted by the failure of the United States to respond positively to suggestions that Great Britain mediate the disputes with Spain.

106. See Onís to José Garcia de León y Pizarro, 18 July 1818, Estado, legajo 5643. These proposals were made in a meeting between Adams and Onís on 11 July 1818, but in his diary entry for that date Adams made no mention of having discussed a line to the Pacific. He did, however, refer to it in a 16 July conversation with de Neuville for conveyance to Onís (see Adams, *Memoirs of John Quincy Adams*, 4: 106–7, 110). In reporting the matter to Madrid, Onís described in some detail how he and Adams had traced out their respective positions on the latest edition of John Melish's *Map of the United States and the Contiguous British and Spanish Possessions* (Philadelphia, PA, 1818), which Onís believed had been produced by the United States in order "to sustain their pretensions." Recent scholarship has endorsed Onís's claim to the point of arguing that the very design of Melish's map fueled desires for expansion by inducing in its American viewers "a somatic craving for territory" (see, for example, Martin Brückner, *The Geographic Revolution in Early America: Maps, Literacy, and National Identity* [Chapel Hill, NC, 2006], 262–63; and John Rennie Short, *Representing the Republic: Mapping the United States, 1600–1900* [London, 2001], 132–37). While it might be agreed that a map is much more than just a map, these suggestions may be unnecessarily speculative and unduly reductive. It is, in fact, unclear whether the positions the United States had reached by 1816 on its boundaries with Spain owed anything at all to Melish's maps.

107. For the February 1818 discussions about establishing a boundary on the Pacific Ocean, see Samuel Flagg Bemis, *John Quincy Adams and the Foundations of American Foreign Policy* (New York, 1949), 309–11, where Bemis assumes that it must have been Adams rather than Monroe who came up with the idea of claiming the Pacific coast for the United States. To question this argument is not to assert that Adams himself did not envisage the possibility of American expansion to the Pacific Ocean. As early as 1811, he had predicted that American settlements would spread across the continent, forming "one *nation,* speaking one language, professing one general system of religious and political principles" (see his 31 August 1811 letter to John Adams in Worthington C. Ford, ed., *The Writings of John Quincy Adams* [7 vols.; New York, 1913–17], 4: 209). But statements of this nature are hardly evidence that before 1818 Adams had thought through all the possibilities concerning the boundary disputes between Spain and the United States and how they might be settled in a comprehensive negotiation to the extent that the Madison administration had done by the spring of 1816.

108. This news had been conveyed to John Quincy Adams by the British minister in Washington in June 1818 (see Charles Bagot to Lord Castlereagh, 2 June 1818, Public Record Office: Foreign Office, ser. 5, vol. 132). For a discussion of how Bagot failed to explain the full complexity of the British position on Astoria on that occasion, see Merk, *Oregon Question,* 31–37.

109. Monroe to Madison, 10 and 20 July 1818, Madison Papers; and Monroe to Madison, 7 February 1819, Rives Collection of Madison Papers.

110. Jackson's justifications for his conduct in Florida rested, in part, on the so-called Rhea letter, a letter that he claimed to have received from Tennessee Representative John Rhea indicating Monroe's support for aggressive actions against Spain. It is now generally agreed there was no such letter, but historians continue to believe that Monroe implicitly condoned Jackson's conduct because it was not essentially different from the course Monroe himself had followed as secretary of state in 1811 in authorizing the activities of George Mathews in East and West Florida. (See, for example, Bemis, *John Quincy Adams and the Foundations of American Foreign Policy,* 314; Remini, *Andrew Jackson and the Course of American Empire,* 350; and William E. Weeks, *John Quincy Adams and American Global Empire* [Lexington, KY, 1992], 109. For the Rhea letter, see Richard R. Stenberg, "Jackson's Rhea Letter Hoax," *Journal of Southern History* 2 [1936]: 480–96.) This argument is untenable. Monroe had not been responsible for authorizing any aspect of Mathews's second mission, the instructions for that purpose having been drawn up by Robert Smith in January 1811, three months before Monroe entered the State Department. Jackson, moreover, was quite willing to disregard the views of the administration when they conflicted with his own priorities, and he had long believed the continuing possession of Pensacola by Spain was a serious threat to American security on the Gulf Coast (see, for example, Owsley, *Struggle for the Gulf Borderlands,* 120–26). It should also be remembered that in the summer of 1818 the Monroe administration hoped to be able to settle all outstanding differences with Great Britain in a comprehensive treaty (see Bagot to Castlereagh, 2 June 1818, as cited in n. 108 of this chapter). If so, it is highly unlikely Monroe would have wished

to jeopardize that prospect by encouraging Jackson to commit hostile acts against a British ally, to say nothing of executing two British subjects in the course of doing so.

111. See Madison to Rush, 24 July 1818, Madison Papers.

112. For Onís's desire for more latitude in his instructions, see Weeks, *John Quincy Adams and American Global Empire*, 72–73. See also "Bosquejo de los relaciones de la España con los Estados Unidos," 6 November 1816, for an internal review of Spain's boundary problems, including the suggestion for making "some cession in the Floridas to create a barrier between the United States and the kingdom of Mexico" (Estado, legajo 5559).

113. For an analysis of Adams's celebrated 28 November 1818 letter to Erving, see William E. Weeks, "John Quincy Adams's 'Great Gun' and the Rhetoric of American Empire," *Diplomatic History* 14 (1990): 25–42.

114. For the relevant correspondence, see Onís to Adams, 18 and 24 October, 16 November, 12 December 1818, 11 and 16 January, 1, 6, 9 February 1819, all in Notes from Foreign Legations, Spain; and Adams to Onís, 23 and 31 October, 28 and 30 November, 2 December 1818, 29 January, 13 February 1819, all in Notes to Foreign Ministers and Consuls. For the text and the ratifications of the treaty, see Miller, *Treaties of the United States*, 3: 3–31. For secondary accounts, see Bemis, *John Quincy Adams and the Foundations of American Foreign Policy*, 317–40; and Brooks, *Diplomacy and the Borderlands*, 131–69.

115. Monroe to Madison, 7 February 1819, Rives Collection of Madison Papers.

116. Madison to Monroe, 13 February 1819, Monroe Papers, Library of Congress.

117. Madison to Jefferson, 6 March 1819, Madison Papers.

118. Monroe to Madison, 7 February 1819, Rives Collection of Madison Papers.

119. Madison to Monroe, 13 February 1819, Monroe Papers, Library of Congress.

120. This, essentially, was the argument made by Onís in a pamphlet he published in 1820 following his return to Spain. In part, the publication was intended to vindicate the minister against charges that he had signed a bad treaty, but its contents stressed that it was no longer possible to defend Florida against the vastly superior resources and unlimited greed of the Americans and that the task of prudent statesmanship was to protect both Mexico and New Mexico from future American encroachments. The alternative, Onís believed, was to risk rupture and war with the United States, which could then lead "to the loss of the whole, or greater part, of South America." An English translation of the pamphlet appeared in 1821 (see Onís, *Memoir upon the Negotiations between Spain and the United States Which Led to the Treaty of 1819*, trans. Tobias Watkins [Baltimore, MD, 1821], especially pp. 135–50).

121. For an account of Spain's deteriorating position in the Pacific Northwest after 1790, see Warren L. Cook, *Flood Tide of Empire: Spain and the Pacific Northwest, 1543–1819* (New Haven, CT, 1973), 434–523.

122. These sentiments were expressed by the *Daily National Intelligencer* on 25 February 1819, on which occasion the editors congratulated the nation on the conclusion of "the tedious and hitherto unpleasant negociations with Spain."

123. On the western boundary, the *Daily National Intelligencer* remarked that it

acknowledged "the United States to be sovereign, under the hitherto contested Louisiana treaty, over all the territory we ever seriously contended for" (ibid.). This amounted to a tacit admission that no administration had ever seriously sought the territory to the Rio Grande.

124. For accounts of these developments, see Brooks, *Diplomacy and the Border-lands,* 170–86; and Griffin, *The United States and the Disruption of the Spanish Empire,* 191–220. The best explanation of the details of the land grants may be found in Miller, *Treaties of the United States,* 3: 40–49.

125. Monroe to Madison, 24 November and 7 December 1819, Madison Papers.

126. Madison to Monroe, 11 December 1819 and 10 February 1820, Monroe Papers, Library of Congress.

127. Madison to Monroe, 28 December 1820, ibid.

128. Brooks, *Diplomacy and the Borderlands,* 180–91. Selections from the diplomatic correspondence relating to the ratification of the treaty may be found in *American State Papers: Foreign Relations,* 4: 650–703.

129. Eustis to Madison, 15 March 1819, Rives Collection of Madison Papers.

130. Especially problematic in this respect has been the entry Adams recorded in his diary on 22 February 1819, in which he expressed an understandable pride in completing the negotiation with Spain but also claimed particular credit for first proposing in it "a definite boundary to the South Sea" for the United States (see Adams, *Memoirs of John Quincy Adams,* 4: 275). Adams's remark is literally correct as far as it goes, but it has led historians to assume that Adams himself was the originator of the idea of a Pacific boundary for the United States at the risk of their neglecting to trace the antecedents of the idea in the history of the negotiations with Spain before 1817.

131. This is not to say France was indifferent to the fate of Spanish America. On the contrary, Louis XVIII and his ministers greatly desired to prevent the spread of Anglo-American influence and republicanism in the Americas and sought to do so by establishing Bourbon princes, preferably from the French line, in the provinces of the Spanish-American empire, a policy that did not appeal to Madrid. Nevertheless, after 1815 France was far less concerned about territorial disputes in the New World than it had been between 1756 and 1803 (see William Spence Robertson, *France and Latin-American Independence* [Baltimore, MD, 1939], 129–77).

132. For a discussion of the descent of the movements for autonomy in other Spanish-American colonies into civil war and counterrevolution, see Adelman, *Sovereignty and Revolution in the Iberian Atlantic,* 212–19, 258–307.

133. This aspect of Madison's presidency has, perhaps, been too readily taken for granted rather than systematically examined. It is, nevertheless, clear, as may be seen by the celebrated and extended reprimand Madison delivered to his secretary of war on the eve of the British assault on Washington in August 1814 that the procedures he and Jefferson had established for the conduct of executive business in November 1801 had progressively broken down, with the result being that there were too many issues of administration policy that were eluding his oversight. (See Madison to John Armstrong, 13 August 1814, Madison Papers. For the system established in 1801 which

Madison continued after 1809, see the circular letter from Jefferson to his cabinet, 6 November 1801, in *The Papers of James Madison: Secretary of State Series* [8 vols. to date, ed. Robert Brugger et al.; Charlottesville, VA, 1986–], 2: 227–29.)

134. This was particularly the case with the edited version of the 30 May 1816 instructions to Erving that was sent to the Senate on 22 February 1819. It omitted all reference to the willingness of the administration to accept a western boundary on the Sabine River while at the same time seeking one on the Pacific (see *American State Papers: Foreign Relations*, 4: 433).

135. See the debates during the first session of the 16th Congress in the spring of 1820 when Clay, and many others, criticized the abandonment of the claim to Texas and called, instead, for its annexation and an end to the effort to persuade Spain to ratify the 1819 treaty (*Annals of Congress*, 16th Cong., 1st sess., 1719–38, 1743–53, 1756–81). For the debate over Missouri, see Glover Moore, *The Missouri Controversy, 1819–1821* (Lexington, KY, 1933), 84–169; and Matthew Mason, *Slavery and Politics in the Early American Republic* (Chapel Hill, NC, 2006), 177–212. As Mason points out, the Missouri crisis exposed many pre-existing sectional tensions in the early republic, but before February 1819 these had not involved either Florida or Texas, which were seen as national security issues rather than as locations involving the future of slavery (see p. 185).

136. In a letter to Monroe on 14 May 1820, Jefferson declared he was "not sorry for the non-ratification of the Spanish treaty," as it could only serve to strengthen the American claim to Texas, which "will be the richest State in our Union, without exception" (Jefferson Papers). Somewhat alarmed by this, Monroe responded that the sectional debate in Congress "was not a question with Spain, in reality, but one among ourselves" over the proper extent of the Union. The opposition to the admission of Missouri he likened to the efforts made by the Northern states in 1786 to accept the Jay-Gardoqui treaty closing the Mississippi to the United States, and he warned Jefferson that "further acquisition of territory, to the South & West involves difficulties, of an internal nature, which menace the Union itself." He concluded, "We ought to be cautious in making the attempt . . . and to take no step in that direction, which is not approved, by all the members, or at least a majority of those who accomplished our revolution" (Monroe to Jefferson [May 1820], Hamilton, *Writings of James Monroe*, 6: 119–23). Madison, too, was concerned about the sectional debate, and in his 28 December 1820 letter to Monroe he hoped the impending acquisition of Florida, once Spain had ratified the 1819 treaty, would "give no stimulus to the spirit excited by the case of Missouri" (Monroe Papers, Library of Congress). The crisis, nevertheless, provoked him into writing his whimsical allegory "Jonathan and Mary Bull" as a defense of the inviolability of the Union (see Robert J. Allison, "From the Covenant of Peace, A Simile of Sorrow: James Madison's American Allegory," *Virginia Magazine of History and Biography* 99 [1991]: 327–50).

137. A useful history of this subject is Marshall, *A History of the Western Boundary of the Louisiana Purchase*, 86–241. See also the following articles by Richard R. Stenberg: "Jackson's Neches Claim," *Southwestern Historical Quarterly* 39 (1936): 255–

74; "Andrew Jackson and the Erving Affidavit," ibid. 41 (1937): 142–53; "Jackson, Anthony Butler, and Texas," *Southwestern Social Science Quarterly* 13 (1932): 264–86; and "The Texas Schemes of Jackson and Houston," ibid. 15 (1934): 229–50.

138. For a recent statement of the case that later controversies over Texas were "crucial in framing a long process" that culminated in secession and civil war, see Joel H. Silbey, *Storm over Texas: The Annexation Controversy and the Road to Civil War* (New York, 2005), xvii–xviii. A brief account stressing how the manipulations of politicians contributed to the expansionism and sectionalism that produced the conflict is Michael F. Holt, *The Fate of Their Country: Politicians, Slavery Extension, and the Coming of the Civil War* (New York, 2004).

INDEX

Adair, John, 58, 146, 156

Adams, Brooks, historiography and family influence, 216n29

Adams, Henry: historiography and family influence, 8, 216n29; *History of the United States during the Administrations of Thomas Jefferson and James Madison*, 6–9, 215n24, 216n29

Adams, John: administration of, 38; and "Plan of Treaties," 14–15

Adams, John Quincy: and claim to Pacific boundary, 205, 290n130; and defense of Jackson, 201; historiography and family influence, 8, 216n29; and Louisiana boundaries, 8; as minister and commissioner at St. Petersburg, 131–32, 264n145; as secretary of state, 195–96, 199–200, 286n91, 287n106

Adams, Louisa Catherine, 216n29

Alabama River, 53, 57

Alabama Territory, 194, 286n86

Alagón, duque de, 204

Alazán, Battle of, 162

Alden, Samuel, 275n105

Alexander I (of Russia), 131, 162, 198, 263n141

Algiers, 131–32, 189

Allen, Ira, 159

Ambrister, Robert, 198

Amelia Island (Florida): British goods at, 259n95; British navy at, 102; return of, to Spain, 121; slave trading from, 97; Spanish garrison at, 95, 116, 259n92; U.S. occupies, 126, 196–97, 259n93; U.S. withdrawal from, 133

American Register, 135

Anderson, Joseph, 129, 130

anti-Catholicism, 227n54

Apalachicola River, 43, 57, 91, 93, 98, 230n97, 230n100

Arango y Parreño, Francesco, 137–38, 265n15

Arbuthnot, Alexander, 198

Arkansas River, 201

Armstrong, John: account of *1803* negotiations, 216n28; as minister to France, 45, 46–47, 48, 49, 234n115, 236n133

Army, U.S.: and Mexican filibuster, 279n144; militia and aid from, 73, 76; posts reinforced, 82; takes in Spanish soldiers, 117. *See also* Fort Stoddert (Mississippi Terr.); Point Petre

Arredondo, Fernando de la Maza, Sr., 95, 104, 253n23, 259n93

Arredondo y Mioño, Joaquín, 168, 283n50

Articles of Confederation, 14, 15, 222n7

Ashley, Lodovick, 112

Astor, John Jacob, 186–87, 189, 190